# A Life Poured Out

PIERRE LUCIEN CLAVERIE, O.P.
May 8, 1938–August 1, 1996
Bishop of Oran, 1981–1996

# A Life Poured Out

## Pierre Claverie
## of Algeria

Jean-Jacques Pérennès

Translated by Phyllis Jestice
and Matthew Sherry

ORBIS BOOKS
Maryknoll, New York 10545

Founded in 1970, Orbis Books endeavors to publish works that enlighten the mind, nourish the spirit, and challenge the conscience. The publishing arm of the Maryknoll Fathers and Brothers, Orbis seeks to explore the global dimensions of the Christian faith and mission, to invite dialogue with diverse cultures and religious traditions, and to serve the cause of reconciliation and peace. The books published reflect the opinions of their authors and are not meant to represent the official position of the Maryknoll Society. To obtain more information about Maryknoll and Orbis Books, please visit our website at www.maryknoll.org.

**Library of Congress Cataloging-in-Publication Data**

Pérennès, Jean Jacques.
    [Pierre Claverie. English]
    Life poured out : Pierre Claverie of Algeria / Jean-Jacques Pérennès ; [translated by Phyllis Jestice and Matthew Sherry].
      p. cm.
    Includes bibliographical references and index.
    ISBN 978-1-57075-706-8
    1. Claverie, Pierre. 2. Bishops – Algeria – Oran – Biography. 3. Oran (Algeria) – Church history – 20th century. 4. Algeria – Church history – 20th century. I. Title.
BX4705.C565P4713 2007
282.092 – dc22
[B]
                                     2007003104

# Contents

Foreword by Timothy Radcliffe, O.P.     vii

Preface     xi

Map of Algeria     xvi

1. From Happy Childhood to Youth as a Pied-Noir     1

2. From University to Novitiate: A Time of Transition     17

3. Le Saulchoir: Years to Grow and Prepare for the Future, 1959–67     38

4. Toward the Joyous Encounter with the Other     62

5. The Time of Responsibilities     78

6. Bishop in Oran: Happy Beginnings, 1981–87     99

7. A Preaching Friar before All Else     119

8. Muslim-Christian Dialogue: An Original Approach     137

9. Christians in the "House of Islam": From Theological Debate to Witness     154

10. An Algerian Bishop in the Midst of Social and Political Debate, 1988–94     170

11. A Church on the Fault Lines, 1994–95     190

12. "The Combat of Life": A Spiritual Portrait     209

13. Witnessing the Greatest Love     225

Epilogue: "I leave you upon this open horizon"     250

A Tribute from a Muslim Friend: In the Footsteps of Saint Augustine by Redouane Rahal     254

Humanity in the Plural: A Reflection by Pierre Claverie, O.P.     258

Notes     263

Index     283

# Foreword
*Timothy Radcliffe, O.P.*

Pierre Claverie, Dominican friar and the bishop of Oran in Algeria, was assassinated August 1, 1996. With him died a young Muslim friend, Mohamed Bouchikhi. At Pierre's funeral a few days later, the cathedral was packed with his many friends, Muslim and Christian. It seemed absurd that this man, who had devoted his life to dialogue between Christianity and Islam, should die in such a violent way. It looked like a contradiction, an annulment, of all that Pierre had sought. He had known for a long time that his murder was probable, but he had refused to run away to safety. But what future could there be for reconciliation between these two great faiths when such a man and his Muslim friend were deliberately wiped out by a bomb?

The story of Pierre Claverie is of a man who lived with hope. His death did not, as I shall suggest below, extinguish that hope but made it shine out more strongly. We have need of that hope more urgently than ever today. Five years after Pierre's assassination, the world was shocked by the horror of 9/11. In London and Madrid bombs have been detonated on public transport, murdering hundreds of innocent people. But this is nothing compared to the ongoing violence in Iraq, Afghanistan, India, and Thailand. All over the world the followers of great and ancient religions are killing each other. Faced with this escalating slaughter, is there any hope for peace?

Pierre Claverie's life and death show that not only can we hope but, as Christians, we must do so. Faced with the prospect of his own death, he did not run away, because he believed that violence never has the last word. That is our faith. He wrote, "Living in the Muslim world, I know the weight of this temptation to withdraw into oneself, the difficulty of mutual understanding and of respecting each other. And I can measure perfectly the abyss that separates us... We would not be able to bridge this gap by ourselves. But God, in Jesus, gives us the means to measure the length, the breadth, the depth and the extent of his Love. Supported by this revelation, we can regain confidence... To give one's life for this reconciliation as Jesus gave his life to knock down the wall of hatred which separated Jews, Greeks, pagans, slaves, and free men, isn't that a good way to honor his sacrifice?"[1] Hope is not a naïve optimism, but confidence that for each of us after Good Friday comes Easter Sunday.

Even at his funeral, just over three days later, there were signs that our hope is not groundless. The gathering of so many Muslim friends, their profound distress at his pointless murder, was a sign that Pierre's quest for friendship across religious boundaries had borne fruit that will endure. At the end of the funeral, a young Muslim woman gave her testimony. It was through Pierre that she had returned to her faith. He was the bishop of the Muslims too. Pierre had been annihilated, but not his message. The crowd of friends around his coffin was a sign of the love that cannot be defeated.

Friendship was at the heart of his mission in Algeria. At his ordination as bishop of Oran, in October 1981, he said, "My Algerian brothers and friends, I owe to you also what I am today. You also have welcomed and supported me with your friendship. Thanks to you, I have discovered Algeria, where, even though it was my country, I lived as a stranger throughout my youth. With you, in learning Arabic, I learned above all to speak and understand the language of the heart, the language of brotherly friendship, where races and religions commune with each other. And again, I have the softness of heart to believe that this friendship will hold up against time, distance, and separation. For I believe that this friendship comes from God and leads to God."[2]

So for Pierre this friendship is much more than friendliness. Pierre was being a good Dominican and a disciple of Thomas Aquinas, in giving friendship this central role. Aquinas taught that our vocation is to live in friendship with God, and this friendship is our sharing in the love of the Father and the Son in the Holy Spirit. It was this friendship that grounded Pierre's understanding of dialogue. Committed religious believers often look on interreligious dialogue with suspicion. It can smack of compromise, of the search for a vague and woolly compromise, in which we surrender what is at the heart of our beliefs in favor of a spirituality of the lowest common denominator. But for Pierre, dialogue was an expression of God's relationship with humanity: "At this moment, the key word of my faith is 'dialogue,' not because this is a strategic choice linked to my situation, but because I feel that dialogue constitutes the relation of God with people and of people with each other . . . May the Other, may all others, be the passion and the wound through which God will be able to break into our fortresses of self-satisfaction to give birth to a new and fraternal humanity."[3]

So dialogue is not an alternative to preaching the gospel. It is the expression of our faith. By daring to open ourselves to the faith of another, to enter their lives and hear with their ears, we show forth our trust in Jesus Christ, who dared to share our human life and who placed himself in our hands. Our dialogue not only manifests our faith in Christ, but it also expresses the hope that we may learn about Christ from others. At his funeral that young woman thanked Pierre for bringing her back to Islam with a renewed faith, and if we are open and humble, then we too may be led deeper into the gospel through dialogue with people of other faiths. Pierre wrote, "We are not and do not want to be evangelical proselytizers who think they honor God's love by a tactless zeal and a total lack of respect for the Other, for his culture, for his faith . . . But we are and we want to be missionaries of the love of God as we have discovered it in Jesus Christ. This love, infinitely respectful of humans, does not impose itself, does not impose anything, does not coerce consciences and hearts. With a light touch, and by its presence alone, it frees what was chained, reconciles what was torn asunder, lifts up what was downtrodden . . . This love, we came to know it and believed in it . . . It grabbed us and transported us. We believe that it can renew the life of humanity if we can recognize and accept it . . . "[4] Our conversation with those who have different beliefs is in itself a proclamation of our faith in the God whose very life is the conversation of the Trinity.

For this dialogue to be real, then, it must be truthful, and "Truth" is the motto of Pierre's religious order. We must not disguise our deepest convictions but dare to share them and to hear the heartbeat of the other person's faith. We must also be truthful about the wounds that we have inflicted upon each other in the past. For one and a half millennia, Christians and Muslims have fought each other, invaded each other's lands, expelled and hurt each other. We cannot create peace unless we face that past without flinching. The reaction of many Muslims to the Second Gulf War was intensified since it was seen as the prolongation of a long history of Western aggression against Islam, going back to the Crusades. Muslims must also understand how Western Christians carry the memories of Muslim armies advancing into southern France and to the gates of Vienna. Pierre insisted on speaking frankly: "The collective unconscious has kept the scars that we have inflicted on each other, and it would be totally self-deceiving to believe that we could easily get rid of them by appealing to good feelings. At any moment, and especially during times of crisis, the warriors of Allah and the Saracens or the Moors invading Europe reappear in the collective mind and the discourse of the West, while the Muslim always recalls the Crusades and colonialism."[5] For most of Christian history and nearly all of Muslim history, each faith has looked on the other religion as "the other" over which it defines itself. Unless we can face that history, we will not be able to overcome it.

This dialogue must be both confident and humble. There is no point in dialogue unless we believe that believers on each side are passionate about the truths that they claim have been revealed to them. As Christians we are confident that the gospel is indeed good news for humanity, and we should be disappointed if our interlocutors were not sustained by an equal conviction. And yet we come to listen in humility, knowing that the God by whose revelation we live is beyond all our words and conceptions. We are always just at the beginning of understanding, and we need those of other faiths and of no faith to help us move a little closer to the edge of the mystery. To quote Pierre again, "There are certainly objective truths, but they are beyond all of us and one can only reach them through a long journey and by slowly reformulating that truth by collecting from other cultures, from other types of humanity, what others have also gained, have searched for in their own journey toward truth. I am a believer, I believe in one God, but I don't claim to possess that God, either through Jesus who reveals him to me, or through the tenets of my faith. One does not possess God. One does not possess the truth, and I need the truth of others."[6]

Dialogue implies vulnerability to the other person. He or she may enlighten me, affirm me, and offer me a welcome and love. But one also takes the risk of being puzzled, challenged, rebuffed, or even hurt. Such are the necessary risks of friendship. Pierre's embrace of that vulnerability found its fullest expression in his death, witnessing to his hope in Christ. It was a moment of grace. Shortly before he died, he made his own these words of Bonhoeffer: "In fact, our battle involves a grace for which we must pay. Grace acquired cheaply is grace without the cross. Grace for which we must pay is the gospel that one must always look for anew. This grace is costly because it can only be acquired at the price of one's own life."[7]

# Preface

A little before midnight on August 1, 1996, Bishop Pierre Claverie of Oran was assassinated. With him was a young Algerian Muslim, a friend of the Christian community, to which he had willingly given service during the summer. Occurring only two months after the murder of seven Trappist monks in Tibhirine, this new event sent a shock wave both through Algeria and abroad. *They* had dared yet again! After these monks and nuns, who had given their whole lives to the service of this land, after all those unnamed Algerians who were innocent victims of senseless violence, now yet again what was best in Algeria had been attacked. For Pierre Claverie did not die by chance, because he was in the wrong place at the wrong time. He had been deliberately assassinated. In the previous weeks and months the same fate befell Abdelkader Alloula (director of the Oran theater), Mahfoud Boucebci, Saïd Mekbel, M'hamed Boukhobza, Youssef Sebti, and others. Artist, psychiatrist, journalist, economist, poet — these men and all those who died with them were members of the Algerian elite. They were among the best the land had produced. Who then was Pierre Claverie, that he deserved to be included on this list? What values had he upheld? Why and for whom was he a menace?

Pierre Claverie was a son of Algeria. From its inception at Bab el Oued in the French colonial world, his entire adult life was spent in this land or, more precisely, on this intangible frontier that separates or unites the two shores of the Mediterranean. Born in 1938 to a family that had been settled in Algeria for four generations — what are called "pieds-noirs" ("black feet") — at the age of twenty Claverie became aware of the drama of entrapment in what he would one day call the "colonial bubble." France at that time was split on the question of its colonial presence in Algeria. Almost forty years later, Claverie wrote, "Perhaps because I had ignored the 'other' or because I denied his existence, one day he leaped into vivid relief. It made my enclosed universe explode, so it crumbled into violence — but how could it have been otherwise? — he had affirmed his existence."[1] This discovery led him to follow a painful path, so that he longed to return to his land one day, but differently. Learning the Arabic language with enthusiasm, he became familiar with Islam, and returned to spend his adult life forming a relationship of rare intensity, practically a kinship, with this land, and above all with the people of Algeria. "The emergence of the 'Other,' the recognition of the Other, the adjustment to the other" were, by his own admission, the beginning of his double vocation, both religious and Algerian. A young Dominican, Claverie was quickly given responsibilities by Cardinal Duval, whose task was to guide the church of Algeria in a delicate transition from French rule to an Algerian Algeria. Astonishingly gifted at human relationships, cordial and warm, Pierre Claverie played an enthusiastic role in the construction of this new Algeria, and during the seventies was regarded as a leader in developing, non-aligned nations. After becoming bishop, he helped the small Christian community of Oran to find its place in this common effort. If matters had stopped at this point, they would tell a fine tale of a life, the tale of a journey from colonial Algeria to Algerian Algeria, "from Algiers to el-Djezair."[2] But Claverie was called to follow a different path.

In the early 1980s, the dream of a socialist Algeria gave way to uncertainty, then to a veritable nightmare. Dubious economic choices, social inequities, and corruption undermined the political stability of the state. Hasty Arabization and political manipulation of Islam favored the emergence of a radical "Islamism," above all among the youth and in the society's working class. The riots of October 1988 and their resulting repression inaugurated a period of violence that to this day has resulted in at least 150,000 deaths in what resembles a civil war in which none are spared. The social fabric has been deeply torn and reconciliation still appears distant, despite several initiatives intended to promote national concord. Far from distancing himself from the national drama because of his minority status — he was a Christian, an Algerian *par alliance* (that is, "by covenant") one might say — Pierre Claverie plunged into the turmoil body and soul. The question of the "other" was the central concern of his life: it was on that issue that his own personal adventure was played out. Far from yielding to threats, he took a stand and denounced those who fanned the flame of rejection and exclusion of the other. He spoke out to uphold militants fighting for human rights, women struggling for emancipation, and all those who were working for an open and fraternal Algeria. When the Christians became victims in their turn of the violence that engulfed the country, Claverie raised his voice in scathing denunciation of "the cowardice of those who kill in the shadows." This came not from concern to defend the interests of the church — what was there left to defend? — but because what was at stake was, in his opinion, the very possibility of a humanity that was pluralist, not exclusive, and that belief lay at the heart of all.

Did Pierre Claverie expose himself too much? Some have thought so, even among those in his own church, where many considered it more prudent to keep a low profile while waiting for better days. But for Claverie it had become a kind of interior necessity to see his choice through to the end, faithful to his recovered land like a certain Galilean who taught that there is no greater love than to give one's life for one's friends. To be present on the "fault lines that crucify humanity" appeared to him to lie within the profound logic of his vocation as he consciously took on the risks. Who could have stopped him then? At his funeral in the modest cathedral of Oran, the crowd of Muslim friends, outnumbering the Christians, were there as visible proof that his message had been heard. In their name, a young Algerian woman bore witness with courage and emotion to what both groups had become to Claverie. Forty days later, during a solemn tribute in the cathedral of Notre Dame in Paris, at the request of the French bishops and his Dominican brethren, the high-pitched cries of Algerian women at the end of the homily confirmed, in a striking manner unseen previous in that place, the deep sense and measure of that life that had been offered up. However moving the ceremony was to those present, though, these tributes could not disguise the fact that the values Pierre Claverie had extolled remain a matter of controversy. Is there really a place for a Christian in a Muslim society? Where Islam predominates, can it allow full citizenship to any other religion? Is it proper for a bishop to engage in society's debates to this extent? These questions are far from being resolved, and the rapprochement of the two shores of the Mediterranean and the values that each side upholds is still fragile and under threat.

I had the pleasure of knowing and frequently seeing Pierre Claverie over the course of nearly twenty-five years, from the early seventies until his death. For a long time I was afraid to undertake this biography, which several of those close to him had suggested I write. Perhaps this was because I didn't want to probe the great pain that his tragic end had given me. But then came a certain serenity, and along with that a desire to share that to which I had been a privileged witness: an ardent life, lived with passion; a taste for the truth that does not exclude a sense of the Other and respects his difference; a joy whose secret could not be found except in giving himself to the very end. Having lived in Algeria for ten years, where I knew and associated with Pierre Claverie, it was easier for me to analyze the context of his life's course and to find those involved. Although it may seem suspicious, I must confess that I found great happiness in attempting to discover the extraordinary mainspring and the intimate strengths of this exceptional life. I have written this book with joy.

In this endeavor, my gratitude goes first of all to Pierre's sister, Anne-Marie Claverie, and to her husband, Eric Gustavson. Both gave me their complete confidence, not only providing access to Pierre's abundant correspondence with his family (more than two thousand letters) but also to their intimate family circle. Perusing photo albums, so evocative of memories, speaking with them about Pierre for hours while walking in the New Jersey countryside where they live, little by little I felt myself become part of what Anne-Marie Claverie loves to call "the weft," the strong web of interconnecting threads to which the life and death of Pierre gave birth. I also owe a great debt to Henri Teissier, archbishop of Algiers, Pierre Claverie's friend for three decades. He opened his archives to me with no reservations at all. His dynamism helped me establish many contacts, and he was kind enough to check facts while leaving me free to draw my own conclusions. François Chavanes of the Order of Preachers also afforded me an inestimable cooperation: he knew Pierre from 1956 until his death and had spent numerous years with or near him. Having organized his working archives in a very rigorous fashion, Chavanes helped me to extract the essential points, with the kind agreement of Bernard Lapize, diocesan administrator, and then that of the new bishop of Oran, Alphonse Georger.

Besides abundant documentation and my own memories, this biography is based on numerous interviews with Pierre Claverie's companions at various moments in his life. In particular, I wish to mention Thierry Becker, Claverie's vicar general in difficult times, and Redouane Rahal, whom Claverie called his "Muslim vicar general." Both helped me to uncover Pierre's astonishing network of relationships in Oran, rich in personalities of all sorts. All of these witnesses were invaluable in helping me to reconstruct fittingly the nuances of a rich personality. The list of people from whose help I benefited is a long one. They will recognize their contributions in the text. I thank them all. I owe a particular debt to Daniel Junqua, Jean-François Cota, and Roger Roche: participants or qualified observers in the evolution of Algeria from the colonial period to the present, Pierre's companions at various stages in his life, each of them helped me find the appropriate tone to speak about him. François Martin and Sister Anne-Catherine re-read my manuscript with patience and skill. I am also deeply grateful to my Dominican brothers and sisters, who have made me welcome in the course of editing these pages, from Kenosha, Wisconsin, to Cairo, and including Chalais, Orbey, and Taulignan in between. Lastly, I am indebted to the great encouragement I received from people whose paths crossed Pierre Claverie's in France, Algeria, or Lebanon, and whose lives were changed by the encounter. Among them I have felt a high sense of expectation, which I hope I will not disappoint.

There is a certain mystery in a life that has been sacrificed. When it is a matter of a man of such passion, given to "make the 'other' exist" and to create ties between human beings, it is hard not to cry out at the waste. I hope that the reader will be able to glimpse, in these pages, that the secret of Pierre Claverie's life and his joy lay above all in that gift.

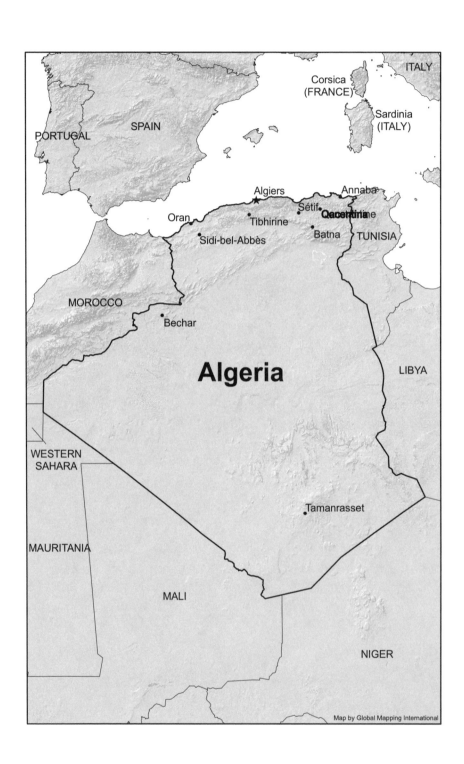

*Chapter One*

# From Happy Childhood to Youth as a Pied-Noir

> I have been witness to a love of more than forty years that unites
> two beings, my parents, so different and yet so close, depending
> on each other, growing together, so united and so welcoming.[1]
> — *Pierre Claverie*

Pierre Claverie was born in Algiers on May 8, 1938, to a family of *pieds-noirs*, French people who had lived in Algeria for several generations. Algeria was his country.

He was full of the joy of life. Did he owe that to his Mediterranean origins? A little bit, without doubt. But much more came from the fact that he was a happy child, loved by exceptional parents. It was to them first of all that he paid homage at his ordination as bishop in the cathedral of Algiers on October 2, 1981: "We grew up trusting in that love that watches attentively and unfailingly over the happiness of others; we grew up with a wonderful freedom that continuously opened the doors of life in front of us, inviting us patiently and persistently to enter, and accompanying us with an affectionate and demanding presence. Yes, love exists; it is possible and I have had the good fortune of knowing it."[2] From this happy childhood Pierre Claverie preserved an outstanding emotional balance that was invaluable to him in his later life.

## A Rather Uncommon Family Story

Pierre was the first child of a family that his parents had hoped would be large. Because of the uncertainties of the war, though, he had only one sister, Anne-Marie, who was born in 1944. These four constituted what the parents called the "family cell," a nucleus in which communication and confidence reigned to an unusual extent: "We are the four fingers of the hand," Mr. Claverie liked to say; "if one fails, the others fall." The maintaining of this family unity seems to have been the most important goal of the elder Claveries, both of whom had, in their own ways, painful family histories.

1

Étienne Claverie was born in Algiers on October 12, 1906. His mother, a member of a large family in Belcourt, a working-class neighborhood of Algiers, was only fourteen years old when she gave birth to this child. The young man was only seventeen. The child of a prominent Algiers family who disapproved of this relationship, he did not marry her and did not acknowledge the child, who remained for life, therefore, an illegitimate child, a bastard. The young mother had to deal with this situation completely by herself and dragged her son about with her, first to Egypt and then to Spain, where she met a Mr. Claverie, who worked for the Saint-Gobain company. He recognized the child as his, so Étienne henceforth had a family name, which he passed on to his own children. But this Mr. Claverie in turn disappeared, and the young mother had to return to Algiers, where she placed her child in the care of his grandmother and aunts to be raised. Later she moved to Maisons-Alfort near Paris, and this time married a man with whom she lived for the rest of her life. But the wound was there. For his entire life Étienne Claverie would attempt to learn more about his childhood, but he never succeeded to any great extent and seldom spoke about it. In a way, he sublimated his unhappiness by doing everything in his power to make his own family happy. Out of the misfortune that was his as a child, Étienne Claverie developed a strong personal morality, marked by a sense of honor and exceptional integrity. His children grew up in this environment. "But," he liked to say to them, "my life began when I met your mother."

Louise Maillard came from a completely different environment: a prosperous family of shipowners, who lived in a beautiful building on the seafront in Algiers. A well-to-do environment, but not any happier: a depressed mother who died young, a father deeply scarred by the Great War, whose second marriage was to a much younger woman. He had a son, Jean, whom his daughter Louise, then fourteen, helped to raise. It was an environment where fine clothes and social events mattered a great deal. It was at the Shell Oil Company Club that Étienne Claverie first noticed this very popular young woman: lively and outgoing, she had "a personality full of sunshine," as her daughter Anne-Marie puts it. But there was no question of Étienne Claverie proclaiming his love. With his keen sense of honor, he did not want to let others imagine that he, the lowborn child, was above all after her money. So he had to be content with watching her, but as often as possible. Suddenly came a stroke of luck, as he humorously told the story later. The stock market collapsed — this was in the 1930s; the family business went bankrupt, and he ran immediately to ask for the hand of Miss Maillard. The wedding took place on April 20, 1936, in the parish church of St. Vincent de Paul in Algiers where their first child, Pierre, would himself be baptized on November 6, 1938.

## The Family Cell, the First Apprenticeship of Life

By this time, Étienne Claverie had found a job at Shell Oil on the boulevard Saint-Saëns in Algiers, where he spent his entire professional career. The young couple went to live in Bab el Oued, at number 4 rue Koechlin, because they did not want to leave behind the elderly parents and uncles who lived in the same building. They never moved from this apartment, even at the height of the Algerian War when Mr. Claverie's daily walk to his office was not without dangers. Despite past misfortunes, or perhaps because of them, the young couple did everything they could to create a happy family. Anne-Marie recalls the atmosphere of this childhood:

> The view from the three balconies of our apartment at Bab el Oued was magnificent. On one side was Notre Dame d'Afrique and the neighborhood of St. Eugene, and, on the other, the sea and the Padovani Baths. We spent a lot of time on those balconies, which served as our lookout post . . . Pierre spent hours teaching me to whistle, an essential part of my education in his eyes . . . We also developed all sorts of rituals, like the one that made it fun to clear the table after meals. We passed one another while carrying glasses and napkins, eyes closed and singing a magical song whose only words, repeated *ad nauseam,* were "Uncle Leo, Uncle Leo" . . . We had marvelous parents who loved us totally unselfishly.[3]

Simply, as we see, the elder Claveries had achieved their goal of giving birth and life to a happy family. Pierre Claverie drew from it a love of life and an emotional balance capable of standing up to anything. The neat regularity of his handwriting bears witness to his temperament. Surprisingly, but also rather typical of his character, he never spoke of his parents' painful past. He was not the sort of man who confided in others. "Trait for trait, I resemble my 'brute' of a father," he wrote to his parents in March of 1959; "we both hide our feelings . . . but if I don't talk more about them, it's not because I don't have any, you can be sure of that."

This family cell, as Mr. Claverie called it, provided the setting and fertile environment in which Pierre's personality grew.[4] It was a group of four: Papie, Mamie, Pierre, and Nane, as they called each other: four people among whom communication and trust developed and blossomed to a rare degree. Later an American son-in-law, Eric, and two little girls, Ingrid and Celine, would join the four, but the fundamental pattern of relationships was already in place. Papie was nearly blind because of a tragic incident in his youth; his remaining eye was just good enough that he could read with the aid of a magnifying glass. But he listened a great deal: to the radio constantly, especially as he grew old, but also to people, and first of all to his family. Introverted without being withdrawn, he had the reputation of being a wise man. His good friends liked to call him "le vieux bonze," the old Buddhist monk. Athletic in his youth, every morning he performed a kind of yoga invented by himself, part of a very disciplined life. As for Mamie, she liked to laugh and was extroverted, thus serving very well as a complement to her husband, who said teasingly to her at times, "Mamie, you are thinking like a child." In fact, they were a very united couple, in agreement on essentials. As they grew older, their mutual love was moving to see. Personality traits from the two found their way into their son: his mother's joy of life and his father's determination. "Pierre took the best of both; it is rare to do so to such an extent," his sister, Anne-Marie, says.

Pierre Claverie was one year old when World War II broke out. Later came the Algerian war of independence from France. In short, during his childhood, the outside world was often in turmoil, but his parents spoke little of these matters at home, expending all their energy to protect their children and provide them with a happy and trusting environment in which to grow. They had joy, a great deal of joy, at home. They laughed; they told each other stories; uncontrollable laughter was common. They went to the beach and, in the summer, spent their vacations together in France. Pierre experienced this life until he reached the age of nineteen and did not seem to suffer from what was, after all, a fairly strict parental control. Though he was concerned about education, Étienne Claverie also knew how to give some free space to his children. But he had something to pass on and he did so, leaving a profound mark on his son's personality. From the day that Pierre left for the University of Grenoble in November 1957 and then for the Dominican novitiate at Lille in December 1958, Papie did everything he could to maintain close family ties through a remarkable weekly correspondence in which, in four typewritten pages, he told about the events of the week, day by day, serious or insignificant, commenting on this or that, blending humor with advice and questions. And Pierre, a young exile from his Algerian homeland, responded: ten letters during his first month in Grenoble! Later there was a letter per week, usually written on Sunday, using carbon paper so the letters could be circulated to the other two poles of this family, his parents and his sister, who also wrote when, beginning in 1961, she left Algeria to study in France. Later, in the parents' old age, there were also weekly telephone calls — at set days and hours, 10:00 a.m. on Sunday for Pierre — but all that was essential was expressed in the correspondence.

Papie had a remarkable writing style, the vivacity of the natural storyteller and a gift for striking phrases. His letters usually started with an affectionate and slightly comical greeting, such as "my doves," "my ducks," "my lady camels," or "my pigeons and my penguin."[5] Pierre usually responded to these salutations with "hello, everyone," or "hello, family," but sometimes with his father's humorous tone: "my dear little old folks" or "my little angels." Mamie wrote her own message ("to my little Pierrot"), and one can feel that she was very much a part of what her husband wrote: Mamie thinks this, wonders about that. The content of the letters was anything but trite. There is talk of the daily life of a young son away from home (colds, socks to be replaced, the packages that his parents are sending him), but also essential matters. For nearly forty years in these letters, Pierre Claverie shared with his family his most personal investigations into questions concerning God, prayer, the religious life, and peace, and also his reaction to movies, books, and events. His parents thus continued to play an intimate part in his life, and their own attitudes changed profoundly on several points, including faith, the relationship with Algeria, the view of Islam. And at a turn of even the most serious discussion came the sense of humor, the witty phrase that gave everything a light touch. Something rather rare for a young man or, later, for someone with big responsibilities, Pierre wrote with the same regularity, two pages a week, whatever his cares, his occupations, or his travels. This correspondence was preserved in its entirety and is one of the sources of this book, along with Pierre Claverie's other writings, my own memories, and accounts received from other witnesses. The correspondence would be well worth at least a partial publication because it covers a slice of nearly forty years in the life both of the world and of the church.[6] It stretches from the beginning of November 1957, when Pierre left Algiers for Grenoble, to June 19, 1996, a month and a half before his assassination. Papie died on April 3 of that same year, four months before his son. Mamie had already passed away on February 11, 1992. Étienne Claverie was well aware of the importance of the letters and preserved them carefully, putting them all together at the end of each year in simple containers constructed out of cereal or cracker boxes and tied up with string so none would be lost. He explained all of this in the letter of January 17, 1965, very much in his usual style:

One day you will find at the bottom of a chest in a cellar some packets, more or less well bound and painstakingly organized. Take care not to throw them away before you have looked into them. You will be amazed by what these pages reveal. First of all history, which you will be surprised to rediscover with such vividness, but also a large quantity of other things, of feelings, of unchanging trust between your parents and yourselves, as well as in your destinies, that will take your breath away, unless you are fools, which, truly, I recognize that you are not.

Here we have Étienne Claverie's usual tone: humor is never far from the deepest feelings. Papie's letters were not all preserved, which is regrettable because of their style and their content, so revealing about the family environment and the events its members experienced. Clearly, for Pierre Claverie's parents, this correspondence was a means to maintain and enhance the ties of the family cell, in order to give to each member the best chance to face successfully the challenges of life. From his retreat in Nice, five years after being forced into exile from Algeria, Étienne Claverie made the following comments to his children: "Definitely we have been blessed and are capable of holding up against any storm. You, above all, for whom the road ahead is still very long. We still can't believe that we have prepared you so well for life. It would be impossible to give a clear recipe to so many families that are disunited" (letter of January 8, 1967).

Blessed, indeed, but these parents had paid the price. Thus, Étienne Claverie, who had become head of public relations for Shell Oil in Algiers, turned down an attractive offer to head the Dakar branch of this company so that he could preserve this family life in which he believed so strongly. Yes, this man was not at all an ordinary one. His exceptional personality and the love which bound him to his wife did a great deal to strengthen Pierre, to give him a solid foundation in order to face, in his turn, the challenges of life. He would indeed need it.

## The Context of an Algerian Childhood: The Colonial Bubble

Pierre Claverie spent his childhood and youth almost entirely in Algiers, apart from summer vacations in France; this influenced his first vision of Algeria, Arabs, and Islam. As a reminder, France gained a foothold in Algeria in 1830 through a military invasion, arriving after three centuries of Turkish administration, during which an Algerian national identity was never really affirmed. The path seemed clear: in the wake of Marshal Bugeaud's soldiers came the first colonists, who took several decades to take root in this country, draining marshes, building dams, looking for crops that could grow in this variable and

semiarid climate: wheat, grape vines, olive trees, and citrus plants were cultivated with some success, but not without difficulty. Large agricultural estates
were created, model farms, recognizable by the grand avenue of palm trees
leading to the master's home. The passing attempts at Algerian resistance
were repressed. The population of European descent grew significantly, and
colonial villages were established in the great plains. By 1930, when the hun-
dredth anniversary of the colonization of Algeria was celebrated with great
pomp, an entire pieds-noir population had become established, coming from
France but also from Spain, Italy, and Malta. The mixture of cultures was most
pronounced in Oran and its surrounding area. Modern cities appeared next
to traditional Algerian medinas: Oran, Algiers, Philippeville, Bône, and, in
the interior, Constantine, Mascara, and Sidi-bel-Abbès. With their beautiful
buildings, their avenues and their gardens, they looked like European cities,
with the sun as a bonus. From it came the designation "Algiers the White"
for the capital, a pleasant sight for anyone arriving by ship. In 1962, when
Algeria won its independence, this population of European descent amounted
to nearly a million people, to which should be added 120,000 Jews, native to
Algeria, but integrated into the French state ever since the Crémieux decree
of 1870. There were nearly eight million Algerian Muslims. Even as colonists
dwelling in the countryside lived side by side with the "Arabs" on a daily basis,
learned their language and worked with them, city dwellers could go for years
closed off in their own world without meeting any, except as a mere backdrop to their daily lives. This is the life Pierre Claverie lived, as he himself
admitted. A sort of juxtaposition.

Algiers at that time had very distinct neighborhoods. The "Arabs" lived
especially in the Casbah and outlying districts. The pieds-noir population occupied the main part of the modern city, and each neighborhood had its own
social characteristics. The residential neighborhoods were on the heights (El
Biar, Hydra), while the business districts were along the seafront and near
the port. Bab el Oued, where the Claverie family lived, was a rather mixed
neighborhood: members of the middle class but also artisans, shopkeepers,
fishermen, many people from Mahon, migrating Spaniards from the Balearic
Islands, and Maltese. It was a neighborhood full of life, sometimes very colorful, where the local idiom ("pataouète") had juicy phrases and accents. There
was a style, a way of behaving, of telling stories, of savoring life, made famous by the epic tales of Cagayous, the Algerian urchin, which were retold
among pieds-noirs along with *kémia* and a glass of anisette.[7] Belcourt, home
of Étienne Claverie's mother, was even more working-class. It is where Albert
Camus spent his impoverished childhood, as told in his posthumous work *The*

Pierre, at age three, with his parents.

First Communion
at Bab el Oued.

Pierre Claverie (left) with the scouts
of Saint-Do in Algiers.

*First Man.*[8] His writings, like those of Jules Roy, help one better understand this Mediterranean mind-set, made up of love of life and exuberance, but also of an acute perception that these pleasures are ephemeral. Claverie later referred to this mentality while speaking of death and the passion for life characteristic of Mediterranean societies.

This was the setting in which Pierre Claverie grew up, a setting and a heritage that affected him profoundly. He truly felt himself to be pieds-noir and never repudiated this heritage, even later when he lived in Algerian Algeria. Although he established a certain distance from the political positions of many pieds-noirs, he remained emotionally faithful to them and showed it. He had their love of life and found it hard to bear the distance from sun and sea while he was studying in France, to the point that his master of studies gave him special permission to go out on the grounds of the priory from time to time, weather permitting, to read and work in shorts.

Like many pieds-noirs, he spent almost his entire youth in Algiers without really encountering "Arabs," as they were called at the time, except for the cleaning woman who came to the house:

> I spent my childhood in Algiers in a working-class neighborhood of that cosmopolitan Mediterranean city. Unlike other Europeans born in the countryside or small towns, I never had Arab friends, not in my neighborhood school, where there weren't any, nor at the high school, where there weren't many, and where the Algerian War was beginning to create an explosive climate. We were not racists, only indifferent, ignoring the majority of the people of the country. They made up part of the landscape for our excursions, the backdrop for our encounters and our lives. They were never partners.[9]

Claverie's understanding of the world of his youth evolved over the years. One can even say that he never stopped thinking about his own experience, reinterpreting it in light of the convictions he acquired over time. Thus, starting in 1991, the expression "colonial bubble" appeared in his writings. It returned frequently thereafter to characterize this enclosed world from which he eventually sought to free himself: "The fact is that I passed obliviously by the Muslims although they constituted nine-tenths of my human environment. I was able to live for twenty years in what I now call a 'colonial bubble' without even seeing the others."[10] More serious in his eyes, Christianity had done little to break down this ignorance about the other: "I must have heard numerous sermons about loving my neighbor, because I was also a Christian and a Boy Scout, without ever realizing that the Arabs were also my neighbors. I did not leave this bubble, as others were able to do, to go to discover this different world beside which I lived permanently without knowing it. It took a war to make that bubble burst."[11]

Pierre Claverie was not immersed in a truly racist climate, because his family environment protected him from that. Besides, many pieds-noirs were far from being exploitative colonists on a large scale, as has sometimes been suggested. It was more a matter of indifference on a day-to-day basis, the absence of awareness, even in people with the best intentions, that an Other was there. The secular ideology of the French Republic, moreover, helped accentuate the distance from the world of the Muslims. Relations were cordial, the French Algerians like to say. This is without a doubt, and it is this which made it more difficult to recognize the ambiguities, as shown by René Lenoir, another pied-noir who, like Pierre Claverie, reflected and followed a path of discovery on this point:[12]

> It took me a long time to see the racism around me. My father didn't talk about Arabs; he lived in his own world of the TSF and music. My mother, from the lower class, was ennobled by her goodness; she had a horror of vulgarity, and I never heard her insult anyone. The Arabs respected and liked her, especially the poor...But then I noticed that adults, neighbors or friends, spoke of the Arabs with fear or disdain. These "Arabs in general," reputed to be liars or fellows quick with their knives, were the people in the depths of the country whom one did not know. Fortunately, there were also "Arabs in particular," the vendor of fresh cheese with whom one exchanged pleasantries on the doorstep, the neighbor woman to whom one entrusted the baby, the gardener who entered our home like it was his own. These were exceptions, but every pied-noir family had its exceptions.[13]

This passage helps one understand the ambiguity of so many situations and the suffering of the French who left Algeria and believe that their relationship with the Arabs has been misrepresented. But, there was also racism plain and simple, as the same author shows:

> My perception of racism became more acute when I mingled with city folk in cafes, trams, and stadiums. The Arab bus conductor was always automatically addressed familiarly as "tu"...The common people among the pieds-noirs liked to use contemptuous terms like "raton," little rat; "bougnoule," wog; "bicot," Arab. With a majority in the cities,

they vaguely felt the rising competition from the common people among the Arabs in workshops, stores, offices . . . [14]

Eventually the question of the Other became the fundamental question for Pierre Claverie, to the point that one can ask whether he might not have had an unconscious longing to make up for something that he missed in his youth. This intelligent and friendly man could not fail to regret that he became aware so late of the ambiguities of the colonial world of his childhood. He would have to leave that environment to break decisively from his previous understanding of it. For the majority of people of that time, the simple fact was that Algeria was French and its regions were French provinces. And that's all there was to it.

## The Scouts of the Saint-Do: Friends for Life

Education was first of all a family matter and taken seriously, in an atmosphere of trust and humor. The elder Claveries knew pretty well what they wanted for their children: conscious of the limits of what the street can teach in a working-class district like Bab el Oued, they also had no illusions about the moral climate of a certain kind of Algerian bourgeoisie. Pierre began by going to the public Rochambeau elementary school in the neighborhood, then attended the lycée Bugeaud, since renamed the lycée Emir Abd el-Kader. Very few Algerian children attended the high school, the most well known in Algiers, "only two or three per class," as the Algerian author Jamal Amrani, one of Pierre Claverie's classmates from the sixth grade on, remembers. "He was always ranked among the best students," Amrani recalls, "and succeeded without giving the impression of working." The two were punished together more than once for provoking uncontrollable laughter, something to which the mischievous Pierre was accustomed. But in general his schooling passed without notable incident, and in 1956 he received his baccalaureate in category C (mathematics) with distinction.

There was also the catechism. His parents were Christians "as one is around the Mediterranean," said Pierre Claverie. Even though they rarely attended church in those days, they still registered their son for his catechism because that was part of a normal education. Pierre distinguished himself on the very first day, as his father laughingly reported, by crossing himself backward! He prepared there for his first communion and confirmation under the care of Abbé Streicher, an Alsatian who was a fervent partisan of French Algeria, like nearly everyone in the parish of St. Vincent de Paul in those days. This priest was present on the day of Pierre's own ordination at Le Saulchoir in July 1965. Pierre Claverie does not seem to have retained significant memories of this childhood religious education. It was quite otherwise with the Boy Scouts, where, thanks to the advice of a colleague at Shell, his father sent him in 1948 at the age of ten.

For many at that time in Algiers, the scouts had a nickname, "the Saint-Do." They labeled thus a group created by the Dominicans of Algiers in the early 1930s and developed through the combined efforts of Fr. Lefèvre and Max Dervaux. Consisting of three Boy Scout troops, three packs of Cub Scouts, a group of advanced scouts, and a company of Girl Scouts, the Saint-Do met at the little Dominican priory on the rue Edith Cavell, between the rue Michelet and the parc de Galland, in a completely European neighborhood of the city. Pierre belonged to "the Saint-Jacques," one of the three troops of the Saint-Do, and worked his way up through every rank from last man in his patrol to head of his troop, to advanced scout. He even became "un écuyer [squire] de France," a rare distinction limited to those who earned all their badges. "Pierre already wasn't like the others: he had a clear sense of his life," remembers Jean-François Cota, his friend in childhood and adolescence. His cheerful and lively temperament earned him the "vigilant squirrel" as his totem, or special name. He lived every aspect of the scouting experience: group life and camps with their games in the open air and their evenings around the campfire. Pierre went to a number of summer camps, from one in Alsace in 1949 to a camp for advanced scouts in the Ardennes in July 1957, which ended with a retreat at the monastery of Orval where the scouts, as he later confessed, made inroads in the monks' beer supplies. "I remember his returns home from summer camps," his sister, Anne-Marie, writes, "camps from which Pierre came back thin as a rake, as our mother said, black from the sun and accumulated filth, and overflowing with amazing stories which made me dream until my turn came to experience similar things."[15] Guy Maigrot, a fellow scout through all those years, remembers:

> Although only a new scout at the time, Pierre was a driving force in his patrol, with an innate cheerfulness and a sense of humor that was caustic but never malicious and which made us crack up . . . From that time on, what never ceased to attract me about him was that gaze from "elsewhere," both profound and vigilant, doubtless revealing his true questions, his lively intelligence always on the lookout . . . He caught on quickly and got to the heart of matters in a way astonishing for a boy of eleven or so.[16]

Is this reinterpretation after the fact, an idealization? Probably not, because this memory is consistent with the personality that we will come to know later. François Chavanes, who arrived as a young religious at the Dominican priory in Algiers in 1954, remembers a boy of sixteen, who was very lively and determined, drawing together his patrol around him "with both authority and gentleness." Pierre also excelled as an actor. In 1955 he played the role of Diafoirus in Molière's *Imaginary Invalid*, performed, as was every annual gala, at the salle Bordes in the center of Algiers. Besides camaraderie and a kind of apprenticeship in responsibility, Pierre received from the Saint-Do the influence of someone who indirectly made a significant mark on his life, Fr. Lefèvre.

Louis Lefèvre had just arrived from Iraq when the Saint-Do was entrusted to him by Fr. Le Tilly, prior of the Dominican priory of Algiers, founded in 1932 at the request of Archbishop Leynaud. A young religious of thirty-five, Fr. Lefèvre had spent five years in Mosul, where he, along with other French religious, took care of the youths enrolled in the séminaire St-Jean, where Chaldean and Syriac clerics were trained. There, among other things, he created a brass band of which he was very proud. The son of a well-to-do family of Neuilly, he liked to associate with the upper crust of Algiers. But he also had zeal to spare and a real influence over young people, to whom he gave a "catechism of perseverance" that helped many adolescents deepen their faith. His persona would be emblematic of the Saint-Do, up until its dissolution in 1963 and even afterward, thanks to a very active network of "old boys of the group Saint-Dominic d'Alger," to which he gave inspiration and life. For all these youths, he was and often remained "Father," the one who knew all of them by their first names and helped them along their paths in life. Evenings around the campfire he brought the scouts together around him, "and Father taught me about God," as Jacques Campredon, a former president of the old boys of the Saint-Do, puts it so well. He had a marked impact on the boys, teaching and confirming them in their faith, to the point that, still today, these former scouts, organized as an association, continue to attend reunions in large numbers and stay in contact with one another through a regular bulletin, *Feux*, created in 1936 and still numbering 650 subscribers.[17]

Fr. Lefèvre left his mark on Pierre Claverie, who said in 1988 at the celebration of the tenth anniversary of his death:

Ten years already, and his blue-eyed gaze rarely leaves me, sometimes mocking with the wrinkles at the corners of his eyes, sometimes somber and profound in attentiveness or reflection ... There is such a weight of presence in this gaze that I am still amazed at Father's absence. All the other things about him seem only the unchanging props of this presence: Basque beret on his head, a belt tightly holding his Dominican habit or his light smock, his square goatee, his head high, a walking stick in his hand, his laced boots on his feet, a smile on his lips. More than his words, I believe that it was this presence that made such a strong impression on me. Discreet and attentive, distant and yet close, unimposing but also intense.[18]

It was thanks to him that Pierre was able to make his childhood faith more profound, but this was more, as he admitted himself, through a sort of presence and example than by formal teaching, which does not seem to have made a great impression:

I must not have been spiritual or devout enough to follow his religious instruction with sufficient attention to talk about it today. I don't re-member a thing ... except the profound respect that formed around him as he prayed or led prayers. Next to him, we were able to discover that one can be proud and joyful to be Christians without being timid or overly anxious about it.[19]

These few modest words allow us to imagine what Pierre received from him. Was it Fr. Lefèvre who led him to the Dominican order? Only indirectly, as he indicated to his parents when he informed them of his decision to enter the novitiate:

He never encouraged me for a single instant to join the order, no more than he held me back from doing so. It would be too simpleminded, I believe, to think that Father is a recruiter who stumbled upon a fool ripe for plucking, and it would be very uncharitable to credit to him something that comes only from me — and a little from the family education that you have given me ... That he guided me, unconsciously on his part, he would tell you himself if you spoke about it one day, as, if you want to put it this way, one follows the guide on an excursion that one has chosen to take ... (letter of October 20, 1958)

Even while acknowledging a debt, Pierre Claverie proclaimed his free choice in this matter. Gradually, in the course of his personal maturation, he distanced himself from some of Fr. Lefèvre's positions, while maintaining his affection for him. Fr. Lefèvre was in fact a rather committed partisan of

French Algeria, like the majority of the Dominicans in Algiers in those days, of whom he was at one time the prior. His partisanship was not so much the product of an explicit ideology — as was the case for others — as of a lack of detachment from the pieds-noir milieu in which he was immersed. Moreover, he seems to have been influenced by reading a fundamentalist journal, *La Pensée catholique,* published by his own brother, Abbé Luc Lefèvre. In 1971, Pierre Claverie wrote to him to express his disappointment with his mental blocks concerning the future of Algeria. Here is what he said about it to his parents, who were friends of Fr. Lefèvre:

> When will he free himself from this negative and reactionary attitude? Ten years afterward, is it not possible to begin to look a little more toward the present and the future? I'm not saying that the past is "unimportant" or that it is necessary to deny the pain, still too acute, of the pieds-noirs. I'm only saying, as you well know, that there is no point in maintaining it by all sorts of outward signs and inappropriate articles. (letter of October 25, 1971)

Fr. Lefèvre, like many pieds-noirs, left Algeria shortly after it gained its independence. Pierre Claverie, however, decided one day to return there, which earned him a rather disillusioned note from his former chaplain. At one time Fr. Lefèvre had dreamed that Pierre might succeed him as chaplain of the Saint-Do. Their paths were going to diverge significantly, but Pierre Claverie always remained grateful to him. From 1983 on, five years after Fr. Lefèvre's death, Pierre did, in a way, as we will see, become his successor. It was for the Saint-Do that he gave a magnificent sermon on the cross of Christ and the gift of his own life at Prouilhe on June 23, 1996, a couple of weeks before his death.[20] With the personal warmth and the clarity of expression of which he was capable, he shared with these old boys of Algeria — his old scouting friends — his thoughts and questions about the new Algeria, Islam, and the ties to be renewed between the two shores of the Mediterranean. Despite their still open wounds, several members of the Saint-Do concretely demonstrated their solidarity with Pierre's choice and today's Algeria by organizing shipments of books to the libraries of the diocese of Oran and to the organization Caritas-Algeria, of which Denis Gonzalez, another old member of the Saint-Do, was in charge. One sees here another of Pierre Claverie's character traits: a personal aversion to ideological confrontation, to the point of sometimes appearing ambiguous. He had more faith in human relations than in overly abstract debates. Did points of view seem irreconcilable? He would break into laughter and talk about something else. But the bonds, the human relations, were not severed.

## A Young Man Facing the Great Choices of Life

Summer 1956: Pierre Claverie had the scientific baccalaureate in hand. He thought about his future and envisaged the possibility of entering a seminary. He first confided his thoughts to Jean-François Cota one evening at the scout camp beside the campfire. His father, to whom he then spoke about it, advised him to pursue his university education before making a decision. Concern to see his son mature? Fear that the idea was just a youthful caprice? Pierre accepted the advice and agreed with his parents that he would reopen the matter after he had earned a *licence*, a bachelor's degree, or an engineering certificate. So he undertook a first year of preparatory classes in Algiers, where he led the life of a normal young man, studying, to be sure, but also living with the exuberance of youth in the environment that Albert Camus describes in *Summer:*[21] He loved music, was passionate about the cinema, and cruised around Algiers on his motorbike. His father had had him take some dance lessons and, says his sister, Anne-Marie, "he could dance the fox-trot, waltz, and cha-cha respectably." In human eyes, everything considered, he was on a typical track.

But things turned out totally differently. After this first year of preparatory classes for schools of engineering, to which he failed to gain admission, Pierre Claverie left at the start of the next school year for Grenoble to continue his preparation for the entrance examinations. He took ship for Marseille on the eve of November 1, 1957. What was he thinking about, leaning on the rail of the *Ville d'Alger*, as the city of his childhood disappeared in the haze? Was he still considering what had preoccupied him during the retreat at the priory of Orval in Belgium, at the end of scout camp in July? Or was he thinking about the way the political and security situation in Algeria was deteriorating? The Battle of Algiers had just ended with the arrest of Yacef Saadi on September 24, 1957. No one now could be unaware that exactly three years before, on November 1, 1954, a nationalist movement had begun a genuine insurrection in eastern Algeria, in the Aurès Mountains. Pierre Claverie was en route to his destiny; he was leaving an Algeria full of turmoil. He would return one day, but a very different person, filled with a passion finally to get to know the land of his childhood and youth. His whole life would be dedicated to reestablishing ties with this country. From this moment of his departure until his return in 1967, the world of his childhood would disintegrate in violence. Personal changes, profound and painful, were in his future also. It was on that day, November 1, 1957, that the weekly correspondence with his loved ones, which would make it possible to trace Pierre's path, week by week, for the next thirty-eight years, began.

## Chapter Two

# From University to Novitiate
## A Time of Transition

> The emergence of the Other, the recognition of the Other, the
> adjustment to the Other became an obsession with me. It is very
> likely what lies at the origin of my religious vocation.[1]
> — *Pierre Claverie*

Pierre Claverie disembarked at Marseille at the beginning of November 1957 after a rough crossing. The rain discouraged him from taking his time, so he immediately went to Grenoble where his first days were spent settling in: finding a place to live, enrolling in the math, physics, and chemistry division of the university. "It's pouring rain, and the weather is getting nippy," he noted in his first letter. "Last night when I went to bed I felt that I was far from Algiers, and that really hit home." In reality, this crossing and the change in climate and environment were only the beginning of much deeper and more painful passages that Pierre was going to have to live through. Arguments about the future of Algeria were stirring up public opinion. They were going to lead to a profound reorientation of his life.

## The Emergence of Algerian Nationalism

When Pierre Claverie left Algeria, the reality of Algerian nationalism had become an undeniable fact. The targets of the first hit-and-run attacks had been large colonial properties or homes in isolated areas: a simple matter of terrorism, people liked to say, as though to reassure themselves. However, the bombs planted in September 1956 at the Milk Bar and La Cafétéria, right in the heart of Algiers, provoked fear both in Algeria and in France. Robert Lacoste, the governor-general, called on General Massu, commander of the Tenth Parachutist Division, and gave him all police powers in the area of Algiers in order to bring the rebellion to an end. In less than six months this had been accomplished and there was renewed hope that the problem of the "Algerian events" had been resolved. The creation of the Morice Line on

17

the borders was intended to prevent the rebellion from acquiring arms from
external supporters. Militarily, France had regained the upper hand. But in
reality a nationalist movement had been working at a grassroots level within
Algerian society for decades.[2] This was a movement that public opinion in
the mother country, and even more in the world of the pieds-noirs, had un-
derestimated, passing it off as merely sporadic terrorism. When the Algerian
War broke out, "nothing had enabled me to foresee it," wrote Pierre Claverie,
"even though people had been laying the groundwork for it for thirty years."[3]
It was, in fact, a historical process that sprang from the very heart of Algerian society. At first France strove to downplay the crisis by speaking only of
Algerian "events," but it was in fact a war, a war of liberation.

The movement had come a long way and enjoyed widespread support
among the Algerian people, where nationalism had developed in two distinct
worlds: the revolutionary world of emigrant workers in France and the cultivated Muslim circles, the *ulema*. In the 1930s there were about 100,000
Algerians in France, mostly laborers who had been driven from their country
by poverty and who took on the most physically difficult jobs. The workers'
world was at that time in ferment with the dream of a world revolution, one
aspect of which would be the liberation of colonized peoples. The French
Communist Party attracted leaders like Chou En Lai and Ho Chi Minh, who
were students in France at that time. It was under the influence of the French
Communist Party that a militant Algerian, Messali Haj, created in 1926 a
movement, l'Étoile nord-africaine (the North African star), dedicated to promoting an anticolonial struggle and, as a final goal, the independence of
Algeria. Dissolved by the French government, the movement was reborn in
1937 in the form of a political party, le Parti du peuple algérien (Algerian
People's Party) (PPA), the future MTLD, Mouvement pour le triomphe des
libertés démocratiques (Movement for the Triumph of Democratic Liberties).
Opinions were divided between supporters of working for independence by
legal means and more radical militants who advocated armed struggle. From
1945 on, it was the latter approach that became dominant, and in 1947 a
structure, l'Organisation spéciale (OS), was put in place to begin the armed
struggle. This first source of the Algerian nationalist movement was strongly
influenced by the Communist workers' movement.

The other branch of Algerian nationalism, the Mouvement des oulémas,
came from a very different world. These were Muslim religious leaders: muftis,
imams, specialists in the Qur'an and Muslim law; they were often prominent
and moderate people who were searching for ways to renew an Islam that

they believed to be too rigid, without going so far as to challenge explicitly the colonial power. They were all fascinated by the currents of the Arab
renaissance that had been moving through the Muslim world since the nineteenth century through people like Jamal Eddine el Afghani. Studying in the
universities of al-Azhar in Cairo, the Zitouna in Tunis, and the Qarawiyyîne
of Fez, Algerian religious leaders became conscious of the state of cultural
submission in which their country found itself and fought to win greater respect for Algerian identity, especially by promoting the study of Arabic. Their
leader was Sheikh Ben Badis, who gave concrete form to these aspirations in
1931 when he created the Mouvement des oulémas, whose password became
a famous slogan: "Islam is my religion; Arabic is my language; Algeria is my
homeland."

Although they stemmed from very divergent cultural and political out-
looks, these two approaches joined forces and crystallized in a nationalist
movement because of the poverty in which the majority of the Algerian people
lived and the repression that intensified after the end of World War II. Having
given many of their own lives to help liberate France from the Germans, the
Algerians were less and less willing to accept their situation as a colonized
people. Thus the PPA called for demonstrations in favor of independence
on May 8, 1945, and some of them became violent. The response to these
demonstrations was merciless, killing between 15,000 and 45,000 people in
the Setif region, depending on the sources. This repression opened the chasm
between France and the Algerian nationalists for good, and it led many of
the latter to radicalize their demands. Finally becoming aware of the poverty
in which much of the Muslim population lived, the French government then
launched a vast building program, the "Constantine Plan," to try to make up
for the lack of housing, schools, and clinics primarily for the Muslim population. But it was too late. Algerian nationalism had already moved on to
revolutionary action and quickly gained support from the Algerian people.
The main directors of the Front nationale de libération (FLN) met in the
Soummam Valley in 1956 to chart a political and military strategy that would
lead to independence in 1962. The French army tried to win popular support through a policy that was called "pacification," in which the concern for
the education and health of the people was real, but the Algerian nationalists
were winning points on the political and diplomatic fronts. Some mistakes like
the deadly bombardment by the French of Sakhiet, a village on the Tunisian
border, did the rest. After nearly winning this war militarily, France lost on
the political front, and not without encountering some serious agitation in
the mother country itself.

## Grenoble: A Young Student at Loose Ends

The French university where Pierre Claverie arrived was stirred up by debates about what was from then on called the Algerian War. After the first hit-and-run attacks of the revolution on November 1, 1954, the French authorities had engaged more and more in a policy of repression that some French political groups denounced. Meanwhile, the French army, confronted with guerilla warfare, tried to isolate the combatants by moving the civilian population to "relocation villages" and then carried out strong-armed "pacification" operations in the mountains. It was what Yves Courrière called in his history of the war "the time of the leopards,"[4] that is of the "paras," the elite French parachutist regiments. In France, not only the political groups following the Communist line but also the socially conscious democratic groups denounced the process of repression into which France was entering. Works like Pierre-Henri Simon's *Contre la torture* (Against Torture), published in 1957, awakened public opinion, which for a long time had been indifferent, to the dangerous deviations from normal French policies. Public opinion was even more sensitive to this because numerous young men were drafted and sent to the front, where sometimes they lost their lives. That's war. All of this greatly stirred up the students in universities, which were like sounding boards for the national debates. Having left his protective family environment for the first time, Pierre Claverie, a young pied-noir viscerally attached to his land, could not remain indifferent.

Enrolled in the division of sciences, he was taking, without any real enthusiasm, preparatory courses for the admissions exams. The situation was very different from the relaxed atmosphere of the previous year in Algiers. There were many students, and the focus on the coming exams was intense. He worked steadily, getting good enough grades on tests, but he was not able fully to commit himself to this uninteresting cramming. He did not really try to hide this from his parents, in whom he confided with remarkable openness in their regular correspondence. His father's letters in response showed that he was following closely. A Citroën for excursions, movies, and detective novels gobbled down one after another did not help at all: he was not happy. While spending winter vacation with an uncle at Monte Carlo, he wrote to his family:

> Since my arrival here, I've dragged myself from one detective story to another without any appetite at all for my work. Thus on Friday afternoon a detective novel; Saturday afternoon *Tu seras seul dans ton cercueil* [You Will Be Alone in Your Coffin]; *Le Temps des gros sous* [The Time

of Big Money]; *Le cave se rebiffe* [The Dupe Fights Back], and *Qui a tué Harry?* [Who Killed Harry?]. A little bite; a few hours and that's all. (letter of January 6, 1958)

The only matter about which he felt passionate, at least to outward appearances, was politics. He attended lecture-debates in the university's lecture halls, and from the very beginning the dominant tone offended his pieds-noir feelings. He found the debates too oriented around the mother country:

> On Friday I went to a lecture on the "Algerian problem." Five different opinions, the invitation had announced. The hall was packed (1500 people), but all were in agreement...Nobody thinks about the fate of the million Europeans in Algeria. NOT ONE of the five speakers even mentioned it. For them, the question does not even come up; we are banished from France. After all, what were we doing down there in the first place? They're still wondering about that...(letter of January 13, 1958)

But the deeds that were denounced had in fact occurred. Starting in 1957, the acts of torture performed by Colonel Bigeard's parachutists had alarmed a segment of public opinion. Challenged, Pierre Claverie set out to learn more. First he read some works defending "pacification," that operation intended to contain the rebellion: Jean-Yves Alquier's *Nous avons pacifié Tazalt, ou le Journal de marche d'un officier parachutiste en Algérie* [We Have Pacified Tazalt, or The Daily Log of an Officer of the Parachutists in Algeria] ("to read and disseminate widely, which I am doing," he said), and *Une autre Algérie française,* by the Count of Paris. But he also read some more critical works, like *L'Algérie en 57,* by Germaine Tillion, whose quality he recognized,[5] and went to hear a lecture by Colonel Pierre Rondot, a specialist of the Middle East. But it is clear that his political feelings lay naturally to the right. In this he reflected the dominant feelings of the pieds-noir milieu from which he came. This orientation meant that he was quickly recruited by a group, le Comité universitaire d'information politique (CUIP), whose purpose was "to fight against progressivism by presenting more realistic and reliable information." "This committee is in fact very far to the right and even has a royalist tendency," he wrote to his parents. "Catholic for the most part, it provides a counterbalance to Jesuit-progressive influence" (letter of January 17, 1958).

It took Pierre only fifteen days to see the organization's intellectual weakness. "In terms of doctrine, the CUIP just doesn't measure up," he wrote on January 30. "Their verbal opposition has covered them with ridicule; only their fists have enabled them to get by, but badly of course." In the minority, these little groups on the right engaged in rather superficial political analysis. Resorting to insulting language (*"les cocos,"* the commies; the *"crétins de frangaos"*[6]), they sometimes came to blows with their opponents. In their pamphlets, they constantly denounced the Communists and the politician Pierre Mendès France. But that fit in with Pierre Claverie's natural political feelings. He was a member of this movement for one semester, participating along with others who raised their voice in opposition in general student assemblies and at the student chapel. Some scapegoats were booed: André Mandouze, a well-known scholar who was a specialist on St. Augustine, and who took a stand in favor of independence for Algeria; *Témoignage chrétien* (Christian Witness), a left-wing Christian newspaper that willingly opened its columns to those who, like Mandouze or François Mauriac, denounced torture in Algeria.[7] From denunciation, these little groups soon moved to action. In March 1958, on Sundays, operations to seize copies of *Témoignage chrétien* at church doors were organized. Following events in Lyon where copies of the newspaper were taken and then burned at the door of the archbishop's residence, a similar operation took place at Grenoble on March 17. Pierre took part and described the event to his parents:

> In bed at 2:00 a.m., I was up at 7:00 a.m. for "Operation Clean the Churches," organized with great secrecy by our committee of the CUIP. By 8:00 two groups of four had been put together, one in a Citroën, the Other in a Peugeot (driven by a retired colonel) — I was in that one — to grab copies of *TC* (*Témoignage Chrétien*) from where they are sold in churches. With my team I "took care of" the five churches in the city center without any opposition, or "technical incident," in any of the churches. At 10:30 we returned with our "harvest" of fifty newspapers which, torn into quarters, will be sent to the bishop. The operation came at a particularly good time because this week *TC* spoke (yet again) about the odious barbaric actions of the army (a communiqué from the Mission de France), about police torture (an article by Rhamdani), about the verdict against Pasteur Mathiot (a supporter of the Algerian rebels — see article by Mandouze) . . . (letter of March 17, 1958)

His political activism would not go any further than that and would be of short duration because on April 18, 1958, Pierre wrote to his parents: "As for political questions, I've dropped everything." But the quality of his political analysis would evolve more slowly.[8] Little by little, one gets the feeling that his heart was no longer in it. What caused this change? His father's reactions in letters, which can be imagined from his son's responses, no doubt played a part. Étienne Claverie was following his son closely and took advantage of a business trip to Paris in late February 1958 to make a quick stopover in Grenoble. He wrote to the family members who were still in Algiers, "You can't imagine the intensity with which you are living with me, a thousand times more than when I am close to you. What would I have here below, if I didn't have you? Pierre unchanged. Has gained much self-assurance and decisiveness. Is still our son and brother. Am pleased with him in every way. Skinny as always, but strong" (letter of February 22, 1958).

This episode enables us to imagine just how much Pierre Claverie's maturation was often connected to exchanges with his father, who questioned him continuously, with a real concern for honesty. The weakness of the arguments of the little right-wing groups, more emotional than coherent, probably also led him to distance himself pretty quickly from them. But his membership in this group, brief though it was, is of interest because it shows the confusion in which many French people of Algeria, feeling abandoned by France and misunderstood, found themselves at that time. This was grasped by de Gaulle, who was applauded for his famous, if ambiguous, statement of June 4, 1958, at the Forum in Algiers, "I have understood you." Another factor was perhaps even more decisive in this evolution:

> Difficult arguments at the doors of the churches with well-behaved gentlemen who cannot really see how, as Christians, we approve:
>
> – of a policy of force against a people who ask for nothing but the right to exist
>
> – of torture, reprisals, etc. (letter of March 24, 1958)

He is referring to an argument, which appears to have been in quite some depth, with a man selling *Témoignage Chrétien,* Mr. Tirard, who sent Pierre a seven-page letter at the end of April to push him further in his consideration of the issues. Had Mr. Tirard discerned true human and Christian material in this young partisan of French Algeria who was just beginning as an activist? Several years later, when Pierre Claverie went to a meeting of the Centre des intellectuals catholiques dedicated to Algeria, he recalled that he had once gone there in Grenoble "with a group of vandals and maybe a homemade bomb" (letter of June 12, 1961). His evolution on the Algerian question was only just beginning.

The other important place in his evolution was the student chapel, where he was involved from the beginning, although he did not feel comfortable there. The chaplain was a Jesuit, Georges Haubtmann, whose goal was to help the students reflect and mature in the troubled political context of the Algerian War. Henri LeMasne recalls the efforts this priest made to shape the understanding of the young students of Grenoble. Pierre Claverie at first went to the chapel to present an opposing point of view in a reflection group on the theme of the church and politics. Invited to plan a chapel meeting on the prologue of the Gospel of Saint John, he admitted, "I really want to go after the Jesuit on duty, who has a reputation as a progressive, on the Algerian question" (letter of January 30, 1958). In reality, this Fr. Haubtmann had a very good understanding of the Algerian question. The moving spirit behind the CCU (Centre catholique universitaire), he certainly was acquainted with his Jesuit brethren of the CCU in Algiers who had been trying for several years to open the eyes of the young pieds-noir students of Algiers to the reality of the underdevelopment of the majority of Algeria's Arab population. The Jesuit Louis Coignet was the moving spirit behind the Association des étudiants catholiques of Algiers, known by the nickname "l'Asso," which was going to play a decisive role in awakening the consciences of some young Christian pieds-noirs. Daniel Junqua, an active member of l'Asso, explains, "The majority of Europeans were not colonists: they lived in the city where the only Algerians they knew were the cleaning woman, the *fatma*, who was also the children's nanny. Some were racists, but all believed in a French Algeria. For them to see clearly, there had to be some spark to start the process." Coignet was a wonderful catalyst for an entire group of young people who remained very closely tied to Algeria and its future. Before even speaking about "colonialism," he first helped the students to recognize the poverty of the Muslims who surrounded them. The secretariat for social affairs, whose driving force was another Jesuit, Henri Sanson, in 1959 published a pamphlet entitled "Le Sous-Développement en Algérie" ("Underdevelopment in Algeria"). Among the Christians of Algeria, some were already involved in social or union work.[9] Later, they had to reflect on the issue of torture and found themselves in political positions close to those of the Communists and a growing share of public opinion in France.[10]

Those in Algeria who had been in contact with these groups of people saw the Algerian question very differently from the majority of pieds-noirs. But these social activists were a tiny minority, soon targeted for elimination by the activists of a group defending French Algeria, the OAS (Organisation armée secrète), who would hunt them down. Their ranks included "liberal Christians" whose role would be important in the rebirth of the Catholic Church in Algeria after independence. Pierre Claverie would become close to them in time, without having followed the same path, but, at this moment, he was on a completely different planet. Despite their undeniable good qualities, his family and the scouts of the Saint-Do had not opened his eyes, and in that he is a reflection of the majority of people around him. It would take several more years, at least four more, to truly change his political vision. Later, confronted by another period of violence, he would write, "Perhaps because I ignored the Other or denied his very existence, one day he jumped in my face. He made my closed universe explode, so it fell apart in violence — but could it have been otherwise?"[11]

What did Pierre really live through in his innermost being during this spring of 1958 as he groped for his true path somewhere between the student chapel where he did not feel understood and little groups of reactionary agitators, whose limitations he had seen? His true mental state breaks through when he tells about the twentieth birthday party his friends organized for him on May 8, 1958:

> Today I am in a "morbid funk." I muse on memories and dark thoughts so I can't focus my attention on any of my notebooks. I thought this morning as I tried to draw up the accounts for the first twenty years of my life that the results are not exactly brilliant. When I think about everything that I still have to do, I feel deeply discouraged. I'm tired of having only one job that consists of setting my butt on a seat and listening to classes and learning the materials and spitting them out again without any conviction at all, and how many more years will this last! . . . Oh, I know that I am preparing for my future, etc., etc. (letter of May 8, 1958)

At loose ends, Pierre Claverie seems to have begun to find his internal compass during a student pilgrimage to La Salette. The chaplain's political preoccupations, included in the plan of activities, continued to irritate him, and he remained resistant to one-sided reflection groups, "an obvious snare into which all the people tormented by Algeria were supposed to fall," he comments sarcastically. Still, something was clearly taking place inside of him on this occasion, making these two days a ray of sunshine in the midst of gloomy months:

> From the mountain's first foothills, sun and blue sky . . . During this pilgrimage I discovered that the religion of catechisms has nothing to do with that religion which should be ours. Not only does one throw over notions that seemed basic, but one makes all truths much more present and what one calls Mysteries more alive . . . We join together as a group

of nine to eat at a pass above La Salette. The air is thin and the wind that blows up there makes us stagger. A few scattered snowdrifts remain. Lunch in the sun. (letter of May 12, 1958)

With the gift of hindsight, how can one come to any conclusion except that he was touched by grace there? It is the spirit that set a process of evolution in motion that would take him a long, long way. As if to put a stamp on this moment of passage, Pierre had a blast with his buddies on the way back: sliding down the slope of dry grass on their rear ends and rolling uncontrollably to the ditches at the bottom. They ran through the entire musical repertoire, "from 'La Claire fontaine' to 'Nini peau de chien.' We were really crazy," he writes. "In fact, people noticed us from the bottom, if only because of our wild shouts" (letter of May 12, 1958).[12]

The month of May was spent preparing for the admissions competitions for engineering schools in June, but Pierre followed the events in Algeria closely: the creation of a Committee of Public Safety on May 13, and in June the call to de Gaulle to "save the Republic." Although continuing to react with the emotional fiber of a French Algerian, he did not get much involved, except for going one night to paint the cross of Lorraine in support of de Gaulle on the sidewalks of the city center. Politically, he had not yet evolved very far, but his heart was not in it any more. On June 5 he began the competitions at Strasbourg, then took those at Grenoble, thinking already of the summer scout camp he would be attending with the Saint-Do. The process of selection was very tough, and he failed to gain admission! "Then the fortunate ones buy us a drink," he comments. "A dinner without joy and then we go to listen to some records to cheer ourselves up. Of course it's been raining all night and still this morning... My plans for the immediate future have been completely overthrown" (letters of June 26 and 30).

What does that last phrase mean? Is he speaking of a setback on his exams, or is it already another matter, which will in fact turn his life upside down? In the course of the summer other plans began to ripen in him. He shared them with his parents after the summer was over, as he was taking his examinations again. This letter of October 20, 1958, announces the major change of direction in his life.

## Finally a True Plan: "To Give One's Life Completely"

In this handwritten letter, eleven half-page sheets long, Pierre announced to his parents his decision to enter either the Dominican novitiate or a seminary.[13] It deserves to be quoted in its entirety because it illuminates his inner debates and exhibits his maturity, but here are the essential passages:

Dear Parents,

Yes, I am beginning this letter in the traditional way because I would be out of line to joke around in light of what I am going to say to you.

You certainly remember the little conversation we had the year I received my baccalaureate on a small matter to which we, with good reason, decided not to return until a specific time that we set as the moment when I received my bachelor's degree or an engineering certificate.

At that time you were able to temper my enthusiasms, which might have seemed emotional, maybe even childish (an imitation as Papa would say), and you surely said to yourselves, "This will pass away as he grows up, like his acne, or when he has a sweetheart . . ."

And Pierre then examined the various elements of his life during his second year at the university. As for a girlfriend, he said he had "played the game to the full, up to the limits of what normal morality can accept, and we were excellent friends . . . I assure you that if I hadn't had another goal in the back of my mind I wouldn't have hesitated an instant to play the game to the end with her; she was worth it." At Grenoble he made some friends, but above all worked to obtain his diploma at any cost.

And yet . . . This year I studied the behavior of those, like me, who were preparing for this examination. I was like an outsider among them . . . First, they are all working to be engineers . . . and as they head toward this goal, they all understand that they will spend their whole lives amidst industrial blueprints or electrical machinery. They are all interested, to varying degrees, in machines and technical progress. They read *Science et avenir* [Science and the Future]. They build radios or loudspeakers, etc. Their studies, without being an ideal for them, are a reason for living. For me, things are different. I have arrived at this level of scientific studies . . . by forcing myself to acquire a knowledge that I know has nothing whatsoever to do with my goals in life.

If I have chosen the priesthood — or let's say a religious vocation — it is to give myself entirely to something that I feel is the most beautiful thing in the world; it is to wear myself out for something that would be worth the effort for others as well as for myself. I know what I lose by this, but I also know what I gain and what I will enable others to gain. Do you see my intentions? Do you believe they can be reconciled with the miserable years I would waste to scrape out, certificate by certificate, a diploma that leads me nowhere?

I am not "giving up" — or rather I am, but not in the sense of running from my responsibilities and my work. I am giving up the life that has been offered to me in the course of my studies. For the rest, you know full well that, if I avoid certain social responsibilities in a religious order, I take on others that are far more arduous.

Having announced his plans, Pierre considered the pain that such a choice might give to his parents, who very much wanted to have grandchildren: "What is hardest for me, right now, is the tear that I imagine in Mama's eyes and the tightness in Papa's throat. There they are: the first trial and the first shock. That's why I was so hesitant to speak of this during our vacation when we were so carefree and, above all, so happy to be together..."[14] He tried, then, to show them that he was not abandoning them, even if his choice was motivated "by a greater love."

There follow some comments on Fr. Lefèvre's modest role in his decision ("as one follows the guide on an excursion that one has chosen to take") and a proposal for a plan of action: first a weeklong retreat among the Dominicans in Paris or in Lille, a retreat "especially necessary," confides Pierre, "because I am throwing myself into the matter armed only with my little faith, a little love, a couple of short retreats, and a great deal of inexperience." If he had been advised not to follow the Dominican life, he would have considered the possibility of turning to the secular clergy of Saint-Sulpice or to the French seminary at Rome, but he was very worried that he would not be able to stick with it there, because "life in a religious community, even if it carries with it little inconveniences because of its human nature, also brings the immense comfort of communal prayer and reflection." Promising to visit Algiers soon, before the big separation from his family that he dreaded, he concluded:

> I embrace both of you as strongly as I love you. You are the best parents that one could wish for (as everyone agrees) and that's why you are giving to them (to everyone) a priest.
>
> I will send you this letter right after I take my oral exam.
>
> Until we see each other again.
>
> Pierre

At this moment, Pierre Claverie provided very little explanation of why he chose the Dominican order. Perhaps it was his connection to the Saint-Do that pointed him in this direction, even though he wished to minimize the

In his twentieth year, a last vacation with his family
on the Mediterranean before entering the novitiate.

influence of Fr. Lefèvre in this choice. But he did not rule out the possibility
of living his plan to "give himself entirely" by another means (Saint-Sulpice
or the diocesan clergy). The fact of the matter is that Pierre's intuition was
correct. Over the years, he found himself completely comfortable with the fundamental characteristics of the Dominicans: the taste for study and preaching,
the fraternal life, and a certain sense of truth. This letter was certainly a shock
for Pierre's parents. Annie Prénat, who looked after them in their old age,
reports that the question of grandchildren, "of little Claveries," had been a
matter of real suffering for them. But they respected their son's liberty. Mamie
outfitted him for his new life, sneaking some of her husband's own suits into
his luggage! The letter (with some excerpts below) that Étienne Claverie sent
a month later to the master of studies of the novices at Lille says a great deal
about the quality of this man:

Algiers, November 23, 1958

Reverend Father:

Last Thursday's plane took our son Pierre toward his new destiny. He
will soon be with you . . . I have waited for this moment to leave behind
a sort of anonymity, which I have not ceased to fear you would interpret

unfavorably...Now that divine Providence has brought everything to pass according to his will, it is time to present ourselves to you and perhaps help you know Pierre better through his parents.

Étienne Claverie then wrote of the two years of "probation" that he had requested from his son, in the course of which he quickly understood that his son remained "always serenely constant in his inner resolution." He added, "But what Pierre has not been able to convey fully to you is the intense emotion with which we accepted his decision. Since nothing, or very little, in his family circle seemed to incline him to such a Mission, we had to recognize a Call without appeal..." And his father then explained that for him religion had for a long time been merely a "formality" that he had not thought about deeply until his son Pierre, in catechism class, obliged him to take it more seriously:

To his great joy, I began to accompany him to church. So that I would be able to talk meaningfully with him about it, I started to prepare for Mass in a superb daily missal that he and his sister gave to me. And that is how, little by little, it became possible for me to perceive a light, to understand better and follow my son's development. My faith is still quite weak and shaky, but I know that the Lord, who never stops giving me evidence of his concern, will allow me to communicate more closely with him through my child, his future servant. The same feelings animate his mother, whom I always represent to my children as the natural link that unites them with God...

Our son is now yours. All of our prayers are with all of you. Once again, may he know how to bless you as he has always blessed us. He is a good and loyal young man...

Étienne Claverie

Then things started to happen very rapidly. Pierre spent a few days at the house of studies of Le Saulchoir near Paris. From there he wrote on October 27, "So, except for the legion of mosquitoes that is attacking my window, I am very, very happy and I can't wait to come home to share with you at least a little of my joy." Fr. Marneffe, the master of studies, sent Pierre immediately to Lille, where he met Fr. Delalande, the master of the novices. He then took the normal psychological tests with Fr. Plé and Abbé Marc Oraison in Paris, and returned to Algiers, heralded by a telegram dated November 6: "Delalande agrees. Will be in Algiers Sunday. Letter follows. Kisses. Pierre."

After those long and painful months in Grenoble, bounced between the scientific studies that bored him and a political agitation that gave him little satisfaction, one word sums up Pierre's mental state: joy. It would be with him for a long time.

## To the Novitiate in Lille: The Opening Up of Horizons

The preliminary evaluations were favorable, so he was admitted very quickly because the novitiate year had already begun for twelve novices who had arrived in October and November. Pierre Claverie took the habit when his turn came on December 7, 1958, and described his feelings thus: "I wish that you could be happy with the same joy that I am feeling and with the same satisfaction and confidence that what needed to happen has come to pass. If only it lasts!" It would.

The first weeks were devoted to a variety of discoveries, both banal and profound. First he had to get to know the twelve brothers with whom he would proceed on this path, as well as the master of the novices, a musician in frail health, who was a little overwhelmed by such a large novitiate but a "very just and profound guy, with a sense of truth, like Papa," comments Pierre (letter of December 14, 1958). As one might imagine, such a group included very diverse personalities, sometimes very different from his own. Pierre became very close to a young American brother, Wayne White, whose background and personality fascinated him. An American who loved France, White was an artist, very cultivated, and a bit of a globe-trotter: he had just hitchhiked back from India! Their friendship was reserved but deep. "Fr. Delalande taught us simplicity," says Wayne White, "starting with that of music. He did not like the baroque and was unhappy with a church too concerned with power: that made an impression on us." This man, whom many regarded as "not up to" the situation, perhaps taught Pierre Claverie more than is generally believed. When Pierre arrived at the house of studies, he had already acquired a spirit of poverty and detachment, as Albert de Monléon, one of his companions, recalls. This was also the time for the amusing discovery of the ways and customs of a novitiate: how to climb stairs or sit down wearing a Dominican robe "without getting the rosary stuck in the rungs of the chair," how to ring the bells or, even more comical in his eyes, how to be the barber of the community. "Pierre was mischievous," White adds, "and all that stuff made us laugh a lot." He submitted with good grace to the various initiations, including to *venia*, the old monastic act of prostration, and seemed to be comfortable with a life in which times of prayer, the teachings of the master of the novices, rehearsals of Gregorian chants, and games of volleyball alternated with each other. One gets the feeling that he entered into all of this easily, without having to force himself. Even the bad weather no longer weighed as much on him as in Grenoble. There was just a little bit of homesickness for Algiers of which he speaks in his Christmas letter in a way which already announces his plans for the future:

> In the common room I found an old book of photos of Algiers. Just imagine: in it one sees a view of Guillemin Square! I look at it nearly every evening. If only they allow me to return to Algiers, at least for a couple of years of ministry! That would be fascinating. In any event, I am going to: (a) learn Arabic, (b) participate in a seminar on Islamic studies that several brothers interested by these questions have organized at Le Saulchoir. (letter of December 25, 1958)

Pierre Claverie was barely twenty years old. Less than a month after his entrance in the Dominican order he had a plan for his life, and it was the plan that he would in fact carry out. As the months passed, his determination continued to grow.[15] His sympathies for French Algeria had not gone unnoticed, and the master of novices asked Pierre to stop leaving in the common room issues of *L'Écho d'Alger*, a daily newspaper that he received, whose arguments in favor of French Algeria might create tensions in the community. As Fr. Delalande said with a touch of humor, it was already enough to have *Témoignage chrétien* and *La France catholique* at the same time. Seeing the justice of the remark, Pierre accepted it and even suggested of his own accord that it might be better if he canceled the subscription. Several of Pierre's fellow novices had a very different approach to the Algerian question: Michel Froidure returned from two years of military service at Aïn Sefra convinced that Algerian independence was inevitable; Michel Perret, who came from a working-class environment, had worked for the release of Jean Muller, a young Christian opposed to the war in Algeria. Pierre Claverie listened more than he spoke. He followed the evolving situation in Algeria fairly closely, thanks to his father's letters, from which he liked to read excerpts to his fellow novices. "They were extremely objective, a thousand leagues from the madness of the extremists," one of them remembers. On May 13, 1959, some novices organized a commemoration of the massive pieds-noir riots of the year before as a joke in which Pierre participated. However, behind his reserve on the subject, he hid an inner suffering, "doubtless too profound to be shared with people who were not pieds-noirs," confides Michel Froidure, who was very close to him. As the months passed, Pierre gradually discovered the problem of being trapped in an ideology as the cultural and ideological diversity of the novices, and even the fathers of the priory, asserted itself. Some were passionately in favor of a renewal of the apostolic mission among the workers or in the scientific world. (On January 25, 1959, Pope John XXIII announced a council of *aggiornamento*.) Others were more drawn to a monastic style of life. On one hand, Pierre Claverie kept a certain distance from all of this, in strong contrast to his simplistic statements during his year in Grenoble. On the other hand, the internal adventure in which he had entered fascinated him, and his favorite evangelical text during this period was Jesus' nighttime conversation with Nicodemus: "How can one be born again?"

In general, for Pierre the novitiate offered an excellent apprenticeship in dealing with the Other, and discussions with his fellow novices were not only about politics. The relationship with religion was another area in which their approaches varied widely. During a vacation on the coast in early June they attended a religious festival in a village, out of which a vigorous argument developed among the friars, an argument in which Pierre recognized that he was fighting a bit against the spirit of the times:

> Lots and lots of people, touching devotion of the people who adorn the fronts of their houses with fishing nets decorated with flowers or strew hay or flowers along the route of the procession. Obviously, "that" is not what religion is. But on our return I found myself in a rather big argument against quite a few friars who had regarded the festival with disdain and a detachment that I found inappropriate. One must respect faith at all its levels ... (letter of June 16, 1959)

Another aspect of his expanding horizons involved working afternoons in a lower-class neighborhood of Lille as part of a program to improve the slums, in which all the novices participated once a week. He discovered there the poverty of the working class in the north. What is interesting to note is that instead of causing him to become nervous or tight, this apprenticeship in diversity seemed to help him relax and open up. "It's funny how a novitiate completely changes the focus of your interests," he recognized (letter of June 28, 1959).

A second matter fascinated him during the novitiate: the discovery of the large apostolic vistas that were opening up before him. He responded enthusiastically to visits from some of the important Dominican figures of the age, who were also concrete examples of actual preachers. In March it was Fr. Joseph Robert, from the Dominican working-class community of Hellemmes, fellow traveler of the Communist trade unionists and close to the Mouvement de la paix (peace movement). In early April, Fr. Marie-Dominique Chenu spent three days with the novices. His reinterpretation of the contemporary church in the light of the Middle Ages and his apostolic optimism excited Pierre, especially because Chenu placed Islam among the great challenges that faced the church (along with the working-class and scientific worlds). Then came Fr. Avril, former provincial superior, relieved of his functions over the issue of worker-priests; the philosopher Dominique Dubarle, a specialist in the relationship between science and faith; André Duval, a historian, who introduced him to the Dominican missions to Morocco and the Arabic language school in Tunis that dated from the beginning of the order; Fr. Duployé, a colorful figure with great knowledge of literature, who played an important role in the renewal of the liturgy in France; finally Fathers Anawati and Fiey, both of whom were living and working intellectually in the Muslim world. He also learned with interest about the Arab Christian communities of the Middle East from some priests visiting from Mosul and then from the arrival in the novitiate of Brother Joseph Atticha, a young Iraqi priest. This was all very attractive to a young man of twenty, whose horizons were suddenly enlarging, thanks more to human contacts than abstract speeches. That did not keep him from reading a great deal at a pace that he himself acknowledged to be "a bit frantic." One senses that he wanted to store knowledge away for the future. He devoured everything: theology, spirituality, literature, the scriptures. He put together files on all sorts of subjects: the Bible, religious life, the liturgy, Teilhard de Chardin, and so on. He seemed impatient to enter into the very heart of his new life. He frequently shared his discoveries with his parents, quoting to them from Thomas Merton's *Seeds of Contemplation* or summing up the theological works of Louis Bouyer. Beyond his own progress, one gets a sense of his desire to help his parents advance in the faith.[16]

The third great discovery of his novitiate, and without a doubt the most important, was prayer, about which he writes at various times in his correspondence:

This morning in my devotions I finally discovered the Trinity, which up to now had seemed to me to be above all a theologian's subtlety. I believe that this is the essence of Christianity: beyond the life of Jesus, his teaching, and his church, he reveals God, not only as God the Father, and gives us the image of what we are called to be: participants in a current of love that unites the Father with the Son through the Spirit. (letter of May 24, 1959)

Pierre Claverie was twenty-one when he wrote these lines! The novitiate is the time of the fundamental apprenticeships of religious life: of gaining knowledge of the history and organization of the order that one is entering; of communal life, with its rules and rituals; of living with the Word of God in one's studies and meditations; of prayer. It is striking that, on this point, he goes immediately to the essential: personal prayer, his devotions. It is, however, often what is the most difficult and takes the longest time to learn. While for many brothers the choral service — praying the Psalms by reciting or singing them together several times a day — is the means of entering into a life of regular prayer, Pierre immediately rooted his life in a personal relationship with Christ. He did not hesitate to speak of it on various occasions:

I am discovering little by little the extraordinary benefits of my devotions. We do this for an hour a day (half an hour, morning and evening). As much as I did it at the beginning because I had to, now I approach it with "a buoyant heart." Even if I remain dry as a stick of wood for half an hour, I leave it "restored." Besides, the dialogue establishes itself quite quickly, in the form of monologues broken by silences. I believe that I do mix quite a few things up, but in purifying this prayer little by little, I will definitely manage, I am certain, to make of this daily hour the joy of my life and of what I will have to say...Perhaps in a few years, perhaps eventually, I will be able to speak from experience. (letter of September 20, 1959)

The enthusiasm of a novice? A little, certainly. But still, whoever knew Pierre Claverie later knows that that was exactly how things were organized for the long term in his life: his prayer, regular and peaceful, was like the permanent breathing of his life, his essential wellspring, his daily grounding of himself in his roots. It is striking that he was killed at the entrance to his chapel, at the same place where he prayed.

## Leaving Isolation: A Foundational Experience

Pierre Claverie was a man who was rather reticent about matters that touched him deeply. All of the witnesses of this period agree that, at the most, one could sense in him an inner suffering. Later, he did not hesitate to speak explicitly of this time in his personal history, regarding it to some degree as a

formative period. Reflecting back on his personal history, he recognized that
something decisive took place here, at the moment of his entrance into the
religious life: a decisive exit from the closed world in which he had previously
existed and which the follies of his year in Grenoble had revealed. Pierre
Claverie liked to use the word "passage" to describe what he lived through
during these years and which began during his novitiate. It took until 1962
and his military service in Algeria for this evolution to be irreversible and for
him to be able to speak of it with a sense of perspective. But it was especially
when his own country, Algeria, was confronted with the same tragedy of
isolationism much later, this time in the context of the Islamist movement,
that he would rethink this personal experience, seeing there the painful yet
necessary path to reach a recognition of the other:

> Two "vocations": an "Algerian vocation" and a Dominican vocation
> have given birth to me. Chronologically, and at the most fundamental
> level, the Algerian vocation was the first. Born in Algiers, I came to my
> religious faith in the midst of the Algerian War. After a happy childhood
> under the guidance of marvelous parents . . . , I watched powerless as the
> world in which I grew up collapsed . . . All that I had lived and learned,
> in both schools and churches, what I believed to be just and good, was
> called into question by the emergence of Algerian nationalism . . . How
> could I have lived in ignorance of this world, which demanded recogni-
> tion of its identity and dignity? In churches, how could I so often have
> heard the words of Christ about loving the Other like myself, like him,
> and never have met that Other who was popping out like a bogeyman
> in our little universe?
>
> In a parallel way, a painful and tortuous spiritual path led me to the
> religious life . . . My thirst for communication, born from the failure of
> a colonial society and a colonial church, found its first relief in a com-
> munity of brothers that was also preoccupied with the Algerian tragedy
> but better prepared than I was to understand the political and spiritual
> stakes involved. Some of the brothers had already taken a position in
> the course of the war, and they helped me to cross over the thresholds
> of my ignorance and fears. Then, I had to understand how we could
> have lived, and lived as Christians, without even asking ourselves the
> question of the other.[17]

As the years passed, Pierre Claverie reached a deeper level in his understanding of his own history, comparing it to the evolution of the Algerian
society that surrounded him. Having himself lived in his youth the tragedy of

indifference toward the Other, he warned against a society built on a foundation of exclusion. Camille Tarot reports this conversation with Pierre Claverie in the 1990s: "I only heard him evoke once, and too briefly, what was the tragedy of his youth as it was for all pieds-noirs, the Algerian War. Having begun by defending it, when he was a young student, at about the age of twenty, he came to understand not only that French Algeria was dead but that it could not be defended because it had been built upon exclusion. In regard to that exclusion he used, I remember, the term "original sin."[18] One finds this same expression, "original sin," in a lecture Pierre Claverie gave on "The Church and Human Rights" at The Hague in 1986.

Another conviction that comes out of this rereading of his own history: this exit from isolationism is painful and usually accompanied by some kind of violence. Having taken a significant step away from what he was in Grenoble toward what he wanted to become by entering the religious life, Pierre Claverie was going to experience deep suffering: on the one hand, he was watching helplessly as the world and certainties of his childhood collapsed; on the other hand, in France he ran up against the lack of understanding by the inhabitants of the "mother country," who were indifferent to the tragedy of the pieds-noirs forced to leave their country. However, unlike many pieds-noirs, who fell into despair and sometimes violence when they saw the French Algeria in which they had been born collapse, he put this crisis to positive use, but he always remembered the cost: "I went through all of these passages, all of these breaks with the past. It's not an easy thing to see your world turned upside down."[19]

In December 1959, he left the novitiate at Lille. He had grown during that time. Named dean of the novice friars, he had had to deal with his first official responsibilities since the master of novices was often ill. He had already completed a decisive passage. The eight years of Dominican studies at Le Saulchoir would provide the framework to help him continue to grow and prepare for his return to Algeria, his country, in a completely different state of mind.

## Chapter Three

# Le Saulchoir

Years to Grow and Prepare for the Future
1959–67

> The rascal has nothing of the mystic about him, and he under-
> stands human problems with a precocious maturity. And above
> all, he has love enough and to spare. Again I ask, Mamie: Where
> does this prodigy of ours come from?[1]  — *Étienne Claverie*

On December 8, 1959, Pierre Claverie took his vows to continue for three
more years. He then entered the house of studies of Le Saulchoir south of
Paris where he ended up spending nearly eight years, with a break of eighteen
months for military service in Algeria. It was a period of intense study during which he took full advantage of the great French Dominican intellectual
tradition, which was at a high point at that time, the period of the second
Vatican Council. But, for him, stimulated by Algeria's winning its independence and the first signs of crisis in the post-conciliar church, this was also a
time of deep maturation, both human and spiritual. Ordained as a priest in
1965, Pierre Claverie was already eager for his future: to return to Algeria,
but with a difference.

## Le Saulchoir, A School of Theology

When Brother Pierre arrived at Le Saulchoir in mid-December 1959, the
community included 153 religious, of whom more than 70 were young brothers still in training. Preparations for the Vatican Council were in full swing,
offering a tardy recognition of the battle that the theologians of that priory
had been waging for more than twenty years. It had begun back in 1937
when Fr. Marie-Dominique Chenu had published his famous manifesto, *Une
école de théologie, le Saulchoir*. This text set up a program which was quickly
condemned and, in 1942, placed on the Index of banned books by the Holy
Office. At stake was a profound renewal of theology and of Thomism, which

38

had become almost fossilized in a scholastic mode of teaching that was more concerned with apologetics than with welcoming new questions. Once World War II was over, some people recognized that society was turning away from Christianity and that France was in fact a nation in need of a mission, a *pays de mission* (the title of a work by Abbé Godin). The French Dominicans played an important role in this recognition and the debates that it provoked. They established a publishing house, Les Éditions du Cerf, launched periodicals like *La Vie Intellectuelle* and *La Vie Spirituelle*, and, under the leadership of Fr. Lebret and François Perroux, organized Économie et humanisme, with its working groups, research projects, and journal. Fr. Chenu, who had an amazing ear for the concerns of the world, saw in this "missionary" stance a profound invitation to renew theology, beginning with its methods. A historian by training, Chenu saw in contemporary events an opportunity for an "evangelical awakening" like that which had occurred in the medieval West, a period of which he was a famous specialist. As rector of the Dominican faculty at Le Saulchoir, he wanted to reintroduce current events into the way of doing theology: instead of attempting to bring the "storehouse of the faith" up to date, it should read and identify the Spirit of God in world history as it was occurring. Vatican II spoke of "signs of the times," an expression that delighted Chenu. Fr. Congar was another figure whose theological work was coming to the fore at this time. His early reflection on the dynamics of *aggiornamento* of the church (*Vraie et fausse réforme dans l'Église*, 1950), his innovative contribution to the theology of ministry (*Jalons pour une théologie du laïcat*, 1953), and his participation in the ecumenical movement (*Chrétiens désunis*) all made him a clerical figure of the highest order and an inspiration for young Dominican theologians. However, their prophetic voices earned both Congar and Chenu severe penalties: a ban from teaching and even exile. Chenu was sent to Rouen and Congar to Cambridge. In consequence, the experience of the worker-priests was painfully halted, causing the French Dominican provincial superiors to be removed from their positions.[2] Even though these great masters were still in exile in 1959, the Dominican faculties of Le Saulchoir were filled with the sense of renewal they had inspired. It was to this extraordinarily rich environment that Pierre Claverie came to study philosophy and theology.

At Le Saulchoir, he encountered many other Dominican students, French but also foreign (English, Spanish, Croatian), with a great variety of attitudes toward the changes taking place in the church. The dominant tone among the student brothers was a desire to go out into the world, which quickly upset the stability of a teaching priory whose style of life had become very rigid during the years of exile outside of France at the beginning of the century. Other brothers, in contrast, had "preoccupied faces," as Pierre wrote humorously about a more traditional group of young religious. Where and how would he find his place? Once again, we find that he was not very attracted by ideologies. His energies were focused on the essentials: above all to work, to take as much advantage as possible of the extraordinary intellectual ferment of this place; then, to make his religious commitment take root and mature through prayer and his apprenticeship in preaching. His interest in Algeria's evolution led him to take only a small part in the internal debates about French society. He left Le Saulchoir a few months before the events of May 1968 which would have important repercussions for that priory, but very early it was evident that the focus of his interests lay elsewhere.

## The Training of a Preaching Friar

The first section of the program of study was devoted to philosophy, for which Pierre Claverie felt little affinity. Nevertheless, he obtained his degree, a "licence," in philosophy in April 1962, in spite of a difficult thesis defense, where "the numerous members of the public who were present at this embarrassment were amazed not to find the usually talkative Brother Pierre," he confided to his parents. He could not have performed too badly, though, because some of his professors suggested that he consider a career in teaching. He rejected this notion totally "unless it is required as an act of obedience." Where his enthusiasm already lay was with preaching. At that time, it was customary to train the student brothers to preach by practicing in front of each other, under the supervision of a more experienced brother. Guided by Fr. Liégé, an exceptional mentor in the art, Pierre approached this activity with pleasure. His debut was brilliant, if one judges by the first responses he received:

> I preached yesterday. I'm going to end up believing that I am gifted... Of course, a lot of justifiable criticism of both form and substance... but a relaxed demeanor, an ease of elocution, a freedom from dependence on the text, the ability to connect with the audience, a likeable voice, although not yet fully controlled. A lot of compliments, especially for a first sermon... Don't imagine that I'm ready for Notre Dame. I listened to a recording of myself in the evening; it was rather pitiful, spoken in a monotonous and nervous voice. (letter of February 16, 1960)

Fr. Liégé, recognizing the danger, criticized him sharply on the next occasion ("some charm, but that's it!"), but Pierre Claverie quickly learned to move beyond his obvious facility to what is essential:

> Sermon by yours truly on Advent. For the first time in my career as a preacher, I had to resort to notes from the beginning. Stage fright, fatigue? I believe that it's truly the first time that what I had to say really moved me. Fr. Liégé says that all our sermons must have as a preliminary condition this conversion of the preacher. He even adds that the faithful will themselves only be converted if that happens. I have to believe that in his wisdom he had things right because people told me that I had never been so "genuine." You're telling me! I served them up a slice of life! Only the presentation left a bit to be desired... They retained less in the way of "ideas" or a clear organization than a spiritual attitude and a call to conversion. This is exactly what I wanted, but I will not repeat this experience for some time. (letter of December 6, 1960)

Did he have in mind the events the French in Algeria were living through? Probably, because in this same period the letters received from the brothers called up for service in Algeria led him to recognize that he "had lived an illusion for a long time." For him, this was a heart-rending reinterpretation.

However, Pierre Claverie did not have the sort of temperament that would have led him, embittered, to turn inward on himself. Le Saulchoir was alive with youthful enthusiasm, and he actively participated in the joys of student life. For a rather long time he occupied himself with the record library at the student center, organizing musical evenings or weekends. He played volleyball in the garden, went on walks with his American friend Wayne White, and entertained himself with literature during the winter and spring vacations he spent at La Chaux, a property in the Massif Central lent by a family friendly to the priory. His precocious maturity led to his selection as dean of the student friars, then of the young fathers, a role he had already assumed midway through his novitiate. Le Saulchoir hosted a series of lecturers who engaged him deeply, including Georges Dumézil, Paul Ricoeur, Vincent Cosmao, and some worker-priests. The Dominicans who were chaplains to Parisian artists introduced the brothers to the comedian Jean-Louis Barrault and the painter Alfred Manessier. In this period movie clubs were also popular, even at Le Saulchoir. Pierre enjoyed seeing films like Fellini's *Nights of Cabiria* and Alain Resnais' *Last Year at Marienbad*. It was quite an era, a new culture that came to them there: one senses in Pierre, as in his fellows, a desire to listen to the life of the world.

Pierre Claverie (center) as
a young friar at Le Saulchoir.

Nevertheless, he remained a serious student, even an insatiable one at times. He took full advantage of the Saulchoir library, the best of its kind in France. Having begun to study Hebrew during his novitiate, he and several others now took up Arabic, forming a group of up to eleven who worked together on Sunday mornings, Pierre soon helping the beginners. He recognized that it is a difficult language, but a very beautiful one. "And I enjoy writing it," he confessed. He also considered studying Spanish, and later German and English. Youthful enthusiasm? Unquestionably, but Le Saulchoir had an intellectualizing element, from which Claverie later came to distance himself. Theology fascinated him and he dove into it with delight. In 1963, the priory celebrated the rehabilitation of Chenu and Congar, who came to speak about the Vatican Council in which they were now participating as experts. Their disciples began to stand at the forefront of the theological scene: Liégé, of course, but also Geffré, Pohier, Jossua, and others. Pierre Claverie succeeded brilliantly on his exams, with a master's thesis in ecclesiology on ministries, which he wrote under the direction of Bernard Dupuy, another of Congar's disciples. The theology of the church and of its mission was one of the areas of theology that was moving the most in the wake of Vatican II. Pierre Claverie perceived this clearly. Dupuy reported of him:

> Pierre was an extremely serious student, attentive, precise but not book-ish. He was perfectly aware that the twentieth-century church was living an era of renewal. He recognized that this new age would affect all sectors of the church, all peoples, all Christian communities. Manifestly, he carried within him a hope for Algeria, which was his country, whose people were becoming his people, and where he knew without a doubt that he would be called to live.

It is important to note that, however gifted he might have been, and he clearly was, Pierre Claverie was engaging in a process that combined belief and intelligence in his faith, unlike some other religious for whom the foundations of belief did not grow at the same pace as their intellectual evolution. Eventually, this failure led to departures from the religious life, which did not surprise Pierre: "There will be others," he commented already in June 1961.

One can judge this maturation by perusing the long letters which he wrote to his parents and which allow a glimpse of his interior life. Prayer always has a central place: "I am a fan of meditation, and I do it for one hour a day, not the way I 'do' Greek, but to be able to live by successive forward motions, more and more in harmony with what I have chosen as my goal" (letter of January 10, 1960).[3]

He spoke all the more gladly with his loved ones since his parents were following him down the same path and beginning to attend Mass regularly. He encouraged them in this and endeavored to nourish their reborn faith with that on which he himself fed, and which he shared as much as possible with them, at Easter, for example:

> Christ is risen. That is the foundation of our joy and our faith. Without this resurrection we are nothing...Christ died not only as a hero of justice or as a just person persecuted (how many others have died in conditions even more atrocious, who were just as innocent as he was); what is so special about this death is that it is voluntary. And it is this voluntary offering, that is nothing other than the unconditional surrender into the hands of the Father, which earns for him (and will earn for us) the resurrection. To be certain of the strength of the love of the Father *that* is the message of Easter...It is this certainty, lived to the ultimate limit of its logic, which created the martyrs and makes us

as Christians bound to bring joy to humanity, whatever cross we have to bear. The whole Christian message is in these lines: surrender to the will of the Father, who is love. (letter of April 2, 1961, concluded by "There it is! The chief has spoken!")

There are in the correspondence pages and pages of this nature, which, at first, might make us think of a young man who is repeating what he has read or heard. At this time Claverie was not quite twenty-three years old. One cannot deny that, as he wrote, he was carried by a specific intellectual and religious environment. Nonetheless, one can sense in him a real entry into the Christian mystery. The best proof of this would lie in the future, when this loving surrender to the will of the Father would be displayed up to the ultimate and (one dares say) joyous gift of his own life. Already the theme of the cross recurs insistently:

The cross represents a choice. Between human ways and the ways of God there is this unfathomable mystery of the cross, and if one allows oneself to be molded by it, one can hope for a resurrection. The cross: this is not just any suffering, it isn't even simply suffering and nothing more. It is this perpetual desire always to choose in terms of God . . . , it is to search to place oneself in the presence of God, to attempt to rediscover in oneself and outside of oneself the reality that we live beyond masks and appearances. To love is to remain open to the Word that God speaks to us through those who surround us. And all of that can be summed up in these words: follow Jesus Christ . . . and this is a very great strength, much more than a moral rule . . . Since this letter will serve you as an Easter prayer, my wish is that you search for this living encounter with Christ . . . And now, my little sermon is at an end. (letter of March 22, 1964)

The result of this spiritual maturation was that Claverie integrated deeply into his being what he was learning, and he felt that the Dominican religious life, whose forms and methods he adopted with ease, was the right place for him. It was in this state of mind, on November 1, 1964, that he professed his solemn vows with due gravity in light of the *usque ad mortem* (unto death) that he pronounced. Later, he would often baffle his fellow disciples because he seemed to have little to do with the questionings that emerged and grew in the late sixties. One must say that Claverie himself was experiencing his own painful evolution.

## The "Algerian Question" Once Again

The first years of his education as a Dominican coincided with the end of French Algeria, in what Yves Courrière has called "the fires of despair,"[4] the barricades in January 1960, then the hit-and-run attacks by the OAS, an extremist organization dedicated to preserving French Algeria at any cost. When he returned to Algeria for his mandatory military service in 1962, it was already independent and Algerian. A new era was beginning. During that period, there were many dramatic events which held his interest fully.

Pierre Claverie had a gut-level attachment to Algeria, a point not always realized by his Dominican brethren from the mother country, who were more sensitive to Algeria's right to self-determination. As a man of the Mediterranean, he was disconcerted by the mentality of the people from the north: "You cannot know how much I would like to return to Algiers. I am beginning to realize that I am 'literally' of 'another race' than the people here..." (letter of February 29, 1960).

Until May 1960, he believed that a military victory over the rebels was possible: "We are not heading for a Dien Bien Phu or a capitulation camouflaged as a negotiation. Militarily, there is no problem. As for the rest..." Much of what he read or heard provoked him, and he did not hide it, writing, for example, to *Informations catholiques internationales* in June 1960 to contest their position on the Algerian question, which he considered too simple. He was certainly not insensitive to the more and more frequent denunciations of torture. In April 1959 thirty priests, reserve officers, had written a collective letter to their religious superiors; in October 1960 the cardinals and archbishops of France continued on the same path, at the instigation of Cardinal Duval, archbishop of Algiers. In November 1960 two Dominican brothers serving in Algeria sent a crushing report, which the master of studies at Le Saulchoir read to the student brothers. It was a harsh blow for Pierre Claverie, who commented on General de Gaulle's speeches: "An Algerian Algeria...the word is now officially out" (letter of June 19, 1960). New realizations came more and more frequently to him. He threw himself into the reading of the Algerian authors Mouloud Feraoun and Kateb Yacine, and reread Camus. And at that point, he understood and confessed, in November 1960:

> I believe that we have been living in an illusion for a long time. Living in our enclosed world, we are no more objective than the Communists. I admit that I discovered the 1945 Sétif revolt in a book. This warning shot, far from making us reflect, incited us to pay even more attention to

defending our rights, and thus gave us the opportunity to ignore quite a few of our obligations. Note that I do not blame: I declare that we gave in to the natural inclination and that not for a single moment did we try to see the problem from the opponent's point of view . . . I do not judge, but I am trying to understand how we could have reached this point . . . We have done NOTHING, we the Claveries, to be specific, to learn about the true conditions of the Arabs. Apart from friendly contacts with all the Arabs we knew and who liked us, we never thought to confront problems head on: why is the European sphere so closed and why does it monopolize three-quarters of Algeria's wealth? It is easy to give an answer of the sort: "The Arabs don't work; we are the ones who built up this country." But let's try to examine these responses more thoroughly: they all come down to the fear of a minority with possessions (acquired legitimately or not) facing an enormous majority that has not ceased to demand (legitimately or not) a place in the sun. Thousands of facts, with which I have been bombarded for three years, are there to show CLEARLY that we have done everything possible to minimize the claims against us and to increase our power . . . The war began unjustly. It is now just but absurd because, on both sides, people ask why they are fighting. It is just because we have understood that the Arabs should receive the same rights that we have . . . The Algeria where we are going to live will be completely different from the preceding one. It is, in my opinion, unthinkable that we should remain part of French territory. It is not with the citizens of the mother country that we have to live and unite, it's with the Arabs, however we may do it . . . In practical terms, the war is over or nearly so: the referendum will accomplish NOTHING but to confuse things. Passions are still high and memories painful . . . (letter of November 15, 1960)

This letter marks an important turning point in Claverie's developing consciousness. We are far from the simplistic declarations that he used to make at Grenoble. He has reached the point of speaking of a just cause and even of a "just war," but it is easy to imagine his inner suffering, so much more acute because some of his fellow students had a very different feeling about the question. One recognizes here a strong ability to analyze, a taste for truth, a real courage. It is in exactly this period that he gave that sermon where what he had to say, according to his own testimony, had "really moved" and even converted him (December 6, 1960). At the end of December he came, unexpectedly, to spend a week in Algiers. He was doubtless encouraged by the master of studies, who was a witness of his painful evolution. He would henceforth be very coherent in his approach to the Algerian question.

The situation was complex and Pierre Claverie forced himself to analyze it rigorously. The first contacts between the French government and the "terrorists" had occurred, secretly, at Melun. Should the National Libera- tion Front (FLN) be recognized as the legal representative of the Algerian people? Many were not so sure. On the pieds-noir side there was panic and some activists turned to indiscriminate violence; hit-and-run attacks multi- plied. Pierre Claverie could understand, having been, in his own words, "on the side of the agitators" when he was a young activist in Grenoble. He pre- pared his parents for the necessity of a return to France, "because nothing more keeps you in Algeria, which is going to become a sort of new land, where retirees will no longer have a place, especially the European ones..." (letter of February 4, 1961). He also helped them to accept the message of Archbishop Duval of Algiers, a message that opened the door to Algerian national self-determination and offended most pieds-noirs:[5]

> Let us not forget that Catholicism isn't a religion of peace and secu- rity in the worldly sense: the peace of compromise and security at any cost...No. It is a sword and often a scandal, as St. Paul says. It is for this reason that the church honors martyrs: it's because they have under- stood that the act of bearing witness, if it is truthful, cannot but come in conflict with the world and lead to death. Perhaps, in Algeria, it will be necessary for Christianity to be born again through a few...(letter of May 8, 1961)

Keeping close track of breaking events, Claverie commented on the Évian agreements and judged "the furious tenacity of the OAS catastrophic and ridiculous." He continued to read on the subject, even though sometimes wounded by what he found, for example in Pierre Nora's *Les Français d'Algérie*, which he considered well documented but one-sided: "When one claims to be working as a historian, one has to try to remain objective; even more important, when one assumes the right to speak about people, one cannot understand them without loving them" (letter of June 12, 1961). His own sensibilities remained keen and his political analyses were often succinct.[6] But, at the most basic level, Pierre Claverie had changed his position: from now on the independence of Algeria appeared to him to be inevitable. However, his evolution was far from complete, as can be seen from his vocabulary: he often spoke of "Arabs," as did the people of the world in which he grew up.

It was only later that he would say "the Algerians," after he established close connections with Algerians, who became his partners and friends.

In Algiers the Dominican community was also undergoing a painful evolution. A prior who had come from Iraq in 1958, Fr. Tunmer, had given up after six months because of the inability of several religious to distance themselves from their identification with French Algeria. A younger prior, Pierre Le Baut, was elected. A pied-noir like Claverie and also a spiritual son of Fr. Lefèvre, Le Baut only accepted his election on condition that the provincial superior reassign to France those who were fundamentally incapable of change. This was done, except for Fr. Lefèvre, who knew how to avoid open conflicts and left of his own accord after Algeria gained its independence. A group of more open-minded brothers established themselves in the priory, reinstalled in a completely new building in the chemin Laperlier. Étienne Claverie frequently attended Mass there. Pierre Le Baut very soon regarded Pierre Claverie as a prime candidate for this new community and proposed to the provincial superior that he come and spend the summer of 1961 in Algiers. Later, it was also Le Baut who arranged his permanent return in 1967. In July and August 1961, Pierre took an intensive Arabic course at the major seminary of Kouba under the direction of Henri Teissier, who would later become very important in his life. These two months in Algiers were very good for him, as can be seen in a letter written after his return to Le Saulchoir in 1961:

> I now have...a sense of balance, an inner calm, a peace that I don't think I have ever fully felt before, or, to be more precise, possessed... These are factors of maturation that not only permit me to brush off a multitude of little matters that often, only a couple of months ago, exasperated or stressed me a little, but to strengthen my internal silence and bring my prayer to life through the large slice of life, in the sense of life experiences, that I acquired in the course of those two little months. (letter of October 15, 1961)

Reading this, one has the feeling that in his prayer Pierre Claverie was "recycling" his interior debates about the Algerian tragedy. Did he have other deep internal battles? If so, he never said anything about them, baffling, on this point, even those closest to him. His conversion to the cause of Algeria may have absorbed him completely, saving him from the doubts that led a number of his confrères to leave Le Saulchoir. On his return to France, Claverie ordered an Arabic translation of the Gospels. He also corresponded with the Little Brothers of Jesus, met during the summer while studying Arabic. Members of this order lived among the lower-class people of Algeria, in the new districts of the capital (Mahieddine and Climat de France), built hurriedly, but quite late, through the initiative of Mayor Jacques Chevallier of Algiers. Stimulated by these contacts, in the spring of 1962 Pierre Claverie volunteered to perform his military service in Algeria, as a teacher.

## Military Service: Return to Algiers, "but with a Difference"

In March 1962 he joined the army at Chartres, where he arrived "in white," wearing the Dominican habit. Contact with his barracks-mates was easy, but very soon the off-color jokes and the obsessions of the young conscripts made him consider all he had learned from his parents: "With papa," he wrote to his mother, "you gave me, not intentionally but simply by living it, an emotional stability, a true and healthy vision of love" (letter of May 23, 1962). More often, without making a show of his feelings, he praised his parents with "Claverie humor." Thus, on a Mother's Day he wrote, "It's with mothers like this that one reaches the bishop's throne or becomes a ballerina at the Opéra, to use a paternal expression about his offspring." At the end of June, he reached his post at the air force base at Reghaïa, east of Algiers. He was in Algiers itself when Algeria gained its independence at the beginning of July 1962. The French soldiers still in Algeria for this period of transition were confined to their bases because their presence might create problems with the celebrating crowds. But Pierre Claverie nonetheless saw something of the event because Fr. Le Baut, prior of the Dominican priory in Algiers, suggested that he wear a religious habit, which allowed him to go out into the streets. Unfortunately, we have no text he may have written about it.

The military authorities proposed that he teach literature at the air force school at Cape Matifou, but the young soldier, without hesitation (already!), refused firmly and chose the chaplaincy instead. He had already met Fr. de L'Espinay, an army chaplain who made a mark on numerous soldiers by helping them to open their eyes to distinguish good from evil during the darkest hours of the repression of the Algerian insurgency. Pierre Claverie assumed responsibility for activities at a meeting place for soldiers in the air force, the Saint-Exupéry Club, rue Foureau-Lamy. There, with his friend Paul Pavat, he welcomed young soldiers who were in need of rest and recuperation or were close to being discharged. "Pierre kept the bar," Paul Pavat recalls, "and together we prepared thousands of servings of steaks and French fries in a very cheerful atmosphere. Even the colonel loved to come and eat at our place."

The atmosphere was lively. Sometimes a young soldier, nephew of the actor Jean-Louis Barrault, delivered theatrical speeches. Another was in charge of a small jazz orchestra. Evenings were above all dedicated to meetings. The pair in charge of the club regularly visited Fr. de L'Espinay at the club for the infantry in Bouzareah: "One could see how Pierre was paying very close attention, and how de L'Espinay was educating him," says Paul Pavat. In July 1962 Claverie successfully organized a short retreat for forty young soldiers at the Dominican priory in Algiers. He published a little bulletin for them, entitled *Le Petit Prince*. Three months later Étienne Claverie, who was still in Algiers, wrote: "In both physical condition and morale, Pierre is absolutely great, overflowing with happiness to see his affairs expanding, his field of action enlarging...His morale is firing on all cylinders, and he is in excellent physical shape. We have cause, Mamie, to be proud of our offspring." Delighted at the opportunities to see his "penguin" arrive at the apartment from time to time, Étienne Claverie developed with his son a very trusting and open relationship, which he shared with his wife: "And then our endless conversations, which continued long into the night, and statements which confirmed to me that our son and brother was becoming more and more, in addition to that, my friend." These conversations enabled him to know his son better and certainly to continue the mentoring role that was always so important to him. He was more than a little proud of him and wrote to his wife on October 9, 1962, Pierre "understands human problems with a precocious maturity. And above all, he has love enough and to spare. Again I ask, Mamie: Where does this prodigy of ours come from?"

Within a few months the military chaplain was replaced, the French army was ready to leave, and Algiers was living in a state of panic, but Pierre Claverie felt at home in that city. And so he continued his activities as if nothing or nearly nothing was out of order — to such a degree that the new chaplain felt a little jealous of this young man full of resources and enthusiasm: he knew lots of people in Algiers, and was able to find preachers even at the worst moments, encouraged by Fr. Liégé, who wrote to him from Rome, where he was taking part in the Council. Should we be surprised by the ambiguous observations that the military chaplain sent to the master of students at the end of Pierre's service in Algeria: "Religious devotion regular and solid. Magnificent generosity. Unwavering apostolic zeal. Tendencies: (1) a tendency to go beyond his strength; (2) an independence of mind that makes it hard for him to accept the point of view of others."[7] Papie, a bit biased, gave as his opinion that the chaplain had "lost interest in his mission." Doubtless the most accurate point of view is that of François Chavanes, Pierre's senior in

Pierre Claverie in uniform as he looked when he returned
to Algeria for military service in 1962.

Algiers' Dominican community, who had watched him grow up since 1954:
"Pierre was someone upon whom one didn't really have an influence." One
can understand that this self-assurance wasn't to everyone's taste! During this
period, Étienne Claverie stayed in contact with his son, but left him his space,
as can be seen in a letter to his wife and daughter, written one day when he
thought about attending Mass at the chaplaincy but changed his mind: "I did
not give in to this desire, fearing (don't tell this to anyone) to be the 'father
who won't let go of his child.' This will make sense to you later, Nane. When
you have some kids, you will understand your uncouth father. You, Mamie,
you understand completely; you are me! . . ." (letter of July 15, 1962).

Every month Pierre Claverie addressed a letter to Fr. Marneffe, master of
the student brothers at Le Saulchoir. In these twelve letters, running from
October 1962 to October 1963, one can already recognize a marked taste for
proclaiming the faith. In October 1962 Claverie took charge of a catechumen, to whom he proposed a rather systematic instruction: "My catechumen
shows himself to be exceptionally intelligent and receptive: pray that he will
always have this attitude that leaves him profoundly open to grace." In November, Claverie threw himself into various short retreats and made his first
observations on the difficulty of each one of us to convert: "How can one be,

at the same time, full of oneself and full of Christ?" (letter of November 2, 1962).[8] As the weeks went by at the chaplaincy, a cheerful team took shape, in which he saw "some soil where one day the Word might spring up." Pierre was soon very busy with little free time, even for prayer, but already he was making preaching the central focus of his life:

> My prayer is often an intention or an offering in the course of a conver-
> sation, rarely a time of silence or of meditation. I have very little energy
> in my peaceful moments, and it already takes a great deal of effort even
> to count the beads of the rosary. My comfort in this area comes from
> the fact that the matters on which I am working are always in a direct
> relation with God... This obligatory interaction with the Word of God
> serves as my support. But I bless heaven to have made it "obligatory"
> because otherwise I wonder where I would be. (letter of November 2,
> 1962)

This burning obligation to preach was also, in his eyes, a form of poverty: "To have nothing of one's own, even time, is much more overwhelming and enriching. It is there that I place my effort at fidelity," he wrote in the letter of December 3, 1962. At the invitation of the Protestants, he wrote his first article, a little text of two pages entitled, "Ce qu'un catholique attend du Concile." One finds there some themes dear to Fr. Chenu, which would become progressively more profoundly developed in his own thought over time:

> The church today is in the process of leaving the "Constantinian era"
> ... She is opening herself to the world instead of erecting defenses; she
> is sending out her message instead of protecting herself with condem-
> nations... May she pull herself out, release herself from the frameworks
> of the West to enrich herself with the thought and the life of people of
> all races. May she recover the primitive enthusiasm of Pentecost...[9]

This seriousness did not get in the way of his sense of humor, as when he wrote to Fr. Marneffe in January 1963 to ask him what clothing he should wear when on leave: should it be military (but he isn't fond of medals, he says), or civilian, or "like an undertaker adorned with a delicate Roman collar..."

Truthfully, it was a strange situation. Pierre Claverie sparkled, exerted himself unstintingly, and successfully made his debut as a preaching friar, and all the while, in Algiers, it was a time of panic. There were shootings in the streets and the pieds-noirs were packing. This emotionally charged letter, written on October 9, 1962, from Étienne Claverie to his wife and daughter, conveys this unhappy atmosphere, at a time when all their European neighbors were moving out:

> The situation is catastrophic... My spirit can't bear up against the magnitude of this desolation. I myself am affected and would drop everything if I did not have hopes of an end point, and above all one that meant I was coming to spend a couple of days with you far from THIS HELL [sic]. Here, I live only for you, bearing serenely, but with a nostalgic distress, the falling apart of this land that is ours, which saw our births, where we have lived and struggled, where our children were born, and which is becoming more and more foreign to me, who loved it so much! It is with a heavy heart that I go through our familiar streets, in earlier times full of the exuberance of the "Hernandez families"[10] of our neighborhood. Nothing, nothing is left. No more familiar faces. All of the balconies covered with rags and soon to be hidden by mismatched folding-screens. Heaps of rubbish on our tidy street... Swarms of urchins in rags, poor kids who are astonished to have some air and space... [11] I walk, far away and indifferent, into our building, which little by little oozes misery and decay..., full of enormous human suffering, which we used to see in the so-called "local color" of the Casbah. I have the strange impression here that I am a body without a soul: I go, I come, terribly lonely, without friends...

This quotation from Étienne Claverie enables us to measure what his son perhaps felt himself, but about which he speaks with the detachment that he usually employs when he is involved: "Everyone is getting ready to leave. Algiers is taking on a strange appearance. When I walk along the rue d'Isly, I don't recognize it anymore. Really, we don't have anything in common anymore with this new world that is being born without us after having been conceived against us for seven years" (letter of October 19, 1962). Henceforth convinced of the legitimacy of Algeria's political independence, Pierre Claverie was no longer very clear about his own place in this country, as one can see in a short passage of November 1962: "I long to return to France... Here, I am no longer at home."[12] But truly, where was he really "at home"? In January 1963 the soldiers' club closed because the French military was moving out. Pierre Claverie finished out his service as chauffeur for the Protestant chaplain and took a leave of thirty days at Le Saulchoir to think about his situation. Étienne Claverie sold the family apartment and said his farewells at the Shell Oil Company where, to his great surprise, the new

Algerian directors threw him a party and gave him a farewell present. Having returned for good to France, he received the following letter from his son:

> I know very well that the situation is painful and that it is impossible for many to change their minds ... But I believe that beyond the different forms of expression, and especially in spite of the wall that these seven years of distrust have erected, one can often reunite with people through their essential goodness. This does not lessen the great size of the barriers but simply changes the way of approaching them. (letter of February 1963)

Having received a brotherly welcome at Le Saulchoir, Pierre continued to correspond with Fr. de L'Espinay, and on February 27, 1963, he wrote to his parents, settled in Nice, this astonishing letter full, at the same time, of both tenderness and political clear-sightedness. Here are some excerpts:

> My dear old folks,
>     Here you are, reunited again, but to "settle the affairs" of the past. Poor little home, as Papa wrote in one of his last letters. To be sure, we will no longer see the panorama from Notre Dame d'Afrique to the sea. To be sure, we will no longer take walks in the breeze of the rue Koechlin, and all of these images will become part of our storehouse of memories ... But I hope that you will very quickly realize how much this separation from walls counts as nothing in comparison to the creation, elsewhere, of a human environment where you have your proper place ... A new human environment (in Algiers) has radically changed the structures of brick to the point that they are unrecognizable. This radical change leaves a place only for "pioneers," for those who, like me, have nothing to lose and who have dedicated their lives to the service of others. You, who founded a family, had to face up to your own responsibilities, and you managed your affairs admirably ... You took your task of founding "a creative and educational family unit" as far as possible ... That was your reason for being on earth and, in the eyes of God, you have surely fulfilled the purpose laid out for you from the beginning ... Thus this departure is unimportant. You go to find your new place, in the midst of those who have been placed in your care ..., all your friends ... I admire the simplicity of that life that you have shown as an example to Nane and me. If only we could hold on to its secret ...

You have not been uprooted because your roots are in human hearts (and not in the earth or bricks), and you will find again all your friends there where you are going. A page is turning: no messing around, no more regrets. The battle that occurred in Algeria was not at your level, nor at mine either. It was and still is at the level of the revolutionaries, the visionaries, the true believers and the crooks, the conflicting interests. There is nothing left that you can do for those people; others will take your place, and I hope and prepare myself to be one of them, in my own sphere. "The family endures," continuing to spread its peace and build bridges. At its level, the family fights its battle; it conquers territories, and from them nobody will be able to dislodge it . . . Big kisses and I'll see you soon.

Pierre

The author of these lines was twenty-five years old! It was barely five years since he disrupted student assemblies at Grenoble with a few over-excited comrades. At Algiers he had witnessed the transfer of power to the Algerians. The struggles to control the new state had been bitter, but one thing was already certain: Algeria was and would remain Algerian. On October 23, 1963, Pierre Claverie returned to Marseille aboard the *Ville d'Alger,* the same ship he had taken on November 1, 1957, when he had left his native Algeria in a completely different state of mind. He had come full circle. At the end of a painful road he was now a different person, who was preparing for a future in this country to which he would return for good in four years. But what an internal battle he had had to fight! Later, thinking back on this stage of his life, he came to the conclusion that every process of leaving a closed world includes, somewhat inevitably, its share of suffering. This would lead him, one day, to hope that the violence into which Algeria was plunged in 1992 might bear fruit as had been the case in his own personal history.

## 1963 – 67: Calls of the Future

The last period of study seems completely focused on the calls of the future. Certainly Pierre Claverie studied, indeed a lot. Theology interested him; he took in as much as possible for his future ministry, putting together systematic files on various questions. He passed his exams with flying colors, achieving the highest average for the diploma in theology. In France, including at Le Saulchoir, this was a time when everything was called into question. The Dominican students had been granted a committee of representation to the college (the CRAC! — the "college," meaning the faculty, in Dominican jargon). This group developed the curriculum with the professors, decided that choral prayer was not very responsive to the innovations permitted by Vatican II and sometimes went as far as rejecting the need for regular attendance in class. They were very eager to participate more in Parisian life: how can we preach to a world that we don't know? the leading spirits of this movement argued. "I admit that all of that puzzles me," Brother Pierre responded, saying he was disconcerted by those who were "rejecting the essential means of all religious life, under the pretext that one has to 'go beyond the law'" (letter of March 8, 1964). This was the period of liturgical reform desired by Vatican II: the beginning of concelebrations and the use of French in church prayers. He rejoiced at all of that, but did not take part in the radical questioning of the traditional forms of religious life, a position that seemed to disturb his fellows:

> Report from a group meeting: it seems that I frighten the younger brothers because I look very serious . . . It also seems that I have a very strong personality and that people don't dare open their mouths after I have given my opinion rather abruptly . . . And in this time of "dialogue" it is indeed unfortunate . . . Finally, when I become a superior [sic] I will have to be wary of my rather forceful ways. There, now you know it all. (letter of April 5, 1965)

One can sense here a man firmly established, capable of taking on real commitments, and he attributed this to his family background: "Fortunately, you helped give me a personality that, on the whole, is well enough balanced at its core without any inner torments. But still, what an adventure!" he wrote on the occasion of his solemn vows in November 1964. But, the questionings at Le Saulchoir did in fact go far. It was badly shaken by the storm of May 1968, and even closed later and transferred to Paris to be closer to the city and its effervescence. But Pierre Claverie had already left: his own questions were elsewhere, and he was never really involved in the "cultural revolution" taking place north of the Mediterranean.[13] Nonetheless he was quite shaken by the departure of several brothers of his circle from the religious life, as shown by this letter of November 6, 1964: "We freely accept to commit ourselves to live near the cross: one never knows exactly what that will entail. But what one does know is that it is necessary to give everything down to the root and essence, a little as though one chooses to be blind, and without being too pretentious about it."

Two things energized him: his preaching, of which he did a great deal after he was ordained to the diaconate in November 1964, and the preparation for his return to Algeria, if his superiors decided to send him there. A pilgrimage to Chartres; church work at Étiolles, the neighboring village to Le Saulchoir; short retreats for groups of Boy Scouts: he gave a lot of himself, sometimes to the point where he was overwhelmed by the various pastoral obligations he accepted, but he received a real personal benefit from it all.[14] As superior of the student brothers he also had to manage some tensions in the priory. But he possessed good physical and emotional health, real generosity, and energy to spare. The year 1965 was marked by his ordination as a priest, on July 4, by Bishop Sauvage of Annecy. On the reverse of his medal of ordination, which had on its front side the washing of feet, were the names of seven brothers of whom more than half later followed a different path. Pierre's parents were there for the occasion, along with Abbé Streicher, the former parish priest of Bab el Oued, and Fr. Lefèvre, with whom differences of opinion on the Algerian question could no longer be kept hidden ("But I admire him very much, in spite of everything," he said). Speaking of his ministry as a Dominican, a preaching brother, Pierre Claverie wrote: "In the course of my preaching, I will insist on the three essential actions of the Easter mystery which are at the heart of our lives: the Last Supper, or the sharing of bread; the cross, or the gift of Christ; the reconciliation, or the victory over death" (letter of March 20, 1967). One often saw these same themes, later, when, as a bishop, he was responsible for teaching his community.

The other motivating force during these years was the project to return to Algeria, in which Pierre believed more and more.[15] In May 1964 Fr. Anawati, at that time director of the Dominican Institute for Oriental Studies in Cairo, told Pierre Claverie that he was "counting on him for Algiers and the Islamic world as a whole." The provincial superior was in agreement and the matter seemed settled until the new master of students, Fr. Besnard, quickly worn out by the climate of dispute in Le Saulchoir, suggested that Pierre Claverie be groomed to succeed him in office. The idea was not new: Pierre Claverie had been "hailed as a future master of studies" very early, remembers Pierre Raffin, a fellow student at Le Saulchoir from 1962 on. It was October 1965. Worried about the changes in the *studium*, the provincial superior, with the support of his advisory council, thought this was a good idea and so informed Brother Pierre. He reacted without becoming too anxious, at least to outward appearance, as can be seen in a humorous letter, written to his sister in *pataouète*, the dialect of the pieds-noirs in Algiers:

> Where you going to spend your vacation? Me, I still don't know: since in Algeria the horizon, it is blocked off, I'm like a duck in a dish of

macaroni; everything is slippery, and I don't know how to orient myself. Fortunately, I try to keep my inner compass out in the air: otherwise I don't know how I would land...But what surprises me is that they want to make me master of studies. I wonder if you can imagine what that is! Me, I always say to myself: how do I know if I would be able to talk to them? How do I know that I will not get old so quickly that I will no longer understand the young people who will come to me to be educated?...Because when I see the others around me, you can't imagine the insecurities that that gives me, just because I seem to hold my own when I chatter in the world outside because I'm a specialist in matters that the people don't know well. But among specialists I'm not at all a shining light: I just know how to flap my mouth. It's always the same since I was little...: "This kid seems intelligent, he's a leader, he knows where he's going, he understands people," and so on. All that because my mother, she gave me sparkling eyes. But monkeys have sparkling eyes too, and people even say of them that they look intelligent and all. (letter of March 1966)[16]

Pierre Claverie wrote this letter just after his meeting with the provincial superior, Fr. Kopf, in February 1966: "After having fought step by step to convince him, I must give in to his reasons and to my duty to obey him."

In fact, for several months his future was discussed, seeming to veer first toward one plan then the other, depending on the moment, according to the pressures placed on the provincial superior. Fr. Le Baut, prior of Algiers, fiercely defended his point of view, but for a time the needs of Le Saulchoir seemed likely to win the day. Pierre Claverie nevertheless decided not to abandon his study of Arabic and attended the meetings of the students of Arabic who wanted to be assigned as a team, and never alone, to the communities of the Arabic world. A little resigned to his fate, Pierre Claverie acknowledged, "It's clear! I'm beginning to see a future take shape that will lead me from responsibility to responsibility, until, God forbid, I fall on my face. I won't be a 'brain,' as Nane says, but a bigwig; that's something else and much less exciting!...Let God decide!" (letter of March 13, 1966).

Behind these debates, one feels the question looming: would Claverie become an intellectual, a specialist, for which he had the ability, or rather a preacher and administrator? In fact, he would never be a specialist, but a preacher and later a pastor, who retained a taste for intellectual reflection but was above all energized by human contact.

Finally, it was the path of the future in Algeria which carried the day, following a memorable intervention by Pierre Le Baut, superior of the Algiers community, who came to a provincial assembly in May 1967 specifically for that purpose. The newly elected provincial superior, Nicolas Rettenbach, settled the matter, judging, "One can always find a new master of studies; the Arabic world, though, that's more complicated." The news arrived at the priory in Algiers by telegram on July 5, 1967, the anniversary of Algerian independence.[17] A couple of days later, Pierre Claverie was there to start a month-long Arabic course with the Lebanese sisters at Birmandreis. This time, he had returned for good to Algeria, where he would go, finally, to meet the other.

Le Saulchoir
27 février 1963

Mes chers petits vieux ...

vous voilà donc réunis à nouveau mais pour "liquider"
le passé. Pauvre petite maison comme écrivait Papa dans une de ses dernières épitres.
Bien sûr, vous ne reverrez plus ce panorama de Notre Dame d'Afrique à la mer –
bien sûr vous ne referez plus cet itinéraire venté de la rue Koechlin – et toutes
ces images vont rejoindre un arsenal de souvenirs ... Mais j'espère que vous vous
rendrez bien vite compte combien cette séparation d'avec les murs ne pèse rien en
comparaison de la création ailleurs, du milieu humain où vous avez été plus.
Papo avait très bien ressenti cette différence et cela lui faisant dire qu'il quitterait
sans regrets. Il n'y a pas de regrets à avoir, en effet. Maman comprendra très vite
combien ce nouveau milieu humain a bouleversé les structures de briques au point de
les rendre méconnaissables. Ce bouleversement ne paraît de place qu'aux "premiers", à
ceux qui, comme moi, n'ont rien à perdre et qui ont consacré leur vie à un
service des autres. Vous, qui avez fondé un foyer, vous avez eu à faire face à
vos responsabilités propres et vous avez admirablement mené votre barque, en
sachant garder la mesure dans les contacts que vous aviez avec l'extérieur. Votre
œuvre de "cellule créatrice et éducatrice" vous l'avez menée à fond, et ce n'est pas
encore tout à fait fini pour Nane. C'était cela votre raison d'être sur terre et aux
yeux de Dieu vous avez sûrement réalisé le dessein prévu pour vous depuis Fruges.
Le reste, votre situation en Algérie, votre confrontation au drame des sept ans de
guerre, votre "exode", sont à comprendre en fonction de votre rôle essentiel et
prennent alors l'importance exacte qui doit leur revenir : des moyens dont vous avez

Extract from a letter of Pierre to his parents from Le Saulchoir, February 27, 1963.

... du extraire le meilleur et surtout que vous avez su vivre dans la paix intérieure, en la rayonnant autour de vous. Alors ce départ n'a aucune importance. Vous allez rejoindre votre nouvelle place, au milieu de ceux qui vous sont confiés — et qui se sont confiés à vous depuis toujours — : les Mejiat, les Maillard, tous vos amis. Et vous pourrez continuer à mener Nane au but. Quand vous aurez accompli cela — et même avant — vous pourrez songer à une nouvelle forme de service qui, tenant compte de l'œuvre accomplie, ne vous laisse pas riches du droit de vous reposer. Je fais entière confiance à Papa pour entamer avec sagesse l'étape ultime qui vous mènera tous les deux — et nous tous, les 4, représentés par vous — à la rencontre de Dieu, riches du don d'amour que vous n'aurez cessé de faire. J'admire la simplicité de cette vie que vous nous avez montré en exemple à Nane et moi. — Si seulement nous pouvions en retenir le secret...

Je ne sais pas pourquoi je vous écris sur ce ton ... peut-être cette la nostalgie de savoir que vous vivez vos dernières heures algériennes ... peut être pour ne pas vous laisser seuls et surtout pour que vous ne soyez pas cafardeux en vous laissant envahir par le sentiment — oh! bien légitime, mais de si peu d'importance ! — de déracinement. Vous n'êtes pas déracinés puisque nos racines sont dans le cœur des hommes (et pas dans la terre ou les briques —) et vous allez retrouver tous ces amis là où vous allez.

La page se tourne, pas de salades, pas de regrets possibles. Le combat qui s'est déroulé là-bas n'était pas à votre mesure, pas davantage à la mienne. Il était, il est encore à la mesure des révolutionnaires, des visionnaires, des purs et des escrocs, des intérêts qui se sont affrontés. Plus rien à faire pour ces hommes par vous — d'autres prendront la relève, je le souhaite et je me prépare à en être, dans ma sphère propre. "La famille continue", continue à répandre sa paix et son esprit d'union — A sa mesure elle mène un combat, elle conquiert des territoires et d'ceux là personne ne pourra la déloger ...

Grosses bises et à bientôt          Pierre

## Chapter Four

# Toward the Joyous Encounter
# with the Other

> Therefore I asked, after independence, to return to Algeria so
> I could rediscover that world where I was born, but that I had
> not known. It's there that my true personal adventure began—
> a rebirth.[1]                                          — *Pierre Claverie*

Returning to Algeria on July 5, 1967, the fifth anniversary of Independence,
Pierre Claverie had changed a great deal — but so had Algeria. His outlook
had changed considerably, little by little abandoning the prejudices and pre-
conceptions of the colonial world in which he had been born. But it had been
an intellectual journey, which had led him, for example, to consider that the
war of liberation was "just," in a manner of speaking, because there were legitimate grounds for it. But Claverie's feelings had not evolved at the same pace,
which still led him to react in an embarrassing way occasionally. Returning to
Algeria to establish himself and live his adult life there, he found himself in
an environment that gave his deepest feelings room to evolve. This explains
the enthusiasm with which he would rediscover no longer the "Arabs" but
"the Algerians," learning their language, visiting their country, the country
that was also his own. He had a great deal to discover: the energies of the
whole populace now being invested in the construction of a new Algeria.

## The Algeria of Houari Boumediene, or the Hope of
## "Better Tomorrows"

The first years after independence were marked by a real euphoria. There was
joy in recovering an identity and dignity, hope for a more just society, the
enthusiasm of a new beginning. An Algerian leadership little by little took
the reins of the country, assisted by outside advisors, enthusiastic for this new
Algeria, a state modeled on socialist self-management of the Yugoslav variety;
they were called the "pieds-rouges" — red feet, in contrast to the colonial
pieds-noirs, black feet. The Christians in Algeria played a role in the renewal,

creating social centers in the lower-class districts or bringing the assistance of their scientific and technical competence to a country where so much needed to be done. It was a period of many shimmering initiatives, encouraged by the effervescent Ahmed Ben Bella, first president of independent Algeria. On June 19, 1965, however, a coup d'état brought an end to these three years, during which a kind of happiness was in the air, as well as unrealistic expectations. Houari Boumediene, an austere colonel from eastern Algeria, took leadership of what came to be called the "revolutionary correction." In place of the bubbling euphoria that had dominated immediately after independence, Boumediene intended to substitute a rigorous program to construct a state and to put the economy on track.

The Algerians responsible for this new policy laid out an "Algerian development strategy" inspired by the theorists of the transition to socialism (Bettelheim, Salama, De Bernis, O. Sik) and by the experience of Eastern Europe. The priority was to create a state, to devise administrative structures and to nurture an environment in which the army and a single political party — the National Liberation Front — would come to play a leading role. Official newspapers (*El Moujahid* in French and *El Chaab* in Arabic) were created to disseminate approved slogans to mobilize the masses, building on a basis of third-world nationalism. With Independence, many non-Algerian leaders had left the country, leaving the state free to assume direct control of key sectors of the economy, including banking, foreign trade, heavy industry, and transport. Agriculture, established since 1963 on a self-governing cooperative model, was taken in hand mainly to limit the ravages of a foreign system badly adapted to the Algerian environment. The nationalization of mines and soon of hydrocarbons was intended to give the Algerian state the financial means to launch an ambitious policy of economic and social development. This policy was in place by 1967 and gave priority to heavy industry, education of the masses, and free access to health care. In the following years, one other aspect of Boumediene's policy became clear, but in a controversial fashion — Arabization. Profoundly stripped of its culture by three hundred years of French occupation, Algerian society was to recover its identity. Access to the Arabic language, which is also the language of Islam, was an essential element of this plan. Two approaches to this question confronted each other, foreshadowing future ideological conflicts: a religious approach that in the course of the years became Islamist, while a secular, socializing approach, at one time dominant but little by little lost ground to the religious radicals.

At that time Algeria was a leader among developing countries. It was a member of the Group of Nonaligned States, which in fact held its conference at Algiers in 1973, an occasion on which Algeria played host to the leaders of the third world — including Tito, Fidel Castro, and Sékou Touré — with great pomp, cheered by the crowds that dutifully assembled along their route. Soon Algeria came to play a decisive role in international affairs, thanks to the talent of Abdelaziz Bouteflika, who served as minister of foreign affairs for seventeen years. Algeria even presided over the special assembly of the United Nations dedicated to raising the price of raw materials. The pan-African festival held at Algiers in 1969 expressed in music and poetry what everyone believed: Algeria was on course toward "better tomorrows."

It was to this euphoric Algeria that Claverie returned. For him, too, it was a time of optimism. He was rediscovering a country, its people, its language, and its scenery. He was also coming to join a church that was taking part in this renewal in many ways.

## First Step: Learning Arabic

Claverie's first priority was the serious study of Arabic. He had been learning the language since his arrival at le Saulchoir in 1960 and his knowledge was already well beyond the elementary level. Now the question was where he should go to get a good mastery of the language and at the same time enjoy access to Arabic and Muslim culture. At his arrival, accompanied by another young Dominican friar, Jean-Marie Mérigoux, Claverie signed up for a summer course in Arabic that was organized by the Lebanese nuns of the Sacred Hearts of Jesus and Mary. For Claverie, it was rather a case of "love at first sight." He reported his early encounter with the sisters to his parents:

> They are wonderful in their own fashion. They wear civilian dress, wonderful, quite elegant, I assure you! They are animated by a very surprising missionary spirit. The Arabs welcome them with a boundless admiration. And when the Arabs know that these women are Arabs, Christians, religious, they are amazed... There is no proselytizing in their attitude, but rather love and a truly disinterested service to the people to whom they have been sent. (letter of July 1967)

The members of this community would come to play an important role in Claverie's future. The Jesuits who had founded the congregation of Sisters of the Sacred Hearts of Jesus and Mary at Bikfaya in Lebanon in the middle of the nineteenth century had intended a female congregation that could take

In 1967, the young Dominican priest Pierre Claverie with the Lebanese sisters
and members of the course in Arabic at Algiers.

charge of educating young girls in the Lebanese mountains. Highly qualified,
often with higher degrees, these sisters ran numerous schools in Lebanon,
Syria, and several other countries like Algeria and Morocco. They worked
with equal vigor in the health field and the promotion of women. At Algiers,
in a completely Muslim country, these women were astonishing. They knew
Arabic better than the Algerians, who found it hard to imagine that one
could be an Arab without being Muslim. They had great facility in their
relations with the people, something not yet common for women in Algeria.
These nuns are professional religious, women for whom prayer and service
are essential, but that does not cut them off from life, as is so often the case
for women in a Muslim milieu.

Claverie was captivated, and the feeling was reciprocal. The little community of Lebanese sisters at Algiers was at that time led by Sister Atina Fadil,
a woman overflowing with zest for life, who adopted Pierre as her "son," to
use her own word. In September Claverie enrolled in their center for Arabic
pedagogy, located at the Voirol Column on the heights above Algiers. The
program there was intense: "I have an enormous amount of work," Claverie
wrote in January. The teaching was good and this was his highest priority. But

Claverie's work load was made heavier because of the many other calls on his time that quickly appeared, including homilies on Radio Algiers (beginning in mid-August), sermons, and encounters with lay groups. In January 1968 Cardinal Duval asked Claverie to preach during Lent at the cathedral of Algiers, but he refused because Sister Atina was protective of him. As Claverie explained: "The Lebanese, who already complain about the multiplicity of my activities (but who also recognize the seriousness of my work), would have been furious" (letter of January 7, 1968).[2]

The sisters' student worked very hard, spending mornings on his Arabic class and afternoons in his room at 92 rue Didouche-Mourad, where the Dominican community had moved in 1962. "In the bus, he recited the lessons to me from memory, according to the Alverny method," Claverie's fellow student Jean-Marie Mérigoux remembers. In spite of his intellectual gifts and industry, the undertaking was difficult, but Claverie fully understood its importance: "It is necessary at any price to penetrate the language a little, which makes it possible to begin to perceive the abyss that separates us. Truly, the Algerian crisis was completely inevitable and the future still isn't clear in regard to relations with the Western nations…I confess that I'm beginning to fall in love with the Arabic language and world" (letter of July 28, 1968).

Later one will encounter that expression again from his pen: "the abyss that separates us." It is interesting to note that he had quickly become aware of its existence. Claverie passed his exams in June, graduating first of the thirty students. "Atina was radiant," he commented, "and received congratulations with undisguised satisfaction." The following year, Claverie enrolled in an advanced Arabic degree program at the University of Aix-en-Provence, while continuing his studies at Algiers. Three or four evenings a week he engaged in Arabic conversation with an Egyptian, Mr. El Badry, author of several books on Sufism and a friend of the famous Egyptian Dominican Fr. Anawati, director of the Dominican Institute of Oriental Studies at Cairo. Claverie made swift progress thanks to intense daily work. At one time there was a question of whether he should spend his third year at the White Fathers' Pontifical Institute of Arabic Studies at Rome, where Fr. Borrmans was eager to welcome him. But the Lebanese sisters did everything possible to keep him. They offered private lessons to help him in his work for the degree and considered giving him the job of teaching Arabic grammar to the beginning students at their center starting in the 1969–70 school year. Pierre succeeded at everything, and was indeed rather fawned upon in this almost exclusively feminine environment.[3] Beyond these facilities, Claverie had a deep stake there, which he explained clearly: "I hold dear my Algerian orientation, and more and more I feel deeply the need to 'Algerianize' myself further, instead of just exposing myself to countries and institutions. The future will tell us how far I may be right" (letter of September 1, 1969).

Dedicating himself to improving his skills, at age thirty Claverie confessed that he worked full throttle to the point of having had enough, as he indicated in a letter written in the summer of 1970: "Every afternoon I worked on my Arabic, for three and a half hours without a break. The Lebanese are really wonderful to give me their time. I have astonishing good luck ... but I really have to force myself to work, because I'm a hundred feet over my head in Arabic ..." (letter of August 5, 1970).

These years of intensive Arabic study gave Claverie access not only to a language but to a cultural world that he desired to enter. The language courses were rounded off with a class on how to penetrate Arabic texts and the Qur'an, offered by Henri Teissier. In the evenings Claverie celebrated the Eucharist in Arabic among the sisters, to whom he was becoming ever closer. He even made a tour of Algeria with them and, in the summer of 1971, they invited him to Lebanon. There, while conducting retreats, he was able to immerse himself delightedly in the Eastern cultural universe.[4] He attained a good knowledge of the language, in which he could express himself with ease "and a good accent," said Sister Marie Melhem, who gave him some special lessons. But Claverie recognized that it had taken him ten years to achieve that result. Enrolled in the Arabic program at Aix-en-Provence, he successfully passed his first-year exams in 1970, but did not go on to obtain his degree, since he was already too absorbed in his many preaching activities.

Still more stimulating for Claverie, the sisters introduced him to some Algerian friends, a step that came to play a major role in his deepening Algerianization. For example, he wrote to his parents:

> This week we have had impassioned discussions with our fellow students at the Lebanese sisters — about those women who formed the core of the Algerian revolution, from the time when they were students and planters of bombs (Djamila Bouhired, Zohra Drif, Malika Khène, and several others who were imprisoned for long terms in France). Behold yet another Algeria that we didn't know anything about. (letter of November 18, 1969)

Here was the human loam in which his deepest feelings could grow the most.

## "My Algerian Brothers and Friends"

The Lebanese sisters had many friends. Among their students were high officials, wives of ministers, magistrates with an urgent need to improve their knowledge of Arabic. All of these, having attended school during the colonial period, lacked a real mastery of the language that was now dominant in the administration, politics, and the schools — where their own children were gradually coming to be instructed in Arabic. Highly professional in their pedagogical methods, the sisters also knew how to be very convivial. Often invited to family events by their Algerian students, they themselves entertained magnificently, regaling their guests with delicious Lebanese dishes but above all with their joy in life and their talent for interpersonal relationships. Claverie was charmed by these opportunities, where he made personal contacts with the people about whom he had had a negative image all the time he was growing up. "In my childhood I was not in a Muslim environment. At the time of independence I had a head full of images of the 'Arabs' butchering the world where I was born. It was only when I returned to Algeria in 1967 that I discovered, beyond the terrorists, human beings. I have had, I always have, Muslim friends."[5]

Later Claverie would tell, during a television interview for French channel France 2 in June 1995, that his stomach knotted when he realized that among the students was a woman who had set off a bomb in an Algiers café that had claimed numerous pieds-noir victims. Others, without being terrorists, had been very active as militant anticolonialists, like Mme Laliam, who later became Minister of Health. As a young doctor she had joined the underground. She was arrested twice, was detained in camps (from which she escaped), and was sheltered by the White Sisters in one of their convents in France.

Another of Claverie's classmates was Malika Boumendjel, sister of the leading militant nationalist Ali Boumendjel, who had been assassinated after being tortured by the parachutist division of the French army. "On another occasion," remembered Henri Teissier, at that time a professor of Arabic for the Lebanese sisters, "a student brought a photo of her brother, killed in combat against the French army during the Algerian War." "Pierre was always very anxious to question participants in the war of liberation," Professor Drif, another close friend of this period, emphasized. Claverie also set out to read *L'Histoire de l'Afrique du Nord* (*The History of North Africa*) by Charles-André Julien, one of the first historians to "decolonialize" the historiography of this country. Pierre found his approach in this book, which soon became the standard reference work on the subject, "very instructive, although very subjective."

The friendly climate created by the Lebanese sisters certainly did a great deal to help Claverie in this mutual process of getting acquainted. "Sister Atina used to read his future in the coffee-grounds after dinner," Mme Chentouf remembered, "and everyone laughed a great deal." Apprehensions fading, he began to have contact with a number of Algerians, among whom he found the Mediterranean cordiality of his youth. There were evening barbecues with one, tea with others, a family outing to Chréa or a weekend at the cedar forest at Kabylia. They all became opportunities to establish contact with the Algerian world — with people, but even more with ideas, which suited Claverie's temperament very well. The sisters even had him meet President Boumediene's family, of whom they knew the elderly mother and his younger brother and sister. The Dominican community in which Claverie lived also had a network of Algerian friends, whom he visited with even more pleasure, and since by this time Claverie had a good mastery of Arabic they blossomed into unexpected and passionate discussions. Even with his dentist, who tended to forget about the patients in the waiting room when Pierre was there: "We talk about the Bible and the Qur'an, messiah and prophecy, Holy Spirit and spirit of Muhammad. What an amazing good-natured man this Hadj Zinaï is" (letter of December 7, 1969).

Claverie remained faithful to this network of friends. Besides the relaxation that he enjoyed with them, he had a debt, which he explained in their presence on the day of his episcopal ordination in the cathedral of Algiers:

> My Algerian brothers and friends, I also owe it to you that I am who I am today. You also have welcomed me and sustained me by your friendship. I owe it to you that I have discovered the Algeria that was still my country, but where I had lived as a foreigner throughout my youth. With you, in learning Arabic, I above all learned to speak and to understand the language of the heart, the tongue of fraternal friendship where different races and religions can speak with one another. There still, I believe that this friendship endures through time, distance, and separation. Because I believe that this friendship comes from God and leads to God.[6]

Through his friends, Pierre Claverie had regained a country and an identity: from this point on, he was at home in this land, since these Algerians considered him to be one of their own.

## An Algerian Church in Transition

The Algerian church, too, changed from what it had been while Claverie was growing up. The pieds-noirs had left the country en masse in 1962, and in many districts of Algiers the churches were deserted. A large majority of the pieds-noir clergy had followed, as much from conviction as from necessity — the majority of priests, close to their flocks, had had little detachment from the ideology of French Algeria. A quite small minority of Christian pieds-noirs had shown solidarity with the Algerian struggle for their independence: in Algeria itself these were called the "liberals" at their trial in July 1957, and in France the networks of supporters were called the "suitcase carriers."[7] Among the church personnel, only the religious orders had remained in large numbers, continuing their service in the schools or health care. Despite the efforts of Archbishop Duval to maintain continuity in the Christian presence, the rupture was deep. Priests and religious had to adjust the form of their presence in Algeria to new realities. Now the community to be served was no longer exclusively — or even to begin with — the Christian community, but a Muslim people. Although many religious already had a very pronounced social commitment, the change was profound. It was sharpened by the arrival of a large number of aid workers, who offered their technical and professional competence for building up a new Algeria, where everything was still to be done in all fields. Some priests, like those of the French Mission, had already cleared the way by working at the port or as medical secretaries in dispensaries. Thus for everyone a new adventure of solidarity began, solidarity with a Muslim country confronted by the urgent needs of development. The Dominican community was just as transfigured as the rest and forged a symbiotic relationship with the Algerian world. The brothers took up professional employment, one at the Ministry of Agriculture, another teaching at a technical school, while a third was even recruited to the Ministry of Religious Affairs, where he drafted a legal statute concerning imams! A less-cloistered lifestyle also let neighborly and friendly relations incubate. In short, the church in Algeria was getting a remake. It would not be long before Claverie was part of it.

Claverie made his first entry through friendship. In September 1967 a group of aid workers invited him to share in their reflection group. The members were committed Christians, but they were not very comfortable with diocesan pastoral approach. These were the years following Vatican II and a wind of freedom and creativity was blowing through the church in movements like Vie nouvelle ("the New life") or the Équipes enseignantes ("Teaching Corps"). Claverie's new group included engineers, doctors, professors who "try to reflect on their faith and refuse to let themselves be 'organized' in the Catholic Action movements. It is a very rich human environment, of the 'prophetic' variety," Claverie commented (letter of November 1, 1967). With his friends Gernigon, Lugan, and du Jonchay, Claverie made several excursions to explore southern Algeria, meditating at the tomb of Charles de Foucauld at El Goléa; he even returned wearing a beard and *cachabia*. In this group, Claverie encountered Pastor Jacques Blanc and his wife, whom he had gotten to know during his military service, when Blanc was his counterpart at the Protestant military center. A figure of wide-ranging intellect, Blanc remained for Claverie a point of reference and inspiration. Later they worked together in the Encounter and Development Association. This group of lay Christians worked seriously and welcomed Claverie, finding him a dependable source of sustenance. For their annual program they organized a Bible retreat (studying the epistle to the Romans) and a theology workshop (theologies of the death of God, a fashionable theme in 1968). On both topics the young Dominican, fresh from Le Saulchoir, had things to share. The meetings took place at their homes or at the parish of El Biar, on the heights of Algiers, where the vicar, Pierre Frantz, soon became Claverie's friend. At the beginning of the seventies Claverie would be the moving spirit of a group reflection, launched by Frantz in his parish, very well attended, on the new face of the church in Algeria — work with mixed couples (in general European women married to Muslim men) whose children were educated in Algerian schools, an effort to put in place a Catholic catechesis adapted for these children growing up in a Muslim environment. It was the sort of thing that stimulated Claverie. Everyone was enthusiastic.

Other ministries were suggested to Claverie from the time he arrived: homilies on Radio Algiers, alternating with Pierre Le Baut, prior of the Dominican community; Bible conferences; meetings of religious. But at the archbishop's headquarters the young leader was regarded with a degree of distrust. "Why does he never refer to the pope?" Cardinal Duval complained, fearing that these dynamic lay groups might import into the Algerian church the revolutionary ideas of May 1968. Everyone was watching everyone. Claverie found the cardinal "charming in private" but "stiff" in his relations with his priests. Indeed, the cardinal had nothing of the Mediterranean spirit — he was more like the statue of the Commendatore in *Don Giovanni!*

Born in 1903 to a deeply pious Savoyard family, Léon-Étienne Duval had grown up in Annecy in the shadow of St. Francis de Sales, whom he revered. A seminary professor, he had acquired a deep knowledge of the church fathers and spoke freely of St. Augustine, another Algerian, whose successor he became as bishop of Constantine and Hippo in 1946. This period of res-idence in eastern Algeria, just after the massacres of Sétif, opened Duval's eyes to the Algerian people's aspirations for dignity and even more for jus-tice. Transferred to the diocese of Algiers in 1954, he lived under extremely excruciating tensions during the Algerian War, the excesses of which seemed intolerable to him. So the archbishop denounced the abuses, following the traditional principles of theology and Christian ethics to which he was so deeply attached. Spurred on by Abbé Jean Scotto, who had friends among the Algerian nationalists, Duval showed himself, gradually, favorable to possible self-determination by the Algerian people. It was still out of the question to speak of "independence." But even though he had not uttered the word, this positive stance drew down on him the opposition and sometimes the hatred of many members of his flock, who in derision nicknamed him "Muhammad Duval." The majority of his clergy no longer supported him. But Duval held firm, reaffirming the law and moral values even during the worst hours of the barricades and the OAS. This won him a very high regard from the Algerian people, for whom he was "the cardinal," that lasted for the rest of his life.[8] In February 1965, along with twenty other priests, Duval applied for and ob-tained Algerian citizenship, not to disown his origins but to underscore his connection with Algeria. "When I came to Algeria," he said to explain this decision, "I came to spend the rest of my life, consecrating myself entirely to the country." A week later, February 22, 1965, Pope Paul VI made Duval a cardinal, thereby signaling papal consent to Duval's plans for the evolution of the Algerian church.[9] But the cardinal had found the years of contention extremely painful, a fact that probably aggravated a certain inflexibility in his temperament — a characteristic that at first disturbed Pierre Claverie very much. The cardinal offered Claverie several responsibilities, all of which he declined. On one occasion: "I saw Monseigneur Duval, as always about the question of the marginals [the lay groups]. He didn't know where to stand. Too bad. He wanted to assign me for next year to the diocesan chaplaincy of the Teaching Corps. I refused. We parted good friends" (letter of July 16, 1968).

Claverie was more at ease with the "great Duval," the bold upholder of political positions, as is clear in this remark of March 23, 1969, after the cardinal had given an interview on Radio Luxembourg: "We found it excellent as a whole. The boss is a little like de Gaulle: a holy monster who only gives unstintingly in times of crisis. Well intentioned, he is completely incapable of dialogue, even when he craves it."

In January 1970 at the time of new year wishes, the cardinal showed himself to be very much aware of Claverie's activities and wished him to be "the Anawati of North Africa."[10] Some months later, he put Claverie in charge of religious broadcasts on Radio Algiers. But one can sense that Claverie was always reserved in his relationship with the cardinal. The situation was quite different with Jean Scotto.

## Deeper Discovery of Algeria: The Year in Constantine

On September 6, 1970, Abbé Jean Scotto was named bishop of Constantine and Hippo. One of the first things he did was to ask Pierre Claverie to be his *socius* — not a private secretary, but his theological advisor. The two men had met in the summer of 1965 at the priests' assembly held at the seminary in Kouba. From the outset, they had gotten along well. Both were pieds-noirs, both had the same communicative and zealous temperament. They encountered each other again and became better acquainted at Algiers in 1968: "More and more I admire this good, unpretentious little man, and can see how badly the press has done by choosing certain aspects of his personality just to be sensational and to excite public opinion," Claverie wrote on August 4, 1969, after a dinner with Scotto at the Dominican priory.

Scotto came from a lower-class sector of Algiers and, during the Algerian War, had been the "bête noire" of the partisans of French Algeria. He supported the cardinal's positions the more willingly because he had helped to inspire them in the first place. Scotto was a pastor who loved his pieds-noir flock very much, but the injustices of French rule appeared to him to be too flagrant to pass over in silence. At times he even gave refuge to FLN members who were being pursued by the French army. After independence Scotto was elected to the Algiers municipal council. His friend André Mandouze, at the time rector of the University of Algiers, often hailed Scotto as "the most firmly established Algerian bishop." Famous for his sometimes coarse language in private, he was nonetheless a spiritual person, a man of God. Was he a man who could manage? This is less clear. The nomination to the episcopate surprised and disconcerted him.[11] By inviting Claverie to join him in his new see, Scotto thought to give himself a better chance of success.

Claverie accepted and in November 1970 started to divide his time between Constantine and Algiers, where he returned for a week each month to continue his Arabic studies. From their first week at Constantine, Scotto and

Claverie sorted out files and deliberated about one of the first decisions that had to be taken — the abandonment of the cathedral in favor of a smaller church. There were only about 150 actively practicing Catholics left in the city of Constantine. Helping the bishop prepare his community for this downsizing, Claverie can have had no idea that he would have to perform a similar operation at Oran ten years later. Claverie also established contact with the various communities of Constantine. It appears that their relations were good, as he told his family: "The priests have asked that I be the theological spearhead for their area studies. I will have my own work independent of Scotto, while still remaining close to him so he can draw pastoral conclusions from our common work" (letter of January 1971).

Between Bishop Scotto and his priests matters were not nearly as simple. The diocese of Constantine had several sacerdotal communities that were deeply engaged and had carefully articulated visions for their presence there. The Jesuits taught at the university and encouraged literacy in self-managing agricultural domains, while priests of the French Mission were deeply embedded in the working-class milieu. Things did not go smoothly between these groups and Scotto — the priests spoke of militancy, of commitment, posing essential questions on the evolution the church must undergo to become Algerian. The church of Algeria was in effect beginning to confront new questions. It did not want to be an "embassy church," that is, a church for foreigners without local roots. But under what circumstances could this church become Algerian? That was the point under debate. Beginning with independence, this debate began in circles like the Study Association, created by Jean Delanglade, a Jesuit close to André Mandouze. During the first years, a certain mystique of fraternal service had led many to engage in a service of development. Priests and religious saw themselves in the attitude described by Serge de Beaurecueil: "Silent bearers of the Word, of a creative word, incarnate and crucified, merely in being, merely in living here, merely in loving, merely in dying here, merely in celebrating the Eucharist, I engage the future of a people in the Light."[12] But this mystique of lying hidden quickly led people to question the logic of an institutional church — all the theology of mission came into play. This led to the enunciation of increasingly radical positions. In their eyes, the church accomplishes its calling when it disappears as a separate reality and, so to speak, it merges completely with the people where it lives. Stimulated by the spirit of 1968, this sometimes led to extremely anti-institutional reactions.

At times the interchanges were sharp; Jean Scotto was baffled and did not really respond to his clergy's expectations. His experience was not at all

Pierre Claverie with his friend Henri Teissier in 1972,
the year Teissier was appointed bishop of Oran.

administrative — he had been rector of several major parishes in Algiers, such
as Hussein-Dey, Bab el Oued, and El Harrach. Scotto's family background
did not help either; he came from a lower-class environment of simple faith,
and he loved Thérèsa of Lisieux very much. Certainly he had taken political stands, but more by following his heart than because he was swayed by
ideas. Scotto was no theologian, and he knew it. Moreover, the austere world
of Constantine upset him. He had just left the euphoric period of independence, rich in projects in which he was deeply involved. At Algiers, he was
a personality; in Constantine he was unknown. He had no friends there and
soon discovered the difficulties of being accepted by local authorities who had
no idea what a bishop was. This was deeply rural Algeria, a core area of the
Algerian people.[13] It was here that Algerian nationalism had recruited many
of its militants and its leaders. Pied-noir bonhomie was not enough to break
the ice.

Claverie heard and saw all of this. Making the rounds of the diocese with
the bishop introduced him to an Algeria of the interior about which he had
known nothing, places like Sétif, Soukh Ahras, El Eulma, Tébessa. These were
the high plateaus, with a continental climate that is harsh in winter, torrid

in the summer. The main crop is wheat, but yields are poor; the majority of the population is poor and lives in *mechtas,* extremely destitute hamlets. In the summer, nomadic bands from the south graze the stubble. Barley cakes, couscous made of durum wheat, and a little milk constitute the normal diet of the *fellahs,* whose character is toughened by the life they lead. For Claverie, this was a different world, utterly unlike the middle and wealthy classes, at ease in French culture, whom he knew in Algiers. In one stroke, the Other took on a new face and raised new questions. The Other is different, he is difficult to encounter, sometimes he even resists. Claverie also discovered a new type of Christian community, a little flock, completely mixed among the masses, accomplishing its service discreetly. Leaven in the dough, there was nothing showy about the Christian presence here. He got to know men and women who immersed themselves completely in the Muslim environment, as much as possible rubbing out their differences so they could serve the community better — one was a doctor, another a teacher. Little distinguished them from the population at large. These circumstances gave Claverie a great deal of food for thought, since here he discovered how far he was from penetrating to the heart of this country. He wrote a great deal in this period,[14] lectures, articles, and retreats — especially the one he would conduct in Lebanon in the summer of 1971. His position midway between the priests (whose questions he understood very well) and the bishop (whose friendship he could not betray) was a little delicate, to say the least. Besides, his own reflections on the questions that were being posed had barely begun. Still, in less than a year, he arranged to take his leave from Bishop Scotto, who "took the blow hard," he recognized, but he promised to continue to collaborate on occasion.[15]

Another factor weighed into the decision to go: the heavy investment Claverie had made in learning Arabic was of little use to him because the church's personnel were still French-speaking, and his work with Scotto gave him little opportunity for direct contact with Algerians. So Claverie installed himself once more in Algiers and resumed a rhythm of activity that he himself characterized as "alarming": Arabic study, retreats, preaching, theological lectures for the Union of Teaching Religious. But the experience at Constantine had left its mark on him. He had traveled thousands of kilometers in the wasteland — he the city dweller. He had encountered the harshness of a daily presence in the Muslim world, discreet and not very gratifying. He had taken the measure of all that he did not know about this country, which was just beginning to be his own. An Algerian friend, from In Salah, encountered during an excursion in the south, had uncovered for Claverie the world of the Ouled Sidi Cheikh, the large nomadic tribe of which he was a member.

Claverie realized that he knew next to nothing about popular Islam, the religion of people who received very little instruction in Muslim formal texts. He made a first attempt to elaborate on this experience more systematically in a study on the relationship with the "other" with its psychological and social characteristics:

> That determines a limitation on our speculations on perfect love that does not exist anywhere. I believe that faith, like charity, comes to graft itself on human behavior and does not violate the normal laws for how things work in our psychology. Both can give meaning to a code of conduct or can even surpass limits judged too hastily to be insurmountable, but they cannot break away from the natural foundation. (letter of November 15, 1971)

One can sense in these lines, so Thomistic in their inspiration, that Claverie was beginning to plunge into deep reflection on how to find a real rapport with the "other." This question, central to his personal history, also came to be the central theme of his future work. But he was still far from having the human experience and sufficient maturity to reach valid conclusions. This process of reflection would take years, with all the human and spiritual enrichments that attended them — the cares and tests, too, because Claverie had reached his time of shouldering responsibility. Upon his return to Algiers in 1972, the priests of a sector of the city elected him as their dean, and thus he joined the bishop's council, where he committed all the energy of which he was capable.[16] Even though he would resign later, one can say that at this point the mutual distrust between him and the cardinal gradually began to fade. Thirty-five years separated the two men, and even more than that, they simply had very different temperaments. On one side was an old bishop, spiritual but finicky about ecclesiastical discipline, an upright man who had suffered a great deal, including at the hands of some of his priests. On the other side was a gifted young religious who loved to be loved and who had yet to confront the tests of life. In the course of the years, a mutual admiration grew, and even a certain affection. But the early stages were not simple. From this distance, one has the sense that the cardinal was both great and humble. Pierre Claverie would gradually find his own course as he grew into the responsibilities that were in store for him.

*Chapter Five*

# The Time of Responsibilities

> The discovery that we are called to make in Algeria is that the truth reveals itself a little when one consents to leave his own home and his own ideas. But that requires living together for a long time.[1]
> — *Pierre Claverie*

In January of 1973 Pierre Claverie took up his first position of responsibility in the diocese of Algiers. He was now thirty-five years old and was beginning to feel comfortable in this land of his birth, which had already changed so much since the coming of independence in 1962. By persisting in his study of Arabic, by traveling around the country, but especially by forging ties of friendship with Algerians, he hoped one day to feel completely at home here. This was by no means self-evident for a non-Muslim, because Algeria too was seeking to recover its identity, making a return both to Arab nationalism and to Islam. What should the role of Christians be in this new Algeria? It was around this question that Claverie's efforts and reflections came to converge in the years to come. Even though he was now taking on responsibilities in the church, he endeavored not to cut himself off from the country that was being born.

## "Les Glycines"

The Diocesan Center for Studies of Language and Pastoral Care, of which Claverie became director, was usually known as *les Glycines*, because it was on chemin des Glycines (Wisteria Street). Claverie succeeded Henri Teissier, who was ordained bishop of Oran in February 1973. Eight years later he would succeed Teissier yet again, as head of the diocese of Oran. In the meantime, les Glycines was a good introduction to responsibility. Although situated in a beautiful district and enjoying a lovely view of the Bay of Algiers, the building itself was quite austere. It had been constructed as a retirement home for nuns, and the atmosphere was serious — it was clearly intended as a place to work! The center, in its new location at les Glycines, had been founded scarcely two years before, created from a merger of the major seminary of Kouba (empty of students since independence) with the Language Center of the Missionary Sisters of Notre Dame d'Afrique, also known as the White Sisters, a group founded in the nineteenth century by Cardinal Lavigerie. Deeply embedded in the Algerian population, the White Sisters had always given great attention to the study of Arabic. The former major seminary brought to the merger a library and a group of professors. The whole consisted of a dozen staff members, with Claverie as coordinator.

The task was not an easy one. The personnel came from different backgrounds and did not share the same views of the church's role in Algeria, a role that to a great extent still had to be defined. Admired in a way, Claverie intrigued them because he was an outsider compared to those who had been working together for the diocese for several years. His unanimous election as head of this establishment surprised him. He confided to his parents:

> I admit that this is the last thing I had in mind ... It astonishes me especially because I've hardly ever even set foot in this building ... Besides, I feel completely unprepared for this responsibility, which I know perfectly well I cannot fill with the same skill as Henri [Teissier], an Arabist of very great skill who has moreover worked in this sector for ten years ... The brothers — *they* may be in agreement. They claim that I can not long evade the positions that are proposed to me ... (letter of December 12, 1972)

Cardinal Duval named him to the position, all the while saying that he thought Claverie was still a little young. Claverie immediately began consultations with his staff. He found some highly qualified colleagues in the establishment. There were several White Fathers, like Jean Fisset and Pierre Georgin, who had excellent training in Arabic and Islamic studies, and Pietr Reezink, who taught Berber. There were also White Sisters, like Lucienne Brousse and Katarina Kirch, who taught both classical Arabic and dialects. In addition, the staff included some Algiers diocesan priests particularly inclined toward pastoral care and some members of the Lazarist order, like Jean Landousies, in charge of continuing education, and Vincent O'Hara. It appears that O'Hara became Claverie's confessor.

Claverie perceived very quickly that the group lacked cohesion, a common sense of purpose. Not all of them lived on the premises. Their attitudes about the proper role of the church in a Muslim country differed widely. Claverie himself stirred certain fears, particularly among some nuns for whom he was

the "man of the Lebanese [sisters]," those Arabic nuns whose brio and remarkable connectedness to Algerian society made some a little jealous. Claverie's
cordiality rapidly calmed apprehensions about him. He soon resigned himself to residence at les Glycines, despite his desire to continue living with
his Dominican confreres in the city center. His door was always open and
people were welcome without an appointment — a policy that swiftly created
a climate of confidence in the new director. In return, Claverie lost no more
time in attending to the objectives he had been assigned for the center: to
create a genuine staff, to develop some sort of communal life where prayer
and human relations could find a place, to favor an opening up to the outside
world and a style of openness that would encourage Algerians to come easily
to les Glycines.[2]

The Diocesan Center for Studies consisted of several sections: The department of Arabic language, where dialects as well as classical Arabic were
taught for the benefit of church personnel and foreign aid workers called to
work in contact with Algerians. One should note that the teaching staff had,
since 1970, put into place its own method for teaching colloquial Arabic,
the "camel method," which proved to be well adapted for those who arrived
in Algeria to enter into the culture of the land. As the Arabization of the
country intensified, many Algerians asked to enroll in the classical Arabic
course.

Second, there was the *Revue de Presse* (Press Review), created by the White
Fathers of Ben-Cheneb Street in the Casbah, a monthly publication that
reviewed the main French and Arabic publications that dealt with North
Africa and, to a lesser extent, the Middle East. Third, there was the language
laboratory, where the foreign students could improve their pronunciation and
vocabulary with the help of several Algerian coaches. Next was the library,
rich in several thousand volumes about Algeria, the Arab world, and Christian
and Islamic theology. Open to the public, it attracted numerous Algerian
researchers, who appreciated its calm and organization. Finally, there was the
theology department (directed by Claverie himself for several years), which
developed courses intended for the continuing education of members of the
Algerian church.

All of this attracted a large and varied public to les Glycines. Algerians attended classical Arabic classes or visited the library, foreign aid workers came
to familiarize themselves with Arabic dialects, priests and religious attended
Islamic studies sessions. The Arabic classes alone enrolled up to 300 people
at a time, a level that later caused some difficulties at the house. As for theology booklets, which Claverie put together with the help of collaborators,

more than 350 people from all over the country used them. They formed more than sixty different working groups. Claverie was never enthusiastic about the organizational tasks that fell to him:

> Mr. Director, here, Mr. Director, there; and I offer you my respects; and I congratulate you on your "promotion." The poor people, if they only knew how much all that bores me and what a slow process it is for me to enter sufficiently into the office to make myself forgotten again. (letter of February 4, 1973)

Nevertheless, he gave his best to create in the staff a team spirit around a common mission. Coordination of the different departments, introduction of an Arabic-language liturgy, welcoming local dignitaries, days of relaxation or meditation. All this took a great deal of time and energy, but it bore fruit, even if the house never attained the level of flexibility and openness that Claverie dreamed of. Religious houses run the risk of turning into ghettoes if care is not taken to avoid it. So, for Claverie, the stake was always to

> do everything so that the other exists and so that we might discover the truth that we hold in common. Through teaching Arabic, to help foreigners foresake old ways of looking at things and understand the Algerians better. Through encounter and (modest) reflection on Algerian culture and society, to go beyond Europe's tenacious and continuing prejudices or superficial impressions. Through a theological reflection that attempts to integrate the experience of encounter with others, to listen to the Word that God speaks to us here in Algeria and to live by it.[3]

If one includes the conferences and retreats that he continued to direct and the numerous Algerian friends whom he saw regularly, one can imagine how busy Claverie was. Reading his correspondence gives the impression that Claverie's commitments were continuing to increase. Still, he never appeared too busy for a visitor who might arrive unexpectedly — welcoming whoever it was with a warm "How are you?" Pierre gave the impression of having plenty of time for you. If he "held on," as he put it, it was thanks to the regularity of his personal prayer life, acquired during his Dominican training, and to which he remained discreetly faithful:

> I ask myself how I am able to prepare my whole circus — classes, conferences, and presence at the center . . . I confess that right now I am spending part of my nights doing it all but, God be thanked, without exhaustion . . . This requires a serious effort of silence and prayer to keep

me from losing my plumb line. In this too, God be thanked, all goes well. The fact that I often have to express my faith is an inestimable help in keeping it alive. (letter of February 18, 1973)

More than these tasks of organization and inspiration, what really excited Claverie about this responsibility was the contacts that the position allowed. In his eyes, the real heart of his task was to create an open place and a climate favorable for encounter and dialogue, where Algerians would come freely, where listening to the Other would be possible and facilitated. That is what motivated him most.[4] Les Glycines organized numerous conferences, to which Claverie and his staff invited a wide range of participants. There were theologians and ecclesiastical officials, to be sure, but also a large number of Algerians with diverse qualifications. One could meet here the philosopher Sheikh Bouamrane, who spoke on "Islam and Modernity," the writer Rachid Boudjedra, Ali Madani (who ran Radio Algiers's Arabic course), the sociologist Claudine Chaulet, who spoke on the conditions of women in the socialist agricultural villages, or the militant politician Tayeb Louanchi. But there were also famous Islamists like Louis Gardet, Fr. Jomier, André Miquel, Maurice Borrmans, and Roger Arnaldez. Also present were W. Zartmann, Albert-Paul Lentin, and Pierre Rondot, political scientists or journalists, specialists of the Arab world. The library was directed by Jean Déjeux, a White Father and author of authoritative works on French Algerian literature; his graduate students attended assiduously. All of these exchanges delighted Claverie, just like his varied encounters in the city — with his neighbor and friend Boukhari, the Pakistani ambassador, Baya Francis, and the Drif family, who were his closest friends in Algiers.[5] These contacts quickly made Claverie a figure of importance in the ongoing evolution of Algeria. This was particularly important as Algeria changed in the 1970s.

## From Boumediene to Chadli: An Uncertain Algeria

The first years of the Boumediene regime were noteworthy, as already mentioned, for volunteerism and optimism — Algeria recovered its political and economic independence with vigor. Put in power by a military coup and supported by the single political party, the FLN, the regime established a solid framework for the society. The communes and *wilayas* had charters drawn up, elaborated by the Council of the Revolution, the country's directing body (in this period there was neither a national assembly nor a council of ministers). Popular assemblies of the communes and *wilayas* (APC and APW) were created and given exaggerated media publicity by a tame press. These measures were deemed to represent the "living strength of the nation" and to guarantee a true socialist democracy — in this period there was very little said about "citizens." The regime considered the year 1971 as the "socialist turning point."[6] In that year the ordinance on the agrarian revolution (November 8, 1971) and then the ordinance organizing the "socialist administration of businesses" (November 16, 1971) created an institutional structure and provided a framework for economic life. Suspicious, the regime reacted negatively to any questioning, dealing quickly with malcontents by charging that they wanted to harm Algeria's independence, "the supreme value, for which the martyrs of the revolution had died." Still, questions were already emerging, as can be seen from a conversation that Claverie had in April 1974 with Fr. Borrmans and Abdelmadjid Meziane, an Algerian intellectual and politician who occasionally collaborated with les Glycines. The conversation was about "the existence in Algeria of partisans, a minority but very sure of themselves, who were allied to Muslim Brotherhood members coming from Egypt."[7] In this period, Claverie heard a lot and took efforts to inform himself. Among his visitors were militants from the Avant-Garde Socialist Party (PAGS), a resurgence of the Algerian Communist Party, which produced a "supportive critique," in the terminology of the time, of Boumediene's regime, but already had begun denouncing the lack of true democratic institutions.

As promoter of the New International Economic Order to the United Nations, Algeria welcomed an OPEC summit in March 1975. These years from 1973 to 1975 saw a massive rise in the price of hydrocarbons, so the country enjoyed a financial windfall thanks to its large reserves of petroleum and natural gas. This wealth permitted the government to launch grandiose economic projects. The second four-year plan (1974–77) was characterized by gigantic investments in heavy industry. Controlled by all-powerful national societies, major industrial complexes were established, including iron works, chemical plants, and mechanical and electric construction. These "industrializing industries," as they were called, were supposed to spur the development of the economy as a whole and prepare for the further launch of consumer industries. It was in this period that the American Bechtel Corporation established a gas-liquefying complex at Arzew, near Oran, which at the time was considered to be the biggest in the world. Although employing an almost Soviet-style propaganda of the type associated with Alexey Stakhanov, the economic results were meager considering the level of investment. Many of these industrial complexes, constructed with imported technology, never attained their planned objectives and helped create a heavy foreign debt that mortgaged the country's future. Even agriculture was sacrificed in favor of this absolute priority to industry. A profit economy was put in place, a situation that favored corruption. A minority of administrators profited from the manna of petroleum, but the mass of the populace had to wait to see their desire for even basic consumer goods like housing satisfied. The situation generated profound frustration among the lower classes and prepared the ground for the Islamist movement.

This period can be credited with a certain amount of real improvement, especially in the realms of education and health. Algeria had an extremely rapidly growing population, hitting the world record birth rate with an average of 8.1 children per woman. At the World Population Conference in 1974, Boumediene opposed all Malthusianism, arguing that "the best contraceptive is development." This high birth rate placed the state under a considerable strain, which it attempted to relieve. A remarkable effort was made to provide both elementary teaching and higher education — hundreds of high schools and colleges were created throughout the country, even in the remote regions of the high plateaus and the steppe. Between independence and 1982, the number of educational institutions multiplied twenty-seven times! Universities were established, not only in the large cities on the coast (Algiers, Oran, Annaba), but also in the interior (Constantine, Sétif, Tiaret). Technological institutes trained technicians and engineers by the thousand. In a break from the past, girls attended these schools in large numbers, creating a de facto diversity in the schools and universities that threw customary gender relations into disorder. Very quickly a new question arose: what sort of employment was there for these tens of thousands of young graduates? The seventies also saw a great effort in the field of public health. The state established a policy of free access to health care, significantly bettering the health of the populace. There was some decline in quality, but in this field too Algeria justly regarded itself as better off than other third-world countries. There was also great progress in general well-being: a free hot meal was served every day in all school kitchens in the country, while electricity and gas brought a real comfort to remote regions, such as the high plateaus.

These considerable changes of course had a profound ripple effect in Algerian society. Hammered home by those who ran the government and an official media that pumped out a socialist ideology of the "Baathist" sort,[8] the breakdown in traditional life under the pressure of urbanization and education accelerated. The corruption and nepotism naturally shocked the mass of the Algerian population, who were rural and imbued with a very popular form of Islam. Thus one of the regime's problems was how to hold onto the society. The issues gave rise to debates among the Algerians. In 1974, Sheikh Abdellatif Soltani, writing in Morocco, published a virulent critique of the Algerian government's socialism. The ideologues of the new Algeria, such as Mostefa Lacheraf or Ahmed Taleb Ibrahimi, exerted themselves in response to demonstrate that Algerian-style socialism was not incompatible with Islam.[9] This was in truth a profound debate that touched the very soul of the Algerian people and was reflected in the National Charter, published in 1976, which attempted to resolve the problem from above — in other words, without any true democratic debate. The Charter affirmed in its first provision, section two: "The Algerian people are a Muslim people. Islam is the state religion. To regenerate itself, the Islamic world has but a single way forward: to go beyond reformism and engage itself in the path of social revolution." That is precisely what President Boumediene's populist regime attempted to do, but in vain. In the mid-1970s it appeared that "Islam more and more became the focal point of socio-political demands," observers declared.[10] Attempts were made to reassure people with statements such as this: "in Algeria Islam reigns but does not govern" (H. Sanson). In reality, the technocrats had been outmaneuvered. The rulers of Algeria were already making two major concessions.

The first of these concessions with far-reaching consequences was the hastily improvised Arabization. Algeria had been strongly marked culturally by the colonial period, as the sociologist Y. Turin has demonstrated.[11] The leaders of the regime emphasized that the reappropriation of Algerian cultural identity was to be effected through the Arabic language. This vision helped contribute to the decline of the Berber languages and the country's cultural diversity. The subject of strong ideological controversies, the Arabization of teaching in elementary schools as well as some sectors of higher education was decreed prematurely, before the country had the resources to put it into effect. So it was necessary to have recourse to numerous Syrian, Palestinian, and Egyptian teachers. These people were often willingly sent to Algeria because they were not wanted in their own countries, given their connections to fundamentalist movements like the Muslim Brotherhood, an organization born in Egypt in the 1920s. Putting such people in charge of teaching naturally had very weighty consequences for Algeria's youth.[12] Meanwhile, Berber culture was officially ignored, even though cultural Berbers were a significant percentage of the population. In the spring of 1980 the popular reaction to the government's anti-Berber attitude manifested itself significantly at Tizi-Ouzou, capital of the province of Kabylia. Large-scale demonstrations broke out there to protest the fact that the government had forbidden a lecture by

the Kabyle author Mouloud Mammeri. This "Berber spring" was a first breach
in the Arab-Islamic ideology the regime had been imposing and a step toward
a vision of Algeria as a pluralistic society.

The second important concession made by the government was to the Islamists. After three hundred years of colonial status, Algerian Islam was above
all a popular Islam, a matter of confraternities, with very few theologians or
qualified imams. The government attempted to substitute in its place an orthodox Islam, reformist in the sense that it would control the imams, who
would receive the sermons they were to give in the mosques on Fridays from
the Ministry of Religious Affairs, and would spread an officially sanctioned
religious teaching to the masses. This task was confided for some years to a
notoriously narrow-minded Egyptian, Sheikh Muhammad al-Ghazali. Some
funds from the Gulf states began to circulate in lower-class suburbs. Going
still further, the Algerian state several years later (1984) adopted a family
code, much more reactionary than those of other Arabic countries, including
neighboring Tunisia.

By the time Boumediene died on December 27, 1978, the state had great
difficulty managing the societal evolution that had taken place.[13] His successor, Colonel Chadli Bendjedid, "the senior person in the highest rank,"
was an insignificant figure and rapidly lost control of the situation. From that
point, the game would be played out between the army and the Islamists. The
democrats were left out in the cold.

Claverie watched these developments very closely, as can be seen in the
lists of speakers invited to les Glycines. He offered sessions on "Islam and
socialism." He was also charged by the Algerian bishops to give an annual
"discourse on the state of the nation" to the Union of Major Superiors of
Algeria (USMDA), a sort of assessment of the situation in the entire country.
For Claverie, it was an opportunity to put his own observations in order and
to weigh the changes that were having an impact on the life of the Algerian
church.

## A Church under Surveillance

A variety of events, both serious and more trivial, touched the life of the
Algerian church in the seventies. In October 1975, the gendarmerie occupied
Notre Dame d'Afrique and the basilicas of Hippo and Santa Cruz, officially
for "reasons of security." Relations with Morocco were tense at the time
because of arguments over control of the western Sahara, and the threat of war

seems to have inspired this takeover. Cardinal Duval, however, resisted the occupation vigorously and managed to get the government forces withdrawn. Still, for Claverie, the incident was the first sign of things to come. "It is evident," he wrote, "that, more or less long-term, this basilica will be too high-profile and too important for the minichurch that we are."[14] In the same period, the Trappist monks of Tibhirine were ordered to evacuate their premises within ten days. In both of these cases no order was ever given in writing, and the government's actions seem to have sprung from the internal conflicts within the government itself.

Yet more incidents and dramas marked the year 1976. In February the White Fathers, who had been reprimanded for working on Berber culture, were expelled from Mekla. In June, the library at les Glycines was sealed and the police interrogated Claverie for hours — in this case, too, it was interest in the Berber language that was regarded as subversive. The pro-Berber faction was at that time taking to the streets, as the "Berber spring" of 1980 confirms. More seriously, on July 8, 1976, Gaston Jacquier, auxiliary bishop and close friend of Cardinal Duval, was assassinated in the street in front of the archiepiscopal headquarters — by a madman, according to official accounts. "The cardinal is devastated, but keeps up appearances with dignity . . . ," Claverie wrote to his family (letter of July 8, 1976). Without prior warning, on August 16 police occupied the building of the Lebanese sisters at the Voirol Column — where Claverie had studied and then taught Arabic. Despite the intervention of the cardinal and of several state officials who were friends of the sisters, they had to concede; their home then became a police commissariat. In August 1976 the weekly day of rest was moved by law from Sunday to Friday, the Muslim holy day. That same summer, diocesan schools were nationalized, forcing radical changes upon numerous teaching orders. Dramatic or trivial, these events, contemporaneous to the debate on the National Charter, were symptomatic of a broader climate of unease. Debates shook Algerian society deeply. Suspicion was in the air and the church in Algeria, still perceived as very closely aligned to France, was a favorite target.

Claverie kept a cool head, unlike other clerics who panicked in this situation.[15] He sought to understand and analyze the situation, often seeing the cardinal, with whom trust gradually increased despite day-to-day disagreements. Claverie was indeed a little worn out by the atmosphere of the archbishop's headquarters, divorced from real life, in his opinion, and he did not hesitate to say so:

He [the cardinal] reproached me for not taking seriously the fact that I am, according to him, "more than a vicar general, the second most important figure in the diocese," and that I have too few contacts with him and with the archdiocesan administration. I promised him that I would put a little more goodwill into my dealings with him, but not with his administration. In short, we parted very amicably. (Letter of October 18, 1976)

Behind the scenes of the back-and-forth of daily life, the question posed over the months was the purpose and form the Christian presence in a Muslim country ought to take. With some simplification, the debate came down to two basic approaches: either defend the social welfare of the church (schools, religious centers, housing) as much as possible, or, better, to consent increasingly to be leaven in the dough, while living precariously as an institution. Claverie attended many conferences, sessions with religious, and retreats, not only in Algeria but also in Tunisia, Mauretania, and Niger, where he was invited in 1975, 1976, and 1977, all of which wrestled with this issue. He was already well known — his thinking was clear and open, his manner simple and fraternal. In this period he launched a group reflection at les Glycines on the significance of a Christian presence in Algeria, a work whose theological synthesis he assured.[16] He was stimulated in this reflection by passionate conversations with his friend Henri Teissier, bishop of Oran, who often came to see Claverie at les Glycines, the center where he himself had been director. As he later reminisced, "Pierre spoke with me about his projects and his difficulties, and for me these evenings of discussion were a breath of fresh air and a support."

In this same period, Claverie threw himself into a more in-depth study of the great Muslim philosopher Averroës (Ibn Rushd), working with a Dominican philosopher from Toulouse, Fr. Pierre Courtès. Their specific study was the controversy between Averroës and Ghazâli. Ghazâli had written a book intended to demolish the doctrines of various philosophies, entitled *Tahâfut-al-falâsifa* (The Destruction of Philosophers). Averroës responded to him with a work entitled *Tahâfut-al-tahâfut* (The Destruction of the Destruction).[17] Courtès's and Claverie's project was to prepare a critical French edition of this work, available at the time only in Arabic and Latin. The translation took several months, but was never published in *La Revue thomiste* as had been planned. One gets the feeling that the project was a little dull for Claverie, because he was above all an active man, someone who loved to share what invigorated him; there was very little of the secluded intellectual about him. He expressed himself on this tension in a letter of January 1, 1974:

> I have more and more "surface," but I know perfectly well that with time I risk becoming nothing but "surface." Increasingly, I feel the need to work and to go deeper, and I'm pulled to the left and the right at the same time. Is it my fate to be trapped in this dialectic? My dream, you will recall, was to be to some degree a Trappist and to center my existence on what I sense to be the most important thing in it and, finally, the most important for the others. And then I find myself more and more "sent out on the road." It must be a sign of my Dominican vocation that this contradiction should exist continually between two aspects of the same vocation. It tells me that Lacordaire dreamed of being able to take the time to think and to write a summa for his century, as St. Thomas did for his... and this summa never saw the light of day because already in his era he was eaten up by the day-to-day combat, often more political than religious.

Eaten up by the day-to-day combat — that was precisely Claverie's situation. But he consented to it, of his own free will accepting invitations and loving them. It is noteworthy that Claverie published very few articles or other written works for their own sake — the majority of his publications were lectures, repeated in writing. But he regarded intellectual work highly and, unable to engage deeply in it himself, he encouraged his fellow workers, like Fr. Antoine Moussali, a Lebanese priest who worked at les Glycines and had developed good relations with Arabic-speaking Algerian intellectuals, or Jean Landousies, who published a theology textbook. For Claverie, this was also a way of anchoring the church further in Algerian society. This sometimes led to surprising developments, like the offer he received in February 1978 from the secretary-general of the Ministry of Labor — to take charge of the Arabization of the ministry staff! Even more oddly, this offer fell at a moment when relations with France were wretched.[18] "This country is unbelievable," Pierre often repeated at relaxed evening gatherings with us, his Dominican brothers, recounting the contrasting events of his week. Sunday evening was always dedicated to a relaxed get-together with his friends Pierre Frantz and Bernard Tramier from the parish of El Biar. In a pied-noir vein, the location Claverie chose for these dinners was the large restaurant Chez Soliveres, on the former Durando Avenue leading to Bab el Oued. While doing honor to the rosé wine from Medea, he recharged his batteries in the cordial ambiance there.

## Christians In the "House of Islam"

The changing and sometimes uncomfortable conditions in Algeria led the bishops of CERNA (Conference of North African Bishops) to try to reformulate the direction of a Christian presence in a Muslim country, where all proselytizing was forbidden, but where witnessing the faith kept all its meaning. Claverie would later be invited to react to the text the bishops had drawn up under the leadership of the tireless Henri Teissier. It was published in 1979 under the title "Christians in the Maghreb, the Purpose of our Encounters" (*Chrétiens au Maghreb, le sense de nos rencontres*).[19]

This work first noted that the service given to the country was no longer a sufficient reason for the Christian presence. During the first years of the Algerian state, many had come to Algeria bringing their contribution to the country's development in a wide variety of ways, as engineers, technicians, teachers, and so on. But in the course of the years, cooperation had become less necessary, as Algeria increasingly created its own expert labor force. A nationalism, sometimes distrustful, also helped thin out the ranks of the foreigners. A number of priests and religious remained, choosing to devote their special attention to the destitute. Weaving and tapestry workshops in Kabylia and the Sahara, a center for rehabilitation of the disabled, a social-work office in the Casbah of Algiers — such riches of imagination and real self-sacrifice allowed the church to be present in the everyday life of the Algerians. In the process, they created true bonds of neighborliness and friendship. The nationalization of the schools, traumatic though it had been at the time, was an excellent opportunity for many congregations to rid themselves of their possessions and to go out to the people in the poorer districts, closer to everyday life, there where friendship could really take root. Imperceptibly, "to live with" became the most important reason for their presence, rather than "to do things," as Henri Sanson noted in 1975.[20] Cardinal Duval ceaselessly emphasized the preeminent value of brotherly love.

Nonetheless, another element complicated an understanding of the Christian presence in the country: Algeria is almost exclusively Muslim and the church found itself here "in the house of Islam." Christianity here is a guest, accepted on sufferance — not merely a minority, *it* is in the home of another. Over the years since independence, Islam made itself more and more strongly felt in daily life. The number of mosques multiplied; Ramadan and Friday prayer were ever more observed; wearing of the veil becoming a social obligation for women and even very young girls, especially in lower-class quarters. Even though wishing to be "a church of relationship with the Other," as Henri Teissier expressed it, encounter was difficult even with friends, because the religious categories were so different. As for the media, sometimes they spouted inflammatory diatribes against Western and Christian proselytizing, always linking it to the Crusades and colonialism. There was, in fact, a sort of dark night of presence, a solitude "borne like a fissure," wrote Henri Sanson.[21]

The bishops' text tended to take into account these difficult questions and to reformulate the doctrinal bases of a Christian presence in a Muslim land. It was expressed in the traditional manner of texts of the magisterium, both reaffirming at length ecclesiastical doctrines and also placing them in a contemporary context:

> The church is convinced that, as highlighted by Vatican II, it is the "universal sacrament of salvation" (*Lumen gentium*, 40). In other words, that it is the visible and efficacious sign of God's plan in regard to every human being and humankind as a whole. Too often, Christians have been tempted to take the sign, the church, as the goal of the entire religious history of humanity. In fact, the goal is the coming of the kingdom of God . . . This kingdom establishes itself above all where the human being is torn away from the power of death in all of its forms, to enter into a share of God's own life.[22]

Claverie found the text too long, too general, and would have "preferred some specific positions on concrete questions," he said to Bishop Duval. Truly, the work was begun only with difficulty. Later Claverie would put his own stamp on it.

## Encounter and Development

Their status as guests in the house of Islam constrained the Christians in Algeria to involve themselves as little as possible in the nation's political life. For many engaged Christians this was trying. From this position came their interest in an association created immediately after Independence by the Reformed Church and CIMADE. This was the Christian Committee for Service in Algeria (CCSA). This organization's initial objective was to recruit and form a cadre of technicians willing to share their expertise in a true spirit of servanthood. Pierre Claverie, as director of les Glycines, had often participated in the training of these volunteers. Roby Bois, at that time secretary-general of CIMADE, remembers his direct and frank manner of speaking, very different from the language of run-of-the-mill Algerians and those who were called "pieds-rouges" ["red feet"; in other words voluntary aid workers, often leftists and revolutionaries at least in theory], and even of members of the CCSA, more "boumedianist" than Boumediene himself. One left Algiers with clear ideas about how hazy the situation was and the complexity of the problems. Pierre had become the "where it's at"; he embodied the presence of men and women in Algeria who were lucid and joined together in solidarity, but never teachers of lessons, never apologists, never judges. They cast into relief for me a presence, discreet yet demanding, of Christians "in the land of Islam," of Christians "in socialism," as another great friend of Algeria, the pastor Georges Casalis, loved to put it.[23]

The need for cooperation diminished over the years, as Algeria formed its own ranks of specialists. So this association, under the leadership of Jacques Blanc, evolved to support liberation movements and certain humanitarian causes more specifically. This refocusing was carried out in 1974. From its earliest stages, Jacques Blanc got Claverie involved. He asked Claverie to accompany him to Geneva, to the ecumenical council of the churches, to present and defend the project.[24] Claverie accepted and participated in drafting the statutes of this new association, which was called "Encounter and Development." He was even nominated to be the first president, but he refused the honor. He did, however, accept the vice presidency, a position that allowed him to remain an important part of an understanding whose importance he had recognized.

Algeria in the seventies played a significant role as leader of developing nations and led the chorus of anti-imperialism. Algerian leaders regarded their own history of liberation from colonialism as a model for other states. Aided by its strong financial position, the Algerian government freely welcomed a variety of delegations from liberation movements, especially African, active in Angola, Guinea-Bissau, Mozambique, and Namibia, and even fighting for the independence of South Africa's African National Congress, which had an office in Algiers. Coming for the most part from Portuguese colonies in Africa, these leaders in exile were very isolated and needed support of all sorts. The Encounter and Development organization put itself at their service, helping to make their causes known, offering them the day-to-day friendship that they lacked. Occasionally their historic leaders came to Algiers, received with fanfare by the heads of government, including Agostinho Neto, Sam

Nujoma, and Samora Machel. These lands achieved independence in 1974 and 1975.

Encounter and Development also spread information about conditions in Palestine, Chile, and Central America and, in association with the Algerian Red Crescent or Caritas, collected and distributed material aid to Saharan refugees from Tindouf and to the earthquake victims of El Asnam in 1979. Explaining his involvement in Encounter and Development, Claverie saw in it yet another opportunity to break out of the closed circle in which his ecclesiastical activities threatened to entrap him:

> The concrete support to these liberation movements or militants in exile, reflection on the reasons for underdevelopment and the mainte-nance of "imperialisms" in our regions, permits us to sustain an effective solidarity with the people who struggle for their liberty or respect for their human dignity... And besides, it's useful to travel down a bit of road outside of our closed and often suffocating Christian and Western world.[25]

Like all organizations, Encounter and Development experienced some in-ternal tensions, and Jacques Blanc relied more and more on Claverie to hold it on course. In November 1976 Claverie accepted the office of president after he was unanimously elected, in large part because of his friendship for Pastor Blanc, whom he held in the highest esteem. Claverie was reelected as president in 1978 and again in 1980. In 1981 Blanc took charge of the World Council of Churches Department of Justice and Service in Geneva, a position he held until his death in 1989. The tribute that Claverie gave to this indefatigable worker for solidarity says a good deal about the ties that united the two:

> In all areas of his activity, Jacques had the gift of sensing, in this cultural ferment into which we have been plunged in Algeria, that which was just and that which merited the effort he put into it. He worked on this intuition, putting to work his reflection and his relations to search out the best point at which to apply action. He did indeed know how to create collaboration by sharing his preoccupations generously and by drawing many into his decision making. Attentive, warm, and head-strong, he could propel those he had embarked toward the other shore, a shore of foolish hope in a more human world. I have never regretted that I followed him in this adventure.[26]

## Cairo or Paris: The Threat of Transfer

In 1978 Claverie turned forty — he was fully mature. His Dominican brothers
of the French province had chosen him in April 1975 as provincial councilor.
In January 1976, Fr. Vincent de Couesnongle, master of the order, had suggested that Claverie take charge of the secretariat for Islam, an office that
coordinates the Dominican presence and activities in the various Muslim
lands. Claverie refused this nomination, "deciding not to disconnect from
Algiers here for some years" (letter of January 5, 1976). On a trip to Rome in
August 1977 to attend the Dominican Roman Days, Claverie discovered that
the curia had not abandoned its plans. The master of the order wanted to renew the community of IDEO in Cairo, where the corps of founders (Anawati,
Jomier, de Beaurecueil) hoped for new blood. As an Arabist and theologian,
with a rich experience of life in a Muslim country, Claverie was a dream candidate. He had the feeling that everything had already been settled behind
his back, and especially that the importance of a presence in Algeria had not
sufficiently been taken into account. He explained himself to the assistant to
the master of the Dominican order, who was in charge of the Secretariat for
Islam at Sainte-Sabine, and to the central curia of the order:

> I have found all your planning a little harsh, to the degree to which it
> gave no regard to the future of the community of Algiers or to my own
> future, neither my tastes nor my abilities. For ten years I have been in a
> country where personal relationships are our sole strength because we
> do not have institutions — and God knows that these relationships are
> slow to establish and fragile. They demand continuity and patience and
> count for very much for our Algerian friends.[27]

The matter was far from being closed; the French provincial returned to it
in the course of a visit to Algiers in October 1977. There he was subjected to
a "heavy bombardment," Claverie wrote to his parents, as everyone explained
why Pierre played a key role in Algiers and would be difficult to replace.[28]
The most interesting testimony, even if the letter is a little forced, is probably
that of Cardinal Duval, because it shows what confidence and what a high
opinion he had come to have of Claverie:

> I said to your provincial that I would not accept your departure for
> two reasons. The first, at the personal level, was because you are happy
> in your work and it is criminal to displace such a person when he is
> giving his fullest [and he added, "it's so rare..."]. The other reason,
> at the community level, is that he is irreplaceable at les Glycines and

is necessary to the diocese of Algiers, and indispensable to the whole church of Algeria. (letter of November 7, 1977)

For good measure, the cardinal even added, "When you said that to me, I suffered a serious gastric attack!" The provincial yielded, at least provisionally, as can be seen in the confidential report he addressed to the master of the order.[29] Besides his attachment to Algeria, Claverie had a strong fear of being buried in a team of scholars whom he thought had too little contact with life and its real stakes. Therefore when the master of the order visited Algiers in March 1978, he negotiated a compromise: Claverie stayed in Algiers, but was charged with helping the Cairo group develop. He busied himself about this task in the course of several trips to Cairo and Rome, forming an association with the White Fathers' Pontifical Institute for Arab Studies in Rome, collaborating with the Iraqi Dominican sisters, creating new flow charts, and so on. The results did not live up to the effort put into them, and Claverie never regretted that he had once again "chosen Algeria."

The threat of being taken from Algiers did not vanish completely. For a long time the French Dominicans had been keeping an eye on Claverie. In June 1978 he demonstrated all his leadership skills when he presided over a provincial assembly at Chantilly. In November he acted on behalf of the provincial prior in negotiations between the Dominican brothers of Casablanca and the bishop of Morocco to transfer the community to Rabat. A provincial chapter was projected and, conscious of what was threatening him, Claverie declined to participate in a preparatory meeting that called together the provincial council and the superiors of communities. "It is not absolutely necessary that I assist in the meeting of crowned heads," he explained humorously, "bearing in mind the fact that these are the ones who will vote in December in the election of the next provincial and therefore, the less I let them see of me the better I'll be pleased" (letter of late June 1979).

There was indeed an attempt at the provincial chapter in December, but it failed before the energetic veto of Jean-Pierre Voreux, superior of the Dominican community of Algiers. In fact everyone, or nearly everyone, was really convinced that Claverie was well suited for his place in the church of Algeria. This included Algerian friends who, on his return, thanked Claverie for having preferred Algeria.[30] That was his country and he was happy there. He had already contributed a great deal to help the church situate itself in a changing and at times uncomfortable context. He would remain there, but under unforeseen circumstances.

## "Monseigneur Claverie"

In March 1980 Cardinal Duval announced that he would retire in July of
the same year. He was seventy-seven years old and had already extended his
episcopate, at the pope's request, beyond the seventy-five year-retirement rule
fixed by canon law. Since the cardinal was like a lightning rod for the church
in Algeria, the Holy See decided to give him a coadjutor, who would take
over at the proper time. Monseigneur Gabriel Montalvo, the new apostolic
nuncio, began consultations in May. Claverie's relations with the cardinal
were at their best, and his name was very soon added to the list of possible
candidates.[31] Pierre himself was thinking of other matters completely. He was
more active than ever, enjoying "heaps of passionate encounters," he wrote,
and preparing for a very busy summer. In July he preached a retreat first in
Cairo and then in Lebanon. In August, he preached to the Dominican sisters
of Notre Dame of la Deliverande in Martinique, whom he had known in
Beirut and Cairo. The exuberance of nature, the rhythms, and the people he
encountered among the sisters at Morne Rouge filled him with enthusiasm:[32]
"It is truly a discovery . . . Apparently they want me to come again next year.
If I can, I won't say no. I admit that I have been seduced by these people"
(letter of July 27, 1980).

Claverie had something of jubilation in his temperament and, in the An-
tilles too, he put to the test his astonishing ability to empathize with people,
their hopes, and their struggles. Once more, he told his parents how much the
happiness he enjoyed he owed to them. The elder Claveries, seventy-three
and seventy-four years old, were living at Toulon, far from their children, with
one in the United States and the other in Algeria. But at the same time they
were very close, thanks to the "immutable confidence," as Étienne Claverie
called it, that united them. Pierre wrote, "Two happy old folks! There is effectively something, and it's certainly some of the happiness that is yours, which
Nane and I imbibe as the best of ourselves and our greatest strength. Hold
the applause" (letter of August 31, 1980).

At the beginning of September, after a meeting of all the priests in Algeria, the nuncio, Monsigneur Montalvo, invited Claverie to dinner and a
long conversation. In November he then unveiled what he had in mind in
the course of a visit of the new Dominican provincial, Jean-René Bouchet.
Bouchet in turn revealed to Claverie the tenor of the conversation:

> "What would you think of Fr. Claverie being named bishop?"
> "It would be the most precious gift that we could make to Algeria."
> "Would you make that gift?"

"It would be a great loss for us. But wouldn't it be necessary for him to have Algerian citizenship?"

"No problem. The matter is well-nigh a plebiscite, and if he is not named immediately he certainly will be the next time."

"That is a kick in the stomach that I was already somewhat expecting," said Claverie, "but not so soon" (letter of November 2, 1980). Despite the status of the matter as a "pontifical secret," the subject was of course debated among those who had been consulted — Claverie's community and those close to him. Regret at the thought of Claverie leaving Algiers was tempered by evidence of the service that he could give to the Algerian church. Claverie himself was amazingly calm, continuing his regular business and accepting reelection as president of Encounter and Development. It was in 1980–81 that he launched the "Papers on Islamology" in collaboration with Sister Lucie Pruvost, a nun who specialized in Islamic law, whose intellectual rigor Claverie appreciated, calling her "a true master, in the academic sense of the term."

"How come we don't see more of you at the nuncio's residence?" Monsigneur Montalvo was asked. "After my provincial's visit, I decided to keep my distance," responded Claverie, adding that "that made the nuncio laugh heartily." On December 22, the Vatican announced that Bishop Teissier of Oran had been named coadjutor to Cardinal Duval, archbishop of Algiers. At the exchange of new years wishes in January 1981, a group of priests of Oran wrote to Claverie, "We are among those who, if you are called, will welcome you happily among us. Have courage, and may the Holy Spirit blow strongly at Algiers."

On May 12, 1981, Claverie was officially informed by the nunciature that he had been named bishop of Oran. He received the news with a mixture of gravity and humor. On May 24, Mothers' Day, he wrote to his parents: "As a gift for Mamie, I bring a miter . . . Yes, I have ended up accepting in the face of 'popular pressure' and after long hours of discussion with Jean-Pierre Voreux, Jean-René Bouchet, Fr. O'Hara, and even a long telephone conversation with the general [of the order]" (letter of May 24, 1981).

Claverie confided to his friend Jacques Blanc, "The miters are flying low at the moment." In late May, the cardinal, who was visiting Rome, wrote Claverie a note in his typical style: "Fratre episcopo ignoto, plurimam salutem."[33] On his return, he gave Claverie two small gold pieces from his family possessions, for his episcopal ring. To Monseigneur Scotto, the first to congratulate Claverie's parents, Étienne Claverie replied in his inimitable style: "Your compliments to us, which astound us, we appreciate but, without any false modesty, please believe that we had not foreseen this and are the first to be astonished. If Pierre had been a professor or a plumber, we would have had some ambition for him, but in the path that is his own, the only thing that matters is that he be a good servant" (letter of June 4, 1981).

The news would not be official until noon on June 5. "Monseigneur Claverie," as the cardinal already called him, had arrived incognito in Oran the evening before. The whole diocese was assembled for the annual celebration of Pentecost.

## Chapter Six

# Bishop in Oran
Happy Beginnings
1981–87

> In Algeria, it is our good fortune to be pretty well stripped of
> our riches, our pretensions, and our self-sufficiency...Let us give
> thanks to God when he restores his church to simple humanity.[1]
> *— Pierre Claverie*

Pierre Claverie loved to stress that the function of a bishop in Algeria had nothing in common with that of bishops in most other parts of the world. "More like being the pastor of a large parish," he said, adding that this was fortunate for him, because in Oran he was able to know everyone, to have few administrative tasks and many human contacts, including relations with the Muslims around him. In fact he, who already excelled in human relations, came "to give himself completely" in this new ministry that the church had confided to him — and to find a real happiness in weaving relationships, in making barriers fall. Nonetheless, the fifteen years of his episcopate were lived in conditions that differed widely over time. The first years were happy and relatively easy. Later, grave questions confronted him, as they did all of the Algerian church and Algerian society as a whole. The day would come when he would have to stake his own life, and eventually give it up. The better to understand this evolution, it is useful to consider these fifteen years divided into several stages.

### The Warm Reception of a Pastor

Monseigneur Henri Teissier, bishop of Oran, liked to organize an assembly of all the Christians of his diocese each year on Pentecost Sunday. This practice provided an opportunity for the Christian communities, widely dispersed throughout the region, to come together at least once a year and to measure both the diversity and the unity of their church. It was at this event, on June 5, 1981, that Teissier presented their new bishop, Pierre Claverie, to the Christians of Oran. Claverie made his entrance into the cathedral of Oran during the celebration of the Eucharist, at the same moment that Radio Vatican made the official announcement on the air. The two events had been coordinated. Actually, many of the people of Oran half expected that Claverie would be appointed, and the welcome they gave him is a measure of the confidence they already placed in him:

> On June 5, I was struck by the power of fraternal brotherhood born of a common Spirit. From all the earth, God had called his people together. From Africa, full of promise, from Europe heavy with history, from powerful America, from Asia fought over by the hunger of the superpowers, these men and women have become brothers and sisters through the power of the Spirit of love. God gives us the amazing opportunity to meet the other.[2]

From this day, Pierre Claverie gained an impression of what was now his diocese — a mosaic of men and women from Algeria, France, Poland, the Philippines, Brazil . . . assembled in that place because they had been born in Algeria or had come to live there by the necessities of a job contract or by marriage to an Algerian. A motley throng, among whom Claverie's passion for discovering and encountering the Other had the chance of exercising itself at leisure. From the beginning it was love at first sight!

The episcopal ordination took place on October 2, 1981 in Algiers Cathedral. The ceremony could not have been more solemn. Cardinal Duval presided, assisted by Monseigneur Montalvo the apostolic nuncio, as well as the bishops of Algeria, Tunisia, and Morocco. A hundred priests were present, along with a majority of the religious and the Christian laypeople of the diocese of Algiers. Numerous Dominicans also attended, and, of course, Pierre's elderly parents, deeply moved to return to Algiers, their home town, on such an occasion.[3] Also present was a large delegation from Oran and many Algerian friends, whose presence gave a special savor to the ceremony. At the end, before bestowing his first episcopal benediction, the new bishop addressed the assembled crowd — in French, then in Arabic. Here are extracts from his address:

> My brothers, my friends . . . "God's folly": that is the expression of St. Paul that comes to me from the Spirit when I consider the choice that you have made, with the assistance of the Holy Spirit.
>
> If it is the apostle, is like another self for the one who sends him,

If I am called to be, in the midst of you, like a foundation stone of the temple that you are,

If I am ordained to carry the Good News of God's love to the world with assurance.

If I must proclaim through my life and through my words that Christ is risen, living, present, and efficacious in the world through his Spirit, then yes, you have committed a folly.

Your only excuse is to believe that God works in us through his Spirit, making us little by little let go of things, so that we might welcome him with a free heart, without shrinking and without tension, hands open, with confidence.

"I believe this because I have lived it...," said Pierre Claverie, passing in review everything in his life that had helped increase this confidence. His parents, "so different and so similar, supporting each other, growing together, so united, so welcoming...We have grown in this extraordinary liberty, which opened before us the gates of life...Yes, love exists, it is possible, and I have had the grace to encounter it. This gives me strength to believe in it now." His Dominican confreres, who had helped him to learn "the contagious power of confidence. There is true happiness in living this quality of relationship." His Christian brothers and sisters of Algeria, who had "taught that the spirit of the gospel is not in power." Last came his "Algerian brothers and friends." It was to them that Claverie addressed his most vibrant appreciation:

> I owe to you what I am...I owe it to you that I have discovered the Algeria that had been my country, but where I lived as a stranger in my youth. With you, studying Arabic, I have above all learned to speak and understand the language of the heart, that of brotherly friendship where all races and religions commune together. There, I am weak enough to believe that this friendship is deeper than our differences, that it survives time, distance, separation. Because I believe that this friendship comes from God...It is certainly folly to believe still in the strength of empty hands and of simple humanity, but following Jesus Christ, I am weak enough to believe that this is a strength.[4]

Claverie closed with the following words: "I trust in God who calls and sends. I also count on all of you. My brothers and sisters of Oran, I have nothing but that to offer you. The Lord will do the rest..." Repeated in Arabic, this address set off an ovation that those present have not forgotten. It was, after all, the Mediterranean, warm and expansive, which was inviting itself into this cathedral, coming to shatter the somewhat stilted solemnity of the pontifical ritual.[5]

The new bishop's installation in the cathedral of Oran followed a week later, on October 9. Once again there was a crowd of the sort one finds on major holidays, with numerous speeches of welcome presenting a mirror image of the diocese's diversity. There were pieds-noirs who had remained in the country, aid workers who had arrived recently, Polish workers, Brazilian or Filipino dam or factory workers, and so on, as well as, of course, the priests and religious assigned to the diocese. Few Algerians, by contrast. "It was still unthinkable for our Muslim friends to take part in these celebrations," emphasized Thierry Becker, adding that at Pierre's funeral these Muslims formed the majority of the attendees. For his installation, the new bishop gave a homily that was anything but a formal address. He gave a sort of "outline discourse," compressed to four pages, which from the outset sketched the essential questions that would confront him in his ministry: What is the church's mission in a Muslim country? What sort of presence should the church have in Algeria in order to be faithful to its calling? And, already, the question of intolerance and respect for the other. Below are some essential extracts from that speech:

*On mission:*

> Yes, our *church* is sent on a mission. I am not afraid to say this and to express my joy at entering with you in this mission. Many misunderstandings, which we have inherited from history, bear on the mission and the missionaries. Let us state clearly today that:
>
> We are not and do not want to be aggressors...
>
> We are not and do not want to be the soldiers of a new crusade against Islam, against unbelief, or against anyone...
>
> We do not wish to be the agents of an economic or cultural neocolonialism that would divide the Algerian people the better to dominate them...
>
> We are not nor do we wish to be among those evangelizers who think they are honoring the love of God through an indiscreet zeal or a total lack of respect for the culture, the faith of the other...
>
> But we are and wish to be missionaries of the love of God, which we have discovered in Jesus Christ. This love, infinitely respectful of human beings, does not impose itself, does not impose anything, does not force consciences and hearts. With delicacy and solely through its presence,

Bishop Claverie of Oran with Cardinal Léon-Étienne Duval, and fellow bishops
Jean Scotto, Henri Teissier, and Jean-Marie Raimbaud and an unidentified religious sister.

Pierre Claverie led a diocese with the faces of many nations.

it liberates that which was in chains, reconciles that which was rent asunder, restores to its feet that which has been trodden down...

We have recognized and believe in this love...It has possessed and swept us up. We believe that it can renew the life of humanity in so far as we acknowledge it...

*On the proper style for a Christian presence in Algeria:*

How are we to listen if we are full of ourselves, of our material or intellectual wealth...? In Algeria, it is our good fortune to be pretty well stripped — but is it ever enough? — of our riches, our pretensions, and our self-sufficiency to be able to listen, to learn, to share from the little we have. We should not be perpetually preoccupied with defending ourselves. What do we have to protect? Our fortunes? Our buildings? Our influence? Our reputation? Our social standing? All that would be derisory compared to the gospel of the Beatitudes...Let us thank God when he returns his church to simple humanity...Let us rejoice at everything that can make us able to welcome and become more available, more concerned to give than to defend ourselves...More than protecting ourselves, we must defend what we consider to be essential to life, to belief, to human dignity and humanity's future. God's love drives us toward this...

*On intolerance and respect for the other:*

We live in a country where the majority is Muslim. In Islam as elsewhere, what counts is humanity before God. This humanity, our own and that of others, is never worse nor better than that of others...This is why I fear nothing more than sectarianism and fanaticism, above all in the religious sphere. Our Christian history includes many examples of this, and we cannot view the development of fundamentalist movements without disquiet. They already divide the church. In Islam, under the name of Muslim Brotherhood, they appear to be gaining in influence. I know enough Muslim friends who are also my brothers to think that Islam knows how to be tolerant, fraternal...Religion is perhaps home to the worst fanaticisms...Dialogue is a work to which we must return without pause: it alone lets us disarm the fanaticism, both our own and that of the other...Brothers and sisters, behold our mission. It is as vast as our life: it will take prayer, dialogue, speech, action...We will pursue this adventure together, letting God lead our pilgrimage.

Pierre Claverie's tone that day had a vigor and a sharpness of purpose that makes it clear that he already thought of himself "in the skin" of a pastor whose charge is to teach and guide his people. Complex questions confronted this church. For example, what is the status of a church that, having disappeared from North Africa with the arrival of the Almohads in the twelfth century and then having reappeared in the nineteenth with colonialism, appears to be aligned with the dominating aims of the West? What social space should it occupy? Or what dialogue should it engage in with an Islam that appears to become more rigid, as indeed is perhaps true of Christianity itself? Claverie's cordiality never encroached on his sense of responsibility, as we will see in the crisis to come. On October 14, five days after his installation, he received a delegation from the Ministry of Religious Affairs that came to demand that he give them a church to be converted into a mosque. "The spotlights are extinguished, the work has begun," he wrote to his family. "I am carried along by a glow of which Papie and Mamie have been the bedazzled witnesses. The betrothal has been a success; now begins the true apprenticeship for life as a couple — my diocese and me" (letter of October 19, 1981).

## The Diocese of Oran in 1981

What did the diocese of Oran consist of in 1981? It is possible to get an idea by consulting the quinquennial report Bishop Teissier drew up in March of that year, when he was preparing for an *ad limina* visit to the Holy See in Rome, which took place in November and in which Claverie participated.[6] The diocese of Oran had been canonically established in 1866 and covered all of western Algeria — in other words, the *wilayas* (provinces) of Oran, Mostaganem, Tlemcen, Sidi-bel-Abbès, and part of the provinces of Tiaret and Saïda (the remainder of which were attached to the diocese of Laghouat, which covered all of the Algerian Sahara). About four million people lived in this region, of whom about 18,000 were Catholic. In reality, though, only about ten percent of these, between 1,600 and 1,800 people, were really connected to the Christian community. A few more than a thousand people were regular practitioners. The Christian Algerians were few in numbers, and most Christians were of foreign origin.[7] The French constituted a large majority at that time, and are still quite numerous thanks to agreements for technological and cultural cooperation between Algeria and France. However, Poles, Brazilians, Filipinos, and Italians were also present in significant numbers; for the most part they were employed in low-level jobs in the industrial sector of the region. There were also a fair number of Christian women married to Algerians and pieds-noirs, often elderly, who remained in the country: these were the Christians who had integrated best with the population. One could also find Christian students from sub-Saharan Africa who lived, not without hardship, at the university city in a milieu that was almost completely Muslim except for a handful of Coptic Orthodox Egyptians, who were placed under the care of the Catholic bishop with their patriarch's agreement. Finally there were Protestants, fewer in number, who had the services of their own pastor, but enjoyed excellent relations with the bishop. Thus it was an extremely disparate church. Claverie, who loved human contact, could not hide his enthusiasm at having to assure a ministry of communion between such diverse groups: "What joy for a bishop, to see what the gospel might do when it takes root in different cultures."[8]

Despite reduced numbers, the Christians were scattered very widely around the region, and nearly every locality of any importance had a small Christian community and a place of worship. The clergy at this time consisted of thirty-five priests, among them sixteen religious, to which should be added eighty-one nuns, who made a considerable contribution to the church's presence in the country as teachers, nurses, monitors of girls' training or of specialized centers for the disabled; they lived particularly close to the populace. The average ages were good: fifty-five years for the nuns and less than fifty years for the priests. It was not a typical church, having as it did few laypeople, but a relatively young and numerous clergy. This Christian community of foreign origin had very close connections with the people in a variety of ways — through professional encounters, through aid workers, contacts as friends and neighbors, above all if one knew a little Arabic. There was also social and humanitarian commitment, where Caritas worked with Algerian structures; some cultural exchanges, like the conferences organized in conjunction with the university by the Center for Economic and Social Documentation (CDES) of the diocese; and, more durably, the mixed Muslim-Christian families that the church tried discreetly to support. The majority of priests and nuns shared these connections daily through neighborly relations in the various districts and collaboration at work; over the years they have come to be regarded as part of the country. "This is not a church of silence," Bishop Teissier is fond of saying. "It's a church of relationship with the other."

Nonetheless, this church had difficult challenges facing it. How to express the sense of its mission, without being suspected of ulterior motives? How to reconcile discretion with the need to have a minimum of structures? How to "account for the hope that is in us" while respecting other pathways to God?

These are the questions, both theological and practical, that the new pastor had to confront. They were the same questions with which Claverie grappled in his first homily in his cathedral.

## An Enterprising Bishop

The new bishop was forty-three years old, full of energy and enthusiasm. Claverie started establishing contacts without delay. In July he had made a first visit to Oran, accompanied by his predecessor and friend Henri Teissier. Claverie benefited immediately from the support and friendship of an Oranais lawyer, Redouane Rahal, whom he often laughingly presented in years to come as his "Muslim vicar-general." Rahal would become one of Claverie's most faithful friends, helping him to evaluate problems from an Algerian perspective and supporting him to his last day. In a tribute after Claverie's death, Rahal declared, "One day I said to him, 'Father, 80 percent of things unite us and 20 percent divide us. Let's put that 20 percent to one side and work on the rest.'" In August, Bishop Claverie made a tour of the Christian communities of the diocese, accompanied by Jacques Biès, the vicar-general, who would work with Claverie daily for nine years. It is worth recounting one of Biès' memories: "Sensing that he had hesitated to accept the office of bishop, I asked him what had decided him. He responded, 'The assassination attempt against John Paul II: a church whose head can be killed like anybody else — this attracts me.'"[9]

After his installation, Claverie resumed the process of making contact. From the first, he found himself at ease, his Mediterranean temperament helping him to feel the ambiance of human relations in Oran, reputed to be warmer than in the rest of Algeria. The *wali* (prefect) received him amicably, sharing with Claverie his concerns about the nascent Islamist movements and giving Claverie his private telephone number, urging him not to hesitate to call. A meeting with the regional inspector of the Ministry of Religious Affairs was more formal but still cordial — Claverie's ease with the Arabic language was a great help. The Poles, the association of French in Algeria, the nuns . . . everyone tried to meet with him as soon as possible: "the circus has resumed," as he wrote to his parents on the eve of setting out for Rome for his first *ad limina* visit and first meeting with the pope. There were many challenges, but Claverie was happy, full of energy and plans.[10]

One of his first initiatives was to launch a full-scale inquiry into the state of his diocese, aided by Jean Merlo, a sociologist friend with experience in

the realities of the third world. Various groups were defined to allow all categories of people to be heard. There were Christian spouses of mixed marriages,
African students, aid workers, factory workers, pieds-noirs who had remained,
priests, nuns. There were a total of about ten of these groups, with a coordinator at their head. At Claverie's initiative, David Butler was in charge of
consultations with the priests. He was a Methodist pastor who had been in
Algeria since 1975 and had established a good relationship with Teissier. "I
learned a great deal in the course of this experience," Butler wrote, adding humorously, "It's at this time that I got my nickname 'priests' confessor'" (letter
of December 15, 1999). Over time, great trust grew up between this Protestant pastor and Claverie.[11] The consultations lasted eighteen months, ending
at Pentecost, 1984. Claverie concluded, in June 1984: "It took a year and a
half for the investigation to cover the entire diocese . . . , many felt themselves
marginalized . . . I expected of this task that it would lead us toward the others,
and, together, toward God, who calls us, and toward Algeria, where he has
put us."[12] These words at the conclusion of the study show what would be the
double priority of Claverie's episcopate: to assure the unity and dynamism of
the Christian community, but also to rejoin the Algeria to which he felt he
had been sent.

Claverie himself lived this double task, watching over but never allowing himself to be absorbed completely by his own community. For him, his
relationship with Algerian friends was a priority and a joy. This gave birth,
in Oran, to a network of friends even more diverse than he had enjoyed in
Algiers. In 1982, he made the acquaintance of Sheik Bouabdelli, a historian,
member of the higher Islamic council, and leader of the *zaouïa* of Bethioua. In
early February 1983, there was a young Algerian university student who wrote
his doctoral dissertation on the role of Islam in Algeria's political structure.
"Fascinating," commented Claverie. Later came a visit to Si Kaddour, one
of Oran's leading personalities, who introduced Claverie to Abbé Bérenguer,
a pied-noir priest of strong personality who had been the FLN's roving ambassador in Latin America during the war of liberation. During a seminar at
the University of Oran on rationalism in the social sciences, at which he was
invited to speak, Claverie became friends with Hassan Remaoun and Abdelkader Djeghloul, both professors at the university; they paid Claverie a moving
tribute after his death.[13] As he had done in Algiers at les Glycines, at Oran
Claverie organized a series of conferences, getting as many prominent Algerian figures as possible to participate. Claverie also had Master Benchehida in
his network, that aged notable, educated in both French and Arabic culture,

equally at home with Victor Hugo or Ibn Arabi. Claverie's correspondence conjures up, here and there, unexpected visitors, like the young "Muslim brother" who called from time to time and to whose home Claverie went for dinner one evening, or the young nomad of El Abiodh Side Cheikh, who did not hesitate to knock on the bishop's door if he chanced to pass by in his travels. Another time, a "bearded one," an FIS militant, came to the bishop's home to hand over some money that his brother had robbed from a French priest. Claverie started an ongoing dialogue with him.[14] Other friends, like Mr. Nimour, knew how to organize evening discussions that made it possible for Claverie to encounter a number of people, exchanging ideas with them passionately but in an atmosphere of trust, around a good pot of couscous. He felt at home in this fraternal atmosphere and spoke of "his country" with a jubilation that was almost sensual: "Marvelous times: the mountain was strewn with almond trees in flower all along the road, under a dark and pure blue sky. A splendor" (letter of January 30, 1983). It is like reading Albert Camus, describing the exuberance of springtime in Tipasa.

## Some Delicate Matters

This network of friends helped enormously when Claverie had to face a number of delicate matters — for which, in Mediterranean countries, the quality of one's personal relations can make an immense difference. The eighties brought the country to a "blockage of the system," as Benjamin Stora described it in his analysis of Algeria's evolution after independence. The ill effects of development choices in the seventies were becoming more evident every day. Agriculture, sacrificed to industrialization and overly bureaucratized, was far from satisfying the needs of a rapidly increasing population. As a result, in 1984 Algeria had to import 40 percent of its grain, 50 percent of its dairy products, 70 percent of its meat, and 95 percent of its sugar. Industry was not in such dire straits; nonetheless, the costs of production were high and productivity was low. Despite enormous investments in this sector, 98 percent of all export revenues continued to come from hydrocarbons. The combination of these results explains Algeria's dangerously growing foreign debt: in 1989 it amounted to $6.5 billion, that is to say, three-quarters of the country's exports. This situation led to refinancing of the debt and to the structural adjustment programs associated with this. These steps included increasing the prices of durable goods, compressing social expenditures that were not directly productive, and so on. Investment planning had already deferred major projects for the sake of social needs (such as housing and leisure). Enormous frustration was on the rise among the people, who saw the emergence of a privileged class that was showing off its luxury in villas along the west coast and in the upmarket stores of Riad el-Fath, a cultural complex built on the heights above Algiers. Young people were especially frustrated: finding work only with difficulty, they could not even dream of owning their own flats, but were still attracted by the West that lay so near. The young plunged into a state of turmoil portrayed in Merzak Allouache's then famous film *Omar Gatlato*. Some extricated themselves from a hopeless situation by turning to the *trabendo,* a local term for the black market for imported products, but they had dreamed of better things. In addition, there was very little scope for democratic expression. All the ingredients were present for a social explosion — which came in October 1988. It was on this fertile soil that the Islamist movements developed.

Upon his arrival at the head of the diocese, Claverie had received a delegation of Muslims from the St.-Eugène district who asked that he cede a church to be converted into a mosque.[15] In itself, this was not an outrageous request. The departure of the pieds-noirs in 1962 had left the diocese with a number of churches out of all proportion to the number of the faithful. The Algerian church had already negotiated with local authorities in a climate of respect to transfer several ecclesiastical buildings. The novelty in this case was that the inhabitants of the district had begun to make the demands themselves. Many of the mosques being constructed in this period were in fact undertaken by associations of Muslims who raised the funds themselves and also eluded the Ministry of Religious Affairs' control. Very quickly, Bishop Claverie discovered that some of these groups had an eye on the cathedral itself, a very large neo-Byzantine edifice in the heart of the city. It was obvious that this building no longer corresponded to the needs of the Christian community. Nevertheless, for some, including the local pieds-noir associations, it was a symbol of their place in the city and the country — it was here that they had been married or had their children baptized. Claverie did not overlook this point, understanding in his very fiber their sensitivity on this issue. On June 10, 1982, he received a delegation from an Association for the Defense of Islam, which came to request the cathedral. The lawyer Redouane Rahal was of particular assistance to Claverie on the legal side of the issue because, in fact, the cathedral was state property. The bishop immediately turned to the inspector of religious affairs for the *wilaya* and to the *wali* himself. Claverie said that he was "prepared to examine every demand that came from the pertinent authorities," but indicated that, if the transfer indeed took place, financial assistance from the state would be necessary to arrange for another location to serve the diocese's needs. This is indeed what occurred: the *wilaya* furnished the necessary funds and facilitated the acquisition of materials. Claverie noted: "I swear that I did not expect such rapid movement. This proves that the authorities were committed to doing things correctly and that everything was already prepared, awaiting an eventual acceptance on our side" (letter of December 27, 1982).

Claverie also did his best to manage this transition in the court of public opinion, especially on the far side of the Mediterranean, where some pieds-noirs associations were inclined to make the giving up of the cathedral a symbol of the abandonment of which they had regarded themselves as victims since 1962.[16] In fact, though, A. Meziane, the Minister of Culture, was also uneasy at the possible exploitation of this situation by the Islamists. So he dealt briskly with the inspection by the Ministry of Religious Affairs and decided to convert the cathedral into a library and cultural center. At the end of May, the episcopal chancery turned over the keys. In exchange, efforts were dedicated to remodeling the parish church of St. Eugene into a modest cathedral. It is here that Claverie's body is buried today. A similar negotiation took place for the bishop's residence, which was also disproportionate to Claverie's needs and above all his lifestyle. In general, "Pierre did these difficult things honestly," commented Thierry Becker, who became Claverie's vicar-general in 1990. But he was also very decisive, especially when the administration of religious affairs attempted to present him with a *fait accompli*. His resolution stemmed from the honesty and cordiality of his relations, but also from a shrewd evaluation of the tensions within Algerian society, which made it possible for him to reach a solution that was both peaceable and possible on the delicate matter of the cathedral.

Over the course of the years, Bishop Claverie would be confronted with the growing difficulty foreigners had finding work in Algeria. This issue affected the church's life, because nearly all the priests and religious were foreigners and depended on a job contract to give them status and a way of fitting into the country. The cancellation of job contracts started in the eighties. Algeria could count more and more on educated nationals to fill positions. At the time, tensions in Franco-Algerian relations also contributed to the problem, but this was rarely the primary cause behind the change. Claverie approached this issue with great determination. One of his initiatives was to create what he called the "platforms of encounter and service" — places where the church put at the state's disposal locales and personnel qualified to respond to the populace's needs. The best example of this program is the initiative at Sidi-bel-Abbès. In this town, as in many others, the Catholic places of worship had become too large. With external financing, the diocese converted church buildings into a clothing workshop for women, a library, and a residence for a community of Franciscan sisters who were placed in charge of these activities in collaboration with the local priest. And there was still enough room left over to arrange a chapel large enough for their needs. "Instead of highlighting our absence, these locations highlight our active presence in the country," Becker remarked. Sister Serena, superior of the Franciscan community, has fond memories of all these proceedings, arranged enthusiastically with Claverie, who "supported, encouraged, and came immediately when he was needed." She received a letter from him on the day of his death. "Your sisterly community is the daily miracle," he liked to say to her because, with imagination and perseverance, all the nuns without a job found a way of integrating that put them in direct contact with the people. Hundreds of people came every day to this parochial center at Sidi-bel-Abbès. Similar operations, on a varying scale, were put into operation at Mascara, Tlemcen, Mostaganem, and Oran.

## "The Pieds-noirs Are Returning..."

When they were still in Algeria, the pieds-noirs had been in the habit of holding a great picnic excursion, called the *mouna*, on Ascension day. In March 1982, a delegation from the Friends of Our Lady of Santa Cruz called on Claverie. This was an association based in Nîmes that gathered together tens of thousands of Algerian returnees each year at a chosen Marian shrine. The delegation came to announce that 700 of them would be coming to Oran for Pentecost in 1982.[17] Santa Cruz is a sanctuary dear to the people of Oran. The basilica was constructed in the second half of the nineteenth century on a hill overlooking the city to commemorate "the miracle of the rain." In 1849, a long drought brought on an extremely deadly cholera epidemic that killed thousands in the city. Desperate, the people of Oran had gone in procession to the hill of Murdjajo, carrying a statue of the Virgin Mary on their shoulders and begging her to intercede to bring rain to save them. Immediately afterward, rain fell in abundance. The faithful acknowledged the miracle by building a chapel and then a basilica. After independence, this isolated location had been abandoned and was rarely frequented.

The idea of this mass visit caught Claverie's interest and he promised to support the project. This operation fell at the same time as the transfer of the cathedral, but the stakes were worth it. Contact was made with the Algerian authorities, who promised to restore the basilica and the city's Christian cemetery, a very sensitive point for Mediterranean people. The work was carried out. "The mayor even told me to choose the color for the walls of the basilica," the delighted Claverie reported. For several years, other groups of pieds-noirs would come "to the country," visiting their childhood homes and discovering what had become of their houses, farms, and churches — a pleasure mixed with nostalgia. The reception they received from locals was good, and welcoming committees were formed. On April 21, 1987, Claverie again celebrated a Mass at the basilica of Santa Cruz, this time for 200 pieds-noirs on a "pilgrimage of reconciliation": "On Monday there was a prayer procession with the pieds-noirs, then Mass at the basilica, followed by the procession in the cloister and the *mouna*. . . . Memories, memories! As you can imagine, everybody wept" (letter of April 21, 1987).

In 1989 a thousand of these visitors were announced. Arriving by car ferry, they were received by the mayor and the *wali* with great pomp. Claverie told of their departure from the port of Oran in these terms: "At the moment of departure, there were as many Algerians on the dock as there were French in the boat. Everybody wept. This shows that fraternal ties can endure and that it is possible to overcome opposition" (interview on Radio Notre Dame, June 16, 1989).

Besides the emotion inherent in these events, it appears that Claverie saw in these rediscoveries yet another occasion for encountering the Other, for leveling the walls of prejudice and mutual distrust.[18] Having received the Friends of Our Lady of Santa Cruz at Oran, Claverie went to Nîmes in 1992 to preside over their annual pilgrimage to Mas de Mingue, where there was a sanctuary dedicated to Our Lady of Salvation; there he met more than 100,000 pieds-noirs reunited around Bishop Lacaste, who had served as bishop of Oran from 1946 to 1972. Lacaste, very highly regarded in French Algeria, had continued as "the father of this entire diaspora," his successor declared. Claverie was well aware of the risk of people making political capital out of this sort of event, but thought his background put him in a good position to speak to them of Algeria and to help them heal some wounds.[19] To commemorate Claverie's visits three years in a row the city of Nîmes later named a street after him, the "Avenue Mgr Pierre-Claverie, êveque d'Oran," a sign of gratitude by the Friends of Our Lady of Santa Cruz for someone who had, in spite of all, remained one of them.

## Return to Saint-Do

Ten years earlier, in 1983, Claverie had renewed his contact with Saint-Do, the Boy Scout troop of his Algerian childhood, with the same goal of healing the wounds of the past. Nearly all the old boys of Saint-Do had left Algeria when independence was declared. The few exceptions included Abbé Denis Gonzalez, whom Claverie had rediscovered among the clergy of Algiers. All had suffered from this uprooting; few had had the heart to return to the country that had been theirs and where they had lost everything. With the support of a small staff, Fr. Lefèvre had managed to maintain a living contact between them. An directory of addresses was created in 1962. The journal *Feux* (Campfires), dedicated to news about one another, was kept alive. Above all, regular reunions were organized at the regional or national level, where "Father" continued his work of spiritual inspiration. Claverie remained outside of this network for a long time. Certainly he had maintained personal contacts with close friends like Jean-François Cota or Geneviève Troncy, but he did not hide the fact that his views about Algeria were very far removed from those of Fr. Lefèvre.

Not everyone at Saint-Do understood his views.[20] The Oran meeting with the Friends of Our Lady of Santa Cruz having gone well in 1982, Claverie agreed to preside over the second large reunion of old boys of Saint-Do, held at Aiguebelle in Drôme in June 1983. "He was rather ill at ease," remembered Geneviève Troncy, "but everything went marvelously." With cordiality and patience, Claverie explained to these former scouting companions what had become of Algeria and the church in Algeria. Without denying the ever-present suffering and wounds of the exiles, he struck a positive note. Before them, he evoked "the houses of stone and the houses of the heart." The message came through. Afterward, Claverie was called "our bishop" in the pages of *Feux*. He returned to celebrate the Eucharist and to facilitate some evenings of discussion about Algeria in the course of the 1986 reunion (Avignon), 1989 (Lyon), 1993 (Oberhaslach), and 1996 (Prouilhe). When weather permitted, he celebrated his liturgies in the open air using the equipment of a scouting camp — a wooden altar, troop pennants, and so on. Claverie officiated, miter on head and cross in hand. Without speaking of himself — that wasn't his style — he confided his own secrets, if one paid attention. Thus, in his homily at Lyon in 1989:

"Whoever wishes to save his life will lose it, but he who loses his life for my sake will save it." In other words: to live and be happy, it is necessary to give life in giving one's life. The person who tries to save his life, that is to say to catch and hold life and the gifts of life in his greedy hands, dies of egotism in his possession and sows death around himself, because he feeds from the life of others. To renounce oneself is not to renounce happiness or life, but to renounce making oneself the center of the world and to build one's happiness by bringing all to oneself. Happiness is found when one gives oneself. Life is found when one gives it. Isn't this what scouting taught us?[21]

Such statements contained nothing beyond the classical interpretation. But when the person speaking also lives his words, to the point of being ready to die for them, that's something else again.

The Mass finished, one could see Claverie circulating among the various groups, breaking into laughter with rediscovered friends, remembering the old jokes of the troop of Saint-Jacques (Claverie's own), eating brochettes "in the Algiers style." Besides these visits to France, Claverie also gave speeches on the evolving situation in Algeria and on the church there. Jacques Campredon, at that time president of the old boys of Saint-Do, describes one of these talks thus:

Pierre's last word was, "One of my principal missions in Algeria is to establish, develop, and enrich a relationship, always, everywhere, and with everyone." These few lines give little sense of the richness, the warmth of Pierre's talk...Thank you, Pierre, infinite thanks for your optimism, not at all complacent, for your openness, your moderation, and your passion. Great power emanates from everything you said to us and from the way you said it to us; a great power which is none other than that of your faith, your experience, and your charity.[22]

At Christmas 1986 Jean-Charles Benoît, another old boy of Saint-Do, decided to visit Algeria to see Claverie. Like many pieds-noirs, he had "promised never to set foot there again," he remembered, but a discussion with Claverie had changed his mind. "Pierre had this gift of encouraging people to be generous," Benoît stressed. An emotional visit, but it went well. On his return home, along with other couples who had taken part in the trip, Benoît decided to found a mutual aid association to support the activities of Claverie and Denis Gonzalez, the head of Caritas in Algeria. For several years they collected and sent books to the diocesan libraries of Oran. They also returned to Algeria on various occasions to renew their ties. Above all, they created a prayer group that regularly brought together more than twenty people "to pray with Pierre," who had said to Benoît, "You know, prayer is something fundamental."

It was the old boys of Saint-Do, meeting at Prouilhe, cradle of the Dominican order, whom Claverie addressed in his last major public homily, five weeks before he was assassinated. Returning to this unsettling text, one cannot help but be struck by this "coincidence": there is a sense that Claverie's existence had come full circle. He recovered, just before his death, the people and place where he had, in part, found the key to his own life, the secret of his happiness. And he shared this secret with them one last time.


## To Encounter, Encourage, Support:
## A Bishop on His Own Turf

During these first years of his episcopal ministry, Claverie was very close to the ground. The best way to get an idea of how he passed his time is to reproduce here the list of activities that he sent to his parents, each week using the notes on his appointment calendar (they have all been preserved). Here is an example, dated December 6, 1983:

> Nov. 29: Death of a Little Sister of the Poor, Sister Bernadette, 53 years old, after a cerebral hemorrhage. Great emotion. The director of religious affairs (newly named) let me know that, if he had been informed at the time, he would have sent an imam for the prayer and the funeral. I celebrated the morning Mass with the whole community and the pensioners. As you know them from having seen them at Algiers, I will not dwell on the value of these women who give themselves to the service of the elderly without counting the price. In the afternoon, my gastric attack was over . . . as I prepared for the days that follow.
>
> Nov. 30: Departure for Ghazaouet (formerly Nemours). Marvelous weather and agreeable route. At midday, a meal with the small local community (15 people) under Marino;[23] it was an excellent meal. Then I had a conversation with two old pieds-noirs who are still there, one as a fishing boss, in partnership with an Algerian. Then we carried on to Tounane, where I stopped to see B., a friend of the sisters, then we descended on Maghnia: Mass in an aid worker's apartment, then drinks with a crowd of others who had come specially, Christian or not, to see the bishop. One of them had become a Muslim the year before: we promised to see each other again. An excellent ambiance. Then a little group of Belgian Christians for dinner and a discussion that lasted far into the night.

Dec. 1: Return to Oran. In the afternoon, the Jesuits invited me to their meeting, which took place in their apartment in Oran. A good atmosphere and animated exchanges. The arrival of Jean Merlo, who has come for the priests' meeting that will take place tomorrow, and during which he must initiate the work to prepare the diocesan assembly in June.

Dec. 2: Priests' meeting. A long time in preparation, it is always an ordeal for the bishop. I had sent a personal letter to each in which I posed some questions on how to envision the apostolic ministry. The morning was spent in discussion on this subject. Then Mass, lunch, and a general assembly. It all went well. It is evident, as we also have some more legal matters to deal with following the issuance of the new code of canon law, some clearly showed their opposition to any form of structuring the life of the church... As I am fundamentally in agreement, I am very badly placed to defend the theses that have been proposed — Jacques Biès would do this better than I! In the evening, a meeting with Merlo and Fr. Tardy to lay out a plan to follow up the diocesan assembly. A good start was made on the work, and I am happy with the results.

Dec. 3: After lunch, I proceeded with Thierry Becker to Sig to visit some families before a community meeting and Mass. I found some pieds-noirs there whom I've never seen before. In the evening, at Mass, in this little community that has doubled in size this year, good exchanges with the pieds-noirs and the Poles. Afterward, I returned directly to Oran...

Dec. 4: Departure for Temouchent, where Jean-Louis Déclais was expecting me. Lunch with a young member of the APC (Municipal Council) and his wife, a teacher. Then we went to some factory workers who are settling in — French and Indians. In the evening, a community meeting (more than 40, of whom 11 were Egyptians, 8 Hungarians, and a variety of others...). A multilingual Mass! Discussion late into the evening.

Dec. 5: Lunch at the French shipyard, at the cafeteria, then a French lesson in the form of an interview with the bishop for a group of Hungarians in a socialist village near El Malah. Return to Temouchent, then Beni Saf, visit to Fr. Martin, Mass for the tiny community; travel with some young military aid workers and dinner with an extremely pleasant mixed couple who have just had a little girl. A good evening. Return to Temouchent with Jean-Louis, then on to Oran alone at about midnight.

Dec. 6: An avalanche of visits and problems to deal with. Visit to the director of religious affairs, whom I already know because he was assistant to Z. Young and relaxed, rather "secularized," he doesn't wear traditional garb. He received me surrounded by his assistants, whom I also know, B., and the imam of the neighboring mosque. Good conversation, dialogue just as one would like it on both sides. We understand each other well, I hope. In the afternoon, a visit to two old ladies with Sister Désirée. Voilà. I have completed a tour of nearly the whole diocese. There remains Arzew, Tlemcen, and Saîda, where I will spend Christmas Eve. Everything is going well. The weather is always good, although it's now very brisk, cold in the morning and at night.

I'll be leaving Oran for Algiers on Thursday . . . I'll return the following Monday if all goes well. There you have it — the publication of *Le Lien* is being actively prepared . . .

Hugs to everyone and take care.

                                                              Pierre

Is it necessary to comment on this letter? It gives a faithful reflection of Claverie's life during his first years as bishop. There is an enthusiasm about encounter, a sense of his responsibility but also a freedom he showed from undue concern for his position. One can also see a taste for going from one person to another, linking worlds too often separated.[24] There is also an absence of prejudice, as can be seen with the aid worker who had converted to Islam ("we promised to see each other again") and the new head of religious affairs. Claverie enjoyed good health, which allowed him to endure and to enjoy all those miles on the road; he loved his ministry of communion. Quite simply, he was happy.[25]

Claverie continued to work in this style to the end of the eighties. In 1988 the atmosphere began to change in Algeria, and Claverie threw himself into the new challenges that this change posed not only for the church but for the Algerian society of which he was a member. Before looking at this, one needs to consider a more private aspect, which is nonetheless the foundation of his public life. But at the foundation of this public life, Claverie profoundly felt himself to be a religious — and wished to remain so.

## Chapter Seven

# A Preaching Friar before All Else

My Dominican brothers, you have taught me the contagious power of confidence. There is true happiness in living this quality of relationship. — *Pierre Claverie*

"I am happy to become a bishop, but I will not give up my preaching ministry," Pierre Claverie confided to his friend Henri Teissier, in agreeing to take Teissier's place as bishop of Oran. In fact, over his fifteen years as a bishop he would maintain a rhythm of preaching, but also a style of religious life and a sense of freedom, that came from his Dominican formation, as he himself acknowledged. But it was not without apprehension that he resigned himself to becoming something other than the simple religious that he had always been. He said as much to his fellow Dominicans as soon as word of his appointment came out:

On a number of occasions, the order has accepted the fact that my "Algerian vocation" is the substance of my Dominican vocation...On May 12, the nunciature informed me that after extensive consultation with the communities, the church was proposing that I "marry" my country once and for all. Concretely, this was not a matter of an effortless change: wouldn't moving away from my brothers and friends involve some harmful separations? I needed time, prayer, and the great friendship displayed by those asking me to go to Oran and those, in Algiers and Paris, who were assuring me of their fidelity, before I could accept. How can I express to you my great need to remain your brother? It was in the order that I made my own first conversions, that I discovered the gospel and the church... If I have remained strong during difficult times, it is because I have always felt the presence of our beautiful and deep fraternity, both in Algiers and elsewhere.

In spite of the physical distance from his community and despite his new duties, Pierre Claverie would remain a preaching friar. One even gets the impression that this was his fundamental identity, which no role or responsibility would ever change.

## The Way of Life of a Religious

"I was a religious before I became a bishop; I will remain a religious even as a bishop," Claverie declared to his vicar-general, Jacques Biès, when he arrived in Oran. Paradoxically, it was as a bishop that he lived the way of life most closely in keeping with his aspirations. During his years as head of les Glycines diocesan center, he had to reckon with the general atmosphere of a place where the work to be done and the various sensibilities diminished his freedom. His two vicars-general — Jacques Biès, from 1981 to 1990, and Thierry Becker, from 1990 to 1996 — were the witnesses and companions of this lifestyle typical of a religious brother to which Claverie returned throughout his fifteen years as a bishop.

The bishop's residence he found at his arrival was a little palace built the century before, and was richly furnished. The visitor was immediately struck by a splendid wooden staircase with a double banister. Henri Teissier, his predecessor, had lived simply there, but the walls still spoke of the special social status reserved for prelates in earlier times. When Pierre Claverie arrived in Oran, the church of Algeria had simplified its ways. But that didn't displease him. He abandoned the large office and bedroom made for the bishop, and lived in a small room at the end of the corridor, "with no furniture but a cot, a table, a chair, a dresser, a sink, and a crucifix," his father wrote to Wayne White in October of 1981, adding with his usual humor that "we were the ones who stayed in the bishop's chamber, which displays the kind of luxury that prelates of an earlier time enjoyed … and we did not sleep any better on account of this luxury." Following a delay in the transfer of the large neo-Byzantine cathedral to the Ministry of Culture, Pierre Claverie would arrange for a small house near the Church of Saint Eugene, which had become the new cathedral, to be turned into the bishop's residence. It was there that he lived until his death, in a daily simplicity that even his friends did not discover until after he died: he had a small room with nothing on the walls but a crucifix, an icon, and a photo of his parents. His clothing could all fit into two small suitcases, and he had a minimum of personal keepsakes: an Oriental-style pectoral cross, which he never wore, and about a dozen photos. That's it. Few of his fellow Dominicans lived in such austerity.

On the other hand, "he placed great emphasis on community life," contin-ues Jacques Biès. "He said, for us Dominicans, community life is an apostolate, through its witness. The fraternal life, with all problems shared in common, the life of prayer in common, the Divine Office and the Eucharist..." (let-ter dated November 17, 1999). It was with Jacques Biès that Pierre Claverie lived out the community life that he loved. Thierry Becker provided a detailed description of this:

> Every day, Pierre gets up at 6:00 a.m. At 6:30, after preparing the table for breakfast, he goes to the chapel. The chapel is at the center of the house, between the offices and the living quarters. At 7:15, we sing Lauds together. We even sing the Canticle of Zachariah, and we expand the universal prayer to all the business, encounters, and worries of the day. Breakfast follows, and that is our opportunity to plan out our day and seek each other's advice.
>
> Pierre then goes to his office, which is on the second floor, and begins working after listening to the news and reading the newspapers in French and Arabic. He is very attentive to events in the news and tries to understand the situation in the country as it unfolds... He might begin working on a talk, a homily, a diocesan meeting, or an editorial for the newsletter *Le Lien*. But he also permits himself to be interrupted continually by the many visitors who come looking for him, and he rarely puts off meeting them until later... At noon, Pierre is back in the chapel, in silence. Fifteen minutes later, the religious sisters and priests of the bishop's residence and of the nearby diocesan center come to sing the midday office... Around 6:30 in the evening, he is back in the chapel preparing for Mass. At 6:45, we sing Vespers and the Mass, in French and Arabic. An exchange on the subject of the day's readings reveals how much the Word of God nourishes Pierre, how it burns in his heart... The joys and hopes, worries and hardships of the day are offered up with the Lord's sacrifice, together with the needs of the diocese and of the entire world... After a frugal meal, Pierre watches the television newscast from the Algerian broadcasting network, griping at the news anchor's dull monologues but wanting to hear, in Arabic, the official account of international events and the commentaries on these.

Pierre Claverie lived this way of life until the very end: the more pressure he was under, the more he seemed to need this very regular rhythm of prayer. He had been faithful in his prayer life since he was a young man. His Muslim friend Rahal said he had always been impressed by Pierre's concentration while at prayer: "In prayer, it was as if he were detached from the world, and abandoned to God." It was at the door of that little chapel decorated with Algerian craftsmanship that he died, his head resting on the threshold. It had been his good fortune to have two vicars-general who understood, respected, and shared the way of life that he had known since his formation as a Dominican.

In this account of the simplicity of his life, it must again be pointed out how ready he was to entertain guests, even unexpected and overbearing ones. All of the persons questioned on this point are unanimous: each of them was warmly welcomed, "as if [Claverie] had nothing else to do," which was certainly far from the case. Those who were part of his daily life, like the Algerian employees of the bishop's residence (Fatiha, the cook, and Tayeb, the housekeeper) or the religious sisters closest to him (Sister Gesuina, who cared for the clothing and linens, Sister Mireille, his secretary, and sisters Jeanne and Renée) emphasize how thoughtful he was in the little things. "Fr. Claverie was not only very outgoing, he was very easy to get close to," confides Sister Claire, a pied-noir like he was. "And he loved life," adds Sister Jeanne, who laughs when she recalls his passion for french fries and meringue cookies, "a real bishop's diet," as Pierre Claverie would say to Annie Prénat when he passed through Toulon. There was nothing unusual about all this insofar as it went — the other bishops of Algeria had lived in their own way. But Pierre Claverie had, perhaps, a special gift for relating to people, a way of breaking the ice. It was a talent that surprised more than a few, like when he did the "duck dance" at the parties for the elderly organized by the Little Sisters of the Poor: "Once again the bishop could be seen doing the duck dance or playing 'musical chairs' with the wife of the Consul of France, among others...Obviously, I came home with a few aches and pains" (letter of November 19, 1983).

On the other hand, he did not conceal his lack of interest in the functions of society life, which he considered a waste of time. Do the priests of Oran know that when their bishop was given advance notice of his candidacy for the Legion of Honor in April of 1993, he declined the offer, and added, "This goes also for my priests."

## Freedom within His Function

Presenting Pierre Claverie to its readers in September of 1995, when he was most actively involved in public debate, the magazine *L'Actualité religieuse* described him in these terms: "Pierre Claverie, the bishop of Oran, is an unusual person. He ignores the fundamental principles of reserved speech; his unseemly tendency to call a spade a spade has irritated more than a few of his listeners. He doesn't mind being contradicted, and when he is, he passionately defends his own ideas. And he seasons everything he says with a liberal sprinkling of humor. He avoids decorum like the plague, and he behaves with his old friends as if he and they were still youngsters." The extent of his involvement in public debate at the height of the crisis in Algeria poses questions that we will revisit later. But even before this, Pierre Claverie had shown great freedom in his way of expressing himself. As a priest, he was hardly "clerical" at all: the humor that his father had taught him helped him to keep everything in perspective. As a bishop, he was certainly aware of his responsibility, and he conscientiously carried it out. Nonetheless, his manner was always very simple, and above all he never forbade himself from thinking on his own and expressing, when appropriate, his disagreement. He was happy to belong to a stripped-down and, in some ways, fragile church, because this seemed to him more in keeping with the spirit of the gospel. "It matters little how many or few we are, as long as we do not fall back into a defensive position. It matters little how meager our means are, as long as these are truly enlivened by the spirit of the gospel," he wrote in the September 1987 edition of *Le Lien*. It was an early intuition of his: "Perhaps it is fitting that the revival of Christianity in Algeria must come through a small number," he wrote during the exodus of the pieds-noirs (letter dated May 8, 1961). And he was annoyed by the temptation to exercise power that sometimes runs through the church, an annoyance he displayed in a letter dated April 12, 1987:

> The pope is completing his difficult tour of Latin America. I wonder if he should now put aside his pilgrim's staff for a while. Some time must be allowed for the digestion of these incursions into complex surroundings, and he should devote himself to meditating on what he has seen and heard...or, rather, on what others have permitted him to see and hear. Perhaps he should make a concerted effort to come to understand what he did not see, what is going on backstage behind the scenery he was escorted through. Basically, it would be nice to see him calm down a little. It must also be said that we are inundated with letters on every subject imaginable, from international debt to *in vitro* fertilization, from the encyclical on the Virgin Mary to the Holy Thursday letter to priests...One hardly has time to open one letter before the

next is tossed onto the desk! Cardinal Duval thinks that a lot of paper is being wasted at the Vatican.

In 1991, he published in the newsletter *Le Lien* a commentary written by one of the priests of his diocese, Jean-Louis Déclais, who was responding to the "Message to the People of God" published at the end of the synod of the Catholic Church dedicated to the formation of priests.[1] Jean-Louis Déclais notes that the document speaks of "priestly celibacy in the church," as if the discipline and traditions of the Eastern churches were in agreement with those of the Latin church on this point. The article was trying to set the historical record straight, and expressed some irritation at the way in which debate on these taboo topics is carefully avoided in the Latin church. Judging that it is better for one to be able to say what one thinks, Pierre Claverie published the article. On account of this, he was required to present an explanation to the papal nuncio, Bishop Ferhat. The incident was quickly resolved "the Claverie way," frankly but cordially. In March of 1993, he invited the nuncio to a celebration on a Ramadan evening in Oran with sixty or so of his Algerian friends. The evening went beautifully, and was all the more enjoyable because it was an exchange that took place in Arabic with a Christian Arab: "Once again I had the opportunity to appreciate our good fortune at being surrounded by so much respect and good will on the part of all sorts of people — from the member of the constitutional council to the farmer, plus the doctor, the lawyer, the former government minister, the sheikh of a Muslim confraternity. This sort of meeting is very reassuring, and it is certainly no waste of time" (letter of March 8, 1993).

The trials that came during the last years of his life brought Pierre Claverie what were perhaps his greatest sufferings on account of the sluggishness of his church. One gathers as much from an editorial he wrote during the summer of 1995, "Une Église empêtrée":

> I often get the impression that my church is closed off in its own upper room, like the apostles were before Pentecost. The book of Acts tells us that they were there "out of fear of the Jews" . . . If I am willing to appear old-fashioned because I have inherited traditions and values that seem antiquated but contain wisdom about how to live one's life, liberty and projection of love, this doesn't make me a defender of stilted language (it was once Latin) or of ecclesiastical discipline (when this puts on the airs of dogma). It is at this point that the "church-as-communion" steps in, and not simply the apostolic magisterium, which is the legitimate interpreter of tradition, but always in the context of communion.[2]

What bothered him the most was not so much the content of the magis-terium's proclamations as the way in which they were sometimes promulgated. So he concluded this editorial by calling for a new ecumenical council that would resume the collegiality intended by Vatican II. He was not the only bishop who was thinking this way, but few of the others were speaking their minds. In this, he showed the lasting influence of Frs. Chenu and Congar, the major Dominican thinkers of his generation:

> "The contestation of religion drives us to reformulate our convictions," he said that same year to some young Dominicans he was ordaining. "Affirming the faith would, then, consist in finding the words to express the experience that brought it into being. Paul and his companions did this in referring to the teachings of the ancient Greeks, but as far as Paul is concerned, it also involved elaborating a local theology, and at his own risk . . . Isn't this as much the vocation of the preacher as of the apostle?[3]

"Elaborating a brand new local theology, and at his own risk": this is a fairly good description of what Pierre Claverie contributed at that time. He had by then acquired an interior freedom that nothing and no one could threaten. His relationship with the nunciature was sometimes delicate, as when he decided not to go to Tunis for the pope's visit in April of 1996.[4] As a bishop, he did not hide the fact that it was sometimes difficult for him to accept all the positions of the magisterium, as was his duty. He even came to the point of thinking about resigning, but he never did so, because of his fidelity to his country and to the church of Algeria.[5] With the worsening of the situation in Algeria, he would play his part as bishop to the full, with responsibility but without conceding his freedom of thought and speech.

## A Genuine Passion for Preaching

Pierre Claverie spoke and preached a great deal. He loved preaching, and looked upon it as his duty. While still in Le Saulchoir as a young priest, he was already preaching a lot. As a young religious in Algiers, he was in great demand: as soon as he arrived, his prior, Pierre Le Baut, entrusted to him the Sunday homilies on the airwaves of Radio Algiers. A religious sister who observed him at the time remarked, "He's got everything: human warmth, the gift of immediacy, solidity and clarity of thought." Even before he had completed his intensive study of Arabic, he was in great demand

Bishop Claverie, always a preaching friar, in a typically expansive gesture during a homily.

among the religious sisters, who felt a deep need to readjust the manifestations and rationale of their presence in Algeria. Pierre Claverie accepted willingly, almost on principle, without spending much time determining questions or themes: "I almost never fix the subjects of my conferences, in order to force myself to address topics I wouldn't choose of my own accord. Of course, I have a limited number of arrows in my quiver, so I can't deal with everything . . . but for the time being, I'm getting by" (letter of February 13, 1972).

So over the years he would build up quite a number of files dealing with a great variety of topics, including theology, spirituality, religious life, Islam, interreligious dialogue — but also with social questions involving Algeria and the third world (development, peace, human rights, socialism). At his death ninety-five folders, some of them quite thick, would be found, containing both the texts of his addresses (written out by hand, without corrections!) and the preparatory notes he made from various books and articles.[6] This makes it possible to get an idea of how much work he put into the preparation for his many speeches — he certainly had a gift for speaking and an amazing ability to present his ideas clearly, but there was more effort involved than his audiences imagined.

Retreats represented an enormous amount of work on his part. After a few well-received retreats he preached in Algiers and Constantine between 1968 and 1970, Pierre Claverie would dedicate almost a month of each summer to giving retreats to religious sisters in Lebanon, then in Martinique. He retained this commitment after becoming a bishop, and it took the place of his vacation. It was always a busy period, with two conferences per day, a homily at the Mass, and at least two hours dedicated to the sisters who wanted to meet with him. The choice of Lebanon and Martinique was due to his special relationship with two religious congregations for women: the Lebanese congregation of the Sisters of the Holy Hearts (whom he met in Algiers when he was studying Arabic) and the missionary Dominican sisters of Our Lady of la Deliverande. The latter of these, founded in Martinique, have houses in Lebanon and Egypt, and were still present in Algeria (in Bordj el-Kiffan, formerly called Fort de L'Eau by the French) when Pierre Claverie arrived there in 1967. He would develop deep bonds of friendship with the superior general, Sister Marie of the Incarnation, and would participate in three of their general chapters. He would go to Lebanon almost every summer from 1971 to 1982.

In 1982, Lebanon was in the grip of war. The Beirut airport was shut down, and Pierre Claverie had to come by sea from Cyprus (he twisted his ankle while disembarking at the port of Jounieh). After returning to Algeria, he wrote a long editorial for the diocesan bulletin of Oran, *Le Lien*, demonstrating that he was not fooled by the "Gemayel solution," named after the new Lebanese president who had been elected amid "a climate of formal legality." In September, Béchir Gemayel was assassinated. Terrible massacres followed at the Palestinian camps in Beirut, Sabra, and Chatila. Observers claimed these were perpetrated by the milita forces of Gemayel's father, Pierre, under the protection of Israeli troops that had sealed off the area.[7] Pierre Claverie's analysis displeased the Maronite hierarchy, and he was declared *persona non grata* in Lebanon, where he would not be able to return for a number of years. This would prompt him to dedicate his summer retreats to the sisters of Our Lady of la Deliverande in Martinique. Was it imprudent of him to express himself frankly? Sister Marie of the Incarnation, who had spent a number of years at the Dominican college of Araya in Beirut, saw things from a different perspective: "His visit brought a touch of the gospel to poor Lebanon, where the people no longer seem to see things clearly because they have suffered so much at each other's hands," she wrote in the midst of the controversy.[8] By this time, Claverie's interpretation of events frequently linked this "frank way of speaking together with an evangelical note," as M. Borrmans put it.[9] He preached in Niger (1975), Tunisia (1979), and sometimes in different countries during the same summer: in the summer of 1980, he preached in Egypt, Lebanon, and Martinique! Once he arrived, it was not unusual for him to preach three retreats in a row, the religious congregations involved having spread word he was coming. One of the congregations he served faithfully was that of the Little Sisters of Jesus, whose spirituality and presence in Islamic countries he greatly admired. He gave two retreats for priests in Canada, in 1986 and 1989, and a few retreats in Europe (to the Dominican nuns of Chalais, to the Dominican friars of Fribourg, and to the priests of the diocese of Bayonne). Pierre Claverie once preached at the annual retreat for priests in his diocese. His account of this experience clarifies what it meant to him, and significantly revises the spontaneous ease that others attributed to him:

> It seems to be a novelty that a bishop would preach to the members of his own flock (something I find astonishing). In any case, it gave me the opportunity to better understand and appreciate what I had barely realized before. And [the priests] also got to know me better, since I spent a week sharing my faith with them. All the same, I now see that this took some courage on my part, since, as everyone knows, no one is a prophet in his own country. I really sweated the first day, and I didn't truly ease into it until the third. It was hard — very hard. But it was worth it. (letter of August 7, 1983)

He explained his interest in these retreats on a number of occasions — above all, he found in them an opportunity to share his faith, which for him was essential. In a retreat he gave in Ainab, near Beirut, in August of 1979, he began in these unconventional terms:

For me, a retreat is the communication of a conviction. I have nothing to communicate except my conviction. Over the years I have communicated it in different ways and under different forms, as the progress of my own life has determined . . . But at bottom, the conviction is always the same . . .

Don't be concerned if I don't talk about religious life. I will speak of it only in passing, because, to tell the truth, it doesn't much interest me. Excuse me: I am a religious, you are religious. What interests me is the foundation of religious life, not its various forms.[10]

What engaged his passion was giving an account of his faith, sharing his conviction with others, witnessing the reality of the Spirit in the lives of others. During a retreat for priests in Canada in 1989, he wrote, "These retreats bring me great joy, in spite of the effort of preparation and the physical and nervous exertion that they represent. I am always anxious and tense the first days, and I'm always surprised to see that the message is received even better than I hoped" (letter of September 19, 1989).

The second reason for his great fondness for the summer retreats is that they gave him a break from the frenetic pace of his duties as director of les Glycines, and then as a bishop. Outside of the two daily conferences that he prepared in advance, and the time devoted to individual meetings, Pierre Claverie lived these days in a spirit of deep recollection, as witnessed by the Lebanese sisters who saw him every summer from 1971 to 1982. He recommended an hour of silent adoration in the chapel each evening, and participated in these himself. He could be seen praying the rosary, smiling peacefully, recounts Sister Thérèse Saad. There are dozens of hours of recordings from these retreats available: his voice is very calm and recollected, but also cheerful at times. Great bursts of laughter emphasize that these months were like a breath of fresh air for him each year. The weekends were dedicated to relaxation and time with friends. In Lebanon, he loved returning to Qnat, the mountain village of Sister Marie Melhem: he sat for hours with her elderly mother, talking with her in Arabic and admiring her simple and deep faith. One day, he confided to her, "You have the good fortune of having roots, but I don't anymore." Apart from his personal history, one can imagine that Pierre Claverie was hinting here at his dream that one day the church of Algeria would have true Arab roots. Occasionally some of his Algerian friends joined him in Lebanon, and they would go together to Baalbek to the north to see the cedar forests. These were happy days. Lebanon was also meaningful to him because it had suffered much on account of war, and it was then plunged back into violence, which he had experienced in 1957 during the battle of Algiers and which he would see again during the 1990s.

## A Platform: Le Lien

Pierre Claverie also exercised his flair for preaching through the monthly editorial he wrote for the bulletin of the diocese of Oran, *Le Lien*. He worked hard on these editorials, struggling with them and revisiting them multiple times, as Sister Mireille, the secretary for the bishop's residence, recalls. Around forty of them were collected for the book *Lettres et messages d'Algérie*, published in 1996. The bulk of these editorials come from his tormented final years, beginning from 1988. But in total he wrote almost three hundred of them, each running around two or three typed pages.

In its essence, this monthly text was anything but a formality: it was the writing, the teaching of a pastor concerned about guiding his community in the decisions it faced. In them, he commented on the gospel in the context of the liturgical season (Christmas, Easter, Pentecost), but also in terms of the contemporary church's life and world affairs. We have already referred to the September 1982 editorial dedicated to Lebanon, which brought him a bit of trouble. From August to November of 1983, he dedicated three long consecutive editorials to Roger Garaudy's conversion to Islam.[11] Like many Christians, he had greatly enjoyed *Parole d'homme*, the book Garaudy wrote as he was leaving Communism for a form of humanism closely resembling Christianity.[12] The elevated media profile of the French philosopher's conversion to Islam, and the explanations Garaudy gave for it, prompted Pierre Claverie to explore publicly three points he saw as essential: Is there, or is there not, a continuity of revelation among the Jewish, Christian, and Muslim traditions, as Garaudy asserts? What is the relationship between science and revelation? And what is the relationship between faith and politics? These extensive editorials made something of a splash, and were reprinted in 1984 by *Islamochristiana*, the journal of the Pontifical Institute of Arab and Islamic Studies (IPEA) directed by the White Fathers in Rome.[13] Two other editorials in 1986 would revisit the issue of conversions to Islam, which were always highlighted by the Algerian press. From July to December of 1985, he wrote another series of five editorials on Muslim-Christian dialogue.[14] In these, Pierre Claverie explained his understanding of dialogue, which will be presented in detail in the following chapter. His chief concern was to face the question honestly, without disguising the difficulties involved and with attention to the importance of the value of reciprocity. He would revisit this theme in the March–April edition of 1990, under the title "L'étape présente du dialogue islamo-chrétien." Beginning in 1988 and the affair of the "great controversy" (see page 141), the editorials in *Le Lien* bear witness to the growing pressure of Islamism upon civil society and the religious minorities in Algeria. In taking a public position, the bishop intended to defend the interests of the church, but he was also concerned about helping it find the true power of the gospel, the spirit that the church needs to face such a challenge in fidelity to the spirit of Jesus: "Far from letting ourselves be shut up within our own apprehensions, our complexes, our limitations, more than ever we will need to draw upon the resources of our faith in order to go out and meet others," he wrote in August of 1993.[15]

Going out to meet others: this remained his goal even during the most difficult moments, and many of his editorials consist of theological reflection on what it means to live as a Christian under increasingly hostile conditions:

> Without idealizing our sometimes difficult daily relationships, both on the personal level and among communities or national groups . . . we can say once more: what brings us together is stronger than what divides us. Or better: the One who brings us together. Because it is my conviction that without Him we would be at the mercy of our natural impulses.[16]

While Algeria was plunged into violence beginning in 1990, Claverie would display a steadfast concern for reconciling the spirit of the gospel and political resistance. In June of 1988, he commented on the attacks that had been conducted against Christians: "It is my duty as the Catholic bishop of Oran to express my most vigorous protest against this polemical campaign of misinformation." His biting editorials would continue to emerge, including those of May 1994 ("Pourquoi?"), January 1995 ("Qui sème le vent"), and November 1995 ("Bravo"), which he wrote after the assassination of Odette Prévost, whom he greatly admired.[17] But it is interesting to note that, regardless of the nature of the difficulty he was facing, he always had a spiritual message, as in his editorial for the summer of 1994, "Priez sans cesse." The first assassinations of religious figures took place in May; Christians were stunned, and their confidence in the country and their place in it was shaken. Pierre Claverie reacted as a pastor, and he strove to remind his community of the essential reasons for the Christian presence there, which went far beyond transitory motivations: "This moment of crisis, trial, and shock may be a unique opportunity to experience the presence of God, and to find, with Jesus and through Jesus, a more intense experience of life and love, as an interior necessity that asserts itself when one loses one's certitudes, defenses, and one's own paltry capacities. Pray unceasingly."[18]

His second-to-last editorial, which he wrote when no one knew what had happened to the seven Trappist monks kidnapped a few months earlier, ends with a summary of the difficult mission that Pierre Claverie believed to be his:

> Our lives are suspended together with theirs in the unbearable anticipation of decisions that are beyond our control. Under these conditions, holding on to our confidence instead of becoming discouraged, maintaining hope instead of giving up, not permitting our love to be extinguished in spite of the fury in our hearts, desiring peace and building it up in tiny steps, refusing to join the chorus of howls, and remaining free while yet in chains...isn't all this a form of living in the Spirit?[19]

In the light of such statements one understands better what sort of audience the editorials of *Le Lien* had gained, well beyond the diocese of Oran and the church of Algeria. For Pierre Claverie, this was an eminent form of preaching.

## "Le Livre de la foi" and "Le Livre des passages"

Pierre Claverie didn't do much writing on elaborately researched long works boasting scholarly bibliographies. He did exert himself to complete a translation of Averroës. He worked on two other longer works, only one of which would be published, and that after his death.

*Le Livre de la foi* (The Book of Faith) is the result of an effort spanning a number of years, undertaken by the bishops of the Maghreb. Their intention was to provide the Christians living in that particular context, not an exhaustive presentation of the Catholic faith (as found in the *Catechism of the Catholic Church*), but a "practical tool" that would help them reflect on their Christian experience in the Maghreb. The context of Islam prompted a special examination of the issue of revelation and the Word of God in the Christian tradition (which provided the book's subtitle). According to Henri Teissier, Pierre Claverie "played a decisive role in this work, directing the groups that wrote the various chapters and overseeing the final draft."[20] Claverie's personal archives contain a wealth of preparatory notes, including, for example, twenty handwritten pages on *Unicité et monothéisme* by Stanislas Breton, or detailed analyses of works by Paul Beauchamp and André Manaranche. The method chosen for preparing *Le Livre de la foi* was to hold discussions on the various topics in the dioceses of the Maghreb, and to compile the comments and suggestions for further synthesis. An examination of Pierre Claverie's files reveals the various stages of the book's development, which occupied him a good deal from 1988 to 1991. After seeking a publisher for some time, the bishops of Algeria reached an agreement with Éditions du Cerf, which announced the book's publication in the summer of 1996. Pierre Claverie personally oversaw the finalization of the book, which was published in September of 1996, a few weeks after his death.

From 1992 to 1994, Pierre Claverie worked on a volume entitled *Le Livre des passages* (The Book of Journeys), referred to more simply as *Le Livre*. This was commissioned by Éditions du Centurion, which had begun a collection entitled *Le chêne de Mambré* ("The oak of Mamre"; see Genesis 13:18, 18:1, 23:19). The idea behind the collection was to gather around a single topic (Abraham, prayer, forgiveness, compassion, etc.) three voices from the three monotheistic religions: Judaism, Christianity, and Islam. Asked to write about the theme of "the Book" from the point of view of Christian theology, Claverie accepted and went to work. In 1992, he received some pages from Monique Lise-Cohen on the Jewish approach, and submitted his own contribution in March of 1994. His section ran to seventy pages, arranged in five chapters: (1) "Jesus Christ, the Word of God"; (2) "Origins and patriarchs"; (3) "Kings, sages, and prophets"; (4) "Gospel and gospels"; and (5) "Contemporary interpretations and encounters."

His contribution was accompanied by an introduction of ten pages. "Living in a Muslim country," he wrote, "we feel more intensely the uniqueness of the relationship that connects us with our sacred books. While the Qur'an presents itself as THE book revealed by a prophet who was its sole and faithful transmitter, I find myself the heir of a veritable library that took a millennium to develop, and the finalization of which in the form of 'canons' is relatively recent."[21]

François Chavanes, who found and examined this unpublished document, emphasizes the density of the manuscript and draws attention to Pierre Claverie's conclusion: the main function of the gospel is to transform the disciples of Jesus into a "living gospel" — "The creative and liberating word that took form with Jesus Christ, and then in the scriptures, does not cease to embody itself in those who live by his Spirit. What they present to their contemporaries is a living gospel."[22]

Why was this called *Le Livre des passages*? Claverie explains in the opening pages:

The Bible could have been called "The Book of Journeys." Isn't the central event, the original experience around which the history and the religious memory of Israel is based — isn't this the exodus from Egypt and the journey to meet God at Sinai? The Passover celebration that commemorates this journey would become the key of the messianic message of Jesus: "go forth... go..." From Abraham to Moses, and then with Jesus, the same injunction urges a departure toward an unattainable destination, a promised land that always disappears from view, because the fulfillment of the promises always leads to a renewal of the journey, the final journey being that of death, the encounter "with unveiled face." For Christians, the Bible becomes the overture to the never-ending symphony that we ourselves write with no guide other than the inspiration, the harmony, that we follow.

Did Claverie himself consider his text as unfinished? He never spoke of it to anyone, and it was only after his death, with the discovery of three diskettes labeled *Le Livre,* that it became known that he had begun this work. The work was never published, because the collection *Le chêne de Mambré* was canceled by Éditions du Centurion in 1994 due to financial problems. Claverie's friend Redouane Rahal had been asked to write about the Muslim approach.

Pierre Claverie's other written texts followed his many public addresses during his last years.[23] Special mention should be made of his contribution at the conference *Monoteismo e conflitto* (Monotheism and Conflict) held in Naples in December of 1995. His contribution, entitled *Les derniers et le règne de l'homme,*[24] is a good summary of what Pierre Claverie intended to be: a witness, rather than a writer or an expert. This was his way of remaining faithful to his vocation as a preaching friar.

## A Taste for Fraternity

Pierre Claverie loved to refer back to what a superior of the Dominican order once told him humorously: "There are two ways to leave the order: get married, or become a bishop." And Claverie added, "whatever the case may be with marriage, I have never had the impression of having left the order, but rather of accomplishing to a certain extent what the order had prepared me for."[25] He was, we have seen, a preacher. He was, moreover, very fond of fraternity, the spirit of which is so strong among the sons of St. Dominic. During his years in Algiers, the little community on rue Didouche-Mouraud was for him a place of relaxation and trust. During times of difficulty, Jean-Pierre Voreaux and François Chavanes, who were older than himself, were faithful companions who provided good advice. As bishop he took every chance he could to spend time with his Dominican brothers. These occasions included many ordinations of young friars to the diaconate and the priesthood, in France or Belgium. He ordained at least twenty friars from 1982 to 1995. Pierre did not conceal his joy on these occasions: "I always feel very close to you in the service I have taken on," he said in October of 1983. "This is not only because of the memories that it evokes, but also, and for better reason, because of the decisive bond that our apostolic religious vocation constitutes, our common service of the Word of God and of the faith of our brothers."[26] He took special pleasure in ordaining brothers who were destined for the Arab world, from Iraq to Egypt to Algeria, and he seized the opportunity to invite his brothers not to forsake his country, Algeria.[27] These Dominican reunions provided him with a platform to talk about his Algerian church and this very special mission of presence in the Muslim world. On these occasions, he gave very well-attended conferences at Froidmont (1990), Lille (1992), Lyon (1993), Montpellier (1995), and Paris (1996). The newsletters of the Dominican provinces gave these contributions substantial publicity, and one might say that his brothers repaid in full the affection that he had for them. In June of 1994, I accompanied Fr. Timothy Radcliffe, master of the Dominican order, who had come to visit Claverie for two days in Oran. The roads were already unsafe at certain hours of the day, but Pierre Claverie himself drove us to Ghazaouet, Tlemcen, and Tounane, where we were happy to meet with the Dominican Sisters of the Presentation. Father Timothy returned to Oran for Pierre Claverie's funeral, and one can say that his death, or more precisely the witness of giving his life, made him one of the most remarkable contemporary figures for his brothers and sisters in the order of St. Dominic.

Pierre Claverie had another opportunity to immerse himself in the fellowship of other Dominicans: the pilgrimage of the rosary in Lourdes, where he was the featured preacher in 1991. This pilgrimage gathers together, at the beginning of October, more than forty thousand people and at least one hundred and fifty Dominican friars who come to hear confessions, accompany the sick, and make themselves available to families. The theme of this eighty-third pilgrimage of the rosary was "Priests, Servants of Hope." One finds in his homilies at that time the themes that would constitute his central points of reference during times of trial:

Instead of sinking into meaninglessness and despair, Calvary and the sign of the cross will become the source of reconciliation and hope. This is the reconciliation God offers to his shattered creation and to a humanity that has gone astray: God comes to restore the covenant, and offers himself in order to restore all things in their right order. He restores justice between himself and creation, which finds in this the source of its life. When Jesus was plunged into injustice, suffering, and death, he did not struggle like someone without hope: he bore within himself the peaceful strength that comes from trust.[28]

Pierre Claverie's words resonated in a special way with his confreres: "We need powerful words," he said in his concluding homily, "words that shake us up and rouse us from our lukewarmness...We have the duty of proclaiming Jesus Christ by recalling the duties of justice and truth." For Pierre Claverie, the time for an even more radical form of commitment was coming. His last trip outside of Algeria, six weeks before his death, took him to Prouilhe and Fanjeaux, where St. Dominic founded his order, after years of trial and of the apparent failure of his preaching. We will revisit this event, which had a special significance for him.

All of this helps us understand better how, as a bishop, he remained a religious and a preaching friar, not out of chauvinism, but because the order of St. Dominic was the venue where he had the foundational experiences of his life, the community where his "true personal adventure began." He was at home here, among others who recognized him as their own.

## Chapter Eight

# Muslim-Christian Dialogue
## An Original Approach

> Today, the touchstone of my faith is dialogue. This is not for
> strategic or opportunistic reasons, but because dialogue is an
> integral part of the relationship between God and human beings,
> and of human beings' relationship with one another.[1]
>
> — Pierre Claverie

Pierre Claverie's approach to Muslim-Christian dialogue was rather personal. True to his straightforward way of speaking, he never concealed his reservations and sense of irritation in regard to the official talks dedicated to Muslim-Christian dialogue, and to the ambiguities maintained by those who specialized in this field. As a young theologian, he was invited to participate as an observer at a conference in Tripoli in February of 1976, but the invitation sent from Rome reached him — the day after its conclusion! He was immediately disappointed, and all the more so because, as he confided at the time, "the Christian delegation was less than brilliant." It had, in effect, been led into a trap. Later on, he would decline this sort of invitation, preferring the dialogue of daily life or exchanges based upon real mutual trust.

## The Mixed Results of "Organized Dialogue"

The expression *dialogue organisé* (organized dialogue) was advanced by Fr. Maurice Borrmans, a renowned scholar of Islamic studies who played an important role in the history of Muslim-Christian relations. The Catholic Church made a decisive shift in this area with the Second Vatican Council. In its Declaration on Religious Freedom (*Dignitatis Humanae*), the council solemnly proclaimed the need to respect every person's freedom of conscience, because everyone should be free to respond to God and seek the truth. *Nostra Aetate*, the council document on the church's relations with non-Christian religions, went farther in declaring that the Catholic Church "rejects nothing of what is true and holy in these religions. She has a high regard for the manner of life and conduct, the precepts and doctrines which, although differing in many ways from her own teaching, nevertheless often reflect a ray of that truth which enlightens all men."[2] While still maintaining that the church remains "bound to proclaim without fail, Christ who is the way, the truth and the life,"[3] the council opened new perspectives on interreligious dialogue. It even sketched out a blueprint for this in relation to the Islamic faith: over the course of the centuries, "many quarrels and dissensions have arisen between Christians and Muslims. The Council now calls on all to forget the past, and urges that a sincere effort be made to achieve mutual understanding; for the benefit of all men, let them together preserve and promote peace, liberty, social justice, and moral values."[4] *Lumen Gentium,* one of the other great documents of Vatican II, went even farther in recognizing that the Spirit speaks "outside of the visible confines"[5] of the church. This, by the way, was the passage that Cardinal Duval loved to quote.

It was to foster dialogue in mutual respect that Paul VI created, at the end of the council in 1964, a Secretariat for Non-Christians. In 1988, it was renamed the Pontifical Council for Interreligious Dialogue, and it included a commission on Islam. Both the secretariat and the pontifical council were made up of around forty bishops, who were assisted by a number of specialist consultants. The mission of this group was to ensure that dialogue with the members of other religions "take place in an appropriate manner," through studies and meetings "aimed at mutual understanding and respect, so that, through common effort, the dignity of human beings and their spiritual and moral values may be advanced."[6] There had already been contacts between Christians and Muslims for many years: in 1926, in Tunis, the Institute of Arabic Literature (IBLA) run by the White Fathers had initiated collaboration on a cultural level; more recently, the Center for Economic and Social Studies (CERES) of the University of Tunis, under the direction of M. Boudhiba, had taken the initiative of sponsoring Muslim-Christian discussions on concrete topics like the challenges of development, human rights, and so forth. Similar initiatives were begun in Libya, Egypt, and Jordan, but they dealt with social challenges as often as they did with religious or theological topics, the conceptual focus of which remained unclear.[7] This is why the impulse provided by Vatican II was so important, and in 1971, the Secretariat for Non-Christians published a document entitled *Orientations pour un dialogue entre chrétiens et musulmans* (Orientations for Dialogue between Christians and Muslims), which was updated several times by the pontifical council that succeeded it.[8]

The first major Muslim-Christian discussions dealing with specifically religious topics were held in Cordoba in 1974, in Tripoli in 1976, and then again in Cordoba in 1977. The discussions in Tripoli brought together around three hundred and fifty Muslims and one hundred and fifty Christians from fifty-five countries, at the invitation of the Socialist Arab Union and the Secretariat for Non-Christians. These discussions had their points of interest, but they also demonstrated that in spite of the best intentions there was no common language or common understanding of essential terms like "revelation" and "prophet." Some people who had little interest in real dialogue took advantage of this to try to claim that the other side had "surrendered." For example, the question of the "recognition" of Muhammad as a prophet was a constant preoccupation for some of the Muslim participants who were overly fond of exploiting an unfortunate comment made by Archbishop Grégoire Haddad during the concluding session. The overly politicized context created by the tumultuous Colonel Qaddafi led the Holy See to issue a clarification, expressing its "consternation."[9] The local meetings were often better, because they involved people who had real relationships of friendship and mutual respect. This was the case in Tunis, where in 1977 the Muslim-Christian Research Group (GRIC) was founded under the direction of Fr. Robert Caspar and professor Abelmadjid Cherfi, and in Rabat, where the La Source Center had for years organized meetings with Moroccan intellectuals in a real climate of dialogue.[10] There were few initiatives of this sort in Algeria, or at least few that were long lasting.[11]

After he was made a bishop, Pierre Claverie was appointed a member of the Pontifical Council for Interreligious Dialogue in 1987. He participated in three plenary assemblies — in 1990, 1992, and 1995 — where he was appreciated for the soundness of his reflection and his openness, as testified to by Cardinal Arinze and Bishop Fitzgerald, at that time the president and secretary of the pontifical council, respectively. He happily met with the bishops living in other Muslim countries, like Indonesia and Pakistan, but also with those living among Buddhists and Hindus. But he quickly displayed an original approach in regard to Muslim-Christian dialogue, as shown in five editorials published in *Le Lien* in 1985 and reprinted in 1986 in the bulletin of the Pontifical Council for Interreligious Dialogue, under the title "Chemins du dialogue islamo-chrétien."[12] This writing displays Pierre Claverie's plain speech, which does not exclude cordiality and even admiration toward people, but departs from the sometimes excessively complacent statements made by some "specialists" in dialogue. In his eyes, these specialists entertained ambiguity and sacrificed some of the truthfulness of the encounter under the pretext of not giving offense, or of doing everything possible to create a favorable environment. But it must be said that the context for dialogue in Algeria is unique.

## The Increasingly Polemical Situation in Algeria

Unlike other Muslim countries, contemporary Algerian Islam does not have access to a great intellectual tradition of its own, as is the case, for example, around Al-Azhar university in Cairo or at the Zitouna in Tunis. Colonization certainly played a role in this leveling of the Muslim intelligentsia, but the policies put in place after independence did not improve the situation. In effect, popular Algerian Islam, which was highly concentrated in the *zaouïas* and fraternities, was damaged by the official socialist ideology. Instead of respecting the traditional, peaceful Islam of the majority of the Algerian population, a headstrong reformist politics contributed to "uprooting traditional popular Islam and corrupting it through ideology."[13] We have already evoked the hasty Arabization entrusted to backward instructors coming from the Middle East. The modernization of Islam was not conducted any better: seminars of Islamic thought were organized regularly in the country, and some of the speakers did nothing but blast the cultural aggression that they ascribed to the West, always linking it to Christianity. There was more of politics than of religion in this. Xenophobia was instilled in children under the pretext of anti-imperialism, and under the guidance of officials who were careful to have their own children educated in the French school in Algiers, or in Switzerland. The press regularly echoed the diatribes against proselytism, of which the Christians, associated with the Crusades, were thought to be guilty. Cases of conversion from Christianity to Islam were lauded, as were those works that "demonstrated" the superiority of Islam over other religions.[14] In spite of its relative openness, the weekly newspaper *Algérie-Actualité* published an article by a professor at the Institute of Islamic Studies of the University of Algiers in which he claimed that every person of intelligence and good will could do nothing other than acknowledge the excellence of the law of the Qur'an, "the incomparable Book that stands as a monument among the various philosophies and political, economic, and cultural doctrines."[15] Such was the atmosphere. One of the official preachers, Sheikh Al-Ghazâli, never missed a chance when he was on television to ridicule Christianity, going so far as to declare that "Mother Teresa of Calcutta and Sister Emmanuelle of Cairo are Islam's worst enemies." These remarks were excessive, of course, and they didn't convince anyone, but little by little they crept into the hearts of simple people who were hardly prepared to sort them out. Pierre Claverie was well informed of what was going on, because he had real Muslim friends. So for example, after meeting with Sheikh Bentounès of the *zaouïa* of Mostaganem, he wrote:

He received me with great kindness, and said that it was his great honor to receive, for the first time since independence, a visit from a Christian leader. A young man of thirty years at the most, this spiritual leader is of an extraordinary spiritual depth, and is at the same time open to the best that the other religious traditions can bring. The essence of his approach is universal love. A Muslim to the core, he is an exemplar of an Islam of dialogue and fraternity... We will certainly see each other again. I feel a great affinity for men of his character. (letter of December 27, 1982)

But the drumbeat of the media created unrest: could there be dialogue without mutual respect and the acceptance of the "other" in spite of their differences? This was the thrust of a series of editorials in 1985 in which the bishop of Oran gave the broad outline of his thinking on dialogue: mutual respect as a condition; the absolute need for reciprocity; the requirement for everyone to enter into dialogue by "accepting that it begins from a basic attitude of inquiry" and openness to differences. Citing the Tunisian intellectual Mohamed Talbi, Pierre Claverie concludes: "So it is not a matter of seeking comforting solutions at any price, out of a pure spirit of conciliation. Dialogue, in the context that interests us, is not a form of politics, or of the art of compromise. It is placed on a higher plane. It presupposes total sincerity, and in order to be fruitful it demands that each person be completely himself [or herself], without aggression or compromise."[16]

Unfortunately, the situation in Algeria would deteriorate even further. In 1988, during the evening of the three days of Ramadan before 'Id al-Fitr, Algerian television aired during prime time a debate called "the great controversy" (*Al Munadhara-l-Kubra*): it was a montage created from a discussion between a Muslim firebrand of South African origin, Ahmed Didât, and an American televangelist, Jimmy Swaggart, who was presented to the viewing audience as "an author and a leading American specialist in Judaeo-Christian religion."[17] Public opinion and the Algerian press were carried away by this spectacle in which Christianity came off as ridiculous: "Exhilarating," read the headline in *Horizons*; "Victory over deceit," added *Al Jumhurryya*, the Arabic-language newspaper of Oran. It should be mentioned that the "specialist in Judaeo-Christian religion" is a notorious huckster, one of those North American fundamentalists without any real biblical or theological training who nevertheless agree to debate, without clarification, classical charges such as the falsification of the scriptures that is attributed to Christians, or falsehoods concerning Jesus, which claim that he cannot be simultaneously the son of God and the son of Mary. Pierre Claverie's Muslim friends were embarrassed:

"In our gatherings for the feast, we talked a lot about these broadcasts," one of his close friends confided to him, "obviously to condemn the spirit in which they were conducted, but the evil has been done." Claverie wrote, indignant and determined to respond: "If only Algeria would not let itself be carried away by the current that too many Arab countries unfortunately find themselves in today! In any case, I have firmly decided to fight so that the atmosphere of coexistence among Christians and Muslims will not deteriorate further: if necessary, I will appeal to the new League of Human Rights in Algeria" (letter of May 22, 1988). In fact, he wrote to the head of radio and television in Algeria "as the bishop of Oran, and in this capacity responsible for the Christian community in the west of the country, together with the archbishop of Algiers." Here are some excerpts from his letter:

> For us Christians who have lived in Algeria for many years, and have long lived with the Algerian people in an atmosphere of cooperation and respectful, peaceful, even fraternal coexistence, it is a great trial to be treated as imposters for believing that God had revealed himself in Jesus, that the gospel is truly the Word of God, and so forth...The very nature of the debate hardly allowed one to seek the truth with serenity...Do you believe that the truth is advanced by this unequal, deceptive, and manipulated contest?...I have too much respect for Algeria and Algerian Muslims not to become indignant at such propaganda, even though it did originate in the Middle East. I am afraid that the policy of the media is creating in this country a climate similar to that which is now expressing itself in the bloody conflicts between believers to whom God, in his mercy, revealed his desire for peace. Does it not say in the Qur'an, "Speak with the People of the Book only in the most courteous manner" (*Al-Ankabut sura,* v. 46)? We did not recognize in the manner of Sheikh Didât what our Algerian friends have accustomed us to expect. (letter of May 19, 1988)

Claverie received only a convoluted reply, but he had the unstinting support of his friends in Oran, and his letter was printed in its entirety by the June 9 edition of the weekly magazine *Algérie-Actualité,* which also opened its columns to a number of complaints sent in by Muslims. Cardinal Duval congratulated him for his "firm yet respectful" letter. More than just a passing incident, Claverie saw in this affair a disturbing sign of the growth of intolerance in Algeria.[18] Regrettably, the future would prove him right. Some of his Muslim friends already shared in his disquiet. One can thus say that his reaction was not dictated solely by the desire to defend the existence of the church in Algeria: what he was engaged in was a struggle on behalf of a pluralistic society.

## A First: A Bishop Delivers an Address at the Mosque of Paris[19]

In December of the previous year, Claverie had the surprise of receiving a visit from the vice-rector of the Mosque of Paris, M. Missoum, who had come to issue an official invitation on behalf of the rector, Sheikh Abbas, to deliver an address at the Mosque of Paris. "What a surprise!" he was to say. In the course of making arrangements, he discovered that Muslim friends of his from Oran had suggested this to the Sheikh. Their meeting was "very cordial," and Claverie felt that his guest had "a desire to confront the Islamists." In effect, Islam barely had a visible presence in France, in spite of the number of Muslims who were either naturalized French citizens or living in France. Being constrained to a de facto underground existence in basements and abandoned warehouses, French Islam was in danger of falling to the fundamentalists, a risk that Sheikh Abbas himself could see. This led to his idea of opening up a discussion in order to dispel prejudices, and letting a bishop speak in a mosque was an innovative step. Sheikh Abbas was a truly enlightened Muslim who had been born in Mila in Algeria and had joined the Mouvement des oulémas in 1938, after studying at the Zitouna in Tunis and at the Qarawiyyine of Fes in Morocco. President of the Supreme Islamic Council in Algeria from 1966 to 1970, he was a gracious and open-minded reformer with a twofold task as rector of the mosque of Paris: to reassure the French about the intentions of the Muslims, and to open up the Muslims in France to a dialogue with the Christian churches, and even with Judaism. "We need a leadership composed of theologians and thinkers who can expand upon the elements of tolerance and progress in our religion. At the moment, we are burdened with self-proclaimed experts who are actually the most ignorant men in the world," Sheikh Abbas had declared in a recent interview.[20]

After checking with the archdiocese of Paris and with the Secretariat for Relations with Islam, the office of the French church in charge of such matters, Claverie accepted the invitation, and the event was scheduled for June 15, 1988. It was a good opportunity for him, because he had a lot on his mind and intended to set matters straight in the cordial but plain-spoken style that he always employed. His friend Rahal accompanied him from Oran. Here is the account that Claverie gave of the event just after the fact:

An esteemed company was waiting for me and Rahal: the admirable old sage and rector Sheikh Abbas, a man of openness and great spiritual depth; Missoum, who comes from Oran, always extremely kind; and Ghaouti Sari, a man of no slight intellectual stature and very friendly as well. There were others with them. We had tea and spoke for a while. Then there was the conference in a room filled to capacity (250 persons). There were Muslims of all nationalities, and also Christians (one-third of those present). It goes without saying that I was a bit hesitant at the outset. The debate was perfect: it showed the tensions that are inevitable with this sort of "dialogue," but it was always conducted with courtesy, and above all with a sense of balance that began with the audience itself, the more tolerant among them calming the more agitated (who were few in number anyway). It lasted for three hours. Present were Radio France Internationale, Radio Orient, and other broadcasters with illegible logos on their microphones, *Le Monde*, *L'Actualité religieuse*, etc. Archbishop Grégoire Haddad, a longtime friend who is very close to the Palestinians and even more to all of the downtrodden in the Middle East (he was living through the Israeli bombings of West Beirut in 1982 the last time I met him) was passing through Paris and made a point of coming to the conference, as did other noteworthy figures. All in all, it went very well... I met once more with the conference organizers, and while some of the participants gathered at a conference table, I returned exhausted to Saint-Jacques, in the company of Sari, the president of the Union of World Religions for Peace. A door has been opened, and I believe that it will remain open and allow others to pass through. (letter of June 19, 1988)

This echo of a spontaneous optimism says something about Pierre Claverie's outlook, about his trust in his Muslim friends, about his commitment in the battle against intolerance that he intended to fight together with them. A more complete understanding of this event can be gained from the accounts of some of the other participants, as well as a more thorough assessment written by the bishop of Oran himself, probably drafted for the Pontifical Council for Interreligious Dialogue or to the nunciature.[21] Here is an excerpt from Claverie's more polished account:

In his introduction, delivered in Arabic, Sheikh Abbas insisted upon the necessity for dialogue among the revealed religions in order to ensure peace in the world and spiritual development on par with scientific progress. He presented Islam as a religion of tolerance and dialogue, rejecting the caricatures of it that are often made, but recognizing the Muslims' share of responsibility for such representations. He reiterated that Islam includes all revelations that came before it, and that, in his opinion, it is therefore capable of unlimited openness toward others.

Claverie also delivered the introduction to his remarks in Arabic, and then gave the address in French. The outline of his talk will be provided in the next section. The debate was long, and at times difficult: "The very idea of the process of dialogue seemed incomprehensible to many of the Muslim participants," he commented. And then, beyond the pious assertions of Islam's inherent concern for tolerance, "the questions revealed a great difficulty in understanding and accepting diversity." But Pierre Claverie added in his evaluation, "the contributions from Sheikh Abbas and his colleagues, as well as those of some participants who were familiar with Muslim-Christian dialogue (including Rahal, from Oran; Sari and Sellam, of Paris; and Archbishop Haddad) fortunately contributed to clarifying the meaning of this, and to maintaining the serenity of the encounter." And in conclusion: "It was a dangerous exercise, but perhaps it was not fruitless in permitting Muslims to hear the voice of another person and test his good will in their own familiar surroundings."[22]

Some of the smaller incidents are worth mentioning. At a certain point, a young Muslim intellectual was speaking in a polemical vein, and Sheikh Abbas leaned toward Claverie and whispered in his ear, "Don't react. I'll take care of it." Friendship came to the aid of this new and complex exchange of ideas. In some ways, this was just a trial run of dialogue. This "debut" brought other invitations to Claverie, which he evaluated with prudence. Channel 2 proposed the taping of a "dialogue with a Muslim"; he suggested as the other guest Mustapha Cherif, director of studies at the school of journalism in Algiers, author of a very daring doctoral thesis on the relationships between politics and religion in Islam, and future minister of Muslim universities. Claverie wrote, "He is a very spiritual man, from a close-knit family, accustomed to Muslim-Christian dialogue, which he practiced during his years of study in Toulouse. I will only accept if he is the one involved in the discussion, because the risk of a mishap would be too great" (letter of September 8, 1988).

## "Pathways of Muslim-Christian Dialogue"

The address at the Paris mosque, the text of his five editorials from 1985 previously mentioned, and a later conference he gave in Lille in 1992, after the Gulf War, give a detailed and nuanced view of Pierre Claverie's conception of Muslim-Christian dialogue.[23] Here are the five essential points:

### 1. A thorny past marked by controversy and exclusion.

At the outset, Pierre Claverie emphasizes that "dialogue has not always been the rule throughout the history of relations between Christians and Muslims — far from it." On the contrary, "polemics and conflict have dominated." So, true to his straightforward way of speaking, he begins by recognizing the difficulties. Beyond the vicissitudes of history, he says, the fundamental problem is the difficulty of "acknowledging and accepting otherness." This is almost a reflex on the part of any social group: in the presence of the Other, turning back in upon oneself is almost instinctive. Pierre Claverie says little about the details of the difficulties at the Paris conference. He had already done so in his 1985 article, in which he evoked the prohibition against Christians practicing their religion openly in Saudi Arabia, the difficulty African Christians had in being accepted and recognized on the university campuses in Algeria, certain pressures on Christian women married to Muslims, the pressure from militant Islam to make sharia the civil law of societies, etc. "I think we have some difficult days ahead of us," he concluded. But Islam is not the only reality under scrutiny: "Believers are not naturally inclined toward tolerance," because they all feel themselves to be "the bearers of a divine message with a universal, worldwide scope. This is shown by the history of Muslims, Christians, and all those who believe that they carry a message of religious or political salvation." This problem is all the more imposing in that it is the result of past conflicts, of wounds and fears inscribed upon the collective imagination. For the Muslims, Christianity is reduced to the Crusades and their bloodbaths; for the Christians, Islam means the Turkish or Saracen invaders of Europe. These are the historical events that have traumatized the collective unconscious on both sides, creating irrational prejudices and fears that are revitalized during periods of crisis, as during the 1991 Gulf War. The first President Bush had prayers for his armies recited in American churches, and Saddam Hussein had the name of Allah put on his banners. "Images are often simplistic caricatures, and unfortunately it is through their very simplicity and even their simplistic message that they have such a great effect on the crowds."

### 2. In spite of this, there have always been points of contact and communication.

These misconceptions are all the more regrettable because, in spite of the difficulties, the Muslim and Christian worlds have always had trade relationships, diplomatic ties, and "even relationships of friendship and respect." As a son of the Mediterranean, Pierre Claverie proclaimed his love of revisiting those moments when the desire for encounter was stronger on both sides than were their mutual reflexes of exclusion. Examples of this include the exchange of letters in the eleventh century between Pope Gregory VII and Al-Nasir, the Hammadite prince of Bejaia; or the good relations in the twelfth century between the Muslim merchants of Tunis and the traders of Pisa. It is true that these were diplomatic or commercial relationships. When it comes to religion, dialogue quickly turns combative, since "there is no instance of communication and searching for the truth that is completely free from the desire to show the error of others." But there are good examples of theological disputes that were carried out in a climate of respect, like the debate between Patriarch Timotheus I and Caliph Al-Mahdi, held in Baghdad around the year 800, which was recorded in Syriac and translated into Arabic. But the examples of theological disputes aimed at detracting from the opponent are more numerous, and include, for example, the treatises by John Damascene or the *Apologetics* by Al-Kindi. "Inheritors of the faith of Abraham, voyagers on the same terrain of the biblical adventure, it is hard for us to understand why we are different, and why, from the beginning, we have sought to impose our own convictions upon one another, resorting by various means to violence or to social, moral, or economic pressure. And yet we see that we are rather similar and called to the same mission received from the one God, which is not that of prevailing over others, but that of building together a more humane world according to his will."

### 3. A prerequisite: learning to recognize the Other as a subject.

From this Claverie draws the conclusion that it is important to move "toward a religion that does not seek to exclude other forms of belief, but recognizes the Other as a free and responsible subject." And he develops an anthropology of dialogue and of one's relation to the other. According to Martin Buber, "true dialogue exists when each participant is genuinely concerned about others in their being and in their individual characters, and turns to them with the intention of seeing the development of a lively reciprocity." From this point of view, a certain conception of tolerance does not really help in the acknowledgment of the Other, because it is not open to reciprocity. This kind of tolerance is the scope of the *dhimmi* status given to Christians by sharia law. Nor is dialogue a technique of approach, in view of converting the Other, which is not respectful of that person's difference. One must consider the Other for whom he or she is, respect his or her values, be concerned for his or her welfare and even acknowledge that the Other bears a portion of the truth. "I not only accept that the Other is Other, a distinct subject with freedom of conscience, but I accept that he or she may possess a part of the truth that I do not have, and without which my own search for the truth cannot be fully realized." In order for there to be dialogue, "everything must begin from a basic attitude of inquiry," Pierre Claverie repeats, quoting Mohamed Talbi. This is difficult within the context of Muslim-Christian dialogue, since Christianity believes in the exclusivity of salvation in Jesus Christ, and Islam believes that the definitive revelation is found in the prophet Muhammad. So both these religions have their own work to do to make room for the question of the other. And even though Christianity seems to have gotten beyond its desire for conquest and domination, it still has difficulty sometimes understanding that there are other authentic pathways to God. Islam, for its part, tends to disqualify the forms of revelation that came before itself, seeing them as partial and incomplete. The conviction that one possesses the truth impedes dialogue, unless one is willing to join others in facing those questions that are common to all, and which Mohamed Talbi raises by citing *Nostra Aetate*, the conciliar declaration on non-Christian religions: "What is man? What is the meaning and purpose of life? What is upright behavior, and what is sinful? How can genuine happiness be found? . . . And finally, what is the ultimate mystery, beyond human explanation, which embraces our entire existence, from which we take our origin and toward which tend?"[24] And Pierre Claverie adds: "Vatican Council II showed Catholics the way in this area, by recovering an essential feature of the gospel message. We do not own the truth: it is the truth that takes hold of us and leads us to discover itself ever more deeply." We will come back to the theological basis of this assertion later.

### 4. Facing our differences instead of avoiding them.

In order to travel farther down the road of authentic dialogue, it is, he says, important to "take into account the extent of our differences," which has not been done sufficiently in the various forums of Muslim-Christian dialogue. The desire has been instead to minimize the difficulties: "The use of a vocabulary presumed to be held in common might allow one to think that real communication is going on, and dialogue has been achieved. Disappointment is not long in coming . . . Even if it were possible to form friendships, it would still be difficult to understand the Other in terms of the principles of his or her way of life and belief. We have not yet adequately measured the significance of the distance that separates us. We have not yet sufficiently purified our-selves from the desire to dominate the other." Two obstacles have prevented there being any great manifestation of Muslim-Christian dialogue. One is that words are not used with the same meanings: "revelation," "scriptures," "Word of God," and "prophecy" have nowhere near the same significance for both sides. This is the reason why, for example, there has been interest in seeing the GRIC (Muslim-Christian Research Group) carry out more patient stud-ies, outside of the pressure of public opinion. The other obstacle is the partial concealment of these difficulties in order to avoid facing the true extent of our differences and trying to overcome the traditional barriers. "Everyone re-veals only what is likely to please the other, or at least be accepted, and what might raise questions is carefully hidden away." But this mistaken form of ec-umenism does nothing to foster encounter and progress. The Christians keep repeating that they believe in one God, but they cannot hide the fact that the Triune God is an essential element of their creed. "Concealing this exposes us to disappointment and drags us down into fruitless arguments. The truth is essential to encounter, but it can be manifested only in an atmosphere of mutual trust and respect."

### 5. An immediate requirement: creating an atmosphere of friendship and trust.

So the first thing to do is to work to establish this mutual respect and trust. At this point in his analysis, Pierre Claverie presents the efforts of the church in Algeria since the country's independence. This effort was guided by Cardinal Duval, who in his teaching frequently quoted a saying of Saint Augustine, himself an Algerian bishop: "Fraternal love is both the first and the last step along the way to the love of God." The church lives its vocation only by stepping out of itself, and it likewise calls all persons to the encounter with the other. This is also the teaching of the council: "The joy and hope, the grief and anguish of the men of our time, especially of those who are poor or afflicted in any way, are the joy and hope, the grief and anguish of the followers of Christ as well. Nothing that is genuinely human fails to find an echo in their hearts."[25] This is the meaning, Pierre Claverie comments, of the commitment of Christians in Algeria for human development and advancement, with a special regard for the poorest and the oppressed. In another text, he speaks with Mohammed Arkoun of "taking up, together, the tasks of our lives and our societies." In sharing together daily life with its joys and sufferings, in praying for each other on the occasion of religious holidays, in fighting together for human rights and the dignity of all, Christians and Muslims can reestablish trust little by little. But "dialogue has hardly started," because "the old demons of polemics, the domination of the Other, and the exclusion of those who are different are constantly renewed from their own ashes." And Pierre Claverie concludes, "Reciprocity is an important element of the trust that must be established among our various groups... We must be simultaneously realistic and truthful, just and fraternal, without ever becoming discouraged."

These are the main points of the conference at the Paris mosque, which can also be found with a variety of nuances in his earlier or later writings on dialogue. Beginning in 1991, Claverie greatly stressed the power of the old clichés that the Gulf War had helped to revive. As for the text from 1985, it ended with this beautiful conclusion borrowed from Mohamed Talbi:

> The apostolate, purified from quarreling and proselytism... becomes, in this perspective, essentially an attentive openness to the Other, a constant search for the truth through the continual deepening and interiorization of the values of faith, and — finally — pure witness... This is to say that the best form of apostolate is the witness of a soul that has won the battle for moral perfection. This is the only fruitful form of the apostolate, and the only one that is compatible with our age. And it can be done without proselytism.[26]

## An Urgent Need: Creating the Conditions for Dialogue

Over the following years Claverie would focus his activity on the last point of his vision: facing, side by side with the Algerians, the challenges to the human person and human dignity. His reservations in regard to "organized dialogue" did not mean that he was uninvolved. On the contrary, he loved to repeat, "We do not yet have the words we need for dialogue; we must begin by creating human connections through which we share with one another the greatness of our cultural heritage." This is what he sought to do, in a variety of ways, during those years in which he saw the growth of "radical Islamism" in Algeria.

One of these ways was reflection, as shown in the writings already quoted and in some other lesser-known works that display the same concerns.[27] In April of 1986, he had given a major speech to the French Institute in The Hague, on the theme "The church and human rights."[28] On that occasion, Mohamed Bedjaoui, a judge at the international tribunal of The Hague and a former Algerian ambassador, had introduced Bishop Claverie in glowing terms that testified to the distinguished reputation he had earned. The conference displayed once more his great forthrightness:

> I admit that I hesitated greatly before accepting the invitation addressed to me ... You know as well as I that on account of its history, the Catholic Church has good reason to remain modest, if not completely silent, on the issue of the defense and promotion of human rights. The church's far too numerous violations of justice and its lack of respect for the dignity of persons, cultures, and other religions (however these may have been justified), are very fresh in the memory of those who suffered them. Even though individual Christians raised their voices to call attention back to the essential gospel message, collectively and as an institution the church helped to sustain a form of power in which it is difficult even today to distinguish political from religious motivations.

Having said this, Claverie added that he remained loyal to his church, because "in the twists and turns of this rather inglorious history I discern signs of hope, and, even better, a solid foundation for work on behalf of human rights." He then explained how the Christian conception of the human person gradually led Christians to adopt a critical attitude toward the powers of this world. He acknowledged that this was a laborious process, because the church has always oscillated "between emphasis on an ideal society that should not be confused with the kingdom of God promised by Jesus, and emphasis on a respect for persons that is in no way confused with the laws of this society." What he is speaking of here is the relationship between faith and politics present throughout church history from the time of Constantine until the present, with all of its progress and setbacks. Apart from his rather technical discussion of this matter, it is interesting to see Pierre Claverie wrestling with the same questions that were being posed at the time in Algeria. This gave rise to bonds of friendship with Algerians who were fighting for human rights, and to whom he would be loyal during times of trial.

His involvement was not only theoretical: through activities in the church of Algeria and his diocese, Bishop Claverie also worked to increase the opportunities for Christians and Muslims to confront common challenges together. So the church in Algeria began to dedicate its energies to serving the needs of the country: creating libraries for students and researchers, rehabilitation centers for the handicapped, facilities for educating women, etc. Establishing these "platforms of encounter and service," as he called them, engaged much of Claverie's energy and attention. He found great joy in doing this, because the service of human dignity seemed to him an intrinsic good. He also expected it to lead to an increase of mutual trust, which he saw as an indispensable condition for interreligious dialogue. With the difficulties that Algeria would face during the 1990s, his efforts would become increasingly practical, almost militant, side by side with his Algerian friends.

This original approach to dialogue has great potential, because it leads to what Fr. Marie-Dominique Chenu called "*intrareligious* dialogue": if each person enters into dialogue from a stance of inquiry, if one is convinced of the necessity of walking side by side with the Other, one is led not to relativize one's faith, but to deepen it "by integrating the truth perceived in the other religion." If one considers well, Christianity offers an encounter with a God who "stripped himself to become like human beings." Over the course of the years, Pierre Claverie would intensify this element in his theological reflection, but above all in his own spiritual life (this will be the subject of the next chapter).

## Requesting Algerian Citizenship

It is interesting to note that it was during this period that Pierre Claverie began the process of trying to obtain Algerian citizenship. In 1965, citizenship had been granted to Cardinal Duval and to about twenty priests and religious who had requested it, wanting to show by this gesture their solidarity with the new Algeria that was being formed. At that time, the young Pierre Claverie had mentioned to his parents the possibility of his asking for dual citizenship, but he was not yet ready to take this step. "Why choose this year?" he wrote on January 21, 1965. "Later I might get naturalized and lose my French citizenship at the same time. But I am not there yet." When did he make the request for the first time? It was probably after he was appointed bishop of Oran, but there are no exact records, and the bishop rarely referred to the matter, and quickly sidestepped it when it came up in conversation. It is uncomfortable to be "between the two shores" of the Mediterranean. In any case, his request was "reactivated" by the justice ministry during November of 1987, and he returned on several occasions to the ministry's office in Oran to complete his application. He explained to his father that he was responding to "pressing requests from the authorities and from friends." He was not doing this to simplify the problems created by his passport, but because, as he said, "it seems that Algerian citizenship for church officials is desired both by the Algerians and by the church" (letter of November 22, 1987). He added that the administration responsible for these applications showed him "remarkable cordiality." His application was complete in December of 1987. He wrote, "Now it's all over except the waiting, which I will do patiently, having no intention of bringing in pressure from friends in high places. I will let the Algerian authorities do the work, because they are the ones who have requested this step in recent months" (letter of December 12, 1987).

Pierre Claverie never obtained Algerian citizenship. It doesn't seem that the application was formally refused, but it cannot be maintained that what was involved was simply bureaucratic delay. Could it have been, instead, connected to the fact that the bishop of Oran was becoming, beginning with the crisis of 1988, a public man whose free and courageous positions received great media attention? Without having a definitive answer to this question, one can suppose that his naturalization was no longer to everyone's taste. But in a way this wasn't the essential thing for Claverie.

Claverie had just turned fifty years old at the time of these events. He was at the height of his maturity. He had changed physically, losing the look of the young intellectual with large tortoise-shell glasses and taking on the confident appearance of a mature man entirely engaged in his responsibilities. His remarks were charged with his powerful human experience: the mourning of French Algeria that had driven him to deep interior effort and conversion; his enthusiastic rediscovery of the country of his birth through assiduous study of Arab language and culture, but above all through his Algerian friends; his accompaniment of the Christian community of Algeria on almost all fronts; and now, his engagement in the serious challenges facing his country. His identity was not a matter of a passport — one could now apply to him the words he had addressed to his parents in 1963, with the somewhat heedless but abundant assurance of youth: "Your roots are in the hearts of other people, and not in earth or bricks" (letter or February 23, 1963). Many Algerians, both Christian and Muslim, now considered Pierre Claverie as "among his own"; many of his Algerian friends recognized him as one of them, and in a way he was "their bishop."

## Chapter Nine

# Christians in the "House of Islam"
## From Theological Debate to Witness

> As long as we do not measure the length, breadth, height, depth—the whole extent of the abyss that separates us, we are not ready to acknowledge each other, understand each other, love each other.[1]
> — *Pierre Claverie*

Pierre Claverie loved to emphasize the uniqueness of the Algerian church: it was a minority church in a Muslim country, but its members did not conceal the happiness at being there. It was an unencumbered, simplified church living as a guest in the "house of Islam," because, unlike the Middle East, there is no traditionally Christian local population there. Algeria is a Muslim country that intends to stay that way, and the church there rejects all proselytism. But then the question arises of what the Christians are doing there, especially in difficult times. Beyond the practical aspect of the opportunity to remain there, deep theological questions arise in regard to this Christian presence in a Muslim environment: if God is not asking for these men and women to be led to faith in Jesus Christ, then what is the church's mission? If their own religious tradition can be considered an authentic pathway to God, how can one continue to believe that Jesus is "the sole mediator between God and human beings," as St. Paul says?[2]

These questions linger at the heart of the church of Algeria, and Pierre Claverie addressed them, too. He made his own contribution to reflection on the matter, but he did this more as a pastor involved in his community than as a theologian honing his analyses in articles and conferences. He contributed to shared reflection when consulted by the church's leadership, but what distinguished him most of all was his personal commitment and the risky decisions he deemed necessary to pave the way for the future. It may be this that led to his death, but he liked to say that "since the first centuries of the Christian era, there has never been a lack of witnesses to the gospel in this part of the world."

## The Church of Algeria as a Community in Exodus[3]

Drastic changes marked the life of the Algerian church after the country's independence, and Pierre Claverie experienced them all, since his life was identified with this country. There had been the immense rupture of 1962, with a massive exodus of pieds-noirs leading to the near disappearance of the Christian population in Algeria. The churches were deserted in a matter of months, and some of them were turned into mosques, Islam having become *the* religion of the country. Almost all of the few Algerian Christians remaining eventually decided to leave the country. At the time, Pierre was a young Dominican student at Le Saulchoir, and he felt the brutality of this rupture less than did people like Jean Scotto, who was also a part of the world of the pieds-noirs and experienced this transition up close. For his part, Pierre Claverie participated more in the euphoria directly following the coming of independence. Everything had to be rebuilt after the destruction of the war of liberation, and the vacuum left by the departure of European experts had to be filled in. Great numbers of aid workers came to participate in the reconstruction, and they received real positions of responsibility. For many, this was a chance to put into practice the socialist, third-world, utopian vision that inspired them, following men like Frantz Fanon, the famous fellow traveler along the road of Algeria's revolution. These were the years that saw the publication of *Populorum Progressio,* the encyclical of Pope Paul VI exalting the holistic and interdependent development "of each man and of the whole man." There were many Christians who believed that "changing the world [is] a task for the church," according to Vincent Cosmao's expression.[4] Pierre Claverie took great pleasure in leading the reflection groups that his friend Pierre Frantz had started with them in the parish of El Biar. The enthusiasm of those years made one forget a little that the church was mainly composed of foreigners.

This initial euphoria was quickly replaced by the austere and voluntaristic government of President Houari Boumediene: the country's plans for development still made foreign technical and cultural assistance necessary, but the country increasingly asserted its Arab Muslim personality. But the church retained a strong presence through the Christian aid workers and through a variety of activities (schools, health clinics, etc.). Many priests and religious chose to serve the country directly, and obtained job contracts in education, the medical field, or in the skilled crafts, which made the cardinal remark with a touch of humor, "I'm no longer the one who decides where my priests will serve; the government does that." At that time, Pierre Claverie was the director of the diocesan center of les Glycines in Algiers, where he worked to help the Christians "equip themselves" to live in this new context. He taught Arabic, gave courses in Islamic studies, and made numerous presentations on Algeria's development plans, explaining why it made sense for Christians to participate in this project of human advancement. One expression was often cited in this period: the church did not want to be an "embassy church," but to participate in the life of Algeria.

One significant transformation took place in 1976, with the nationalization of the schools. This measure was not directed against the church, because the government was more concerned about taking control of the Islamic institutions, but for the church it would mean a substantial loss of social presence. This was a veritable crisis, in the course of which Pierre Claverie accompanied several religious congregations that had to make serious adjustments. He did not hide his admiration for these nuns who overnight had to leave their own activities to place themselves at the disposal of the Algerian institutions, with a special fondness for service to the poorest. In spite of their ejection from places of responsibility, the Christians still felt useful to the country, and they lived out their involvement in it as an evangelical service. The stripping down they were forced to endure was even, for them, a sign of fidelity to their vocation as disciples of Christ. But this stripping down was not yet complete: during the 1970s and 1980s, Algeria called upon foreigners less and less, except for specified, short-term technical operations. This led to the departure of most of these families, and it emptied the parishes of their people. Many of the priests and religious saw their labor contracts terminated. The Arab Muslim identity asserted itself more each day, sometimes in a way that was very unpleasant for non-Muslims. The Algerian church became acutely conscious of the fact that its contribution to the country was very marginal, and no longer sufficed to justify its presence. "We are not necessary to Algeria, or rather, we are of only occasional value to it," Henri Sanson wrote at the time, adding "we are sinking deeper into the darkness . . . In this darkness, we feel unusual questions rising up within us: What is Christianity good for?"[5] Pierre Claverie was not insensitive to this slow erosion, but he never displayed regret for the church's loss of influence. A young bishop, he was entirely occupied with his ministry of communion: the majority of Christians in his diocese were foreign workers from the Philippines, Brazil, and Poland, who came by the hundreds to work on dam construction projects or at the petrochemical complex in Arzew, near Oran. He occupied himself above all with cementing relations between the communities of his diocese and the Algerian world. It was apparent that the concrete and daily activity involved in building these bridges engaged him more than did any abstract reflection on the significance of the Christian presence in the country. But he did make his own contributions to this intellectual reflection, through the regional conference of the bishops of North Africa and through the Pontifical Council for Interreligious Dialogue. He distinguished himself in this by his frankness of speech and by his insistence on the need for reciprocity: "Coexistence must be negotiated in complete truth and justice, and with reciprocity of rights and duties."[6]

The decade of the 1990s was a time of trial for the Algerian church, a trial that was also borne by the native Algerians themselves, who were the victims of violence. It was in the heart of this trial that Pierre Claverie best expressed the sort of reflection that came naturally to him. This was a matter not of theological generalities and the endless elaboration of concepts, but of a vital message that was simultaneously human and supernatural, which formed the basis of life and for which one was ready to die, if necessary. Although he belonged to a church that often found itself pushed to the margins of society, he felt that he was a full participant in the challenges facing Algeria. Evoking the crises confronting his community, but also the many gestures of concern made to him by his Algerian friends, he concluded his Christmas letter for 1994 in these words: "For these reasons, and for many others, I am going to stay here. I even find genuine happiness in remaining... There are some who will understand what I mean."[7]

But apart from his personal feelings, he believed that some essential feature of the gospel message was at stake in the unique destiny of the church of Algeria.

## "Christians in the Maghreb: The Meaning of Our Encounters"

Through the various periods of its recent history, the Algerian church was prompted to reflect upon the meaning of its presence in the country, given the new realities facing it.

This church thought of itself first of all as a "local church by virtue of solidarity."[8] Although it was essentially composed of foreigners, the church did not think of itself as a foreign element in the country, because most of its members had freely chosen to associate their own lives with the destiny of Algeria. These were the wonderful years of cooperation, during which the Muslim religious identity was eclipsed by socioeconomic realities that affected Christians to nearly the same extent as they did the Algerians. There was widespread optimism. Inspired by the ecclesiology of Vatican II, which emphasized that the church exists primarily "for the sake of the world," the goal of Algeria's Christians was that of "entering, as human beings and as Christians, in the development of the Algerian people."[9] The fact that their Algerian counterparts were all Muslims was certainly an issue, but this was set aside to some extent. What did it mean for the church to be the sacrament of salvation among a people that intended to remain Muslim? Evoking the dogmatic responses to this question, which were still dominated by the classic approach to mission (in particular, the Vatican II decree *Ad Gentes,* on the church's missionary activity), Henri Teissier, then the bishop of Oran, decried the fact that "unfortunately, the church's overall view of its mission does not always seem to connect with the concrete reality that we live in." For the Christians in this situation, the meaning of their life with and for Algeria was expressed succinctly by Cardinal Duval: "Fraternal love, practiced in truth, is a manifestation of the mystery of God."[10] As a natural optimist, Pierre Claverie spontaneously recognized his place and his role in this vision of the Algerian church.

But the multiplicity of the pathways to God remained a fundamental issue: "Does the church have a mission in our meetings with persons and groups that intend to remain outside of Christianity?" In walking together with others, one discovers more and more how different they are. And Islam resists; it seems almost unshakable in its unique identity. Since it believes itself to be the seal and completion of revelation, it has difficulty in truly entering into dialogue, as Pierre Claverie frequently pointed out. The Christians felt the need for a different interpretation of their presence in the midst of non-Christians, and the idea of "reciprocal conversion" surfaced. This is the era of the publication of the text referred to at the opening of this section, "Chrétiens au Maghreb, le sens de nos rencontres": "Many among us could testify to the 'conversions' to which they have been called through their presence among the people of the Maghreb . . . All of us, Christians and non-Christians, are called to enter into a process of conversion, each one following the particular path specific to each . . . This dynamic could be seen, in spiritual terms, as the place where reciprocal conversion takes place."[11]

This was not a matter of relativizing faith in the salvation of Jesus and of saying simply that all religions are equally valid, but of recognizing that the pathway to God that others follow can contribute to everyone else's spiritual growth. "This reciprocal openness and contact among Christians and non-Christians brings the kingdom of God to earth in as much as one converts oneself in this way to a greater fidelity to God's call," comments Henri Teissier, the principal architect of this text.[12]

Pierre Claverie was already contributing at this time, as a theologian, to the creation of documents for the bishops' conference, under the lead of Bishop Teissier, "a workaholic who brings us all to our knees," he wrote humorously. After "Chrétiens au Maghreb" was finished, Claverie thought it wasn't incisive enough. Being skeptical of syntheses that blurred the reality of differences, he believed it was preferable to acknowledge, right from the beginning, "the abyss that separates us." "Recognizing the existence of the abyss that separates us, whatever its nature may be, means measuring the road we must travel for an eventual encounter. Yes, a great abyss separates us."[13] Claverie would also be called upon to help draft texts as part of the Pontifical Council for Interreligious Dialogue, as he was when work began in 1986 on the text that would be published under the title "Dialogue and Proclamation." This document has a complicated history: in 1984, the Secretariat for Non-Christians had published its "Reflections and Orientations on Dialogue and Mission," a text cited frequently by the short title "Dialogue and Mission."[14] The aim of the document was to explore the issues of the kind of dialogue pursued by the Catholic Church after Vatican II, in the spirit of the conciliar declaration *Nostra Aetate* and of the encyclical *Ecclesiam Suam* by Paul VI, which had been published twenty years earlier. "Dialogue and Mission" revisited classic themes such as "seeds of the Word" (no. 27), but it did not broach the fundamental issue: if the church recognized the validity of other pathways to God, then what was to be made of the assertion that Jesus Christ is the only savior? As soon as they took up this task, the experts of the Pontifical Council for Interreligious Dialogue were forced to include the Congregation for the Evangelization of Peoples, which was responsible for the mission *ad gentes* and insisted upon the duty of proclaiming the gospel. The two groups brought up significantly different issues. Thus four drafts involving a number of years of discussion would be required to reach the final version of "Dialogue and Proclamation," published on June 20, 1991.[15] The text affirmed that "the pilgrim church advances toward the fullness of divine truth in a dialogue of salvation with the believers of other religions, which leads to deeper involvement and to conversion to God." So it followed a positive approach to the other religious traditions, seeking to discern the effects of divine grace and of the action of the Holy Spirit. "Dialogue and proclamation are thus two means of accomplishing the same mission,"[16] concludes this text which, in spite of its meanderings, represented an important step in the evolution of the Catholic Church's reflection on this subject.[17] Pierre Claverie's archives show that he contributed to this reflection, through a variety of notes drafted from 1987 to 1990. A scheduling conflict prevented him from participating in the plenary assembly of the Pontifical Council for Interreligious Dialogue in December of 1987, but he participated in the meeting in the spring of 1990, where he was chosen as the chair of the French-speaking group and the co-chair of the plenary assemblies, and was also charged with supervising the work of the committee that drafted the final document. He had a frontline view of the diversity of approaches, which sometimes resulted in blockage, and he took an interest in the debate: "Almost everything is done in English, poor me! Work continues day and night throughout the week. The atmosphere is excellent" (letter of May 2, 1990).

Nevertheless, there were real tensions, which were due not only to the participation of two Roman dicasteries with different viewpoints, but also to the fundamental difficulty of the problem: "Religious pluralism is a more significant challenge for the Christian faith than modern atheism is," wrote Claude Geffré, whose reflections had a significant impact on Pierre Claverie during that period.

## Islam and the Theology of Non-Christian Religions

Pierre Claverie participated in this laborious debate with his usual frankness, and solicited clarifications right from the start:

It seemed important to me to dispel what weighs so heavily upon interreligious dialogue, that one might imagine that the involvement of intelligence and faith is deliberately limited. Our Muslim counterparts often criticize us for not being entirely ourselves in dialogue, and for using it as a strategy of evangelization. It would simplify things if we were to say clearly that all Christian activity is undertaken in view of evangelization, which would obligate us to understand, live, and explain well, in a spirit of dialogue, what we mean by "evangelization."[18]

In his eyes, dialogue should begin with the partners "making themselves present" to one another. They should be able to take part in the fullness of their convictions and traditions, without concealing their true beliefs in any way. Dialogue, therefore, is not static, with each participant remaining ensconced in his or her positions, or trying to draw the Other into them: "it asserts itself as a quest for divine truth, which one never completely possesses."[19] This presentation of one's genuine beliefs, instead of ideological posturing, is often difficult on account of the burden of history and the clichés held by each side. But if this self-presentation is accomplished in the context of projects stressing interdependence (development, human rights, etc.), the mutual trust and appreciation created allow the counterparts to live out their differences in a climate of respect and to face fundamental issues together.

Thus the Christians living in the Muslim world could not help but consider the place of Islam in the "economy of salvation." The Christians living in Asia, like tiny islands surrounded by seas of Buddhist and Hindu believers for millennia, posed the question in an even more radical form. In all probability, most of these men and women would never come to know Jesus Christ explicitly. But the church has always affirmed that God wants to save all people, and that salvation has been won, once and for all, by Jesus. The question was no longer the classic one of the "salvation of the infidels." It was a matter of understanding the meaning, in the economy of salvation, of these other pathways to God. These are the questions that the document that was being prepared, "Dialogue and Proclamation," intended to reexamine in a new light. Pierre Claverie drafted extensive notes, but his writing shows him taking stock of the issue rather than bringing any genuinely new contribution. Despite his excellent education, he had never specialized in fundamental theology, preferring to remain on the level of the common person (as in his many theological conferences as director of les Glycines) and to focus on preaching (e.g., his editorials for *Le Lien* and his numerous homilies as a bishop). He was more a preacher and a pastor than a theologian. So in this area he basically adhered to an exposition of the subject made by his fellow Dominican Claude Geffré in 1985.[20] In reviewing the theology of the major non-Christian religions, he seems captivated by the idea of "differentiated revelation," as presented by Claude Geffré. For him, the fullness of revelation in Jesus Christ does not exclude the possibility that the fruits of the Spirit of God in the history of other religions could contribute to the complete manifestation of salvation:

> The individual figure of Jesus awaits a universal expansion. "So the church's vocation is properly that of realizing the concrete universality of Christ... We are called, therefore, to pass beyond the narrow ecclesiocentrism that rendered us incapable of discerning the presence of God beyond the visible confines of the church... The church as sacrament of salvation is the sacrament of the presence of God in his various and unexpected forms down through the ages... Our task is not so much that of discounting the differences of the other religions and trying to

bring them to Christianity, but of bringing their seeds of holiness to the true God, toward whom they tend eschatologically.[21]

Pierre Claverie adopted this idea without seeking to go any deeper. What may have been new in his approach was his interest in the work undertaken by certain Muslim scholars, notably Mohammed Arkoun, who was prompted to consider the meaning of the various religions and the economy of salvation outside of dogmatic formulations, "because it is in their historical origins that the religious creeds take on meaning and value," Arkoun wrote.[22] What were the meanings of the unicity of God, of prophecy and salvation? These fundamental concepts have a history that ought to be better known: one could reason, for example, that the Muslim insistence on the unicity of God was a response to the debates between Jews and Christians from the fifth to the seventh century. The assertions of the Qur'an, like those of other religions, should be placed back within their context — only recourse to history can resolve the stalemate of dogmatic positions that prevent any real dialogue from taking place. "In this way," Pierre Claverie adds, "the words that too often trip up our dialogue will regain their original heft and their true significance." A plan for an entire line of work was suddenly revealed, and Pierre showed lively interest in what it entailed: a history of dogmatic proclamations, juridical codifications, spirituality, etc.:

> This reflection on Islamic history would be intended, in the first place, to better discern, from the Christian point of view, the salvific dimensions of a differentiated economy of salvation. This is what would give such reflection its authentically theological dimension, and it seems to me that this theology could provide a more appropriate ground for dialogue than the contrasting of dogmatic theologies or simple comparative studies. This is because it engages us in the movement of our common history, and it seeks out the original experiences that cannot be fully captured by the theological expressions that have been crafted to account for them.[23]

Jean-Louis Déclais, one of the priests of his diocese, was involved in a project of this type at the time. He was looking for the connections between the Qur'an and the Judaeo-Christian tradition, through certain central figures like David, Job, and Moses.[24] Claverie was enthusiastic about this sort of research, even though he knew it had attracted few scholars, especially in the Muslim world, where there was a dire lack of such counterparts, as he emphasized.[25] In reality, this was only an initial undertaking in historical-critical studies on the original texts — there were many other such initiatives to be explored, for both Muslims and Christians, if one takes seriously the bishop of Oran's statement "I need the truth of the other."

## For "A Church That Offers Its Life"

In fact, Pierre Claverie did not invest himself entirely in these intellectual responses, since he judged that concepts could be elaborated, and meetings could be multiplied, but "we must recognize that today we are at a bit of a standstill," he stated bluntly at a conference held at the El-Kalima center in Brussels in February of 1988.[26] Instead of contributing to the theological debate that he nevertheless respected, he took another tack — that of giving oneself to following the way of Jesus:

> The life, passion, and resurrection of Jesus open for us the pathways of encounter and reconciliation; they create the conditions necessary for encounter and reconciliation. The presence of Jesus today in the midst of our battle against the forces of death that isolate and weaken us, the power of his Spirit, who propels us out of the tomb, can contribute to freeing us from fear... Giving one's life for this reconciliation, as Jesus gave his life in order to tear down the wall of hatred that separated Jews, Greeks, pagans, slaves, free persons — isn't this a way of celebrating the sacrifice of Christ?[27]

Ten years before his death, Pierre Claverie had already found the theme that would occupy him constantly from that point on and guide his conduct: the only way to extinguish the fear that grips us is to break down the walls that separate us, is "recall the manner in which God spanned the abyss of separation" and follow:

> We have more need than ever for men of reconciliation. But a new covenant cannot be struck at any price. It is not enough to say "love one another" and to act as though differences and fear were nonexistent. Nor is it enough to condemn violence... At a moment when each human grouping, each people, each culture and religion is under pressure from others and strongly tempted to turn in upon itself or exalt itself alone against all others, the church can and should propose the means of universal coexistence.[28]

So what was involved was, for him, nothing less than the mission of the church. This was what the church was here for, its vocation, and, in consequence, the only pathway befitting the disciples of Jesus. One may point out in passing that these existential touches that go to the heart of the gospel message are often expressed by Pierre Claverie on the occasion of homilies for the priestly ordination of his brothers, or of men close to the Algerian church.[29] On these occasions he went right for the essential, imparting to his brothers the secret of his own life:

> Living in the Muslim world, I know the weight of the temptation to turn in upon oneself, and the difficulty of mutual understanding and respect...I understand the extent of the abyss that separates us. We cannot span this abyss on our own. But in Jesus, God gives us the ability to measure the length, height, depth, and breadth of his love. We can rediscover trust with the support of this revelation.[30]

Pierre Claverie would continue to express his point of view on interreligious dialogue and the theology of non-Christian religions, but more as a "witness," with the force of a life lived with conviction, than as an expert.[31] There was something growing deeply within him, and he would testify to this with peaceful assurance.

The disagreeable attacks against the church in some of the Algerian media outlets in 1988 (see the previous chapter) led him to react vigorously, but they also rooted within him the conviction that Jesus, in freeing them from the Law, ushered his disciples into a religion of the Spirit that gave them extraordinary freedom. In his eyes, this religion of the Spirit is at work beyond the visible limits of the church:

> Doesn't being Christian mean offering one's being to the indwelling and transforming action of the Spirit? Much more than new teachings or rituals, Jesus instructs us or, rather, initiates us in this mystery. It is a passage from death to life, from the flesh to the spirit, or, better, the infusion of the spirit into the flesh...Jesus brings us with him into the heart of chaos through the cross, to which he delivers himself and which he asks us to carry with him...In the face of the powers of death that torture and crush the flesh, we struggle together with Jesus, and like him we revolt against falsehood, injustice, contempt, the stupidity of the bloated and moneyed. And in all those who rise up to liberate creation and restore its dignity, to permit humanity to grow in unity, we

recognize the action of the one Spirit who does not cease to bring to birth and rebirth the flesh which is threatened by death...

Against all legalism, literalism, and fundamentalism, the Spirit keeps open a wound of love that nothing can heal or assuage... This form of belief brings happiness with it. It is not a petulant and fleeting joy, but the profound peace of adjusting oneself that permits one to risk one's life without fear.[32]

The increasingly spiritual tone of his remarks did not exclude a return to the question of the theology of religions. In October of 1991, participating in a colloquium at the Institute Catholique in Paris on the theme "Proclaiming Jesus Christ and the Encounter with Non-Christian Religions," he said he was "deeply impressed" by the reflection of Jacques Dupuis, a Jesuit from India. Claverie recommended one of Dupuis's books to the Christians of his diocese: *Jésus-Christ à la rencontre des religions.*[33] In taking stock of the Catholic Church's new approach to the non-Christian religions after Vatican II, Pierre Claverie asked: "While it used to be said that Muslims are sometimes saved through their consciences without consideration of their religion, or worse yet, in spite of it... could one say today that it is their religion that saves them? And then what place is occupied, in God's will to save all people, by Jesus Christ and the church?"[34]

He notes that it is difficult to give a simple response to these questions, and the magisterium has not definitively settled them, but the church, while reaffirming that "Jesus is the only savior," recognizes that "the faithful of other religions can be associated with this salvation offered by Jesus Christ... And if the mystery of Christ is also present among these religions, then we can receive new illumination from them on our own revelation, which we have not yet fully discovered or understood."[35] There is nothing original or new in this statement. Pierre Claverie's originality, his personal touch, lies in his final remarks: "The church does not seek to 'win back' the faithful of other religions: it sees the work of God in them, and turns toward God and toward them, like Jesus, arms spread open as on the cross. It does not place itself between God and humanity as an obligatory intermediary, but offers its life for all wherever it is present, for the salvation of all."[36]

While the theology of religions was at pains to find formulations that would be acceptable to all, Pierre Claverie tried to breach the wall of dogmatic definitions, which often introduce separation. In following Jesus, who offered himself up out of love, the Christian is invited to offer his or her own life for reconciliation, like seed sown in the earth:

Much more time is still needed for these evangelical convictions to penetrate the barriers of human nature and ecclesial structures. The temptation to appropriate others or to impose oneself upon them is often stronger than the desire to serve and to love. Our situation in Algeria presses us more than elsewhere to enter with Jesus into this apparent folly of the cross, which is, in reality, the only wisdom: it is that which substitutes the logic of love and life for the logic of power and death.[37]

Pierre Claverie had become a proponent of a "confessing church," to take up an expression cherished by Dietrich Bonhoeffer, who directly inspired him, as will be seen later.

## Toward a New Face for the Algerian Church

These attempts to rethink the church's mission in a Muslim context came at the end of twenty-five years during which many things had changed in the Algerian church and its relationship with the country. This church had certainly survived the seismic shock of the departure of most of the Christians with the coming of independence, but the Arabization and Islamization of society seemed to be pushing it to the margins, if not outside of the country entirely. Although its numbers had been drastically reduced, it was still there, discreet and alive, as shown by a survey of the diocese of Oran conducted ten years after the one of 1983–84.[38] The aid workers had practically disappeared, and with them the preschool and school-age children; there were few Oriental Christians left; the Christian spouses in mixed marriages had to practice increased discretion in their surroundings, and hardly met together anymore; the pieds-noirs had grown old and were often baffled by the desire to make the church authentically Algerian. The only groups that were relatively stable were composed of students who had come from sub-Saharan Africa, who found vital support in the Christian community, and of the permanent staff, nuns and priests, whose numbers had dropped by only a third. In 1994, the diocese of Oran still counted fifty-five religious sisters and twenty-three priests, most of whom had been able to adjust after the loss of their job contracts and had found interesting ways of integrating positions in Algerian society. "So there was a poverty of means, but an extraordinary human richness," Pierre Claverie said with his habitual optimism in 1987, adding, "The church has every right to insist upon coexisting with a different world: everywhere in the world today, the challenge of pluralism has been raised. What we are living through here with the Algerians could be helpful to everyone's future."[39]

But the situation was fragile, as emphasized by the elevated average age of the priests and religious sisters, and by the precariousness of their status. Together with this was the risk of the church's turning inward and closing itself off in its worship and meetings. Pierre Claverie worked against this constantly:

> The danger [of turning inward] is not an illusion, and we must fight continually to maintain our vitality, our assurance, and our hope. Now, the grandeur and power of Christians come from the quality of their relationship with God and with others...It matters little how many or few we are, as long as we do not fall back into a defensive position. It matters little how meager our means are, as long as these are truly enlivened by the spirit of the gospel.[40]

The bishop of Oran also delighted in the international character of his community, but he was not unaware of the fact that most of these Filipino, Brazilian, and Polish laborers were staying only for the duration of a contract. But he was not discouraged. The essential thing, in his eyes, was to "employ all my human resources so that my Christian community will be grafted onto the tissue of Algerian society."[41] Paradoxically, adversity would assist him in this.

The violence that gripped the country after the invalidation of the results of the January 1992 elections would gradually extend to the Algerian church, affecting its friends first and then its own members (see the following two chapters). But this shared crisis would lead to a strengthening of relations between the Christians and their Algerian friends. In his contribution to the plenary meeting of the Pontifical Council for Interreligious Dialogue in Rome in November of 1995, Claverie said that "dialogue has reached a depth that has been unequaled until now": "What gestures of friendship we receive from people who are close to us, or whom we don't even know! It is as though we needed imminent danger to make us more simple, more friendly, more human...Everyone feels the need to make his or her own life part of a fraternal network, and is awestruck at the signs by which this expresses itself. Ordinary life doesn't exist anymore."[42]

There was also the wonder and gratitude on the part of friends and neighbors at the fact that the Christians were not leaving the country, in spite of the risks they ran. After the first attacks against Christians, Sister Claire and Sister Jeanne, who lived in Oran and were close to Pierre Claverie, were approached by their neighbors, who offered their condolences: "So then, my sisters, you are going away?"

"No," replied the sisters, "we are staying."

"Oh, thank you, and forgive us!"

There were also gestures of delicate concern: a bouquet of flowers, offered by an anonymous hand; neighbors who did the grocery shopping to spare their friends the dangers they faced in the open street. "We are surrounded as never before by a protective Muslim shield," Pierre confided shortly before his death.[43] Without a doubt, these trials brought the church closer to many people in Algeria.

The excesses of the Islamists would even encourage some Muslims to take a closer look at Christianity. Under the direction of Cardinal Duval, the Algerian church had always been reluctant to accept conversions. For one thing, it did not want to engage in proselytism, which did not prevent some Muslim leaders from regularly and unjustly accusing the church of practicing it. For another, breaking from Islam in a Muslim country leads to a sort of social death — rejection by family, neighbors, and aid workers is practically assured, even outside of phases of political Islamism. So exceptional moral strength and personal equilibrium are required to withstand such conditions, which explains the reluctance on the part of bishops in the face of candidates for conversion. In receiving a young man who was asking to become a Christian, Pierre Claverie expressed his dilemma: "There is a fairly large number of people seeking other ways under the pressure of Islamic radicalism. But in a Muslim country, these people must hide...even as the conversion of a European to Islam makes the headline of the local paper! Tolerance has its limits" (letter of January 29, 1990).

The phrase "fairly large number" is a bit excessive: there were at most a few dozen cases in the entire country, and most of these had already been baptized by Evangelicals, who are more assertive in proselytizing than the Catholics. The bishop of Oran would nonetheless welcome these converts to a greater extent than his priests and the other bishops of Algeria thought fitting. And he spoke of the matter with great frankness, as when he explained himself in this interview from September of 1995:

[We do not seek] to make converts, certainly not. The history of relations between Christians and Muslims has been marked enough as it is by conflict, right from the start; our objective is to endure, in solidarity, so that mutual discovery can take place in an atmosphere of serenity. Are we evangelizing? Yes, in the sense that we propose the revelation that God is love. I know that this proposition can be rejected and misinterpreted, that I risk being persecuted on this account, but I also know that this proposition is part of the essence of being a Christian. For this reason, the church has a place wherever there are divisions, both between human groups and within each human person, wherever there are wounds, exclusion, or marginalization.[44]

He was not unaware of the risks he ran in saying such things, since the country's intelligence agencies were always very aware of what was happening. His position was consistent with his view of dialogue: for true encounter and dialogue to take place, each person had to be able to exist in the fullness of his or her convictions. Although he had done nothing to encourage these people to convert, he was moved by their spiritual experience: "It is an extraordinary thing for us to live together with these people who have made a journey of conversion, and this helps us to rediscover for ourselves the gospel's liberating power."[45] In the context of violence carried out in the name of religion, the Sermon on the Mount was the most startling discovery for these converts, he emphasized. Faithful to his own convictions and respectful of those of others, Pierre Claverie bore witness once again to his profound interior freedom.

It is important to point out with regard to this delicate matter that some open-minded Algerians accept this perspective of religious pluralism within their society. This was even a part of their struggle for a "pluralistic society," a struggle in which Pierre Claverie joined them, for both religious and political reasons. In his haste to see his country evolve toward a greater respect for the other, he probably overestimated the possibilities that this crisis had opened: "If in this crisis for Algeria, after passing through violence and the deep divisions in society, religion, and identity, we could only arrive at conceiving of the other person's right to exist and of the respect that is owed to the truth that he or she bears, then the dangers to which we are now exposed will not have been in vain."[46]

The question of pluralism remains one of the great challenges facing Algerian society. Progress on this issue still will require more courageous men and women capable of breaking this taboo.

## Chapter Ten

# An Algerian Bishop in the Midst of Social and Political Debate

### 1988—94

> It is time again for us to take our part in the sufferings and hope of Algeria, with love, respect, patience, and lucidity.[1]
> —*Pierre Claverie*

The year 1988 marked a turning point in Algeria's contemporary history: following riots provoked by social unrest, the one-party regime that controlled the political life of the country since independence would collapse, opening the way to a multiparty system. At the same time, political Islamism would take center stage, posing new and destabilizing questions to Algerians. The victory of the Islamic Salvation Front in the municipal elections in 1991, followed by the invalidation of the legislative elections in January 1992, broached a political crisis that would gradually lead to violence. For Pierre Claverie, the moment is no longer one of academic discussions about dialogue; "living together with respect for each other's differences" became the central theme of his approach. Month after month, and especially during the black hours of violence and intolerance, his links with Algerians bearing the same convictions would deepen. In these forms of engagement, he was faithful to what had become a profound conviction: that facing common challenges together would bring progress in dialogue and encounter with the other. His "difference" as a Christian Algerian seemed to him nothing but an advantage: "Coexistence in the midst of our differences is more than ever the order of the day," he wrote in February of 1990.[2] This solidarity in debate would become solidarity in trial: the more the social and political situation deteriorated, the more exposed he would be himself.

## The Political Turning Point of October 1988

Street demonstrations in protest against price increases broke out in Algiers on the evening of October 4, 1988. In the working-class neighborhood of

170

Bab el Oued, cars were burned and shop windows broken. "An adolescent scuffle that got out of hand; it's just an isolated incident," one government official remarked at the time. In fact, within forty-eight hours the demonstrations escalated to riots that spread through most of the country. In Belcourt, another working-class neighborhood in the capital, the Islamists formed a cohort of seven to eight thousand sympathizers at prayer time on Friday. A state of siege was declared on October 6; tanks were sent into the streets and the army opened fire on the rioters. Hundreds of people were killed and thousands arrested, and there were many cases of torture. The ruling regime would never recover. The Islamists were about to seize power, "like picking a piece of ripe fruit."[3] One cannot understand the violence of these riots in October of 1988 without taking into account all of the elements of social upheaval that had accumulated over almost three decades of underdevelopment. First were the demographics: 60 percent of Algeria's twenty-five million inhabitants (up from under ten million in 1962) were under twenty years of age. Then there was urbanization: the percentage of people living in the cities had risen from 30 to 50 percent, without a corresponding expansion of infrastructure — the lack of housing, water, and leisure activities was the citizens' daily lot. Unemployment was extremely high, and mainly affected the young people, who either fell back onto their own resourcefulness or sank into idleness (Algerians called these jobless young people *hittistes*, literally "those who stand against walls"). Corruption was rife at all levels, and shocked ordinary people. Without denying the achievements of the Boumediene years, for example in the areas of education and health, it must be recognized that the quality of life in Algeria was poor. And Algerians were dissatisfied that their freedom of expression and initiative had been confiscated by a political class that showed itself unable to satisfy their expectations. As in all similar situations, the young people were the ones who touched off the social explosion.

The government made an effort to react: on October 10, President Chadli announced a referendum to ratify a plan for political reform that would end the monopoly of the National Liberation Front, which had been in power since 1962. Approved by a wide margin, the new constitution cleared the way for a multiparty system. A number of new parties sprang into being, including the Islamic Salvation Front. Taking advantage of the weakness of a regime incapable of meeting the current situation, the Islamists obtained legal recognition of their party in September of 1989. They became the leading political party representing change. Legendary nationalist militants like Ben Bella and Aït Ahmed returned from exile. After a long winter, civil society was

Bishop Claverie with Jean-Jacques Pérennès, O.P. (left),
on the day of the author's ordination, June 1989.

bursting out: groups for the defense of human rights and women's associations were formed, and raï music and Berber cultural associations blossomed after years of suppression. Daily and weekly newspapers multiplied, putting an end to the monotony of the official press, represented by *El Moujahid* in French and by *El Chaab* in Arabic. "The Algerian individual is becoming a subject of history, and no longer simply a subject of a regime," wrote Benjamin Stora.[4] In short, hope had come back to life. The aspirations of the people, and especially of the young, had been pent up too long, and now they would overtake a government that had become fossilized.

Kasdi Merbah, a former head of military security, became prime minister amid the fast-paced changes that took place in October. Together with technical consultants like Sid-Ahmed Ghozali, former president of the national oil company Sonatrach, he launched sorely needed deep economic reforms. These included moving from an economy subsidized by oil exports to an economy administered according to real economic criteria, limiting foreign debt, and creating jobs through economic growth rather than through the state budget. But the implementation of such reforms presupposes a firmly established government — and there was nothing of the kind in place. The effervescence of the political situation concealed only poorly the fragility of this young democracy; the old ringleaders of the National Liberation Front were still in charge, and they had no intention of relinquishing their privileges. As for the new political parties, apart from the Islamic Salvation Front these were still fragile in the face of the general atmosphere of conflict shaking the foundations of Algerian society. The army remained the true arbiter of the situation.

Pierre Claverie followed all of this closely, as his correspondence shows. Thanks to the Christian communities of the Oran region, which he visited constantly, he was very well informed about what was going on. On October 12, 1988, at the end of the week of rioting, he wrote, "Calm has returned. Everything is back to normal amid expectations of the promised reforms. The markets and bakeries have been restocked, and anxiety has diminished. One can breathe again. The army still occupies the intersections, but the state of siege was lifted this morning in Algiers. This is the first time in recent history that Algeria has faced this sort of trial" (letter of October 12, 1988).

He also had many contacts within Algerian civil society, friends with whom he discussed current affairs and refined his own analysis of these. For example, during a dinner with the rector of the university of Oran, he met a lawyer who was promoting a league for human rights in the western part of Algeria. A few days later, he had lunch at the home of a militant member of the Ettahaddi party, the former Algerian Communist Party, and noted, "she is an extraordinary woman, a true militant for the rights of the poor." In keeping with the effervescence that characterized the country, his network of relationships had become quite varied. People liked to invite him as a guest, and each time he came the discussion on Algeria's evolution was lively and stimulating: "I really love the people I meet and with whom I find myself on the same wavelength. The problems we bring up are both fascinating and disturbing" (letter of September 25, 1988).

He and his friends would find themselves facing together an entirely new challenge: the rise of a movement that came to be called "radical Islamism" (B. Étienne). Algeria is a Muslim country. We have seen that Islam was an essential factor in the reconstruction of Algerian identity in the colonial era. The people were deeply and sincerely religious. But this kind of Islam was really different. It was a political form of Islam, which had to some extent spread throughout the Arab world after its defeat by Israel in 1967 and 1973. These defeats had led to a profound crisis in Arab nationalism, which became more of a vague invocation than a practical force. The quality of life deteriorated in most Arab countries, leading to bread riots from Cairo to

Casablanca. The political class, enriched by petrodollars, flaunted its privileges everywhere, provoking bitterness and anger on the part of the people. This was the backdrop against which political Islamism extended itself; it was in the first place experienced as "the hope of a return to ethics" (B. Stora). One can understand this better through the main character in a then recent novel by Yasmina Khadra, À *quoi rêvent les loups?*[5] The young Nafa Walid, from a working class background, dreams of nothing but making films. But in Algeria, no such career is possible without an influential contact (*ktef*). So after a small role in a film, he becomes the houseboy for a family of sharp business people. He witnesses the debauchery of these *nouveaux riches*, whom he drives at all hours of the day and night to private clubs of a luxury that is unimaginable for ordinary people. Disgusted, he tries to leave Algeria by using his savings to register for a scholarship abroad. But he is never able to leave. After moping around in the cafés of Bab el Oued, he is finally signed up by the militant Islamists, who seem to him to be concerned about others. Aid associations and soup kitchens spring up around the mosques, fostered in part by a state that is remarkable only for its ineffectiveness. Through a succession of events the young Nafa Walid would join the underground: he begins by participating in street demonstrations, then takes on more delicate tasks (collecting money, transporting weapons), until, one day, he becomes a killer. It is a fairly good composite sketch of those who went down the path of Islamist violence.

Among his many visitors, Pierre Claverie received a young Islamist whom he called affectionately "my budding young imam," and in whose home he would have lunch in March of 1989: "They are a very likeable couple, and contrary to appearances or to the attitudes they display, they are very open-minded," he wrote.

Was he being naïve or overconfident? In fact, the troops that political Islam was recruiting in Algeria were just ordinary people of this kind who had become disoriented. As in the novel by Yasmina Khadra, it was through mutual help associations that Islamist leaders gained a foothold among the masses. In Algiers, they did so through the mosques of Kouba, Belcourt, and Bab el Oued, or in soulless, recently built developments in cities like Badjarah. This strategy of infiltration paid off, because the Islamists made huge gains in the municipal elections of June 12, 1990: with 54.3 percent of the vote, they crushed the National Liberation Front, which obtained only 18.3 percent. Behind the scenes, in fact, were some genuine strategists like Abassi Madani, who had become a seasoned politician after university studies in London, and Ali Belhaj, the fiery preacher of the Es-Sunna mosque in Bab el Oued. In any case, it was the first time that an Arab country had authorized a party whose stated goal was the establishment of an Islamic republic. For many Algerians, it came as a shock.

## Facing Common Challenges Together

This victory for the Islamists in the municipal elections was nothing but a first step toward seizing power. They saw themselves acquiring a majority presence in parliament. With his tremendous personal equilibrium and fundamental confidence, Claverie's reaction was calm and measured, as he emphasized the positive aspect of these elections:

> So, then, we now find ourselves in an "Islamic" country...Algeria has held a number of surprises for us since independence. Hard and fast socialism, half-hearted liberalism with a single party, and now a victory for the Islamist party in the municipal and regional elections...This vote was above all a success for democracy: in effect, in spite of some slight excesses, for the first time in its history the Algerian people freely chose from a list of candidates. There were worse outcomes to be feared! Now it is time for us to judge the practicality of the fidelity of the Islamic Salvation Front to its promises. (letter of June 18, 1990)

He was not unaware that many saw the growth of political Islamism as a threat. This included the democrats who were just beginning to organize themselves, women who were fighting for emancipation, and the "secularist" intellectuals who rejected an abusive role of custodianship for religion. The Christian minority in Algeria were also among those who found the idea of an Islamist regime disturbing. But Pierre Claverie refused to retreat into a ghetto mentality: before defending the specific interests of the Christian community (freedom of worship, social and educational activities, etc.), he preferred to concentrate on the common challenges that Christians and Muslims had to face in Algeria. So in the spring of 1990, he published a long document in which he tried to identify what, in his eyes, these common challenges were.[6]

Rather than sticking to the general principles and issues involved in dialogue, Claverie tackled the fundamental questions facing Algerian society, with an earnest desire to enter into relationship with Algerians "beginning with their own aspirations for the future, in a genuine intra-Islamic dialogue, and not on the basis of what is convenient for us or the terrain that we would have chosen."[7] The essence of the debate was the role of religion in society.

The policy of the Islamic Salvation Front was clear: Algeria was an "Islamic land" and was therefore obligated to submit completely to the sovereignty of God, instead of chasing after foreign cultural and political models, which in the eyes of the Islamists was the source of all their troubles. The danger of such assertions, Claverie wrote, was that of "consecrating a government or a set of policies by setting these up as a divine model." He expressed himself all the more freely on this subject given the fact that he had often recognized and acknowledged how Christianity itself had suffered through this combination of religion and politics.

As the political project of the Islamic Salvation Front was that of submitting all of social life to Islam, the very idea of secularism no longer meant anything, much less the Western idea of secularism. It had arisen from a desire for the emancipation of civil society from institutional religious supervision seen as excessive. At the same time, non-Muslims could enjoy the status of a tolerated minority (*dhimmi*), with the right to worship according to their convictions, but they could not attain full citizenship. Another consequence was that democracy, as a social contract ratified by the various components of the country through elections and laws, was called into question. As the Islamists considered sharia as "the sole source, if not the sole form, of legislation acceptable for a Muslim people," discussions increasingly turned to bringing the legislative systems into line with this immutable law. In fact, Pierre Claverie notes, it was only recently that the Catholic Church had accepted democracy and ceased considering the French Republic as a threat. And it was in Algiers in 1890, during a famous toast proposed by Cardinal Lavigerie, that the signal of the church's support of the Republic was given at the behest of Pope Leo XIII. And even though the West had something of a headstart in this debate, it was also faced with the question of what values could be taken as the foundation for a social consensus: is there such a thing as a "republican morality" shared by all, which can provide the basis for societal decisions? On the issue of women, "we have not yet found the point of equilibrium," he wrote, emphasizing that this subject that was so sensitive for an Islamic regime was also an embarrassment for the Catholic Church, which hardly dared even to discuss the admission of women to the ordained ministry. So without equating these various viewpoints, he emphasized that there were many areas in which Muslims and Christians would both profit from common reflection.

What is striking about this text is that instead of falling into alarmist rhetoric and pointing a finger at the other, he orients his reflection toward the common challenges to be faced. There is naivety here, since in passing Claverie makes the necessary clarification.[8] Let's say, rather, that he was animated by the conviction that "mistrust is the source of fear and violence" and that facing common challenges can be the best terrain for a genuine dialogue. During the summer of 1990, in an editorial entitled "Au nom du Fils," he insisted: "Without idealizing our sometimes difficult daily relationships, both on the personal level and among communities or national groups in their extreme diversity, we can say once more: what brings us together is stronger than what divides us."[9]

This approach won him great sympathy from many of his Muslim counterparts, because, as his lawyer-friend the schoolteacher Rahal said, "Fr. Claverie never spoke of Islam in a wounding or scornful way. Also," he added, "he had excellent training in classic Arabic studies, having studied the original sources." During this same year of 1990, Claverie agreed, after deep reflection, to record a discussion on dialogue with a Muslim for the French television network Antenne 2, taking precautions to avoid any deviations. He did this as much for the French as for the Algerian audience. In the period of 1989–90, in effect, French public opinion was in an uproar over the headscarf controversy in the high schools, and it was also the time of the Rushdie affair, with the death sentence issued by the Iranian mullahs against this English writer of Indian origin for having written *The Satanic Verses*, which they saw as insulting Islam. Many Muslims suffered on account of this image of Islam, as did the Christians who were accused endlessly of wanting to defame it, as Pierre Claverie emphasized in a letter in which he added, "The misunderstandings persist in spite of the still too-limited efforts for comprehension and conciliation on both sides. Our two planets are still light years away from each other" (letter dated March 29, 1989).

What he was striving for was to stimulate reflection on both sides of the Mediterranean. The program was broadcast on September 30, 1990, and led to discussions with his friends in the region of Oran, on sensitive topics like pluralism, secularism, the reinterpretation of the Qur'an, etc. It was a fresh illustration of the "Claverie method": speaking together truthfully, but against a backdrop of friendship and mutual respect.[10] This was how he conducted himself during these years of the rise in political Islamism.

## Standing Together with Democrats for "Pluralistic" Society

Having won the municipal elections, the Islamic Salvation Front would gradually gain more ground, stepping up the political pressure and organizing large demonstrations to demand the immediate application of sharia law and the abandonment of bilingualism, since, in their eyes, Arabic was the only language worthy of a Muslim country. Finding itself backed into a corner, the government arranged a parliamentary vote for the uniform application of Arabic. The democrats tried to respond by organizing their own demonstrations, but they were inexperienced and divided into factions, only one of which — the Socialist Forces Front, headed by Aït Ahmed — had any significant influence. Disorder began to spread. In June of 1991, the Islamic Salvation Front called for a general strike, and a state of siege was declared. The two main leaders of the party were arrested and imprisoned. Legislative elections finally took place at the end of December, and the Islamist party obtained 188 of the seats in the first round of voting. It seemed that a massive victory for the Islamic Salvation Front was assured for the second round. The Algerian democrats faced a dilemma: must one "cede liberty to the enemies of liberty," in the words of Robespierre? What would then become of democracy in an Algeria governed by Islamists? The specter of Iran haunted their imaginations, with its steady flow of executions and everything that hard-line mullahs had imposed upon society. The Algerian democrats, above all the women, were not prepared to undertake such an adventure. Many of these women, like Khalida Messaoudi, literally joined in resistance.

There were, however, some intellectuals who provided assurance that this passage through Islamism could be one stage of a Muslim country's transition to modernity, a "constructive step backward," as Lahouari Addi, an Algerian political analyst, wrote. He added, "The coming to power of the Islamic Salvation Front brings significant political risks, but for Algerian society this is also part of a long-term investment. As the expression of a medieval interpretation of Islam and devoid of realism or of a vision of the future, the Islamic Salvation Front, once in power, would have hastened the painful separation of religion and politics in the collective Algerian imagination."[11] François Burgat reasoned along the same lines, calculating that "nothing prevents us from stating now that this new voice [of the southern hemisphere] will produce responses that will be even less constructive than those of the now wearied protagonists of the great saga of nationalism."[12] But Addi was writing from Princeton in the United States, and Burgat from Aix-en-Provence. The democrats on the ground in Algeria were less confident. Pierre Claverie clearly shared the concerns of these Algerians, but he called them not to give in to panic: "Algeria is not Iran," he wrote. "We should strive to avoid any exaggerations that could lead to extremist reactions. Although I am very pessimistic about the future of democracy in Algeria, I still think it is possible to build something worthwhile together. After the shock of the elections, many Muslims are reexamining their religious views."[13]

Without entirely agreeing with the "Orientalists," specialists who analyzed the situation from afar and provided advice, Pierre Claverie also expected Islamic culture to make a leap forward by virtue of these trials. In fact, he was not in favor of calling off the elections, as Bishop Teissier recalls, adding, "because he was in Oran" — and Oran seemed to be a bit more sheltered from the threat of Islamism. On January 9, 1992, Pierre Claverie concluded his monthly editorial this way:

> I don't expect anything good from any religious government, whether it be Jewish, Christian, or Muslim. But I retain my trust in the Algerian people, and even in some of those who are looking to an Islamic solution. This is not Iran, nor Sudan, nor Saudi Arabia. I am a proponent of democracy — although I acknowledge its limitations — and of respect for individual rights. And so I support, with some reservations on account of the uniqueness of the Christian approach, those who defend democracy and human rights.[14]

In Oran, there was widespread surprise when as in the other towns the Islamic Salvation Front made a good showing in the elections. Two days later, on January 11, 1992, the day before the second round of voting, the elections were called off and the army "dismissed" President Chadli and gave control to a High State Committee, which was under its direct control. This committee called upon one of the historical leaders of the Algerian revolution, Mohamed Boudiaf, in exile in Morocco since 1962 following a disagreement with Ben Bella about the army's seizure of power after independence. He was a progressive and well-rounded man who enjoyed a genuine historical legitimacy, which was essential in Algeria. The Islamic Salvation Front was dissolved on March 4, and suspected members of the party were arrested by the thousand and deported to detention camps in the Sahara, by virtue of the state of emergency declared by the High State Committee. Far from limiting the influence of the Islamic Salvation Front, this brutal and extreme measure solidified its popularity.

Once again, Pierre Claverie tried to understand what was happening and shared his analysis. In his eyes, the essential problem lay in the fact that the National Liberation Front had long held onto power illegitimately while pretending to exercise it "by the people and for the people," as proclaimed by the logo displayed every day on the front page of the official newspaper *El Moujahid*:

In reality as time passed it confiscated power for the use of its cronies, and for the profit of its leaders, many of whom were moved more by ambition and corruption than militancy. A certain class had found in the party the means of social and economic advancement — was this, perhaps, because it had no real political legitimacy to claim?...The Islamic Salvation Front tried to undo this entrenched disorder. In the name of religion, it would establish an Islamic government. It is possible that the intention of its main leaders was indeed that of restoring right order, with God's justice as the basis for human justice. This is a legitimate ambition, but it is even more dangerous than that of the founders of the National Liberation Front, because God is there as a fallback, a guarantor, if the leaders lose their way and become corrupt.[15]

So what Claverie saw as urgent was escaping this polarization of political life that locked these two parties in opposition. Instead, advancement in real democracy should be fostered at all levels of political and social life. Speaking at the annual meeting of bishops and major superiors in Algeria, held on March 26–27, 1992, Pierre Claverie unflinchingly condemned the way in which the government had acted:

Once again, order has been reestablished by those who have long held power. Their manner of speaking has changed, and it may be that their intentions have as well. Could it be that they want to safeguard the birth of democracy, and to protect it in its early stages from the dangers of anarchy and religious fascism? Could it be that the foreseeable dictatorship in the name of Islam would have brought a burst of civil and revenge and violence without providing any solutions for our economic and social crises? But the fact remains that, for the sake of avoiding a religious dictatorship, we are now in a (temporary?) phase of military dictatorship that is firmly maintaining the established order, with the same men continuing to enjoy both power and profit.[16]

So in spite of his customary discretion, Pierre Claverie was no longer keeping his political sympathies to himself. One reason for this greater openness was the growth of his daily contact with men and women he admired and collaborated with in a variety of services for the Algerian people, especially on behalf of the poor. It was his work with these companions that convinced him that the real battle to be waged was that for a "pluralistic humanity."[17]

## From Islam to Islamism: An Understanding but Critical View

The victory of the Islamist party in the Algerian elections came during the first Gulf War. On the one side, the Americans and their allies were styling themselves as the champions of freedom and international law; on the other, Saddam Hussein presented himself as a figure of resistance against an unjust world order, and that is how Arabs in general saw him. The real reasons for the conflict — which had a distinct odor of petroleum about them — quickly disappeared behind quasi-religious considerations with strong emotional and symbolic associations. In short, "Saladin is not dead," wrote Pierre Claverie in denouncing this step backward.[18] For years he had criticized the power of the clichés in circulation and used against one another by Christians and Muslims, and he was dismayed to see them back in use in this disastrous confrontation. The electoral victory of the Islamic Salvation Front in Algeria reinforced some irrational views in the West, particularly in France: so, then, here was Islamism at the gates of Europe...So in all of the media outlets to which he had access, Pierre Claverie did all he could to defuse the situation, explaining from an understanding but critical perspective the state of contemporary Islam: "We must be genuine, and get to know each other with our strengths and defects," he wrote. "This presumes that we leave behind our images of each other, including the ideas conveyed by traditional theologies, in order to make contact with living reality: real, living believers, who are neither Crusaders nor terrorists; real, living Islam, which is not entirely hemmed in by Islamist rhetoric, but is also seeking itself amid the assaults of modernity."[19]

He had two objectives in mind: helping the West to give up its fears in the face of Islam, and supporting those working within the Muslim world for Islam's evolution toward modernity. Pierre Claverie did this above all by constant dialogue with his Muslim friends, and by presenting the reality of the Muslim religion — of which he had both scholarly and experiential knowledge — in a variety of talks and articles. For example, at a colloquium in September of 1991, he gave a remarkably up-to-date assessment of interpretations of the Qur'an.[20] One finds here a scholarly depth that he rarely let show in his daily life. Nevertheless, he preferred to turn his analysis toward current affairs. He was never an "Orientalist." The spread of Islamism in Algeria was for him an opportunity to try to understand the origin of this phenomenon that was so perplexing in a country so close to Europe and, in many ways, marked by Western culture. As he noted, Islam had always had a significant presence in the contemporary history of Algeria — the *ulema* had been one of the sources of the rebirth of Algerian nationalism. During the war of liberation itself, Islam strongly influenced the struggle against colonialism: the combatants called themselves *mujahideen,* and the dead became *chouhada* (martyrs). "Contemporary Algerian Islam is an Islam of resistance," Pierre Claverie concluded, and for him, "Islamism [was] the result of this Islam of resistance."[21] But like any social reality, Algerian Islam is complex and is subject to a multitude of interpretations and uses. Thus after independence, the socialist leaders of the country "reinterpreted" — meaning "exploited" — Islam in a reformist vein, providing for each socialist development (the agrarian revolution, the state monopoly on education, etc.) an "Islamic counterpart": for example, family law, a return to Friday as a day of rest, and obligatory religious education (*tarbiya islamiya*) in the schools. A factor in preserving identity during the colonial period, this reformist Islam reinforced its hold on society over the years, as shown by the growth in the number of mosques during the 1970s. But another, combative form of Islam appeared in the 1980s, after the failures of socialism and the spread of corruption; a "moral jihad" sprang up, claiming that it would purify society and reestablish true Islam to its rightful place. Encouraged by other Muslim countries, this purifying form of Islam attracted young people and added them to its ranks: "Young people hungry for justice and truth and completely dedicated as militants for a religious revolution found meaning for their lives in having a cause to defend."[22] Rather than raising the alarm, Pierre Claverie preferred to understand and explain. And he rightly emphasized the strong emotions that accompanied this renewal, making it difficult to conduct a calm discussion.

The bishop of Oran took advantage of every opportunity he had to speak of and encourage those who, from within Islam itself, were trying to further its advancement in relation to modernity:

> Intellectuals who affirm that they are Muslim — such as Ferdjani, a Tunisian; Arkoun and Malek, Algerians; Asmmaoui and Zakaryya, Egyptians, and many more — are seeking to open a breach, through their writings, within systems that are sealed up in the name of Islamic tradition. They want to take on the challenge of modernity while still maintaining their faith in Islam. Those who look at the Muslim world from the outside pay attention only to the most traditionalist theologians: the West does not listen enough to these other intellectuals.[23]

Taking care not to give offense, he recalled on occasion the efforts that Christianity had had to make within its own history to separate itself from the political exploitation of religion. But being honest to the core, he did not conceal his questions about the possibility that Islam might one day succeed in separating religion and politics:

> Must the forms of Islamism be considered as serious perversions of authentic Islam, a consequence of the global crisis affecting Muslim countries, among others? We think that, in the case of a true crisis, the Islamist reaction takes its cues from the consistent interpretations of traditional orthodox Islam. This is not, after all, the first situation of its kind in the long history of Islam.[24]

But here again Claverie did not become strident, preferring to focus his energy on what he called, together with Mohamed Arkoun, "the taking up in common of our lives and our societies" in all those areas where Muslims and non-Muslims found themselves seeking to understand, educate, and nurture. He also expressed on occasion his admiration for dialogue in the context of prayer, promoted in Algeria by Christian de Chergé, prior of the Trappist monastery of Tibhirine, together with the Sufis of Algeria.

In a context in which some were quick to cast Islam as the villain, Pierre Claverie strove to defuse the situation without betraying or downplaying his own convictions. He even thought that the tendency toward violence among some Muslims might become an opportunity for Islam to pose new questions and take steps forward. This approach can be seen in his address to the Pontifical Council for Interreligious Dialogue in November of 1992: "The discussion about modernity is being enlivened by the combined influence of the Western media and the backward step represented by Islamism. Under these circumstances, dialogue is more profound than it was when it consisted of abstract expressions of principle."[25]

## "In Oran, life goes on..."

During these years of the rise of Islamism, Pierre Claverie's calm and serenity were impressive. It was as if he had placed his life in the hands of God. "In Oran, life goes on," he wrote regularly in letters to his family, which display a constant sense of humor, as in these comments he wrote on May 8, 1991, his birthday: "The weather (today) is exactly as Papa always said it had been on the day of my birth: a torrent of rain during the wait for the joyous event for which Mamie was in labor. And Mickey Mouse came into the world... and here he is a few years later, a bishop. Fate certainly throws some strange surprises our way."

Was this a way of finding some escape at a time that was rather painful in terms of his family situation? Mamie, who had developed Alzheimer's disease, had needed to be placed in a specialized rest home in Toulon in January of 1990. This was a great suffering for Pierre, who drove her there himself, and wept over it.[26] She died there on February 11, 1992. Pierre would remain faithful to his brief visits with his father, between trips. When together, they picked up their conversation as though it had never been interrupted. Papie was almost blind by this time, and listened to the radio all day. Pierre hid nothing from him, including the spread of the violence that surrounded him. In Oran, in spite of the uncertainties weighing upon the country's future, he continued to work together with the priests and nuns of his diocese on the "platforms of encounter and service" that were so important to him. "Nothing about our plans has changed," he stated in regard to projects underway in Mascara and Sidi-bel-Abbès, adding all the same that these amounted to "a wager on the side of hope." At that time, he also tried to make his local church more international, less dependent on its French past. He called in an Egyptian seminarian, appointed as pastor of the cathedral an American religious priest, and prepared to ordain a young man from Poland. His collaborators even found him a bit hasty in his work, and criticized him for not listening to them enough. Was he already fighting against the clock? One could imagine so. He was also in greater and greater demand outside of the country, and had to make difficult choices in order to remain sufficiently present to his diocese.[27] With the beginning of the attacks in the spring of 1993, he would be thrust, little by little, to center stage.

Mohamed Boudiaf's ascent to leadership of the state at the beginning of 1992 had raised great hopes among the people, all the more so because he quickly attacked the corruption that was rotting away the regime and the functioning of the entire country. But these hopes were soon disappointed when Boudiaf was assassinated in Annaba on June 29, 1992. It was a young soldier of his personal guard who opened fire, but the Algerians were convinced that the coup had been engineered by the "political-financial mafia" whose privileges the new president intended to dispute. The real architects of the assassination would never come to light. A strange climate settled over Algeria, such that one couldn't always understand very well who had been killed and why. This uncertainty would poison the future and favor those who killed in the shadows. The principal ministers inherited the government: many of these were technical experts, like Sid Ahmed Ghozali and Belaïd

Abdesselam, who tried to put the Algerian economy back on track. But the measures that had to be taken (privatization, a free market, etc.) came with a high social cost that the weakened state could not permit itself without seeing the entire population take to the streets. Servicing the foreign debt became so costly that the International Monetary Fund suggested programs for structural adjustment. Algeria was at an impasse that was made worse by the drop in the price of oil after the Gulf War. "It would take an economic miracle to avoid a worst-case scenario," Claverie wrote. The only ones who claimed to offer an alternative were the Islamists. Since they had not yet been in charge of the government, they still had a great deal of credibility in the eyes of many, although their management of the municipalities had been brought into question immediately. "They don't even know how to take out the trash," Pierre Claverie confided to one of his friends.

Forcibly deprived of their electoral victory and with their backs against the wall from unlawful imprisonment and even torture, the Islamists would try to take power by violence. They made their first attacks in the spring of 1992, against the forces of the ruling regime: police and soldiers. Actual commandos who had learned guerilla warfare in Afghanistan carried out dangerous operations — they attacked garrisons, like the one in Guemmar on the Tunisian border, which they assaulted at the end of 1992 in order to seize the weapons there. They freed thousands of prisoners from the jail in Lambèse. What made a strong impression on public opinion was the aim of these operations: the Islamic Salvation Front was adopting the tactic that the Secret Army Organization, or OAS, had employed thirty years earlier: "The OAS strikes wherever it wants to." After their attacks, they took cover in the backcountry, where a disquieting uncertainty reigned, punctuated by clashes over influence between groups like the Islamic Salvation Army (a branch of the Islamic Salvation Front) and the Islamic Armed Forces, commanded by mysterious emirs who were authentic "warlords." In February of 1993, General Khaled Nezzar, the defense minister, narrowly escaped an attempt on his life. In March there began the assassinations of intellectuals, journalists, and artists: the economist Djilali Liabès was killed on March 16; author Tahar Djaout on May 26; the psychiatrist Mahfoud Boucebci on June 15; and on June 22 the economist M'hamed Boukhobza, whose throat was slit in front of his children. Director of the National Institute of Global Strategy, Boukhobza presided over the committee for evaluating the economic policies instituted by President Boudiaf.[28] "What they are killing is thought itself," wrote the International Committee for the Support of Algerian Intellectuals, which was founded in Paris in June of 1993 around the figures of Jean Leca and Pierre

Bourdieu, both known for their intellectual and human ties to Algeria. On June 21, 1993, the Algerian bishops asked the Christian communities of their dioceses to pray for peace, and to engage in "any activity in favor of peace that might be possible, taking the situation into account."[29]

## Choosing to Speak Out and Practice Solidarity in the Face of Violence

It was at this time that Pierre Claverie took the step of making known his personal and public position against the violence. He reflected at length upon Cardinal Duval's actions during the war of independence, and often went to visit him at his residence of Notre Dame d'Afrique, where he had retired after handing over the reins to Bishop Teissier in the spring of 1988.[30] On August 15, 1993, Claverie released a statement entitled "An Appeal from a Bishop of Algeria," published by the Algerian press under the title "We cannot remain silent." This is what it said:

> Together with the Catholics of my diocese, I wish to express the consternation and horror that take hold of us amid the escalation of violence in this country that we love, and to which we are linked by birth, marriage, friendship, work, and the sharing of hopes and difficulties over many years.
>
> There are not many of us, and we have almost no influence in the crisis that has shaken Algeria for five years now. We strive through prayer and active solidarity to maintain a climate of dialogue and fraternity with our many Muslim friends, whatever their views or tendencies. We are also coming to the defense of the truth when the media distort our shared reality.
>
> But we cannot remain silent over our disquiet and fear of seeing a political conflict degenerate into a civil war, which will produce no winners, because everyone's hands will be stained with his brothers' blood. Neither religion nor any ideology or political project can justify the daily deaths to which public opinion seems, unfortunately, to have resigned itself.
>
> We pray that God will enlighten with his wisdom those who are now in power and those who are lashing out against them in violence, so that dialogue and peace may permit the just resolution of the problems facing the Algerian people, and in particular those who are most deeply affected by the economic crisis. We humbly call upon the reason and

faith of all believers, so that dialogue may take the place of death and repression.[31]

This text clearly displays the fundamental elements of Pierre Claverie's approach: he speaks in the name of the solidarity of his church, modest though it may have been, in standing with the Algerian people; he issues an appeal for dialogue and denounces the recourse to violence carried out in the name of a "religion, ideology, or political project." And was there, between the lines, a questioning of the strong-arm tactics of repression used by the security forces (the famous "ninjas")? It should be noted that Amnesty International had just published a report denouncing the practice of torture by the security services. The powerful and feared Kasdi Merbah, former prime minister and ex-boss of military security, died in an attack on August 23, 1993, in spite of his bodyguards and armored car. No one was safe anymore. Although it was very brief and was published in the middle of the summer, Pierre Claverie's appeal did not go unnoticed, as he recounted humorously in a letter to his father and sister:

> This "media-star" bishop continues to do his thing by releasing a communiqué that has been published by the Algerian press and picked up by news agencies outside of the country (AFP, BBC, Hollande). One newspaper gave it the title "The Bishop of Oran: 'We cannot remain silent.'" Radio France introduced it with the words "The Algerian episcopate rises to the call"...I have recorded a number of telephone interviews that will be broadcast throughout this week, and every day people call me on the phone to thank me...I am sending you the text of my appeal; it will explain why I chose to speak out. The situation is not good, and the violence is becoming more widespread and more radical. There is an urgent need for dialogue: the more time passes, the more the extremists on both sides run the risk of cutting off any chance of a peace process. (letter of August 19, 1993)

Pierre Claverie had a warmth about him and a way of speaking that sometimes induced others to listen to him more closely than they would to someone else.[32] He thought that he could contribute to a better understanding of the drama that Algeria was living through: "A special correspondent for AFP kept me occupied for part of the morning. I am happy to participate in this sort of exchange, hoping that they will be able to take into account the unique perspective we can bring to the crisis because of our experience and our profound relationships with the country" (letter of November 22, 1993).

With violence breeding more violence, the situation worsened over the months. The Algerian army, which was heavily equipped on the Soviet model, struggled to find the resources and strategies capable of handling the guerillas' tactics: attacks on the markets, ambushes along country roads, the desperate actions of suicide bombers ready for anything. In the summer of 1993, dozens were killed when a military convoy was ambushed in Chréa. Whenever the army encircled a guerilla hideout, it took the severe approach and destroyed it completely, using tank battalions if necessary. The country settled into violence; human life was seen as worthless, and Algeria buried her children by the thousands. Her most talented offspring, like Dr. Belkenchir, a pediatrician; Ahmed Asselah, director of the school of fine arts in Algiers; Abdelkader Alloula, director of the theater in Oran; and many journalists were the targets of assassinations between October of 1993 and March of 1994. In a diary entry from that period, the journalist Mohamed Balhi wrote, "The 8:00 p.m. television newscast has turned into an obituary, and one watches it with the stomach in knots."[33] Pierre Claverie was particularly shocked by the assassination of Alloula on March 14, 1994: "We have lost one of our leading figures in Algerian culture and theater," he wrote. "He was a free-spirited man, it is true, unafraid of proclaiming his anti-Islamist ideas. He was close to the children, heading an aid organization for children with cancer. One cannot really understand what causes such senseless acts, except for religious madness, which in the end is the worst kind" (letter of March 15, 1994).

Not even foreigners were safe anymore: the escalating violence had broken new symbolic ground on September 21, 1993, with the kidnapping and assassination of two French surveyors working in the region of Sidi-bel-Abbès. Pierre Claverie went to the hospital's candlelit viewing room to pray before the departure of the bodies for France. Announcing their action, the Islamic Armed Forces issued an ultimatum for all foreigners to leave the country by the end of November. The Bishop of Oran refused to panic ("we put the threat in its proper perspective while still taking the necessary precautions," he wrote), but he had already factored the possibility of his death into his view of his mission. In December of 1993, twelve Croatians, Christians, had their throats slit in Tamesguida; they were working on a construction project near the monastery of Tibhirine.[34] "It's going poorly here," Claverie wrote to his family on the eve of a great march organized by the democrats seeking to mobilize against the violence. The season of Lent soon came for the Christians, and the bishop of Oran entitled his editorial for the February edition of *Le Lien* "In the Face of Death." Here is its conclusion, which displays a clear change of tone:

In traveling down some of the roads of this diocese where dozens of victims have fallen to terrorism or repression over recent weeks, I told myself that this Lent should be a time for all of us to look death in the face. What place does it have in our lives? Why are we so afraid of it? We are walking with Jesus down the road to Easter, and we will carry out with devotion the rites of Holy Week, in "worshiping" the cross. We recognize in this the path that Jesus once followed to true life, and along which he still leads us today. Is this simply a bit of liturgical theatrics before the "happy ending" of the Resurrection? Or what if these rituals, with their daily or weekly celebrations of the Mass, were an initiation into the giving of our lives, into the love of which we sing so airily that it is "stronger than death"? Then Lent would take on an importance and a seriousness far beyond that of abstaining from food, cigarettes, or some trifling pleasure or object of desire . . . It poses to us the essential question: what are we doing with our lives?[35]

Three months later came the first assassinations of Catholic religious, posing to the church of Algeria radical questions about the meaning and the prudence of its being there. It is impressive that Pierre Claverie had already taken the only theological stance capable of giving a response to these questions: the church is here for love, following the example of Jesus. That's it. It is also clear that this crisis had clarified his place in the country, "his" country: "Pierre is not here as an observer, or as someone standing on the edge between France and Algeria, or between Christianity and Islam," emphasized one of his Algerian friends, Mr. Guadni, president of the league of human rights for western Algeria. "Pierre is where he belongs." And he would not shrink from the consequences of such recognition, which he had long expected.

## Chapter Eleven

# A Church on the Fault Lines
## 1994–95

> The church carries out its vocation and its mission when it is present wherever humanity is torn, crucified, and fragmented… We are indeed where we belong, because it is only in this way that one can see the light of the Resurrection, and together with it the hope of the renewal of our world.[1]     — Pierre Claverie

May 7, 1994. A beautiful spring evening. I was having dinner with Henri Teissier, archbishop of Algiers, in a *trattoria* in the Rome neighborhood of Trastevere. There was a synod of the African bishops taking place in Rome. Teissier enthusiastically told me about the atmosphere at the synod, and added in an offhand remark, "and it's so nice to be able to walk down the street without having to look out for who might be following you." The relief was short-lived: the following day we received the news of the death of Brother Henri Vergès and Sister Paul-Hélène Saint-Raymond, who were killed in the library they maintained for the young people of a working-class neighborhood in Algiers. With their deaths, the church of Algeria entered a time of trial that would see it lose nineteen of its religious men and women. As of the writing of this book, Pierre Claverie is the latest of these martyrs.

For Claverie, a period now began when he would exert himself to the utmost, including in the arena of public debate, considering this a service he was obliged to render to his church and his country. At a time when danger threatened everything for which he had lived and fought — respect for the Other, the acceptance of differences, dialogue — it wasn't a good idea any more for him to protect himself. As a bishop and a son of Algeria, he was listened to, so he made use of his voice in solidarity with his many Algerian friends who were also the resistance. His editorials became scathing, denouncing "the cowardice of those who kill in the shadows." Of those stunned by the violence, he remarked, "It is their astonishment that astonishes me: Those who sow the wind . . . " But this wasn't all he had to say: while recognizing that his church was shaken by this trial, the bishop of Oran expressed his conviction that it was right where it should be. Discreetly present at first like a faint melody, the theme of being present at the foot of the cross, "along the fault lines where humanity is crucified," became the dominant theme of his speech, before becoming the last act of his life.

## A Season of Martyrdom

Shock spread at news of the assassination of the two religious in the Casbah. It came on the same day as a "march for dialogue" through the streets of Algiers, and the same day, May 8, as the birthday of Pierre Claverie, "a birthday that began in joy and ended in tragedy," as he wrote to his family. He added that "until 10:30 p.m., the bishop's residence was deluged with telephone calls, telegrams, and visits from distressed and ashamed friends." The Marist Brother and the Little Sister of the Assumption, sixty-five and sixty-seven years old respectively, who had lived for decades in Algeria and were fluent in Arabic, these two religious were the epitome of unselfish service: the library on Ben-Cheneb street, where they offered their service gratis to young people who were only too happy to find a few books in Arabic to pass the time or prepare for exams. Located in an old Moorish house in the upper Casbah, near the tomb of the patron saint of Algiers, Sidi Abderrahmane, it was a model of discreet integration: its purpose was to render a service, and nothing else. So the communiqué released by *El-Ansar*, a weekly newspaper published by the Islamic Armed Forces, seemed completely incongruous: "As part of the effort to expunge Jews, Christians, and miscreants from the Muslim land of Algeria, a brigade of the Islamic Armed Forces carried out an ambush to kill two crusaders who had long sown evil in Algeria." The neighbors who had come to them for help filling out administrative forms, or simply for friendship, were dismayed and chagrined — such callousness! " 'There is no greater love than to give one's life for one's friends'; Henri and Paul-Hélène did this every day," Archbishop Teissier said at the funeral Mass. This was held at Notre Dame d'Afrique, in the presence of a large group of Algerian friends and, of course, of the entire Christian community, which was closing ranks. Ninety-one years old and in deep distress, Cardinal Duval made a very simple statement at the end of the ceremony: "Our dear brother Henri and admirable sister Paul-Hélène were authentic witnesses of the love of Christ, of the absolute selflessness of the church, and of fidelity to the Algerian people." That said it all.

But life had to continue, albeit in a new context:[2] "It is a shock for many of my friends who did not think things would come to this. Nor does it surprise me anymore," wrote Pierre Claverie, who would strive to accompany and guide his community through what it now faced. He set the course in two of his editorials. His first reaction was one of indignation: "Why?" he asked in the May edition of *Le Lien:*

> We knew very well that there are some who consider us dangerous and harmful influences, the remnants of a colonial past and incorrigible enemies of Islam... We have read and heard this so often, and recently too, in part of the press and on the radio and television, that we grew accustomed to it...
>
> We continued nonetheless to believe that the trust and friendship of so many Algerians would protect us. As one of those closest to us said, "This cannot happen in the land of Saint Augustine and of the emir Abdelkader." Those who know us well know that we are not crusaders or the spies of foreign governments.

And the bishop of Oran enumerated the services provided for the people of Algeria in the schools run by the fathers and sisters, in the centers for the handicapped or the homes for the aged. The Algerian church went even farther, striving in a number of ways to "promote the value of Algeria's culture and the riches of its civilization."

> If one were to tell us that we should have nothing to do with all of this, I would admit it under great protest, because it would be the sign that ethnic, religious, and cultural purification were at work in Algeria as in Bosnia...
>
> But in reality, saying this does not go far enough: without a doubt, Brother Henri and Sister Paul-Hélène were assassinated in Algiers because they were religious... Those who assassinated them considered them enemies of Islam... Is their Islam so fragile that they could be afraid of a sixty-five-year-old man and a sixty-seven-year-old woman?...

Taking up his responsibility as a bishop, he concluded with these almost inflammatory words:

> And the cowardice of these killers in the shadows is so abominable! I would understand if someone were to take aim at me; as a bishop I represent, perhaps, in the eyes of some, a contemptible or dangerous institution. I am in a position of responsibility, and I have always defended publicly what has seemed to me to be just and true, what fosters freedom

and respect for individuals, especially the less fortunate and minorities. I have fought for dialogue and friendship among peoples, cultures, and religions. All of that probably merits death, and I am ready to run that risk. This would even be my homage to the God in whom I believe. But I don't understand very well the reasons for taking offense at Brother Henri and Sister Paul-Hélène.

This indignant editorial, which extended his earlier protests at the practice of some who taught hatred of others to young people, was followed by another text of a very different tone. This expressed the trial that the Algerian church found itself in, and the profound meaning that could be given to this. It was entitled, "Pray ceaselessly":[3]

Many among us are shaken...Shaken in their nervous resistance... shaken in the brutal questioning of their decisions...libraries, education for women, cooperation...Are we still wanted? Shaken finally, in certain convictions they have acquired after years of trial and difficult interior and collective conversions. We had thought the moment had arrived for new relationships between Christians and Muslims, founded on mutual respect and trust...We had led along this path a good number of churches still obstructed by prejudices left over from centuries of conflict...Encounter and dialogue had become the watchwords of our presence...The times of trial really are when our weaknesses come to the surface, and when it becomes important to find what it is that draws us forward and urges us to meet life. It is also, perhaps, the moment for us to recall that we are believers...in a God who "compromised" himself in human history to the point of sharing in the human condition: this is the folly of Christianity, and it is our faith. Believing this does not mean confining religion to the domain of worship or of the observance of legal prescriptions. God gives himself to understanding, service, and love in all the dimensions of human existence, with its good and bad moments. Each one of our actions can therefore acquire meaning...

Jesus tells us and proves to us that God is passionate, that his name is Love...What could be more foolish than going to one's death with nothing but a defenseless and disarming love that forgives in the act of dying? And what could be more senseless than recruiting one's followers from among the fishermen of Galilee, the publicans, prostitutes, and the misfits? And yet that is the line of believers to which we belong — not the accountants of what is permitted and forbidden, nor the warriors of a religion of conquest...Jesus alone can lead us along the path of the living God: on our own, we cannot cling to the "wisdom of the Greeks," which Paul opposes to the "folly of the cross." Our life becomes rich and fruitful when we run the risk of this unique form of folly that runs throughout the gospel with a jubilant audacity. It is the power of the divine Spirit that alone can lead us to embark on this journey... And that is what prayer is. Pray ceaselessly!

From this point on, these two themes would continually circulate through the thought and expression of Pierre Claverie during the months of trial that the church would face. The bishops would be forced to shut down some of their communities, reorganize the Christian presence, and evaluate, step by step, to what point those in their charge could endure. In October, two Spanish religious sisters — Sister Esther and Sister Caridad — were assassinated in Bab el Oued. At the funeral, Sister Esther's father stated, "I forgive my daughter's killers, and I thank the Algerian people for allowing her to be who she was." Saïd Mekbel, an Algerian journalist who would be assassinated later, published a very moving comment in *Le Matin*, beginning with these words: "May it please God that all of us together have the interior freedom to offer our forgiveness, together with the fervor of our friendship, and that we maintain the courage to continue establishing peace."[4] In December, four White Fathers were assassinated in Tizi-Ouzou, in Kabylia: once again, these were men with deep roots in the country, thoroughly steeped in Algerian culture, and loved by those around them.[5] Many innocent Algerians also died, like the five Boy Scouts killed in Mostaganem in November of 1994. This was the period when some of Pierre Claverie's childhood friends, former members of the Saint-Do scouting group, created an association "to aid Pierre and the activities of the diocese of Oran." There was definitely a lot going on. But another and more political battle was in store for him, a battle in which he would have willingly been left out of.

## The Sad Affair of Sant'Egidio

In November of 1994, a group of Italian Christians, the Sant'Egidio community, discreetly held talks in Rome aimed at fostering peace negotiations in Algeria. This was the period when President Zeroual tried to restore contact with the Islamists by freeing the main leaders of the Islamic Salvation Front. His approach prompted strong reactions from the Algerian public.[6] Nevertheless, at the end of a second meeting in January of 1995, the Sant'Egidio

initiative concluded with the signature, "Platform for a peaceful political solution to the Algerian crisis," also known as the "Rome platform." The main
signatories were the Algerian opposition parties and the Islamic Salvation
Front. In Algeria, the effect of the news was explosive: the government immediately condemned the initiative, which it considered a form of interference in
the country's internal affairs. Algerian public opinion was hardly more favorable, and the people gave voice to their disapproval in street demonstrations.
The Algerians were very sensitive about the sovereignty they had acquired
at such great cost, and did not look kindly on the fact that the Algerian
crisis had been taken to foreign soil, as the press unanimously emphasized.
The democrats, finally, were upset because this was the first time that the
leaders of the Islamist parties had been brought to the negotiating table —
and had come away without being required to make an explicit renunciation
of violence.

For its part, the Algerian church found itself in a very delicate situation:
how could it explain to the Algerian public that the initiative of a Catholic community, and moreover one in Rome, did not necessarily involve the
Christians of Algeria and their hierarchy? The apostolic nuncio in Algiers was
summoned to the Ministry of Foreign Affairs, and the bishops of Algeria were
questioned on this "Catholic" initiative about which they had not even been
consulted. Since November 26, 1994, at the end of the first meeting in Rome,
a group of lay people, sisters, and priests living in Algeria had called the attention of the Sant'Egidio group to the consequences of such an initiative.[7] The
bishops had also made their reservations known. "We simply offered the Algerians an opportunity for dialogue," Andrea Riccardi, the community's leader,
had replied, deciding to go forward with the project. "We did not need this
sudden burst of attention," Pierre Claverie wrote. He would be drawn in to
involve himself quite openly in a political dossier.[8]

What is the community of Sant'Egidio? It is one of the wonderful outcomes
of the postconciliar Italian church. Its name comes from a small church from
the neighborhood of Trastevere in Rome where the community meets to pray,
near an ancient cloister where its offices are located. But the community
cannot be reduced to a few buildings — it is the fruit of the initiative of
young Italian Christians who, in the period following the council, wanted to
take the gospel seriously. They placed themselves at the service of the many
poor people in several Roman suburbs — there were almost 600,000 of these,
living in severe hardship.[9] At first the group was composed of a young Italian
university student, Andrea Riccardi, and a few other young people close to
Carlo Maria Martini, the rector of the Rome Biblical Institute and future

archbishop of Milan. Less politicized than other young people after 1968, and less emotional than the members of the charismatic movements, these young Christians would mark out an original path in which concrete action on behalf of the poor would go hand in hand with prayer, each reinforcing the other. They began by teaching children, then opened soup kitchens and centers for isolated elderly people and AIDS patients, and the community gradually expanded to thousands of members who are active in a number of places in Italy, and even outside of it. Each of them gives a significant part of his or her time — several hours each day — to these service works, and receives Christian and spiritual formation from the community, a stimulus to live the gospel message. Each evening, hundreds of them gather in their church for a beautiful vespers prayer: they sing psalms and listen to a commentary on a passage from the Gospel. It is a simple, joyful, fervent service. A number of religious studying or working in Rome join them, finding among them the atmosphere of a living Christian community.

Over the years, the community began to embrace other concerns, beginning with interreligious dialogue. In 1986, it began a yearly celebration of an interreligious day of prayer for peace in conjunction of the day of prayer presided over by the pope in Assisi. Through this initiative Sant'Egidio developed extensive contacts with Orthodoxy and the Muslim world. It is how the community paved the way for John Paul II's meeting with the Orthodox patriarch of Romania, Teoctist, in May of 1999. At the beginning of the 1990s, through the auspices of one of their friends, Bishop Beira of Mozambique, the community got involved in mediation efforts for the factions of a civil war that was ravaging the country. A peace agreement was signed at their offices in Trastevere on October 4, 1992, after twenty-seven months of negotiations. This won them their reputation as peacemakers, or "the UN of Trastevere," and led to their involvement in the peace initiative for Algeria, a country with which the community had been trying to establish relations for a long time.[10]

Who were the partners that Sant'Egidio had brought together? These were extremely varied — the best known were Ahmed Ben Bella and Hocine Aït Ahmed, two historical figures who had returned to politics after many years in prison or exile, after which they founded their own political parties: the Movement for Democracy in Algeria, and the Socialist Forces Front. Only the latter of these carried any political weight. There was also a veteran of the Algerian government, Abdelhamid Mehri of the National Liberation Front, a party that had seen its political influence diminish significantly. There were representatives from very marginal parties, like the (Trotskyite) Workers' Party and Ennahada (a middle-of-the-road Islamist party). And there was the highly controversial Abdennour Ali Yahia, president of one of the Algerian leagues for human rights, who would come to be seen as the advocate for the Islamists. In the absence of democratic forces, the only party that seemed to have any clout at the negotiating table was the Islamic Salvation Front, represented by its foreign delegates, Anwar Haddam and Rabah Kebir. Both of these would later run into difficulties with authorities in their countries of residence, the United States and Germany, on account of their ambiguous statements about terrorism. This party had been outlawed in Algeria since March of 1992, and its main leaders, Abassi Madani and Ali Belhadj, had been imprisoned. Sant'Egidio provided them with an unexpected forum. Mario Giro, who conducted the negotiations on behalf of Sant'Egidio, considered as positive the fact that the Islamic Salvation Front had signed the "Rome platform," "this effort to establish peace with the government." "With the Rome platform," he added, "the Islamic Salvation Front has come alongside the other opposition parties, and is thus obliged to join in the discussions, make concessions, and return to a certain measure of legality."[11] The future would show that things were not quite so simple as that. What did the document say? It established a sort of process for breaking the impasse and restoring dialogue. Apparent guarantees were given, but these concealed profound ambiguities. Thus the signatories committed to accepting "the primacy of legitimate law" (section A, line 7) — but what was legitimate law? For the Islamic Salvation Front, this could only mean *al-Qanûn al-sharîî*, Islamic law, and not *al-Qanûn al-madani*, or civil law. This is more than a simple misunderstanding: "This paragraph represents the very foundation of the ideology of the Islamic Salvation Front, and of its strategy for seizing power," Pierre Claverie emphasized.

The bishops of Algeria had long followed the situation on the ground, reading the Arabic-language press and listening to the preaching of the fundamentalists — but their view was not really taken into consideration. This was all the more insulting in that they had been the ones — and Archbishop Teissier in particular — who had helped Sant'Egidio make its first contacts in Algeria a few years earlier.[12] It was a little like the betrayal of a trust. In any case, a discreet encounter between the negotiators for Sant'Egidio and the bishops of Algeria took place after the signing of the accord, on January 30, 1995, at the Rome headquarters of the White Fathers. It was a difficult discussion, with the bishops being accused by Sant'Egidio of having become the servants of France and of sharing, de facto, the all-out intransigence of the Algerian government. The accusation of being on France's side (*hizb franza*) never failed to cause a stir in a highly nationalistic Algeria. Pierre Claverie spoke a great deal over the course of the meeting, which lasted an hour and a half, but he didn't get the impression that anyone was really listening to him. On the same occasion, the bishops met with the pope and with Archbishop Jean-Louis Tauran, the Vatican "foreign minister," who assured them of the Holy See's support.[13] Vatican diplomats would discreetly urge Sant'Egidio to hold back, but Catholic media outlets, which were insufficiently informed of the details and seduced by the prospects for a Christian-sponsored peace agreement, would continue their simplistic promotion of the Rome platform.[14] Taking note of this campaign, Pierre Claverie chose to speak out in the media on a number of occasions in the spring of 1995 — too often for the comfort of those around him, who were afraid of seeing him come to the forefront in a country where the church had to take care to remain discreet.

## A Springtime Media Blitz

Pierre Claverie was effective in the media: he hated officialspeak, and he presented himself with human warmth and courage. So it should come as no surprise that, in a situation as complicated as that in Algeria, he was often called upon to help explain things. He welcomed these opportunities, taking every chance he could to express the Algerian church's message of fraternity, which, in his eyes, was of universal import. Beginning in 1990, he gave up most of the usual preached summer retreats in order to be present in Algeria while the priests of his diocese went on vacation. On the other hand, he accepted a number of invitations throughout the year, attracting large audiences. During the pilgrimage of the rosary in Lourdes in October of 1991, 8,000 persons attended his conference on the church of Algeria, and more than 40,000 came to hear him preach. In May of 1992, he participated in the Terre d'Avenir forum of the Catholic Committee against Hunger and for Development, and in May of 1994, in the National Forum of Christian Communities in Angers. His notable appearances also included his participation at the "Frat" (the Fraternel, an annual pilgrimage for young people) in Lourdes, where he was a sensation with the 7,000 young people of the movements, campus ministries, and diocesan schools of Île-de-France. A question-and-answer session on the Eucharist with these thousands of young people in the Basilica of Saint Pius X remained emblazoned on the memories of those in attendance. In speaking with an original voice on the question of the Other, which is not unique to Algeria, Pierre Claverie had a sort of "diocese without borders" that gave him a greater hearing than his own diocese, which numbered only two or three hundred Christians. In this period he had a genuine audience in the region of Marseille, where he gladly engaged in public discussions with men like Souheib Bencheikh, the mufti of Marseille, and Jean-Pierre Courtès, who was engaged in promoting dialogue among Christians and Muslims in groups such as the Club de Marseille.[15] A "secularist bishop" and an "Algerian Christian," he was an unusual figure who captivated the young North Africans who invited him to participate in discussions on Radio Gazelle and at the Maison de l'egravetranger. For Souheib Bencheikh, the son of Sheikh Abbas, who had invited Claverie to the Paris mosque, Pierre was a valuable ally in the struggle for an open, aboveground form of Islam in France. The two would meet once more for a final conference in Bastia in June of 1996.

At the end of February of 1995, Pierre Claverie gave a conference in Montpellier on the topic "Christians in Algeria today." Despite his proficiency with the spoken word, he arrived clutching a nine-page manuscript in which he drew a picture of the political and social situation in Algeria, in order to make better known the justifications for a Christian presence there. His argument was arranged in five points:

First, the violence did not begin with the interruption of the electoral process by the army in 1992; it had been underway before this, in the Islamist pressure on the population aimed at imposing a social organization in conformity with sharia: the separation of the sexes, even at school, the closing of the bars, "places of pleasure and debauchery," and the demand that "women remain at home in an atmosphere of chastity, modesty, and humility," etc.[16]

Second, the type of democratization undertaken in Algeria, in part under pressure from the West as a condition for financial aid, had resulted in the end of the National Liberation Front's monopoly on power and in the overhasty initiation of multiparty politics, with the first new party formed being the Islamic Salvation Front. And an attentive analysis of the legislative elections of 1992 did not permit one to conclude that the Islamic Salvation Front had won a landslide victory, as some had been quick to do: with forty-one percent of voters failing to go to the polls, the Islamic Salvation Front, although it was the dominant party, received only 29 percent of registered voters.

Third, this led to the interest in civil society, which had not sided overwhelmingly with either the Islamists or the government, a form of government that was still too uncertain after the resignation of President Chadli. "In the reigning climate of violence in the country," Claverie emphasizes that "projects continue forward, construction sites are being opened, housing is being built . . . In this situation, merely to continue with everyday activities is an act of resistance and hope." He went on, "The Algerians register their disapproval by living, working, and continuing the activities that bring meaning to every death-haunted hour ... It is within this context of resistance that the activities of our church take place," and the church in Algeria knew the cost of this, because a number of Christians had already been killed: apart from the eight religious assassinated in 1994, twelve Croats had paid with their lives for the fact of being Christian.

Fourth, in such a context, the Rome platform opens up no real prospects: for one thing, it is founded upon the Islamists, who have been discredited by their violence and by the barbarity of their actions, and have already lost a good number of their followers. But more importantly, it downplays the hope for the future that is represented by the democrats, as fragile as they are at this point because of the work still to be done to separate religion and government.

Fifth, in this very complex context the church's presence takes its meaning. The Algerian church is respected worldwide, due in large part to "the emblematic figure of Cardinal Duval." It is all the more beloved on account of the fact that, in spite of the risks, it decided to remain in the country in concrete and daily solidarity with the Algerians, for whom each day is an act of resistance. Above all, the church is there as "a modest sign of the covenant of love that God offers to a people," a love that is expressed more effectively the more powerless one is. And Pierre Claverie cited a wonderful passage written by his Jesuit friend Bernard Lapize, who had recently returned to Algeria, precisely because this time of trial was also a time for selflessness and compassion.[17]

The conclusion of this talk in Montpelier deserves to be cited at length, because it expresses the deepest motivations for Pierre Claverie's involvement:

> The last reason, which seems to be the most foolish of all, is for me the most persuasive. Jesus died with his body torn apart between heaven and earth, his arms extended to gather in the children of God who had been scattered by the sin that separates them, isolates them, and pits them against one another and even against God himself. He placed himself upon the fault lines created by sin. Thrown out of balance and ruptured in body, heart, and spirit, individuals and social groups found healing and reconciliation in him, because he took these things upon himself. He places his own disciples upon these same fault lines, with the same mission of healing and reconciliation. The church carries out its vocation and its mission when it is present wherever humanity is torn, crucified, and fragmented. In Algeria we find ourselves on a seismic division that extends throughout the entire world: Islam/West,

North/South, rich/poor, etc. We are indeed where we belong, because it is only in this way that one can see the light of the Resurrection, and together with it the hope for the renewal of our world.

From this time on, the theme of the "fault lines" found frequent expression in his writings.

Should it be surprising that Pierre Claverie's words attracted such interest? His statements contained a refined political analysis that furthered the understanding of Algeria's apparently baffling situation, together with "an evangelical tone" (M. Borrmans) which alone was capable of justifying the continued presence of the Christians despite the threat of death. Claverie received a flood of media requests for interviews: in February in Marseille, he appeared on Radio France Internationale, in the newspaper *Midi libre,* and on a number of local radio stations. They all had questions on the Rome platform, which had won over those who understood the situation only from a distance. He replied as completely as he could, in spite of understanding the danger that his words might be twisted. "The way to peace is through political negotiation," he told *La Croix* in March of 1995, "but not at any price whatsoever." In May he returned to Paris to ordain two young Dominican friars to the priesthood, both of whom were destined for the Arab world. He repeated in his homily what had become his leitmotif: "Our mission places us at the heart of humanity's distress and divisions."[18] At the Dominican convent of Saint-Jacques he gave a second presentation of his talk at Montpellier, and at the end of the week he fielded questions from members of the Catholic media. He met with the editors of the Malesherbes publishing group, which produces *La Vie, L'Actualité religieuse,* and *Croissance.* He gave a talk to the staff of the newspaper *La Croix,* and met with the directors of Bayard-Presse, which publishes both *La Croix* and *Le Pèlerin.* Other encounters included the team that produces *Jour du Seigneur,* a religious program broadcast on Antenne 2, for which he recorded two hours of programming on tolerance; the Catholic Committee against Hunger and for Development; and interviews with Radio France Internationale and Radio Notre-Dame. And all of this between May 18 and 24! Had he, then, fallen into the snare of stardom?

All of his closest friends had this thought, to some extent, at the time. His correspondence with his family affords a better understanding of his decision. On the last day of this media marathon — May 24 — he wrote, "Fatigue has begun to set in. The end of this trip is approaching . . . Fr. Kopf will accompany me to Orly, and I will arrive at La Sénia [the Oran airport] as usual. So there you have it. *I believe that this was worthwhile, and that these working meetings will lead to a modification of the editorial line of the major Catholic media on the subject of Algeria*" (emphasis added).

To understand this last sentence, one must recall the substantial one-sided support from some of the Catholic media for Sant'Egidio's perspective on the situation in Algeria. In April, Claverie had responded to a simplistic presentation of the issue in *L'Actualité religieuse*.[19] Through imprecise reporting, these media would present Claverie and Archbishop Teissier almost as the enemies of dialogue.[20] On July 29, 1995, *Le Monde* carried the headline "The Algerian bishops are torn between desire for peace and loyalty to the government." For a number of months, they would be presented as *éradicateurs,* a term that until then had denoted the members of the Algerian military who favored the elimination of the terrorists, as opposed to those who favored dialogue. The only French newspaper that presented the situation in Algeria in a less simplistic manner was *Témoignage chrétien,* whose advocacy on behalf of Algeria went back to the war of liberation.

Had Claverie been imprudent in his extensive media appearances? When he returned to Algeria, he was confined to his residence for a number of days, for "security reasons."[21] It is clear that for him this was a form of solidarity with the Algerians' resistance to the violence that was preying upon them.[22]

## To Leave, or to Stay?
## A Question of Presence on the Fault Lines

Should one stay or leave? This question was posed by many. But for Pierre Claverie this was not a consideration at all, at least as far as he himself was concerned: Algeria was his country, and he was a bishop charged with leading his community, come what may. But the climate of violence and the string of assassinations put the members of the Christian community to a difficult test. In June of 1994, after the death of the two religious in the Casbah, Claverie canceled his summer vacation plans: he remained in Oran, and encouraged the priests and the sisters to go on vacation to restore their strength. He used this time ordinarily devoted to summer vacation to crisscross the diocese again and again, listening to and encouraging everyone he met: "We are assessing the situation and the 'morale of the troops,' and are making some decisions for the coming months. I am astounded by the courageous serenity of these men and women who remain trusting even though they understand the dangers facing them. They find great support among their Algerian friends, who are doing all they can to be present to them and demonstrate their friendship," he wrote in a letter dated May 29, 1994, in which he acknowledged that "we are in too deep to find easy protection."

He received a number of his Algerian friends at his residence — they, too, needed support, as this statement from the spring of 1994 shows: "Today was calm, with just a few visits from some traumatized and worried people. We truly must fight hour after hour to help people not to give up." His friend Oum el Kheir commented, "Pierre was not only the bishop of the Christians; he was the bishop of Oran." These encounters were sometimes the occasion of unexpected encouragement, as he relates in a letter dated March 21, 1994:

> A great barricade at the entrance to the Mitidja, in El Affroun. A gendarme made a sign for us to pull over. This dialogue followed:
> "Hello! Your papers, please ... You live in Oran?"
> "Yes!"
> "Do you work at the Lycée Pasteur?"
> "No, I am the bishop of Oran."
> "Ah! Do you know the sister who works with the deaf-mutes?"
> "Yes, of course."
> "Where is she now? My sister used to work with her, and she would like to find out where she is so she can write to her. My family loved her very much."
> "She is retired now, and she lives in France."
> "Will you give me her address?"
> "I don't have it with me."
> "Well then, please tell her that the gendarme Moulay and his whole family sends a hug to her."

"So, it's not all about terror here, after all," Claverie concludes.

At other moments, to defuse the tension ("there were some worrisome spots along the way"), he commented on the beauty of the countryside they were passing through: the almond trees were in the bloom of spring, and the evening sky was tinged with various shades of blue. More than ever, he savored the joys of friendship: "In these hours of gloom, ordinary life comes into sharp focus. As I travel throughout the diocese visiting these small, dispersed, courageous communities, I find the countryside even more beautiful, and the people even more welcoming and attentive. They are often more worried for us than we ourselves. What gestures of friendship and solidarity we receive each day from people close to us, or from those who don't even know us!"[23]

In January of 1995, the bishops met with the leaders of the religious communities, "a rather tense encounter," Pierre Claverie related, "because these leaders were beginning to worry, although at bottom the great majority of them are holding firm despite the evident dangers." This was the period when the consulates were pressuring their foreign nationals to return home, and imposing security measures on those who stayed.[24] Nor could families conceal their concern. The Algerian authorities insisted that security measures be put in place. One of the reasons for the visit of the Algerian bishops to Rome in January of 1995 was for them to explain the situation to the heads of the religious congregations. The stance that immediately asserted itself was that the church would remain, because it did not consider itself as a foreign presence — but the outlook for its personnel in Algeria would be considered on a case by case basis; some of them could hold out, albeit nervously, while others could not. The bishops were there to assist with this discernment. Some would leave, and a number of communities would be shut down, but the majority of the permanent members of the Christian community would remain. The diocese of Oran would even continue to undertake projects, to create initiatives for serving the country, like the library of agricultural science opened in Mascara in April of 1995. This exercise of solidarity at a time of trial earned unexpected expressions of gratitude for the bishop of Oran.

Returning one day from a visit with the Dominican sisters in Tounane by a dangerous road, he received a visit from a close friend who had brought — as a gift from another Algerian friend — a bottle of champagne. "Moët et Chandon brut! O astonishing, wonderful Algeria," he wrote (letter of January 27, 1995). Other friends, instructors at the university of Oran, came by with their children and gave him "the bread of friendship, made at home." All the same, these were very difficult months for him in his responsibilities as a bishop. In a rare disclosure of his personal struggles, he said one day to François Chavanes, "My first prayer each morning is that no member of the Oran Christian community be killed that day." Chavanes comments, "I thought at the time, and I still think, that he could have continued, 'but if it must be, let me be the one, and let me be the last.' And that's what happened."[25]

## From Death to Resurrection: The Paschal Experience

Pierre Claverie did not make it through these months solely on the basis of his psychological resilience. His writings from the spring of 1995 convey an extremely profound spiritual experience. At the meeting of the major superiors of Algeria in March, he stated, "At issue here is a demonstration of fidelity, rather than of strength. It seems more important than ever to look upon the

Algerians with respect, trust, and goodwill, as from God's perspective. We must retain a contemplative outlook amid the turbulence of discussion."[26]

That year, because of the dangers of traveling on the roads, he stayed in Oran for Easter. His memorable homilies for the Easter vigil and Easter Sunday were entitled "À travers la mort" (Through Death):[27]

> In hearing us speak of the resurrection, those who do not share this hope might dismiss us as daydreamers. [They might say] You have said, "death is conquered"? Either these words mean something else, or you are fooling yourselves. Look around you . . . and especially here in Algeria, right now: death, alas, is everywhere. And not only with its familiar face in the slow decay of old age or the more brutal onset of illness, but with the horrible aspect of the daily victims of barbarous violence . . .
>
> The daily confrontation of violent death dispels all of [our] illusions, these forms of evasion from the only universal reality which one must resolutely face: death. We who recognize in Jesus the "well-beloved Son," the glory of God in man fully alive — we see in death the hour of this glory's revelation, the visible face of the resurrection. On a number of occasions during his travels throughout Palestine, Jesus demonstrated his willingness to face the unavoidable. He knew very well that his message and his actions would bring him condemnation from the political and religious authorities. He believed that these persons trapped humanity in a state of fear . . . He declared that there is no greater love than to give one's life for one's friends.
>
> This is possible only through trust in a God who is life and who gives life, a God whom one can call Father even in the midst of suffering and death. With him, and like Jesus, we can fight against the powers of death with the weapons of life: love, justice, peace, freedom, truthfulness, trust, compassion. With Him, and like Jesus, we can expose our lives without fear to those who kill the body but cannot kill the soul . . . Life is an indefinite resurrection in which it is death that validates each day, what is essential in our words and actions. "No one takes my life from me — it is I that give it away."
>
> Jesus permits us to transform the passive suffering of death into an active gift of ourselves through which life is renewed and intensified . . .
>
> In doing all this, together with Jesus we will give our life without fear of losing it, in the hope of the resurrection and for the coming of the Kingdom of the living.

This paschal approach to death and this tone of serenity returned in the homily for the ordination of young Jesuits in the church of Saint-Ignace in Paris, on June 10, 1995:

> The passion of Jesus becomes the passion of the apostle. It is a passion for God and for humanity, for snatching from the power of death those whom it crushes. It is a passion of love for the work of God, which is accomplished through our hearts, our hands, and our minds. It is a passion for the Body of Christ, which is the church, being created in the Eucharist and in the senselessness and contradictions of history. And when the time of distress comes, it is also the time for living the Passion together with Jesus, in the midst of the world's divisions and violence, with no other weapon than that of giving of our lives to the utmost, in the trust that the Father of all love will accomplish his work of resurrection in our crucified flesh.[28]

In reading over these reflections, one gets the idea that Pierre Claverie was prepared for the ultimate sacrifice. The spring of 1995 was certainly for him the occasion of intense interior progress. In April, he preached a retreat for the priests of the diocese of Bayonne, at the Benedictine abbey of Belloc: "I found the environment of the retreat very calming," he wrote. "In spite of the work that the conferences and meetings demand of me, I am happy to have these long periods of prayer and reflection in such a place" (letter of May 15, 1995).

In the summer of 1995, he addressed the Little Sisters of the Sacred Heart. He also spoke to the Little Sisters of Jesus Algeria on the Christian meaning of offering one's life, and of the term "immolation," which has fallen into disuse today, but which Sister Madeleine, their founder, had used in the prayer that the sisters recite each day.[29] After the political and media whirlwind in the spring, a certain peace had returned to him, a peace that he gladly shared by reading to his audience a poem written by Hawa Djabali in homage to the White Fathers assassinated in Tizi-Ouzou, "Une longue fidélité" (An Enduring Faithfulness). This poem, Claverie comments, conveys better than any speech the profundity of the covenant that Christians had established with Algeria. It also spoke, in a certain way, about him.

These are the ones who remained...

They knew the monotonous rhythm of the carding of the wool,
The crackle of the bright red flames in old ashen hearths,
The wooden cradles slung beneath the rafter beams,

The deliberate movements of old women setting out dried figs,
    couscous, and chickpeas,
The enormous clay pots, round and smooth and artfully made, arranged
    against a richly patterned wall.

They knew the olive harvest season, the laughter of women and their
    tears;
They knew the barley and the wheat, and the hand mill groaning,
    groaning ceaselessly;
They had seen the hard times, and had tasted the miserable cakes of
    acorn flour,
Had drunk from the enamel jug passed round a circle of old men.
They knew the humiliation of the old, the desperation of the young,
The women's stubborn drive to stitch life back together, whatever it
    might be worth,

To strengthen the home and keep alive the old familiar ways, the
    ceremonies of tenderness,
Unyielding against the heartless mayhem approaching from the west.
They rose at dawn to scents of lavender, blue mint, wild thyme, among
mountains bearing the names of women, where torrents ran unseen
    through forbidding chasms
Where hordes of monkeys flailed and brayed at the wild boar . . .

They knew our filthy institutions, our roach-infested hospitals,
Our orphans dressed in uniform, without a face, expressionless at
    twenty,
Their tanks beneath them, and beneath their tanks the village.
They saw the villages overrun with the white garb of those
Who renounced all work and all of humanity;
They heard pundits on the radio proclaim
That incense and excrement burn just the same.

At the moment when we left to save our lives, our children, our voices,
This scrap, this song, this land at land's end that is still our own —
They remained.

We have asked ourselves why.
There was no answer; it was a long fidelity.
One cannot praise fidelity or blame it;
It is folly, a great folly to love this way,

Humbly, day after day, amid pleasure and sickness,
Amid virtue and shame.

Beyond the suffering that came before we went away,
Should we weep for these lives consumed by love
Until they reached the threshold of old age?
Muslims and Christians wished paradise for them.
I am an atheist. Eternity is other people.

Let this Other be me,
Let the monumental memory within me —
Where every smile, every voice, every moment shared,
every kind welcome, remains alive —
Bring these others inside me.
Let my words speak for them, let their will be my peace,
Let me dispel their doubt, and let them assuage my pain,
And thus until others receive me in turn, if I must leave too soon,
Until we can offer them dazzling white cities full of laughter, where
        rivers run,
Women proud beneath the stars, and children happy.

One day we will walk again along the beach
To watch the sun sink down upon the sea;
We will play in the springtime beneath the orange trees,
The young will have work, and lovers will meet,
And the children will stream from the schools like the birds of January;
I will follow the rose-hued waves of the oleander
From the wellspring down to the sea;
There will be the scent of bread, there will be books and friends,
And we will make music one day, Charles, in Algeria.[30]

Claverie read this text to his audience with evident joy, repeatedly in-
terrupting his recitation to emphasize, "See what it is that binds us to this
country and this people: it is a covenant." The time had come for him to put
into practice what he had recommended in August of 1982, in a retreat on
the Beatitudes he gave in Lebanon: "In difficult moments, instead of seeking
out consolation, I believe it is better to dispose ourselves to radical demands;
this is the price of hope."

# Chapter Twelve

# "The Combat of Life"
## A Spiritual Portrait

> Holiness is, above all, a great passion. There is an aspect of folly
> in holiness, the folly of love, the very folly of the cross, which
> makes a mockery of human calculation and wisdom.[1]
>
> — *Pierre Claverie*

In following the evolution of Pierre Claverie over these times of great difficulty, one begins to wonder if this man of speech and action was not primarily a mystic. He spoke very little about himself, even to those who were close to him, but one catches glimpses of him in the many retreats he gave to religious sisters and priests, notably in Lebanon, Egypt, and Martinique, retreats in which he displayed something of his own spiritual journey. In his archives, a thick file of around eight hundred handwritten pages contains the texts of seventeen different retreats, each lasting a week, presented between 1971 and 1990. In general, the same retreat was given on three or four occasions, with some changes at the level of detail. An adjacent file collects the notes taken from readings that he used on these occasions, and introduces us to his favorite authors. It is thus highly interesting to leaf through these files.[2] Beginning in 1990, Pierre Claverie preached fewer retreats outside of Algeria because of the deterioration of the situation within the country, but this allowed him to express himself more extensively through his editorials in *Le Lien,* which became more urgent: he denounced, called to account, encouraged. While they became more militant, these also became — paradoxically, it might seem — more spiritual. Unlike in his earlier editorials, he cited significantly fewer authors, but he spoke much of the cross of Christ, of the paschal mystery, and of the love that should inhabit the hearts of those who wish to be Jesus' disciples.

## Human Experience as the Proper Realm of the Spiritual

So Pierre Claverie preached a great deal, so much so that those around him sometimes asked themselves why he spent one month each year outside of Algeria, giving four or five retreats in a row, instead of going on a much-needed vacation like everyone else. The contents of these retreats were completely written out, and this called for a considerable effort of preparation. In the early years, Claverie addressed traditional subjects like faith, hope, charity, and the religious life — but he did so in a very direct way, as seen in these comments from the summer of 1968, on one of the first retreats he gave to the Franciscan Missionary Sisters of Mary in Algiers:

> It seemed that I "knocked the wind out of them" — even though my intention was the contrary! It should be said that I had a wonderful group of sisters, and all I really had to do was to present myself simply and express my faith. Personally, I found the experience fascinating, and I would be happy to do it again . . . later on, since I'm worn out now . . . In fact, these situations are complex, and one cannot make oneself understood without entering into the problems of others: after hours spent listening to the sisters who came to talk to me, something relatively coherent finally emerged. (letter of August 26, 1968)

At the time, Pierre Claverie was a young priest and still spoke more of the things he had been taught than of his own experience, but one could already sense in him the desire to join in the life's journey of others, with their battles, victories, and weariness.

Very quickly, the usual subjects would give way to a personal approach in which he would, instead, convey what spiritual experience was in his eyes: bearing such titles as "An Experience," "Humanity," "Life," and "Memory," the retreats of the 1970s sought to go to the essence of the believer's path, leaving behind anything that was merely peripheral. "My ambition is to communicate my conviction," he said to the Sisters of the Holy Hearts in Ainab, Lebanon, in 1979, at the beginning of a unique retreat that he presented this way:

> I'm not going to make an examination of conscience [he was speaking to sisters formed in Jesuit spirituality!]. I don't like introspection . . . I can't do it. I discover myself in confronting realities outside of myself . . . It is not within myself that I discover truth, but in struggling with the realities of life. I am trying to place the combat of life on its true terrain: life is a combat that takes place beyond the confines of religion. That doesn't interest me much, because religion is the domain of the greatest misunderstandings, the place of the most bloody confrontations, as you know . . . Beginning with realities that I haven't chosen, how do I face

these things as part of my life? I think that the Christian faith isn't a question of religion, but a matter of life and death... It is therefore necessary to anchor the faith in a living, fleshy reality... if not, one remains on the level of abstract ideas.[3]

The entire retreat was devoted to fundamental themes of human life: freedom, love, suffering, the Other, these realities common to all which, in the eyes of Pierre Claverie, are the true terrain of spiritual experience:

The first step toward God is always that of taking stock of what we are called upon to live through in our lives. It is through this that we experience God. God reveals himself to us only to the extent to which we plunge into the realities we have been given to face... He does not reveal himself through books. The Old and New Testaments are nothing other than the record of the experiences of God that men and women have had throughout their own history.[4]

The sisters who participated in the retreats were deeply affected by these ideas: it was the 1970s, and many of the religious orders were in crisis because of certain rigidities in traditional religious life, and the process of *aggiornamento* had not yet borne fruit. And now these sisters were hearing something, someone inviting them to the freedom of the gospel: "Pierre's importance lay in who he was, and not so much in what he said. It was enough to just look at him,"[5] comments a sister living in Beirut. He spoke little of himself, at least directly. Nevertheless, he sometimes implied that the spiritual path he was suggesting was the same one he was following himself. This was the case, according to François Chavanes, with the 1985 retreat entitled "Dialogue" (a retreat he would give a total of eleven times!):

My role is that of accompanying you as discreetly as possible. I propose to you a journey in the faith, in *my* faith [emphasis in the original]... It is up to you to take from this exchange what catches your attention and applies to you, and to use it for your good, if you find it useful. It is a journey through realities that are simply human, and also through the gifts of faith and of religious experience.[6]

Even when he addressed more classical religious topics ("The Rosary," "With Mary," "The Eucharist," "A Retreat with Saint Paul"), he would include this essential intuition: the spiritual is not something apart from life, a sort of dusting of piety on top; it is played out in the thick of life, in life at its most tangible and concrete — "it is a matter of life and death." Perhaps it was this that led him to agree to give a conference in Brive in October of 1994 to the Fraternité Edmond-Michelet: this sort of "saint in the world" never failed to fascinate him.[7]

## "Happy are they who have discovered that they are loved"

Pierre Claverie preached on the Beatitudes a number of times, and he loved to explain that he had invented an extra one, "Beatitude Zero," which comes before the rest because it affects all the rest: "Happy are they who have discovered that they are loved," or again, "Happy are they in whom others have believed." He thought that even before one spoke of religious faith, it was appropriate to establish the starting point in a fundamental human reality: a human being does not develop and grow normally without the experience of being loved; it is this that allows one to develop trust in one's surroundings. Without this initial experience, a person lives in fear and anguish, but with the gift of trust a person can begin to blossom. Here Pierre Claverie is speaking from his own experience, because he had the good fortune of growing up in a family characterized by mutual trust and love. In a number of places in his correspondence, he expresses how indebted he was to the trusting love that he received. But he knew that this wasn't everyone's experience; when he met individually with the retreatants at the end of the day, he saw the wounds that many of them bore on account of their family history or of the accumulated frustrations of a religious life that was not always especially nourishing. And so he tried to lead his listeners into this secret place where all can learn to live in trust, in spite of their wounds.

In his eyes, the Christian faith brought the believer to this sort of trusting relationship with God: God, in effect, created human beings out of love, and was the first to trust in them by endowing them with freedom. Even today, God still speaks to the hearts of all through the voice of conscience, and proposes to them a way of life, or more precisely, a way to escape the forces of death that threaten every living being. Those who obey this voice allow themselves to be led, without always knowing it, by the Word of God, for "The message of creation is this: nature is inhabited by an active presence; the Word of God sustains it in being, giving it meaning and fruitfulness."[8]

What distinguishes the Christian above all is the belief that God has spoken and continues to speak to people through his "Word made flesh," through his well-beloved Son, true God and true man: "This is what faith is — radical trust in the man we call the Son of God, and thus also radical trust in his Father."[9]

There is no such thing as complete solitude if we have this certitude of adoption that permits us to address God as our Father. This trust is, then, a source of joy, peace, and strength: "Trust is exercised and reinforced amid everyday trials. The act of faith or trust is precisely that: an act...One 'extends trust' more than one 'has trust.' It is therefore in concrete actions that we embody our intention to extend trust. And thus it is that trust is strengthened," he adds in this retreat, entitled "Life."

Given in 1979, this retreat bears witness to a process of maturation. Pierre Claverie had, by then, freed himself from books and systems in favor of his own vision of the believer's path that would "speak" to his listeners, because it was a living, passionate man who was speaking, and one also capable of truly listening to others. "Pierre approached others with his own poverty; that's rare here," another sister comments. Many of the sisters retained the lesson that trust is something one exercises, not something that one has.[10] One finds in his notes from this time the remark by Louis Évely, "Jesus knew how to find in each person the neglected child who has ceased to grow because others have ceased to believe in him or her."[11] Claverie spent a lot of time listening to other people's troubles during retreats, but also under normal circumstances in Algiers and Oran, where his door was always open to anyone, at any hour. Many discovered, together with him, that wounds could be an occasion for spiritual growth: "God reveals himself at the end of a personal journey, and it is only through this journey that one may discover that there is someone who unceasingly brings us from death into life: this someone is God."[12]

Trusting in God grants the believer the audacity to live under his gaze, in the safety of his presence, "like a child close to his or her mother." This serene sort of trust is, in fact, difficult to acquire, and it is only when we enter into prayer that we realize the difficulty, Pierre Claverie notes. Prayer demands that we silence our constant interior monologue in order to enter into dialogue with God, to the point of talking to him as we would speak to a friend, or better, of remaining in his presence without using words. Arriving at this sort of "living under his gaze" presupposes real self-denial, which should not be confused with artificial mortifications. Citing the Orthodox theologian Evdokimov, Pierre Claverie uses words very rich in meaning for those who had seen him pray: "Ascesis is a disciplined repose, the discipline of interior calm and silence, in which a person regains the ability to pause for prayer and contemplation, even amid all of the noise of the world — on the metro, in the crowd, at the crossroads of a city."[13]

Pierre Claverie had himself acquired, through a long and regular practice of prayer, an ability to remove himself from the grasp of the world's confusion and — at least apparently — from his own concerns, in order to be present to God. Arriving at this confident attitude also presupposes, he notes, measuring to what extent we live under the gaze of others: if we are not careful, we automatically seek to please others, and we live a superficial existence: "Before being seized by Jesus Christ," he said at one of his retreats in the persona of an imaginary sister, "I lived on the surface of myself...I had the impression of being drawn and possessed by the views of others. The opinion of others was more important to me than the quality of my actions. I was possessed by the desire to please."[14]

In order to liberate oneself from this sort of slavery, one must follow Jesus on the path of humility, which consists in seeking, not the glory that comes from human beings, but that which comes from God, as Jesus did. This attitude frees one from the judgment of others, and permits one to exist "in the presence of God, who does not judge, but rather sets us free." This is Jesus' enduring lesson for his disciples: that almsgiving, prayer, and fasting should not be done in order to be seen by others, but for God alone, who sees in secret. "Whatever you do, do it above all for God," Pierre Claverie summarizes. "Live beneath his gaze — that is enough."[15] It is enough, but it demands conversion, a detachment from oneself that is difficult, even impossible, to achieve without the grace of God and the gift of the Spirit.

This is why it is only the Spirit, "who comes to our aid in our weakness," who brings about true prayer within us. The Christian attitude of prayer is above all that of a child, "the astonished discovery of the fatherhood of God":

> One does not pray to have a request fulfilled — this would be like making a bad beginning of a dialogue or encounter by putting oneself first or using the Other for one's own purposes...God doesn't need us to tell him about what's going on, he is not there to carry out our plans, and he knows better than we do what we need. So the right way to begin is to welcome him by recognizing and respecting him as the Other, making room for him so that he can be himself. *Prayer, therefore, consists first of all in granting God's request,* by making ourselves capable of receiving him [emphasis added]. We know that he is standing at the door, knocking.[16]

This theme of prayer was a constant in the teaching of Pierre Claverie, as it was also in his own life. At a time of great difficulty, he would invite those around him to "pray ceaselessly":

Seize even the slightest opportunity to open the door, your heart, your hands, to take the time to let Jesus imprint the image of his face upon you...This moment of crisis, of trial and shock, may be a unique opportunity for you to let God touch you, and to immerse yourself, with Jesus and through Jesus, more deeply within the joys of life and love. This is almost a necessity that arises within us when we have lost our certitudes, our defenses, and our paltry resources. Let yourself be seized by Christ once again.[17]

## "There is but one path along the way, one path beside your own" (Rumi)[18]

In this filial relationship with God, receiving love takes precedence over giving it, as St. John writes in his first letter: "This is love: not that we have loved God, but that he has loved us...We love because he first loved us" (1 John 4:10, 19). Transposing the bedrock experience of every human being, who becomes capable of love by first being loved, Pierre Claverie emphasizes the challenge that detachment from self represents for everyone: "The essential value of our life lies in passing beyond our limitations, in extending beyond ourselves through love...This is the foundation of our life, whether we are believers or unbelievers, Christian, Muslim, or Buddhist."[19]

There is no spiritual life without conversion, without letting go of oneself. And sin is likewise "the desire to make oneself the center of the world, the desire to be oneself for oneself, on one's own terms, before others and before God, to see everything in terms of oneself."[20] The Christian who believes that this sort of conversion cannot be attained without the gift of God's assistance is led to desire this gift, to ask for and try to welcome it every day, in the midst of "the combat of faith." Without this combat, he writes, believers risk:

> behaving as if God did not exist, in living life on our own...We must maintain a certain detachment in life, or we will become indifferent to anything that does not concern our interests and our egoism. This begins by reserving for ourselves a little space where we can be alone in peace, far away from everyone else...We then are annoyed when someone comes to bother us, or simply to ask us to leave our solitude for a moment to render some service...Little by little, we begin to close ourselves within this solitude...And this is because of a lack of faith, because we lose the lively awareness of the presence of God, close and attentive, and that we have nothing to fear from others...Just as it did

with Abraham and the apostles, faith makes us foreigners and wanderers on the earth, never still, always moving toward God, always in exodus toward others.[21]

To designate the effort by which all progress in spiritual life is made, Pierre Claverie uses an expression that is almost entirely absent from traditional spiritual literature, but would be of great value to him in his preaching: *l'ajustement* [English "adjustment," used here with the connotation "restoring the proper relationship"]:

> It is in and through Jesus that the *ajustement* of human beings with God and with one another is realized. Without this *ajustement*, the world is shattered and human beings torment one another. It is in Jesus that the reconciliation of the world is begun. He comes to heal [*rajuster*, cf. *ajustement*] those who have been deformed in body, mind, or spirit. The work of the Spirit is manifested in him when the deaf are made to hear, the mute to speak, the lame to walk, those cast down to be lifted up, the estranged to be reconciled. In each one the right [*juste*] relationship is restored — in body, in heart, with self and with others. And at the origin of this is the Spirit, who makes this person a child of God.[22]

This word, *ajustement*, which recurs frequently in the writings of Pierre Claverie, is intended to emphasize that it is the Spirit of God alone who can restore what has been disfigured and ruined in human beings. Rather than being an active effort, the spiritual life consists instead in letting oneself be taken up and transformed by this Spirit, "Who transforms everything within us to make it conform with the plan of God. The Spirit is the one who puts us into right relationship with the Father."[23] One sees here Claverie's desire to bring freedom from the excessive weight of moralistic exhortations upon the spiritual life of many religious men and women. But the primacy accorded to the reception of the gift of God should not lead the believer to adopt an attitude of passivity, because this usually involves an active effort to dispose oneself for this gift, to seek to remain *ajusté*, in harmony with him who is the source of life. Thus Pierre Claverie attests that

> a spontaneous impulse of trust moves us to seek out signs of the presence of God, to discern his will for us, to go forward to meet him — because he is coming — to refuse to content ourselves with performing the ceremonies or obeying the rules, but to determine together with him what it is that we must endure or undertake to be *ajustés* ["adjusted"] to his love.[24]

This might be the right place to bring up a question that can be asked about everyone, but which is difficult to answer in the case of Pierre Claverie: what were his struggles? Everyone has to struggle, from time to time, with issues of personality or of family history; everyone has victories and defeats, wounds and healings. But in the end, we know very little about Pierre Claverie. There is no one in particular in whom he is known to have confided. His happy childhood and youth, his profound equilibrium, his "unstumbling" journey through life seem to have spared him the false starts that are the experience of many. Of course, there was the trial of seeing the Algeria of his childhood crumble, of seeing the bursting of the "colonial bubble," as he called it. He never concealed the suffering this caused him, and those who were close to him saw the toll it took. But then everything fell back into place for him — almost too easily, one might be tempted to say. One would rightly conjecture that his responsibilities weighed upon him — all the time he had to spend reconciling the sensibilities of various groups and dealing with bureaucratic inconveniences. But for him this was a way of giving his life, another central theme of his spirituality.

## "There is no greater love than to give one's life for one's friends" (John 15:13)

In a conference on the Eucharist that he gave in 1981, Claverie noted, "Faith is an act of abandonment and of unconditional commitment to following Christ." Abandonment *and* commitment: this is a difficult combination, especially for a man like him, naturally more inclined to commitment than to abandonment. It is, however, toward abandonment that he himself had to go. A very meaningful anecdote related by one of the religious sisters of Oran witnesses to the progress he had made: during one of his earliest retreats, in the enthusiasm of his youth, his presentations were crammed with citations from writers on spirituality: Jacques Leclercq, Jean Sullivan, Olivier Clément, Louis Évely, Fr. Varillon, and even Roger Garaudy, author of *Parole d'homme,* which had greatly excited him — it seemed that no one went without mention. When the time for questions came, one of the sisters asked him, "And what about the Cross in all this?" "Fr. Claverie grew thoughtful," the sister telling the story recalls, and then after a moment of silence he said, "Yes, it's true, I'm not there yet."[25]

The last of the retreats that he wrote out in his own hand, in 1990, bears witness to the journey he had made: entitled "Come, Follow Me," it is entirely centered on the person of Jesus and on what it means to be a disciple. At that time Algeria was in the throes of agony, and the theme that keeps recurring is that of struggle in the life of Jesus: his love for God and for human beings led him to oppose all those who obstructed the full blossoming of life lived in accordance with God. With no other weapons than his word, Jesus denounced the perversion of the religious authorities, the indifference and disdain for the lowly on the part of those who were rich, who worshiped money, who thirsted for power and prestige. He also opposed those who fostered violence. He denounced falsehood in all of its forms. This led him to speak and act in ways that led his adversaries to arrest him, judge him, and condemn him to a most cruel death. And following in the path of Jesus, Claverie emphasizes, means engaging in a struggle like his own, and "giving one's life that others may live." At the end of a retreat on the Eucharist in 1981, he had already made a passing reference to the parable that Jesus presented during the days before his death: "In truth, I tell you, unless a grain of wheat falls to the ground and dies, it remains alone; but if it dies, it bears fruit in abundance" (John 12:24). "For me," Pierre Claverie then commented, "the grain of wheat that dies is the central axis of the Christian life; if you read over your notes, you will see that this entire meditation on the Eucharist has taken its direction from this saying."[26]

Saying this is one thing, and preparing to live it is another; this is what he had to face beginning in 1990, when Algerians were falling to violence by the thousands. Living the vocation of a disciple then took on a special meaning: "In following Jesus, we are sent out to be servants of the Good News of reconciliation between God and all of humanity. This ministry does not make us intermediaries between God and humanity, but mediators, entirely dedicated to God and entirely dedicated to the world, placed with Jesus in the place where history and the Kingdom of God intersect. Now, this intersection is a cross."[27]

So anyone who wants to be a disciple of Jesus is brought to take one of the spots along the "fault lines":

The Cross is at the center of this mission [of Jesus]. Jesus died with his body torn apart between heaven and earth, his arms extended to gather in the children of God who had been scattered by the sin that separates them, isolates them, and pits them against one another and even against God himself. He placed himself upon the fault lines created by sin. Thrown out of balance and ruptured in body, heart, and spirit, human and social relations found healing and reconciliation in him, because he took these things upon himself. And he places his own disciples upon these same fault lines, with the same mission of healing and reconciliation.[28]

One of the consequences of the stance of Jesus "on the fault lines" is the refusal to exclude anyone. Pierre Claverie explained this to the Little Sisters of Jesus in the summer of 1995:

> Algeria is a place of divisions: among Muslims, between Muslims and the rest of the world, between the North and the South, between rich and poor . . . There is an increasingly deep divide among people just an hour away from us by plane. It is at fever pitch now; it is terrifying . . . And this is the church's rightful place, because it is Jesus' place . . . The Cross is the rack of the one who does not choose one side or another, because by joining humanity one does not reject part of humanity. So one visits the sick, publicans, sinners, prostitutes, the deranged . . . everyone. The mission at hand is that of holding both sides together . . .
>
> Reconciliation, therefore, is not a simple affair — it comes at a high price. It can also involve, as it did for Jesus, being torn apart between irreconcilable opposites. An Islamist and a *kafir* (infidel) cannot be reconciled. So, then, what's the choice? Well, Jesus does not choose. He says, in effect, "I love you all," and he dies.[29]

He goes on to say that this is the Christian wager: "knowing how to take a position deliberately without taking sides." It's also a form of crucifixion, he adds, because "it would be easier and less frustrating, in a way, to belong to a single group."

This position, "folly for the Jews, and scandal for the pagans," he knows, is difficult for Christians themselves to adopt, and the church is often tempted to provide reasons for sidestepping it:

> Could it be that our religion is simply the celebration of generosity and of the practical value of charity? . . . Could it be that we reserve the cross for the decoration of our churches, or for the most important occasions? Could it be that we think we would be better off living otherwise and elsewhere than with the crisis facing us? Perhaps . . . Who can know what faith really means at the moment of the greatest decisions? What is the place in our lives that faith in Jesus Christ has come to occupy — and how far are we prepared to go in trust and abandonment?[30]

Pierre Claverie repeatedly spoke out against the church's temptation to be simply "a multinational charitable organization," an aid organization that "does good things" but shrinks from the ultimate testimony, which is that of giving one's life in love:

> Martyrdom, in its original meaning, is a testimony to the highest form of love. It doesn't mean chasing after death or seeking suffering for the sake of suffering, or creating one's own sufferings because it is by spilling one's blood that one draws close to God...It means accepting life's difficulties, accepting the consequences of one's commitments. This is what happened with Jesus: he accepted the consequences of his commitments.[31]

But accepting the consequences of one's commitments can also mean facing a violent death, as was the case for Jesus, who did not seek out death, but bore all of the consequences of his freely accepted duty. Pierre Claverie's message for Easter of 1996 included this passage:

> We in Algeria now know what it means to "die a violent death." With tens of thousands of Algerian men and women killed, we face every day this vague menace that is manifested from time to time in a specific form, despite the precautions taken...And so here we are, faced with the radical question of death, and thus of the meaning of our lives...The mystery of Easter obliges us to look in the face the reality of Jesus' death and of our own, and to take stock of our reasons for confronting it.[32]

One can live out this gift in different ways — as Jesus did, by taking positions that led to his death at the hands of those who wanted to silence him, or by giving of oneself in the little things of everyday life. This is what Pierre Claverie [following a tradition of spiritual theology] calls "white martyrdom":

> White martyrdom is what one strives to live each day, the giving of one's life drop by drop — in a look, in being present, in a smile, a gesture of concern, a service, in all of those things that make one's life a life that is shared, given, bestowed upon others. This is where openness and detachment take on the meaning of martyrdom, of immolation — in letting go of life.[33]

For Claverie, this way of life had an eminently eucharistic meaning, a eucharist lived as the giving of one's life past the point of no return, and not simply as the memorial of a bygone event. "The Eucharist, that's us. It is not so much a memorial as it is Jesus accomplishing, in us, today, the offering of his life."[34] And, "Jesus' Passover is accomplished in his body, the church, which through the one sacrifice of Christ also passes from death to life. And we witness to and participate in this until the end of time. Let us take care that we not neglect this commitment to martyrdom."[35]

## The Spirituality of Presence in the Muslim World

This decision to "take a position without taking sides" can be found in Pierre Claverie's way of living out, spiritually, his presence within the Muslim world. In 1983, he had preached a retreat which he would present again on a number of occasions. It was entitled "The Religious Life and Islam." Their existence as a Christian minority surrounded by Muslims posed questions for many of the Christians of Algeria, especially for those who, like many of the religious sisters, lived in the lower class areas and participated in the major events of Islamic life: Ramadan, the Muslim feasts, the return from pilgrimage to Mecca. What Christian had not been approached at some point by a very sincere Muslim friend who, for the sake of friendship, wanted him or her to share his or her faith? The Christian, therefore, needed the support of a spirituality of presence in the Muslim world, and not merely theological analyses of religious pluralism. Pierre Claverie often spoke of his own life and of his almost complete ignorance, when he was young, of the religious world of Islam. He recalled that upon his return to Algeria, he "discovered wonders" that he had passed by without seeing all throughout his youth. What was, then, his spiritual relationship with Islam?

In the first place, it must be recognized that he was always more attuned to Muslims as persons than to Islam as such. Earlier we have referred to his great emotion at meeting with some of the leaders of the *zaouïas* in the Oran region, to whom he was introduced by his friend Rahal. Meeting with these religious men made a tremendous impression on him. He was also very aware of the simple faith of ordinary people who faced the difficulties of daily life with a real sense of abandonment to the will of God. Pierre Claverie readily received visits from people in difficulty, listening to them and admiring their spiritual qualities. Referring to "the Muslim act of faith, which consists in deliberately abandoning oneself to the will of God," he expresses his hope that "the Muslims' faith will awaken in us [Christians] the sense of God's presence and action in our lives."[36] And he was not insensitive to Muslim prayer, which set the rhythm of daily life ("we are in the midst of a people of prayer," he wrote[37]), or fasting, pilgrimage, etc. Nevertheless, he does not seem to have developed for himself a spirituality of presence in a Muslim environment, as had Massignon, Fr. Voillaume, or Little Sister Madeleine, to take a few examples. Their spirit of *Badaliya*, of a hidden and spiritual offering of one's life for the Muslims, inspired a number of his contemporaries, from Serge de Beaurecueil to Christian de Chergé, the leader of the *Ribât-as-Salâm*.[38] Although he believed in the value of this form of shared prayer, carried out in the secret of one's heart and in the eyes of God alone, he never involved himself publicly in this direction. His temperament inclined him otherwise.

He was more of a theologian, and thus inclined to uphold the critical requirements of truth. So his own view was that "the contents of the various forms of revelation, contrary to appearances that would depict them as close to each other ('all are children of Abraham') reinforce incomprehension and misunderstandings."[39] With his thorough understanding of the Arab language and Muslim culture, he was critical of a "deceptive" closeness, a naïve ecumenism that blithely repeats that we are all "people of the Book" and yet comes to an impasse at "the abyss that separates us." How could real reciprocity even be imaginable when Islam, which presents itself as the definitive fulfillment of divine revelation, could not consider the possibility of other valid pathways to God? According to this view, Jews and Christians were simply "awaiting conversion." So although he retained all of the cordiality of his interpersonal relationships, Pierre Claverie refused to be led astray by simplistic and misleading propositions. Moreover, he responded with the fullness of his Christian faith when confronted by the great dogmas of Islam. For example, he would say, "When I hear the muezzin issue the call to prayer by chanting 'Allah Akbar,' 'God is great,' I pray — but I continue, 'Yes he is great — but he has made himself small.'" Or again:

> The Christian God is ONE, but not a solitary unity. He is a communion ... He does not propose to us merely that we live in righteousness by witnessing to his oneness and obeying his law; he proposes that we share in his own life, by giving us his Spirit. And this is where the radical difference lies. This God does not content himself in sending books and prophets to guide humanity. He enters into humanity himself, in order to permit human beings to participate in his own life.[40]

The overlapping of Ramadan and Lent in 1993 and 1994 gave him an opportunity to produce a pastoral exploration of the meaning of fasting and charity for a Christian living in the Muslim world. Behind the apparent similarities (abstaining from food, caring for the poor, dedicating time to prayer, etc.) there are profound differences, due in part to the deviations seen in

Ramadan, which gives rise to excessive consumption and often gives rise to sluggishness in daily work. Claverie concludes that for the Christian, Lent should not be "a pious exercise combined with a low-calorie diet," but rather "an arena of combat where we are obliged to come out from ourselves to take our place at the foot of the cross with Jesus."[41]

The personal effort this probably involved was that of trying never to hurt the other person while remaining true to his own convictions and assuming the accompanying responsibilities. In his retreats, he always invited the Christians living in Algeria to come to an ever deeper understanding of the human environment around them, and thus, if possible, to learn Arabic. But above all he recalled that there is a universal language — that of goodness. Those who are called to live in Algeria should consider themselves as "given" to the Algerian people, because "the covenant with God passes through the covenant with the people to which he gives us. It is a covenant lived in the way Jesus lived his covenant with the men and women of Palestine — as a servant, and not as a master; in giving one's life rather than lessons; in a self-effacing humility that seeks and acts for the welfare and increase of the Other, and finds its joy in this self-effacement and this growth."[42]

He reminded the Christian communities he addressed that their essential mission was that of being a cell of love lived out in faith: "Our sole value lies in the quality of what we are. The church has just one mission: the expansion of the love of God. And this love cannot be communicated without being received and interiorized with humility. Besides, this is what the Qur'an says is admirable about the [Christian] monks — their humility."[43]

Paradoxically, it is at the moment of the greatest trial, when some Muslims were seeking to kill (not only Christians) "in the name of Islam" and "in the name of God" — it was then that Pierre Claverie brought forth, more than a theology, a spirituality of presence in the Muslim world. He decided not to draw back from this division, which was not only between Christians and Muslims, but also among Muslims themselves. It was not an easy matter at that time to avoid painting all Muslims with the broad brush of extremism, especially for someone who took a look from the outside. But it was not by any means an easier matter for a Muslim to practice his or her faith when other Muslims had so greatly distorted it. Wanting to see reconciliation triumph over these opposing positions, Pierre Claverie refused to judge, and simply appealed to the attitude of Jesus, who would not choose one side over another, and in doing so, died. Convinced that the disciples of Jesus could follow no other path than that traced out by their master, he consented in a certain way to the death that seemed to be awaiting him: "An Islamist and a *kafir* cannot be reconciled. So, then, what's the choice? And Jesus does not choose. He says, 'Myself, I love all,' and in saying this he dies."[44]

In this, Pierre Claverie echoed the witness of Christian de Chergé, who prayed for his executioner, "my last-minute friend," and said he hoped to see him again, "a couple of good thieves, we two, in paradise, if it please God."[45] Pierre Claverie met the times with the same spirit, as shown in a letter he wrote on July 29, 1996, three days before his death:

> The death of these monks who were our brothers and friends for so long has wounded us once more, but has strengthened our ties with the thousands of Algerians who are sick of violence and eager for peace. Their silent message has resounded in the hearts of millions throughout the world. We are remaining here out of fidelity to the cry of love and reconciliation that the prior of the community left in the spiritual testament in which he lucidly foresaw his own death. I am taking precautions, and I have the protection of the security forces, but it is God who remains the master of the hour of death, and only God can give meaning to our life and to our death. Everything else is just a smokescreen.[46]

## "Holiness is, above all, a great passion"

One of the first homilies that Pierre Claverie delivered in Oran as a young bishop was for the feast of All Saints in 1981. It expresses well the passion and the sense of freedom that he possessed:

> Holiness is, above all, a great passion. Nothing is more foreign to it than the small-minded legalism of those who seek to save their lives, to assure their salvation, by observing laws, rites, or rules. It has nothing in common with the conformism and the gloomy virtue of the guardians of religious and moral orthodoxy. How many saints have been made unrecognizable by turning their lives into models of piety, virtue, or to regularity! . . . Now, there is an aspect of folly in holiness, the folly of love, the very folly of the cross, which makes a mockery of human calculation and wisdom. Without this passion of God, without this passion from God, the saints become incomprehensible.[47]

Passion for God, passion for his fellow humans — it should come as no surprise that this spiritual man lived out his commitments and his struggles to their very end.

## Chapter Thirteen

# Witnessing the Greatest Love

*The value of my life lies in my capacity to give it away.*
*— Pierre Claverie*

The last months of Pierre Claverie's life were marked by a new upsurge of violence in Algeria. This struck Algerian society itself, with deaths in the tens of thousands, and it also struck the church in a way that astonished many Algerians and the rest of the world: how did one dare to touch these nuns and monks, these people of prayer? Pierre Claverie began this period showing signs of weariness, but he would once again marshal his forces and continue his witness to its last stage, that of giving his life. The decision to speak out and to give witness was, for him, an act of resistance and of solidarity with those in Algeria who refused to go along with the violence, especially when it was carried out in the name of God. Claverie would be assassinated himself on August 1, 1996, in the company of a young Muslim, Mohamed Bouchikhi. At his funeral, the world would be made aware of how deeply rooted he had become in the hearts of his Algerian friends.

## Signs of Weariness under Strain

September of 1995 brought a new trial for the church: Sister Bibiane and Sister Angèle-Marie, two members of the congregation of Our Lady of the Apostles, were assassinated in Belcourt, one of the working class neighborhoods of Algiers, on September 3, 1995. They had been living in this neighborhood since 1964, and worked at the center for women's training operated by the municipal government. After their funeral, Pierre Claverie wrote to his father:

> This time, the aftermath was marked by a great serenity. Their death does not dampen the determination of those who remain here. At the Mass and at the cemetery, Algerian representatives (from the department of religious affairs and of foreign affairs, from the municipal council of Belcourt, some of the sisters' aid workers, etc.) expressed their sorrow

and their condemnation of such blind violence. The pope sent, not only a message, but a personal legate. (letter of October 9, 1995)

After this fresh wound, Pierre Claverie canceled a Mediterranean cruise on which he was scheduled to give a talk, believing that "it would be indecent to be visiting the Greek islands if anything serious were to happen in the diocese." "Nevertheless," he added, "I am beginning to feel the need for rest ... So I will try to spend a week at home around the end of September or the beginning of October." This was a very unusual admission for him. We have seen that Pierre Claverie almost never took a vacation. Until the beginning of the violence in 1992, his breaks consisted of the retreats he gave outside of Algeria, and an evening's relaxation now and then with some friends. At the end of September in 1995, he spent a week in Toulon with his father, who was now eighty-nine years old. He had been a widower for four years, was almost blind, living alone, and his children lived overseas — Pierre in Algeria, and Anne-Marie in the United States. Fiercely independent, Étienne Claverie had refused to go to a rest home, and remained in his own home — under the splendid care of Annie Prenat, a friend of the family — until his death. His children and grandchildren came to see him as often as possible: Anne-Marie came during her vacations, and Pierre passed through when he was traveling, even if he could stay only a couple of days. They had always spoken intimately with one another, and so these visits gave rise to passionate discussions in which Pierre concealed nothing about the situation in Algeria from his father. "My son, you are taking risks," his father told him, but without pressuring him. "I am doing my duty," Pierre replied. This week in September would be their last long visit together. "I had a good rest, and spent hours chatting with Papie, who is as attentive as ever to what is happening in the world and perceptively analyzes these great events," Claverie wrote upon his return (letter of October 15, 1995).

Pierre was also planning his first-ever trip to visit his sister in the United States, where she had been living with her family for more than twenty years. He had not yet made the trip because the two saw each other every year when they visited their parents in Toulon.

His editorial in *Le Lien* for September of 1995 reflects his feelings of weariness. Entitled "Against All Hope," he describes "the sort of poverty that seems to be that of the church today."[1] There was, in the first place, the fact that this church belonged to "a country that has a bad image, and inspires, at best, a sort of pity." Algeria, which was once considered one of the leaders of the third world, now found itself "among those 'banana republics' where a junta maintains power in order to preserve its privileges, crushing a population whose last resort is terrorism."

Next there was the incomprehension that the Algerian church met with abroad, with reactions that ranged "from categorical rejection (Muhammed Duval), to excessive admiration (as a prophetic church), to doubt (What are they still doing there?), to suspicion (they are preserving their influence by catering to the powerful)." The last view echoes the accusations brought by Sant'Egidio against the Algerian bishops, who were lumped together with the "butchers."

This church, he saw, was also poor in its ability to express itself: "In Algeria, we must suffer in silence the absurdities or the preaching of the self-proclaimed Muslim savants who denigrate, distort, or ridicule our convictions . . . And we can scarcely clarify things even outside of the country when the situation seems to have become too distorted . . . It is rare that one asks the Christians in Algeria for their opinion and analysis on the drama they are experiencing."

The last kind of poverty, "the most painful to endure," was the departure of friends, who were leaving in spite of their sometimes excessive praise for the prophetic character of this church: "certain friends are abandoning us." Pierre Claverie evokes the departure to "other countries, other missions, other responsibilities" of members of religious institutions "who have learned so much from the Algerian experience." He concluded, "Let us pray that ecclesial solidarity not be lacking among us in these crucial times." One must keep in mind the enormous tenacity that the bishops of Algeria had to display in order to obtain a few candidates for their church, to make up for those who had left or been killed.[2]

His weariness was also due in part to a certain sense of disappointment in the face of political developments. In effect, the situation was still chaotic, and both the government and the Islamists were still engaging in their doublespeak:

> Here things continue as before and the presidential elections are being prepared in an astonishing atmosphere of terrorism, repression, the charade of ordinary daily life, and grotesque political debate . . . The political game has become so murky that nothing is believable anymore, no matter the declarations of good intentions on either side. Meanwhile, vehicles are detonated, fights claim dozens of victims, killers execute people for reasons that are not always clear, and the security forces engage in spectacular operations against the no less spectacular "armed bands" that sometimes number hundreds of men . . .

In reading this, one gets the impression that the lack of clarity was weighing upon him no less than the daily insecurity, to which he had grown accustomed without deceiving himself, but without panic:

> There aren't many foreigners left here, except in the high-security industrial areas, like Arzew... The rest, like ourselves, dispersed throughout the countryside, take precautionary measures, but we know very well how laughable these are in the face of terrorism. We are protected in our homes. The authorities would like to protect us in our movements as well, but we are not very enthusiastic about traveling with escorts who would draw even more attention to us. No matter how little Arabic one might speak, one can still move around incognito... unless one is a target, and in that case no one else could provide safety anyway. In the case of a false roadblock, nothing remains but to pray. I have not yet encountered one of these "false roadblocks" set up by the armed bands — it must be said that I always take the most highly trafficked routes during the safest hours of the day (never at night anymore, nor in the early morning, nor at evening). With all of this, life continues almost normally: no problems at the episcopal residence yet, with a constant flow of visitors and a steady stream of work. (letter of October 15, 1995)

Why was reconciliation so difficult? Participating at a conference in Naples in December of 1995, on the theme "Monotheism and Conflict," Claverie gave free rein to his heart as he did only on rare occasions, in evoking the musical performance given at the end by an orchestra from Fez that performed music from Andalusia:

> Under the direction of M. Briouel, this magnificent ensemble of renowned soloists performed two *noubas* (*Rasd* and *Hijâz el kebir*) with a virtuosity that enchanted the sizable audience. As is well known, Andalusian music was born in Spain in the twelfth century, in the melting pot where Jews, Christians, and Muslims shared a common culture that they created together, each with their own heritage from the Orient, the West, and from the northern and southern Mediterranean. Woven together from magnificent *mwassahats* or *zajals*, the melodies develop according to a precise form (*sajarat at-tubû*) but with some leeway for the performers' interpretation. These are the cream of the classical culture of the Maghreb. That evening, the vocal soloist (M. Bajeddoub) was joined by a Jewish singer, also a Moroccan one, who performed a duo in Hebrew and in old Spanish, on the same poetic and musical themes. We

were thus drawn into a mental stillness in which our thoughts mingled together through sharing the emotions that the performers expressed so admirably. How is it that moments as intense as these are also so fleeting, and that the fraternity found here quickly disperses again into *yahoudi, moro,* or *kafir?*[3]

It is rare to see Pierre Claverie permit himself to become so nostalgic. He had meditated so often upon Jesus' confrontation of human violence, and he now found himself, in a way, in the same situation: the logic of his life could now lead only to a similar confrontation. New developments were about to draw him back into a struggle that took on the form of resistance for him.

## Resisting to the End, Like Bonhoeffer

Claverie's reading was never casual, and neither was the attention given to what he read. In October of 1995, Pierre Claverie dedicated his editorial in *Le Lien* to Dietrich Bonhoeffer, the young German pastor who resisted the Nazis and was imprisoned and then executed by hanging in 1945. Published after the war under the title *Widerstand und Ergebung* (English translation, *Letters and Papers from Prison*), his letters from prison had a considerable impact, as did the monumental biography dedicated to him by his friend Eberhard Bethge.[4] Pierre Claverie had read these works as a young Dominican. And here he was taking them up again, thanks to an article in the newspaper *La Croix*: Bonhoeffer seemed almost to have been placed directly in his path in order to help him face what was to come.[5] And, in a rare move, Claverie made him the subject of his entire editorial "Thy Kingdom Come!"[6] Here are some selections:

In the evangelical struggle for the coming of the kingdom of God, he [Bonhoeffer] occupies an exceptional place, and his message speaks to me now as an appeal in the midst of the turmoil that we are experiencing. We are not the first to face violence and death empty-handed, and with nothing but the force of our convictions. And we are not the only ones to be doing so either. In the moments when we might be tempted to give up, to run away, or to shut ourselves up in fear, how can we not listen to the voices of those who countered death with the offering of their lives, in giving witness to their faith in the omnipotence of love and life? . . .

Here and today, in Algeria right now — there is nowhere else for us to bring about what God is asking of us as believers, and what we believe to be our highest truth: living, by the Spirit of Jesus, in a filial relationship with God the Father, and in openness to universal fraternity . . .

And so begins the hand-to-hand combat with reality, its resistance, its opacity, its harshness, and, in time, with death. Our faith does not exempt us from all of this. On the contrary, it plunges us into it, together with Jesus. Our life takes its meaning and its fruitfulness from following Jesus down the pathways of the world: "the terrain of Christian life is not the solitude of the cloister, but the enemy encampment itself" . . . If there are cloisters, this is not for the sake of solitude, but for the sake of a deeper relationship with Jesus and, through him, with God the Father and with the world. "In fact, our battle involves a grace for which we must pay. Grace acquired cheaply is grace without the Cross. Grace for which we must pay is the Gospel that one must always look for anew. This grace is costly because it can only be acquired at the price of one's own life." [translation by Timothy Radcliffe]

Half of the editorial consists in quotations from Bonhoeffer. Here are some of the particularly exquisite passages included:

We can pray for the coming of the Kingdom only by being entirely of the earth.

The hour in which we pray, now, for the kingdom of God, is the hour of our most profound solidarity with the world, an hour in which we clench our teeth and our hands tremble. The kingdom comes to us in our death, our solitude, our waiting; it comes to where the church remains in solidarity with the world, awaiting only the kingdom of God.

One can imagine these words from Bonhoeffer bringing new resolve to Pierre Claverie at a time when his deep spiritual life did not shelter him from distress: "In fact, our battle involves a grace for which we must pay."

## Continuing to Fight, in Many Ways

On November 10, two sisters of the Sacred Heart were attacked in Kouba, a neighborhood in Algiers with a significant Islamist presence. One of the sisters survived her wounds; the one who died, Sister Odette Prévost, was very close to Pierre Claverie, having worked with him for years at the diocesan center, les Glycines, where she taught Arabic and worked on the *Revue de presse*. She had participated in the summer retreat that he had given to the members of her congregation. All of a sudden, in an atmosphere of political falsehood in which assassins shamelessly attended "peace negotiations," Pierre Claverie unleashed his fury in a scalding editorial that would frighten those around him. It was entitled "Bravo!"[7] Here are some selections:

> Bravo! The heroic combatants for justice have struck again. They must have spent a long time analyzing the prevailing political situation in the country, composing their strategy, choosing high-profile victims capable of shifting public opinion and changing the balance of power or the course of history, observing their designated victims for days or weeks to determine how they spent their time, mapping out their movements, evaluating their ability to respond to attack, choosing the necessary weapons ...
>
> And while the two unarmed women were walking to meet with a friend who would accompany them to Kouba, where they were going to pray for peace once again that Friday, our two heroes fired from their hiding place, killing Odette and wounding Chantale in the shoulder and face, and in the arm she reflexively raised to defend herself in a pitiful gesture of self-defense.
>
> Bravo! to you who have chosen this kind of war, which you sometimes call jihad, a holy war against the enemies of God, the tyrants and the exploiters, the corrupt and the hypocrites, the unbelievers, the Jews, and the Christians (according to the Islamic Armed Forces).
>
> Bravo! to you, the political leaders and courageous emirs who have constructed programs and strategies to overthrow the *taghut* (tyrant) and to bring about the ideal society ... You even grant yourselves the luxury of giving your contribution and support to dialogue, democracy, pluralism, tolerance, to respect for the opinions of others, to the rights of individuals and of religious minorities (the national "contract" of Rome) ...
>
> Bravo! to you who know so well how to foster confusion ...

Was it an angry editorial? Undoubtedly so. But it continued by recalling some fundamental principles: we cannot defend a just cause through underhanded means; we must not drag God into our human conflicts; we should seek truth without letting ourselves be misled by simplistic slogans, or even by the "scientific" analyses of the specialists. "Above all, let us rediscover the utterly clear lesson that our faith teaches us through Jesus Christ: without respect for the human person, no moral, social, political, or religious project can obtain our participation."

Claverie was in Rome in November, participating in a plenary meeting of the Pontifical Council for Interreligious Dialogue. This gave him the opportunity to meet again with the pope, who "inquired for a long time about the news from Algeria," and to brief the Secretariat of State on the situation of the church there. He also met with the heads of the religious communities present in Algeria and went to see his Dominican brothers at Santa Sabina, where he had lunch with the master general of his order, Timothy Radcliffe. In spite of the dire situation back home, he continued to contribute to the Pontifical Council, providing an assessment of the evolution of dialogue in Algeria since the previous plenary meeting in 1992 — since, that is, the country was plunged into violence. After describing the country's hardships and the price paid by the church there, Claverie concluded:

> Nonetheless, dialogue continues to make progress at all levels, reaching a depth never before equaled. The dialogue of life itself unites us through mutual assistance and solidarity, which are even more necessary in order to overcome the difficulties (of supplies, employment, etc.) but also to dispel fear. The eleven religious order victims have sealed with their blood a new covenant with the country, as the thousands of testimonies we have received bear witness. As during the war of liberation, the church's presence in the midst of this crisis reinforces and legitimizes its rightful place in an overwhelmingly Muslim Algeria.
>
> The "dialogue" of service and cooperation is also moving forward. Whether in the area of charity, or of training the young, or of the advancement of women, we are working together with the Algerians . . . We are the last foreigners to demonstrate a willingness to provide help, while the foreign embassies are exerting pressure to send their nationals back home.

Emphasizing that religiously motivated violence provoked a dismay among some that led to theological or spiritual conversations, he concludes:

> The "dialogue" of religious experience is even stronger. This is because, in the face of suffering and death, the cry for God does not know language, religion, or borders. We find ourselves together before God in poverty and supplication, and we pray for one another. In this desert, the presence of God is revealed to all of us as our only recourse, and all

renounce their self-sufficiency. This experience of being stripped bare is what nourishes our deepest exchanges and our most substantial hope.[8]

In December, Pierre Claverie was in Italy again, in Naples, for the conference on monotheism and conflict referred to previously.[9] He went "dragging [his] feet," scarcely inclined to spend his time in academic debates while those close to him were in danger of death. Besides, the others around him thought he was leaving too often — that year he went abroad at least once a month. He was greeted very warmly by the organizers, and again encountered Roger Garaudy, with whom he had clashed at the time of Garaudy's highly publicized conversion to Islam. Also present were the vice-rector of Al-Azhar University in Cairo, the rector of the Gregorian University in Rome, and other Jewish and Muslim participants with whom he got along well. Pierre Claverie even recorded a program together with the vice-rector of Al-Azhar on the topic "Who is Mary for Our Two Religions?" "We gave the overview in Arabic, and why not? The technicians were astonished!" he wrote with great delight to his father (letter dated December 19, 1995).

His address at the conference was entitled "The Least of All and the Kingdom of Man." It consisted of a reflection on God's stance in favor of the lowly and the poor. In his eyes, religion becomes a factor of oppression and violence whenever it forgets the essential link between God and the humble:

> In these times when the religions are threatening to rise to power once more, on account of a variety of nonreligious causes, recalling the importance of the lowly, of the least, and the last can prevent distortions and straying off course . . . The kingdom of God must not be confused with a particular human regime seen as being invested with divine authority: no political system is certain to fulfill the divine promises. Religion cannot be used as guarantor for any government. It is, instead, the critical yeast within all possible systems, which prevents them from closing in on themselves in self-sufficiency and turning themselves into idols. It opens up a horizon of hope, proposing the ideal of the always-to-come kingdom that is to come, where the ultimate achievement of justice offers perspectives for fighting against the injustices that now exist . . . But in order to do this, it must remain the religion of the least.[10]

It is interesting to note the delicate way in which Pierre Claverie criticizes the Islamists' presumption to take control of society by striking at the root of the problem: the penchant for the religions to forget their primary vocation, that of freeing people from fear by restoring the bond (for this is the meaning of the word *religio*) between them and God. This approach has the advantage of not singling out Islam, because it also includes the deviations seen in the history of Christianity. At the same time, the contemporary witness of the Algerian church takes its place in the long list of witnesses (martyrs) who over many centuries "have joined their own lives with those of the most poor, in a gratuitous and unconditional covenant, for the sole sake of loving, freeing, setting aright, and restoring trust to that which has been shattered. They remind us that the Master gave his life by placing himself upon the fault lines of humanity, in order to heal these rifts and restore what had been broken."[11]

The bishop of Oran made a great impression on the chief organizer of the conference, Italian university professor Enrico Ferri, who afterward devoted himself, with intelligence and spirit, to making known in Italy the thought and witness of Pierre Claverie.[12]

The photocopied message for Christmas of 1995 that Claverie sent as his holiday greetings to his many friends and acquaintances expresses well his state of mind — that of standing firm over the days and months, continuing to live and perform his duty in a spirit of resistance. And, he wrote, just as the women had gone to vote en masse for the first time ever, so also "we have decided to join this resistance, without taking sides but by taking a position of fostering hope through the many activities by which it continues to express itself."[13]

## "To Live and to Die . . ." in the Light of Easter

Pierre Claverie loved life and continued to make plans for both himself and his diocese, in spite of the precariousness of the situation. While putting the finishing touches on a forthcoming selection of his editorials, he showed interest in a variety of book projects proposed to him by a number of publishers: "I admit that I truly do want to set down in black and white that which our Algerian experience brings us to live and believe. The conferences I have attended and my editorials in *Le Lien* have permitted me to give shape to a certain number of intuitions which I must now put into order," he wrote on March 18, 1996.

This was the period during which Éditions du Cerf was preparing to publish *Le Livre de la foi* (Book of Faith), of which Claverie had been the architect. It also seems that he was planning to write a book under the title *Ce que je crois* (What I Believe), which would summarize the major stages of his journey as a believer. He had agreed to write for Éditions de l'Atelier a book on his experience of dialogue, with its issues and difficulties. But with the end of March, events would take a sharply different turn. During the night of March 26, seven monks were kidnapped from the Trappist monastery in Tibhirine by an armed group that had previously approached the monastery on Christmas Eve of 1993. This first visit from an emir of the Islamic Armed Forces had prompted the monks to reexamine, prayerfully and in common, the fundamental reasons for their presence there. Despite the risk, they decided to stay, in fidelity to their vocation and on account of the close ties they had established with their Algerian neighbors who had worked with them on their farm.[14] In his journal, Brother Christophe, one of the Tibhirine monks, reports this conversation between the prior, Brother Christian, and one of the neighbors: "You know, we are like a bird perched on a branch," Christian said.

And the neighbor replied, "See there, the branch, that's you, and we are the bird; now if the branch is lopped off."[15]

A few days later, Pierre Claverie gathered all of the priests of the diocese in order to "set the course" in a context that was sorely trying each of them. Among other things, he told them, "Your mission does not stem from your own responsibility, but from that of your bishop. What you do, you do because I ask it of you. If what I am asking of you is too heavy, you must tell me so. One cannot do anything whatsoever at any age...My concern is for your well-being in your assignments."

After the death of the two French surveyors, who had come to the country on a limited contract, the diocese of Oran had not seen any more victims—but everyone was living in an atmosphere of insecurity, especially on the roads, where "false roadblock" ambushes often led to deaths. In such a situation, it was important that everyone should feel that the decision to stay was not a purely subjective one, but would be made in the context of the church. This involved the commission extended by the bishop, as Pierre Claverie emphasized.

The news of the kidnapping of the monks was a great shock for him: "Another heavy blow," he acknowledged. "The only thing to do now is pray that they were taken in an act of desperation, and that they will not be killed...We have certainly not seen the end of our suffering..." The guests staying at the monastery that night had included a number of people from his diocese, including a religious sister and his own vicar-general, Thierry Becker. They had come for the twice-yearly Muslim-Christian prayer meeting, the *Ribât-as-Salâm*.

A few days later, his father, Étienne Claverie, died at the age of 89. "It's for the best," Pierre Claverie told those close to him, as though relieved. "He was a wise and just man, and I owe a great deal to him," he wrote a few weeks later to Sister Marie Melhem, who had hosted the Claverie family in Lebanon during happier times. A private funeral was conducted in Toulon on Saturday, April 6. Anne-Marie, her husband, Eric Gustavson, and their daughter came for the occasion from their home in the United States. Eric Gustavson recalls that Pierre seemed different: apart from the gravity of the event that had brought them together, there was something "almost ascetic" in his behavior. For some time he had been eating less, and he would not take a second glass of wine. Had he received threats? Was he already fixated on the "journey" that awaited him?

Claverie had always been a disciplined man who never let himself lose control, and now he was called to a certain abandonment. One senses this in his editorial for February, written just before the kidnapping of the monks. It was entitled "Lent 1996." Here are a few of its passages:

> It is a matter of living authentic lives, tearing life away from what holds it captive in order to give it over to him who is the source of its freedom and fruitfulness. More than an effort to earn a divine reward, what God invites us to is abandonment. But we know well that this abandonment cannot be achieved without self-denial, because we often prefer the chains of slavery to the risks of freedom...Prayer is just as central as this sort of fasting during Lent, because it is here that we are stripped of our resources and offer our lives in abandonment, saying "Abba, Father"...All of this is to prepare us to enter together with Jesus into the mystery of Easter, open to the presence of God and ready to do his work.[16]

Pierre Claverie now had the possibility of his violent death explicitly in mind, as he wrote in March. While some were urging the Christians in Algeria either to leave or to take cover for awhile, he saw a crucial opportunity at hand. It was not a matter of "playing Russian roulette with life, in needlessly exposing it [to danger]," but of becoming ever more conscious of one's reasons for living and dying: "In all our lives there comes a time when our decisions reveal who we are and what we carry within us."[17] His determination was founded upon his living solidarity with thousands of Algerians who also faced the specter of a violent death. But it was founded even more solidly upon the paschal mystery:

The mystery of Easter obliges us to look in the face the reality of Jesus' death and of our own, and to take stock of our reasons for confronting it...Jesus teaches us to look this hour in the face without trying to escape it. Whether it is peaceful or violent, the culmination of our life or its untimely end, we must integrate this death as the reality that most fully reveals the significance of our life...There is no life without losing what we have, because there is no life without love, and no love without detachment from all our possessions...This is not a death wish, but a passion of love...Together with Jesus, we reject the logic of violence and power, which contradict love and life. That is precisely where the cross stands, and not in any sort of suffering whatsoever. Taking up our cross in the footsteps of Christ, as he explicitly asks of us, thus means deliberately joining the gift of our life with his own, to continue God the Father's work of creation.[18]

At that time, the Christians were engaged in a genuine battle, above all against their own tendencies, "not permitting our love to be extinguished in spite of the fury in our hearts, desiring peace and building it up in tiny steps, refusing to join the chorus of howls, and remaining free while yet in chains..." as he wrote in a heartrending editorial for May.[19]

## "Letters and Messages from Algeria"
## "The Bishop of Oran Refuses to Remain Silent"[20]

During that same period, Éditions Karthala published a collection of his editorials under the title *Lettres et messages d'Algérie*. The initiative for the book came from René Luneau, a Dominican based in Paris, who was editing a collection entitled *Chrétiens en liberté* ("Christians in Freedom"). Struck by the depth of his editorials, Luneau wrote to Pierre Claverie at the end of September 1994 to propose the idea of collecting these, with some other texts, in a book. These writings seemed to him "so radically Christian" that it would be a shame, he wrote, for them to be read only by those who received the bulletin of the diocese of Oran. But he added, "If, for any reasons you might have, it should seem preferable not to pursue this subject, I will accept this regrettable outcome." The response came ten days later, and was composed simply of two lines: "I have received your letter with its proposal for publication. If this can be useful, I am indeed willing. But I will need to be instructed on how to proceed!" He added only this: "The situation has hardly improved at all, and the horizon seems to be obscured, but we have held an assembly of the mini-diocese that we have become, and hope is not dead." This is a fairly typical response from Pierre Claverie: when the truth was at stake, he took it as his duty to become involved. So he signed a publishing contract in September of 1995, and the book was published on April 26, 1996.

Karthala arranged for Pierre Claverie himself to present the newly published book at a conference at the Dominican priory of Saint-Jacques in Paris, on May 9. The event attracted such a large crowd that it had to be held in the priory church. At the end of the conference, an Algerian approached the microphone and said, "You should be aware that this man's life is in danger." In his correspondence with his family that he still continued, although less frequently since the death of Papie, Pierre Claverie remarked upon the evening in these terms: "I was deeply moved by the testimonies that followed my presentation, these unexpected and heartrending expressions of sincerity and friendship: there was a university professor from Tunisia, an Algerian exile, a Trappist from Zaire, a Dachau survivor, and the sister who survived the latest attack, which claimed the life of Sister Odette in Kouba" (letter of June 10, 1996).

Surprised by the attention the book received, he anticipated and accepted the consequences this would have: "This book will mark a turning point in my life," he remarked to Thierry Becker.[21] On the evening of May 10, he was Daniel Bilalian's guest on the 8 o'clock news broadcast of the France 2 television network: "I am nervous on the outside, but deep down I am very calm," he wrote. Once again, many thought he was being imprudent. In Oran, those close to him tried to dissuade him, but in vain. In the face of his insistence, his aid workers made him repeat his responses to the questions that would be posed to him. "I think you are speaking too much. We need you," his friend Pierre Frantz, who greatly admired him, said as he drove him to the airport. "I cannot remain silent. What I can do is be a witness to the truth," Claverie replied. His answers on the television broadcast clearly show what this action meant to him:

> *Pierre Claverie:* I am responsible for an immense region in the northwest of Algeria, with a population of seven million Algerians, with [Christian] communities dispersed throughout all the towns of the region, and now even more than before I must ensure contact with these communities, which is why I travel through the area so much and meet with so many people.
>
> *Daniel Bilalian:* Do you consider the risk you are taking here in Paris by speaking publicly this evening on France 2 — and why are you taking this risk?

Claverie makes a point on the worsening Algerian situation in Paris
on May 18, 1996, meeting with religious press personnel.
(Photo by J.-M. Magerolle, CIRIC)

*Pierre Claverie:* I am taking this risk because I want to emphasize through this broadcast that the relationships of solidarity that we have sought and established over decades are still important to us at this time of deepening crisis among cultures and religions, this time of exclusion and marginalization. So, then, we intend to communicate a message of peace by the simple fact of our existence.[22]

During May 10–15, Claverie presented his new book in Lille, Versailles, Lyon, Grenoble, and Marseilles. At each town, journalists from all the press and broadcast outlets were there to ask him questions: *France-Culture*, Radio France Internationale, Vatican Radio, Radio Fourvière, *Le Figaro, LCI*. Media interest was all the greater because there had been no news of the kidnapped monks for a month and a half. The press in France was in a frenzy with the speculation on what might have happened. Prayers were said for the monks every day in the churches, and in Paris, Cardinal Lustiger had lit seven candles in the sanctuary of the cathedral of Notre Dame to symbolize the church's constant prayer for them. The bishop of Oran had become the de facto spokesman of the church of Algeria. This provoked great annoyance, and even more so among Christians than among Pierre's politically minded friends. Speaking out in the French media was viewed unfavorably in Algeria. The Algerian consul in Grenoble reproached him for, among other things, bringing the Algerian government into question as violence raged through the country.

Was Pierre Claverie so naïve that he did not imagine his comments would be dissected and discussed?[23] Were his actions simply a matter of his "desire to be loved"? "Our experience of the church here is a grace that we must make known," he said to Thierry Becker, his vicar-general and close friend. "This reduction to the essential, this setting down of roots, this espousal, this is a grace—because we had no other choice."

Camille Tarot provides another interpretation of what was happening: "We feared for Pierre Claverie, and all the more so in that we felt that he was increasingly committed to his struggle for a peaceful, democratic, and pluralist Algeria. Toward the end of his life his activity increased — he wrote, published, and appeared on television, even in France. But what was even more remarkable was how his voice carried—wherever he went, his presence had an effect."[24]

Just after his return to Oran, Pierre Claverie received word of the death of the monks, which was announced on May 21 by the Islamic Armed Forces. As their bodies had not yet been found, he held onto "a slender hope." The regular diocesan celebration of Pentecost took place on Friday, May 24, "in an atmosphere that was not very festive, on account of the probable death of the monks, but was very serene and determined." "Whatever happens, I'm staying," he said to the newspaper *La Croix* on May 25. That was the day he was put under heightened security. Bodyguards and two police cars accompanied him wherever he went. On May 26, they went with him to Sidi-bel-Abbès for an important meeting. On the 28th, he went to Algiers for a meeting with the other bishops, and for a last visit with Cardinal Duval, who was very old and having difficulty recovering from a hip operation. Pierre Claverie found him "very weak, but perfectly lucid and present." "He says that the death of the monks has nailed him to the cross. Poor cardinal, who has given so much to Algeria!" he wrote upon his return. Cardinal Duval died two days later; his funeral was held on June 2 in the basilica of Notre Dame d'Afrique, together with the funeral for the monks, whose remains had been found. There was immense shock throughout all of Algeria. Eight days later a ceremony was held in their honor in Oran, and Pierre Claverie commented upon this with an emotionally touching sense of restraint in his last letter to his family:

> The 10th: a number of visitors and, in the evening, a celebration in the church in memory of Cardinal Duval and our Trappist brothers. There were more than two hundred Algerians, in addition to the handful of Christians. All the classes of society were represented. They came to show their sense of outrage, and their solidarity with our little community. It was extremely moving for me to see these men and women participate in these prayers in an astonishing silence. I didn't recognize

half of them. All had tears in their eyes. After the end of the prayers with the playing of a recording of the Salve Regina, the great evening prayer of the monks, we met for tea and soft drinks in the center's courtyard. The sympathy was extraordinary. The message of the church in Algeria seems to have been heard by many. Our brother monks did not die in vain. (letter of June 19, 1996)

During the ceremony, Pierre Claverie offered a vibrant homage to the cardinal, "the spiritual father of the church of Algeria,"[25] and to the monks:

They were a shining light for us, because they achieved in a radical way what each of us tries to live out amid the concerns and annoyances of everyday life...Their death is an accomplishment, and a call...The spilling of their blood, mixed with that of the thousands of Algerians who have been the victims of violence in recent years, seals a new pact between us: this is a covenant that nothing, not even death, can destroy...As for us, we will journey down the road they took. The light that has been kindled will never be extinguished.[26] The silence and the hidden and humble lives of these monks now speak of fraternity and peace in the hearts of millions of men and women throughout the world. One can kill the body, but one cannot kill the soul; this is what Jesus tells us in the Gospel according to Saint Matthew: "Do not fear those who can kill the body, but cannot kill the soul."[27]

All of his remarks tended in this same direction: his determination to be a witness was absolute.

## In Prouilhe with the Saint-Do, in the Footsteps of Dominic

At the end of June, Pierre Claverie met with his former companions in Algeria's Boy Scout organization, the Saint-Do, the national reunions of which he led every four years. That year the gathering was held in Prouilhe, in Languedoc, which was no ordinary place for a Dominican, as it was here that Dominic had begun his preaching among the Albigensians and had formed his first community from women seeking to escape that sect's grasp. To this day there is a community of Dominican nuns there. Pierre Claverie had never visited Prouilhe, and was moved when he arrived. Upon his arrival on Saturday, June 22, Sister Christa-Marie, the prioress of the community, suggested to Pierre Claverie that he spend a moment in the room occupied by Saint

At a press conference in 1995 (Photo by A. Pinoges, CIRIC).

Dominic in the neighboring village of Fanjeaux, and then drove him there herself. Fanjeaux represented a time of trial in Dominic's life: confronted by political violence and lacking recognition from the church, it was only through the sheer power of prayer that he persevered. Sister Christa-Marie left Pierre Claverie alone for over half an hour in Saint Dominic's room, which had been turned into an oratory. "I was not reborn, but I was touched," he told her on their way back. At the priory, the nuns were waiting for him to join them for vespers and for an encounter with the community. "Pierre seemed illuminated," said Sister Dominique, who was meeting him for the first time. "It was as if he was bathed in the light of a grace obtained for him by Dominic." He then spoke to them of the church's mission in Algeria, adding with tears in his eyes, "It costs us dearly." He then went to meet his friends from the Saint-Do for an evening get-together.

The following day, Sunday, June 23, there was a pontifical high Mass. For the occasion, a crosier was borrowed from the Dominican bishop of Pamiers, Albert de Monléon, one of Pierre Claverie's classmates at Le Saulchoir. Pierre preached that day like never before, with an astonishing power in his voice, with a spiritual depth and a sense of freedom that no one who heard him there could forget. He spoke of a world in tatters — that of Dominic, and our own. When Dominic arrived in Languedoc, it was amid a crusade proclaimed by Pope Innocent III against the Albigensians. The barons of the north took advantage of this as an opportunity for pillage and massacre. Dominic was furious. He quickly became convinced that the only way to fight heresy was through the example of a life lived in imitation of Jesus, in poverty and fraternity. This led to the idea for his first community, called "holy preaching." But it would be 1215 before he could gather his first group of friars. In the meantime he lived through years of hardship, a veritable "descent to hell," as one biographer wrote. He was misunderstood, and was powerless in the face of the violence: "while every word was suspect, at least his life itself spoke clearly."[28] In his homily, Pierre Claverie made the connection between Dominic's time and his own: "The Dominican order was born in the course of a war, in the midst of a rupture (the Albigensian heresy), in a place of division...and during a crusade. Dominic had the inspiration to found his order, and heard the call of God in a ravaged world."[29]

At that time, defending the truth already meant running risks:

Dominic had already been seriously threatened along the road from Prouilhe to Fanjeaux, the citadel of the Albigensians: "I am not worthy of the glory of martyrdom; I have not yet deserved that sort of death," he said to those who wanted to kill him. Jourdain de Saxe, who retold the story, adds, "Those around him became accustomed to his smiling presence, and gave up the plan of killing him."[30]

In this context, "on the whole relevant," Pierre Claverie comments, "Dominic was, in the first place, a man of mercy and compassion":

He truly shared in the suffering and misfortune of others. He also had a great veneration for the cross of Jesus. He saw in this the love of God planted firmly on the earth, heart and arms open to draw humanity into the bosom of his mercy. He saw in it the blood spilled by the Lamb of the Covenant in order to reestablish the sinner in a state of justice, in a just relationship with God and others. He saw in this the suffering of the innocent person unjustly condemned and abandoned, but still closely accompanied by God.[31]

We have already seen all of these themes in the writings of Pierre Claverie, but here they have an unequaled power and coherence. He also spoke in a more personal vein, addressing several hundred persons who were returnees to France from Algeria:

Throughout the dramatic events in Algeria, I have often been asked, "What are you doing there? Why do you stay? Shake off the dust from your sandals! Come back home!" Home...Where are we at home?... We are there for the sake of the crucified Messiah. We're not there for any other reason, or for any other person! We have no interests to protect, no influence to maintain. We are not driven by any sort of masochistic perversion. We have no power, but are there as at the bedside of a friend, of a sick brother, silently holding his hand and wiping his brow.[32] We are there for the sake of Jesus, because he is the one suffering there amid violence that spares no one, crucified again and again in the flesh of thousands of innocents. Like his mother Mary and Saint John, we are there at the foot of the cross where Jesus died abandoned by his followers and bitterly mocked by the crowd. Isn't it essential for Christians to be present in desolate and abandoned places?[33]

Here the message of Pierre Claverie is summarized and concentrated in one essential point, the cross of Christ. In reading his words, one gathers that he no longer paid any heed to the "good advice" being offered to him. And he suffered at seeing that his church was not sufficiently focused on this essential reality:

> What would be the place of the church of Jesus Christ, which is the Body of Christ, if it were not above all present there? I believe that the church dies in not being close enough to the cross of its Lord. As paradoxical as it might seem, Saint Paul clearly demonstrates that the power, vitality, Christian hope, and fecundity of the church come from this. Not from anywhere else, nor in any other way. The church deceives itself and the world when it positions itself as a power among all the rest, as a humanitarian organization, or as a flashy evangelical movement. In this condition it can glitter on the outside — but it cannot burn with the fire of God's love, which is "as strong as death," as the Song of Songs puts it. It is truly a question of love, of love above all and of love alone. It is a passion for which Jesus has given us a longing, and to which he has marked out the way. "There is no greater love than to lay down one's life for one's friends."[34]

The audience was stunned. Those closest to him understood that, in a certain way, Pierre didn't belong to himself anymore.[35] But a festive luncheon gave him the opportunity for a moment of relaxation with some of his childhood friends, like Geneviève Troncy and Jean-François Cota, who, like him, was born in Bab el Oued, and went through the scouts with him. It seems that it was to Jean-François that Pierre first spoke of his desire to become a priest, "one summer evening at camp, before a sinking fire." Their reunion was emotional.[36] This visit to a renowned Dominican site together with his old friends from the Saint-Do, just six weeks before his death, was like the closing of a circle in his life. It was among them, in effect, with Fr. Lefèvre, that Pierre found the key that would give meaning to his life. And he had come back to visit them where Saint Dominic's own vocation had ripened in the midst of trial. His homily in Prouilhe is one of Pierre Claverie's greatest writings.

At the end of the afternoon, he flew from Montpellier to Bastia, where he attended a conference organized by Communist activists on the theme of bringing together the two shores of the Mediterranean. A number of his good Algerian friends were there. Claverie was delighted to have attended. On Tuesday, June 25, he returned to Oran. Those close to him thought he looked concerned, and he seemed to have lost weight. As most of the priests of his diocese had gone on vacation at his own request, he spent the month of July visiting his various communities: Sidi-bel-Abbès, Ghazaouet, Tounane, Mascara, Hennaya, Tlemcen, Arzew.[37] The religious sisters of Oran had all moved in with the Little Sisters of the Poor, or into the diocesan center near the bishop's residence. It was the middle of the summer, and around him there remained only those who had accompanied him day in, day out over the years, surrounding him with great affection: Sister Gesuina, the laundress for the bishop's residence, and Sister Marie-Noëlle, both of them members of the order Notre Dame des Apôtres; Fatiha, the cook; Tayeb, the chauffeur and clerk for the bishop's residence; Sister Renée and Sister Marie-Louise of the congregation of the Filles de Notre Dame d'Afrique; and Clément, a young student from Mali. These would be the first witnesses of the dramatic events about to unfold, and they would be the last to express tenderness toward him.

## August 1, 1996: Pierre and Mohamed

On August 1st, Pierre Claverie went to Algiers to participate in the delegation meeting with Hervé de Charette, the French foreign affairs minister. He went grudgingly, not liking to be too closely associated with French interests in Algeria. He had staked his own life in Algeria. "Go along, at least for our sake," his friend Rahal had said to him. The closing of the consulates had, in effect, made it very difficult for Algerians to obtain visas. Claverie also wanted to explain to the minister why the French men and women religious wanted to stay in Algeria, in spite of the pressure upon them to return. He was received by de Charette around 10:00 a.m., in the company of the bishop of Constantine and the vicar-general of Algiers, who was representing Archbishop Teissier. Teissier had gone to visit the families of the murdered monks in France. "What struck me about Bishop Claverie, whom I had never met be-fore, was his tranquil assurance, his energetic determination to remain in this country that was his own and that he loved so deeply. I was also impressed by the tremendous kindness in his eyes," the minister later said.[38] Pierre Claverie did not go with him to Tibhirine, as some newspapers reported at the time, returning instead to the diocesan center in Hydra, on the hillside of Algiers. One of the people he met there was Djamel Amrani, a childhood friend who had been his classmate in Bugeaud high school.

After lunch, he decided to return to Oran, where there were few priests left during the summer months to assure the celebration of the Mass for the com-munities of nuns. He had an open ticket, because the time of his meeting with the minister had not been specified. With this encounter already finished, he went to the airport with Jean and Hélène Donet, a pied-noir couple of Oran, who had come to explain to the minister the situation of the French citizens who had remained in Algeria, whose representatives they were. The vicar-general of the diocese of Algiers, Fr. Belaïd Ould-Aoudia, drove them to the airport, picking up along the way a friend of his who worked for Air-Algérie, to help his guests get seats on the flight to Oran. For weeks, Claverie had not been allowed to move around without an escort, and he had to take the safest and quickest routes. But because all of the escorts were attending the French minister, they departed alone in the car belonging to the archbishop's residence. Pierre Claverie took advantage of this freedom to make a leisurely visit of the sites of his childhood. From the diocesan center, they drove up the heights of El Biar, with its breathtaking view of the Bay of Algiers, then down Laperlier Road, flanked by flowering bougainvillea vines, past where the Dominican priory had been established after Algeria's independence. Passing the cathedral, they saw Galland Park and Édith-Cavell Street, where the Boy Scouts of the Saint-Do once gathered. Many of Pierre's childhood memories were associated with these places. Then there was Didouche-Mourad Street, where he had lived while he was learning Arabic. They went by the military parade ground and the shepherds' road, arriving at last at the airport, which had once been called "White House" — white, as in "Algiers the White." The weather was good, and the sky had that intense blue that is characteristic of the Mediterranean. Pierre was delighted, and teased Jean Donet, boasting about the superiority of his birthplace, Algiers. For a moment, his worries seemed far away, and he was happy.

There was a large crowd at the airport — all the domestic flights were in great demand, because terrorism had made the roads too unsafe. There wasn't a seat to be had, not even for the Air-Algérie agent, who was dismayed at

Pierre Claverie's daily companions and coworkers with his vicar-general Thierry Becker.

Mohamed Bouchikhi, Claverie's driver, friend, and companion in death.

being unable to help the bishop of Oran. It was 5:00 p.m., and the 11:00 a.m. flight had still not taken off. Some of the people in the airport had been waiting since the previous night. Finally, three boarding passes were given without explanation to Pierre and the Donets hours later, just before the take-off.

Mohamed Bouchikhi was waiting for them in Oran. Mohamed was a young Algerian friend of the Christian community in Sidi-bel-Abbès, which had helped his family in difficult times. The oldest child in a large family, he was happy to help out the diocese by taking its Peugeot 205, which he loved to drive, to the airport, or on errands. That summer, he had asked to replace Tayeb, the employee at the bishop's residence, who was on leave. And this was his first day in his new full-time job. He had a beautiful, brilliant smile. He was not unaware of the risks he was running by helping out Christians, but this had been a heart-felt choice. He recounted that on the day the news came that the monks had been killed, he and a friend went out on a cliff overlooking the sea, and wept. Pierre Claverie had perceived his great delicacy of soul. It seems that they secretly shared some of the same threats.[39] Pierre Claverie had only said, "You see, for a man like Mohamed, there is no question but that staying in this country is worthwhile, in spite of the danger to one's life." The plane from Algiers finally landed at 10:25 p.m. Mohamed was there, together with an escort of two policemen. They returned together to the bishop's residence, after dropping off Jean Donet and his wife. "Pierre seemed deeply preoccupied," the Donets recall. At 10:45 they arrived at the entrance to the bishop's residence, opened the gate, and said goodnight to the escort. "I'll go with you to the house," Mohamed told Pierre, who, apart from his briefcase, was carrying three large mobile phones for the communities of religious sisters which were extremely isolated in the interior. At 10:48, they entered the episcopal residence, and switched on the lights in the foyer. There was a big explosion, and both men were killed instantly. Claverie fell with his head resting on the threshold of the chapel, and Mohamed fell behind him, at the foot of the stairs. The nuns who heard the noise rushed from the neighboring house. Pierre and Mohamed lay, their blood mingling, in the wreckage of the entrance. The powerful bomb had been planted behind a metal door, usually guarded, that opened onto an alley.

The police quickly arrived at the scene, with the *wali* (prefect), the firemen, and the various security authorities. The bodies were carried off on stretchers shortly before midnight, in the presence of some friends who had come in haste. Everyone was stunned. The news began to spread, and dismay spread with it. "For the church in Algeria, cruelly attacked once again, a new page has been added to the martyrology," Pope John Paul II wrote in a telegram received the morning of August 2. The Algerian president, Liamine Zeroual, deplored "this barbarous act, carried out in total disregard for human values and the sense of hospitality." The news made the front page of the morning newspapers — national and international — on August 2. "He did not want to leave Algeria, in spite of the threats," read the headline in the Algerian newspaper *Liberté*. "He courageously assisted this people, his people, to discover its proud and indomitable spirit," a political activist, Zazi Sadou, told *El Watan*. Sadou and Claverie had participated together in the international conference on "The Mediterranean, at the Crossroads of Solidarity," in Bastia at the end of June. "That this Algerian voice has been silenced is, in the first place, a crisis for Algeria itself," wrote the editorialist for *Le Monde* on August 6, under the title "The Death of an Algerian." The most moving tributes in the book of condolences placed in the episcopal residence came from his Algerian friends, who were crushed and humiliated. Hundreds of friends and strangers repeated the same message: "Be assured, Bishop Claverie, that your death is not in vain. We will continue to fight so that the values of love of neighbor, solidarity, tolerance, and respect for the other person will triumph" (signed "Yamina").

Mohamed Bouchikhi was buried the next evening, according to Muslim custom, in Sidi-bel-Abbès. A Christian delegation was present and surrounded his family. Claverie's funeral took place on August 5 in the cathedral of Oran. The presider was Cardinal Bernardin Gantin, the pope's personal representative for the event. He concelebrated the liturgy with the bishops of Algeria and Morocco, the priests of the diocese, the master general and provincial of the Dominicans. A number of Algerian ministers were at the head of a large assembly, composed mostly of Algerian friends, both familiar and unknown. Many wept.[40] Moving tributes to Pierre were delivered after the singing of the Beatitudes and the *Magnificat*. A traditional couscous was offered by his friends from Oran in the courtyard of the episcopal residence after the ceremony. Pierre Claverie was buried in the cathedral, dressed in his alb and wearing his pectoral cross, and around his shoulder the stole that he loved so much, bearing the simple Arabic words *Allah mahabba* ("God is love").[41] Flowers are brought to his tomb each day by friends and strangers, and his memory remains alive in the hearts of both Christians and Muslims who had the good fortune of knowing him. "But who didn't love that man?" Sister Gesuina still says to this day.

# Epilogue

# "I leave you upon this open horizon"

It was with these words that Pierre Claverie ended his last letter to his family. It was dated June 19, 1996. He was not sure he would be able to go to Prouilhe, because there was a strike, but at last this was lifted. But the words carry beyond their immediate occasion: they are like the signature of a life, a message he left for us. The press discussed the circumstances of his death at great length, advancing all sorts of hypotheses, not all of them very well founded. A trial was conducted in March of 1998, at the end of which seven persons accused of conspiracy to commit murder were convicted and given harsh sentences. Recently their case was reconsidered, and their sentence reduced. An emir of the Islamic Armed Forces confessed that the bomb had been planted "to cause fear," and said that "Bishop Claverie died through an unintentional combination of circumstances."[1] But whose word can be trusted in a country in which more than 150,000 persons have been killed, and thousands of others have disappeared, without the truth ever fully coming to light? Not even the assassination of President Boudiaf has ever been elucidated. Algeria is still too tightly in the grip of violence to permit the light to shine peacefully there. And as far as Pierre Claverie is concerned, instead of taking opposing sides over the uncertain question of who killed him, isn't it more helpful to ask for what and for whom he lived? What were the values for which he was willing to die, if necessary? Answering this could bring fundamental meaning to our own times. More than definite facts about a death — which is important in itself, but presupposes a great deal of progress in Algeria — what we most need now is meaning in life, and reasons to live.

The central message of Pierre Claverie's life clearly points to the question of the Other. His entire life was the story of an encounter with the country in which he was born, and with its inhabitants, among whom he had lived at first without seeing them. After the amazement of first waking up to them, as his outgoing personality had inclined him, he quickly came to measure the great extent of the barriers that race, religion, and the weight of history raise among human beings. He spoke of this even as "the abyss that separates us." Instead

250

of losing courage or settling for superficial dialogue, Pierre Claverie committed himself to pursuing encounter on the deepest level possible, without sacrificing the truth. This brought him both joy and disappointment. Above all, he was able to witness personally at least twice in his own life that when no room is made anymore for the Other, violence holds sway. It is clear that the question of otherness is central for our time. Nationalism and fundamentalism have marked the end of this past century, even in Europe, which had thought to have exorcised its demons with its entrance into modernity. The return of violence in all its forms comes as a reminder that our societies are incapable of promoting a pluralistic, nonexclusive humanity. Jean Leca is therefore correct when he stresses that we must not deceive ourselves about the reasons for the assassination of Pierre Claverie: "Claverie did not die because he 'happened to be there,' a victim of the blind violence of war...He did happen to be there, of course, but this is because he had desired and accepted this exposed position..."[2] The fight for a pluralistic humanity was, in his eyes, one of the greatest challenges of modernity, as shown by Enrico Ferri, for whom "the real danger represented by Pierre Claverie was that his experience seemed authentic: there was something unquestionable about it. This is why some wanted to silence him."[3]

Claverie occupied his exposed position with a sense of fraternity — but he was not naïve. "Lucid and passionate, engaged and respectful, the words of Pierre Claverie vigorously cut through the evasive officialspeak on all sides...What impressed me about his approach was his concern for completeness and for respect for complexity," wrote Camille Tarot. "He neglected nothing, and tried to look at a problem from all angles: political, economic, cultural, philosophical, religious. He was neither a single-issue man, nor someone with a single point of view..."[4] He completely assumed his responsibilities as a bishop. One of his strong points was his emphasis that without careful attention, religion quickly becomes a means of exclusion. While denouncing this deviation in some manifestations of contemporary Islam, he did not hesitate to recognize the past sins of his own church in this area, out of concern for the truth and to encourage his Muslim friends in their struggle against intolerance. This honesty of his touched hearts and souls, as shown by this homage paid to him by a young Algerian woman at his funeral: "My friends, I have been deeply touched; I am the Muslim daughter of Pierre Claverie...My friends, we must get a grip on ourselves. We must stand up for the Algeria of our bishop."[5] During a recent state visit to France, the president of Algeria, Abdelaziz Bouteflika, extended this praise to the church of Algeria in its

entirety. Evoking "the surge of terrorism that indiscriminately strikes intellectuals, leaders, and innocent villagers, foreign nationals, and religious figures,
whether Muslim or Christian, as shown by the killing of numerous imams,
the assassination of Bishop Claverie of Oran, or the unspeakable massacre in
Tibhirine, a genuine affront to Algeria, a land of hospitality, and to Islam, a
religion of tolerance," the Algerian president added, "Permit me here to pay
special homage to the rare self-sacrifice shown by the church of Algeria at
worst moment of the storm, in pursuing unflinchingly its mission of witness
and of human solidarity in my country."[6] Camille Tarot was right to say that
"the destiny of the church of Algeria extends beyond itself on all sides."[7]

A witness to the entire world, this testimony was also a lesson for the
church, which was reminded that one cannot place oneself on the "fault
lines" of the world without consequences. This solidarity comes at a price.
At the height of the violence, in October of 1995, Claverie quoted Dietrich
Bonhoeffer, another resister: "At the present stage of our combat, what we
are being given is the grace that costs. Cheap grace is grace without the
cross. Grace that costs is the gospel, which must always be sought anew. It
costs because it comes for human beings at the price of their lives."[8] Here
Claverie places us at the heart of the Christian mystery: a God who gives
himself up for the sake of love, "a scandal for the Jews, a folly for the pagans,"
as Saint Paul said. In following this demanding path, Pierre Claverie and his
companions had the conviction that they were following in the footsteps of a
certain Galilean, who showed the way to give one's life: "When the time of
distress comes, it is also the time for living the Passion together with Jesus, in
the midst of the world's divisions and violence, with no other weapon than
that of giving of our lives to the utmost, in the trust that the Father of all
love will accomplish his work of resurrection in our crucified flesh. At this
moment, the apostle of Jesus accepts and accomplishes, by perseverance, the
free gift of his or her life."[9] At the end of a century deeply marked by violence,
it is useful to recall that there is only one way to break the infernal cycle of
violence: a love capable of forgiveness.

It was precisely to this realization that Pope John Paul II invited the church
and the world in organizing, on May 7, 2000, among the celebrations for the
Jubilee year, a "commemoration of the witnesses to the faith in the twentieth century." Among the thousands of people gathered around him at the
Colosseum, there were the families and friends of the recent martyrs of the
church in Algeria — the relatives of the monks, of the men and women religious, and of the family of Pierre Claverie. As evening fell in that spectacular
place, where so many men and women had died for the faith during the first

centuries of Christianity, we heard once again, in a momentous silence, the singing of the Beatitudes, first in Italian and then in Greek: "Blessed are the meek, for they shall inherit the earth; blessed are they who are persecuted for the sake of justice, for theirs is the kingdom of heaven." Then there was an evocation of a number of twentieth-century martyrs: a Russian Orthodox patriarch who had died in the gulag, a German Lutheran pastor who had been killed by the Nazis, a Chinese Catholic who had died during deportation, two young seminarians from Burundi who had been killed for rejecting ethnic cleansing, Bishop Romero of El Salvador, and others, including Christian de Chergé and the monks of Tibhirine. And the pope read a prayer asking God to welcome all these witnesses to himself, and "to extend his infinite mercy to their killers as well." And so, amid our tears, we understood better the meaning of the sacrifices made by our brothers and sisters: thanks to them, there is a way out of the infernal cycle of violence. Following Tertullian, who said that "the blood of martyrs is the seed of the church," we have understood better, in our turn, the fruitfulness of these sacrificed lives: thanks to them, the horizon remains open.

# In the Footsteps of Saint Augustine
### Redouane Rahal

By their prescient view of the course of history unfolding before their eyes, certain persons emerge from the common lot of mortals through demanding actions on behalf of humanity or of the truth, in response to the circumstances and events they experience. These persons, who are often moved by profound moral reflection, do not hesitate to accept their responsibility, out of love for the truth, to denounce injustice, intolerance, and exclusion at crucial, historic moments. Truly spiritual persons, they build on human realities in order to combat the dark instincts that devastate humanity. History teaches us that these exceptional persons are often misunderstood and not accepted by their contemporaries, because the courageous and just actions that they call for disturb certain consciences and certain interests.

Bishop Claverie was one of these exceptional persons in his effort to bring people together, no matter what their faith or background, and in fighting to have the right to be different accepted without constraint, by the sole means of sincere dialogue and without reservation. His assassination under tragic conditions in Oran on August 1, 1996, together with his chauffeur Mohamed, is at the same time a sign from God and a symbol of the common spiritual struggle of humanity. The mingled blood of a bishop and a Muslim, both descendants of the prophet Abraham, cannot be interpreted as anything but a common destiny intended by God.

A religious man before all else, and one who lived his faith intensely, Bishop Claverie was also a man with a restorative way of communicating, through his exceptional gifts for understanding and comforting the soul, both spiritually and fraternally. His contact with the Other enriched both himself and his counterpart. The many relationships he was able to establish in Oran with all sectors of society made him a man of dialogue who did not think of himself or his situation, but focused upon the work he had to do for and within the reconciliation of races and cultures. His awareness of himself as the religious man who was to go beyond himself gave a greater sense of responsibility to

The tomb of Pierre Lucien Claverie, O.P., in Oran

his struggle on behalf of humanity. Through the grace of purity of spirit, this sense of responsibility was guided by an interior light. There was no room in him for flattery, and he expressed his ideas without making concessions and with tremendous intellectual honesty. Living deeply the drama taking place in Algeria during the 1990s, and with his denunciation of extremists on all sides, who claimed to be acting in the name of God but in reality were betraying God, Bishop Claverie brings to mind Saint Augustine, who opposed the Manicheans and Pelagians of his day.

Born in Algiers in 1938, during the colonial period in Algeria, Bishop Claverie encountered practically no Muslims among the Catholic Boy Scouts or in secondary school. He realized all on his own that the Arabs, meaning the Algerians, were ignored, completely left out of his surroundings and his community. This indifference pricked his conscience at a time when he was still seeking his path for the future. Later on, meeting Fr. Scotto would help him to assess the relationship between colonist and dominated. At the time, the Europeans lived their own separate lives, with the Algerians around merely as part of the scenery. It was an attitude that could only provoke anger, resentment, and hopelessness. Besides, as René Char put it, the dignity of a single person can scarcely make itself felt, while "the dignity of a thousand

persons takes on the allure of resistance." This painful situation, which pen-
etrated the depths of his conscience, drove him to the decision to fight for a
more convivial society in which indifference and exclusion would be banished
forever. After the fashion of Saint Augustine's City of God, he dreamed of
a more humane earthly city in which more virtuous persons would be more
closely united through their greater awareness of their moral responsibility.

The idea of good will, which was a key issue for Saint Augustine, was also
dear to Pierre Claverie, who hoped above all for earthly peace to be worthy
of the peace of the next world. The soul suffering on account of its quest for
the source of this peace can be comforted only by commitment to the truth,
which is the only way of finding meaning in everyday activities. This was the
path that Bishop Claverie chose. For him, justice and love of the Other are
what defeat evil and suffering. Through his regular writings in *Le Lien* (the
monthly bulletin of his diocese), or through his addresses at conferences in
Algeria or elsewhere, Bishop Claverie marked the stages of his intellectual
development through reflection that was deepened by his personal experience. He peacefully continued the development of his increasingly humanist
thought, but he did not hide his dismay over the tragic spread of fundamen-
talisms across the world. For him, in the presence of a humanity in crisis only
love was capable of overcoming hatred, whatever its source. Like Saint Augustine, he was certain that love was a Credo capable of transforming human
beings. This is why he would join in any struggle for the triumph of truth and
justice.

To this end, he loved to meet with certain Algerian Muslim sheikhs who
reflected the true Arab-Islamic tradition, founded upon tolerance and the
respect of the other. This is why he enjoyed visiting, whether in Algiers or
in Paris, the late Sheikh Abbas Bencheikh El Hocine, then the rector of the
Mosque of Paris. He was the one who had invited Claverie to give a conference at his mosque in 1988. Or there was Sheikh Mehdi Bouabdelli, a
member of the Islamic High Council and the head of a Muslim confraternity, whom Claverie often visited in Béthioua, thirty kilometers east of Oran.
His contacts and encounters reflect Bishop Claverie's Mediterranean spirit.
Speaking of this region, the great historian Fernand Braudel said, "The Mediterranean is an ancient crossroads. For millennia, everything and everyone
flowed through it: people, animals, ships, ideas, religions, the practical arts,
even plants...It is a history that has accumulated in layers as thick as those
of the history of faraway China." It is not an exaggeration to say that Bishop
Claverie was the product of this Mediterranean, the crossroads of the greatest
of humanity's civilizations. It is this Mediterranean that must have influenced

his religious and spiritual choices. Because of his thorough understanding of the fundamental texts of Islam, Bishop Claverie was destined to play the role of a bridge between cultures and religious communities that were different, but that worshiped the same omnipresent God.

He honored me with his friendship for twenty-five years. I saw him regularly, almost daily, during his ministry in Oran, and our discussions were always characterized by great sincerity and fruitfulness; he remains alive to me, because apart from being a bishop, he was a great man, in the noblest sense of the term, a great soul consumed with concern for people tested by any sort of difficulty, a man who deeply loved the land of his birth, Algeria, because his knowledge of its long history gave him hope that a great future could be shaped from the sacrifices of the past. For him, Algeria's position in the Mediterranean gave it a privileged place in the dialogue of cultures and civilizations.

In spite of his physical death, Bishop Claverie remains alive because his message of fraternity is always relevant. It us up to the rest of us to make this message bear fruit, and to spread it for the sake of peace in souls and spirits. In his day, he was a man with the courage of his convictions, and he will always remain an example of tolerance and love, and a great point of reference. Algeria, which brought forth Saint Augustine and Sheikh Ben Badis, was likewise honored to have brought forth such a man as Pierre Claverie. Both he and they traveled the same road of the struggle for justice and for the respect of the diversity of the Other.

# Humanity in the Plural

## A Reflection by Pierre Claverie, O.P.

This reflection arises from my own experience. I am not a politician. Born in Algeria, I have witnessed the developments in this country, in sharing in the lives of the millions of Algerians now plunged into a crisis that is apparent to all. It seems to me that I am once again living through the same painful sort of time I have seen before. I spent my childhood in the "colonial bubble," in which relations between the two worlds [European and Algerian] were conspicuously absent. The social environment I lived in was a bubble in which the Other was ignored, in which the Other was seen as part of the landscape or of the decor that we had set out in our collective existence.

Perhaps because I ignored the Other or because I denied his existence, one day he suddenly leapt right in front of me. He burst open my sheltered universe, which was ravaged by violence (but could it have been any other way?) and asserted his existence.

The emergence of the Other, the recognition of the Other, the accommodation of the Other became an overwhelming preoccupation. It is likely that my religious vocation stemmed from this. I asked myself why, throughout my entire childhood as a Christian (no more so than others, attending church just like the rest) and hearing sermons on the love of one's neighbor, I had never been told that the Arab was my neighbor. Perhaps I had been told, but hadn't been listening. I told myself that from now on there must be no more walls, no more barriers, no more divisions. The Other must be allowed to exist, or we expose ourselves to violence, exclusion, and rejection.

And so after Algeria won independence I asked to return, to rediscover the world in which I had been born but had ignored. This was the real beginning of my personal adventure — it was a rebirth. Discovering the Other, living with the Other, listening to the Other, letting oneself be shaped by the Other, does

Reprinted with the gracious permission of Éditions de l'Aube, which published this text in the first edition of *Nouveaux Cahiers du Sud*, January 1996. Written for a meeting of the Club de Marseille, the text was reprinted by *Le Monde*, August 4–5 1996, after the assassination of Pierre Claverie.

not mean losing one's identity or rejecting one's values; it means conceiving of a "humanity in the plural," without exclusion.

Developments in Algeria following independence went entirely contrary to my hopes. In both political and religious terms, the thirty years following independence saw reflex reactions that created fronts that excluded others. In the realm of politics, anyone who doesn't belong to the front doesn't count. But a similar situation developed in the area of religion, in support of political power. Either one is on the inside and therefore exists, or one is not and thus exists at best as a guest whose presence is tolerated, but without truly being part of society.

The statements one hears today, which are supported by armed violence, are not new in Algeria. There exists here a culture of violence — violence is a reality everywhere, but it is more or less regulated by civilization.

This is paradoxical, because in the countries of the Maghreb — Algeria, Tunisia, and Morocco — the foreigner rarely meets with anything but warm hospitality. What impresses anyone who visits the Maghreb or lives there for a few years is that there one is really welcomed. It is a human society, retaining an emphasis on the personal that is sometimes often lacking when one arrives in Europe. But this situation holds true only for those who are passing through the Maghreb. It's much more complex if one lives there. The religion there is a traditional, usually confraternal form of Islam, deeply rooted and earthy, retaining practices and ideas contrary to Islam. The part of society that practices this form of Islam remains welcoming and peaceful, and this includes most Algerians.

At the same time, orthodox (reformist) Islam has contributed to uprooting traditional popular Islam and ideologizing it. Of course, this was done to mobilize the Muslim people against foreign aggression and intrusion, which were all too real. But it gradually became an instrument manipulated by those in power, who battle against the traditional and confraternal form of Islam. It is no surprise that, little by little, this Islam stripped of its profound human and spiritual values became a political component, and has now become an instrument of violence. This took place for reasons that are not religious, but it was justified in religious terms.

Of the extremely disturbing images shown on television, one in particular has made its mark on Algeria. Even the children talk about it and play-act it among themselves: it is that of an imam kidnapped by armed groups and forced to justify the actions of these groups by issuing fatwas, or judicial decrees. Completely disoriented by what was happening in the hinterland and no longer capable of deliberately advocating anything at all, he gave in. So the imam was put on television to deliver his message, somewhat dazed and with spastic gestures: "Look how far we have come — now it is time for us to draw blood; this is the judgment of God, the law of God." It is excessive to say that this is the judgment of God and the law of God. But this is what happens when one turns religion into ideology. What we are experiencing now is the result of developments that did not begin yesterday, and that have contributed little by little to forming a culture of exclusion and violence.

There is a crisis that has pitted those who have let themselves be shut up inside this culture of exclusion against others who, drawing their inspiration from other sources or following other developments, try to resist this closure and confinement. Profound questions are being posed as never before among Algerian Muslims themselves. Paradoxically, this crisis that has emerged out of a confinement is also the first step toward a new openness in the contemporary history of Algeria. In this, religion and identity go hand in hand: being Algerian means being Muslim, a natural state of affairs that raises no questions. Europeans and other foreigners have become Algerians, but in a somewhat different sense — one is never completely Algerian unless one is truly Muslim. Thus religion and identity go together.

And now, in a formerly peaceful Muslim country in which religion has been part of culture, personality, and history, people are coming to say to you that you [Algerians] are bad Muslims, that you have never been true Muslims. In the name of this ideological Islam, persons and groups are brought into question. What, then, is Islam? Are there different kinds of Islam? One then becomes aware that there are different possible interpretations, whether tolerable or not, orthodox or not, but they exist, and sometimes they assert themselves by force. This is not a purely intellectual question that is discussed at conferences, but one that touches the roots of identity: Who am I right now? In what group will I find my identity? It is a matter of integrating, here and now, one's history — and this is true for the Islamists who have gone into the mountains to join armed groups, just as it is for those who resist this form of Islam. It is a question of integrating, here and now, one's identity.

This deep form of inquiry directs Algerians, not toward a group (because there are multiple groups), but toward their individual judgment. A choice must be made: some go into the mountains, some support the government, some are democrats. It is now necessary to make a personal choice, and to me this heralds the arrival in Algerian society of what Mohamed Talbi calls "modernity," the emergence of the individual. One can no longer be satisfied with belonging to a group and equating one's own identity with a group, because the groups have fragmented. One must make a choice, and thus there is the emergence of a new phenomenon, and, it may be, of another way of living together.

From this experience of confinement, followed by crisis and the emergence of the individual, I have acquired a personal conviction that humanity is found only in the plural, and that as soon as we presume — and in the Catholic Church we have had this sad experience throughout our history — to claim that we possess the truth or to speak in the name of humanity, we fall into totalitarianism and exclusion. No one possesses the truth; everyone is seeking it — there certainly are objective truths, but they exceed our grasp and can be attained only through a long journey during which we piece this truth together by gleaning from the different cultures and instances of humanity what others have sought and obtained in their own journey toward the truth. I am a believer, I believe there is a God, but I do not presume to possess God, neither through Jesus, who reveals God to me, nor through the dogmas of my faith. One does not possess God. One does not possess the truth — and I am in need of the truth that others have found. This is my experience today with thousands of Algerians, as we share together in life and in reflection upon the questions that we are all asking.

There is talk of tolerance, but I see this as a minimum, and I don't much like the term, because tolerance assumes that there is winner and loser, ruler and ruled, and that those who hold the power tolerate the existence of the others who don't. Clearly one can interpret the word differently, but I have too much experience of its meaning of condescending acceptance in Muslim society to really embrace it. Of course, it is better than rejection, exclusion, and violence, but I prefer to speak of respect for the other. If only, after Algeria's crisis of violence and of deep divisions in society, religion, and identity, we can finally realize that the Other has a right to exist, bears a portion of the truth, and is worthy of respect, then the dangers to which we have exposed ourselves will not have been in vain.

# Notes

## Foreword

1. "Un grand abîme nous sépare," *Le Lien* (October 1986).
2. *La Vie Spirituelle*, special issue (Paris: Éditions du Cerf, October 1997): 702–3.
3. "Donner sa vie plutôt que de l'arracher aux autres" (speech to the forum of Christian communities of Angers, France), in *La Vie Spirituelle* (October 1997): 808.
4. Homily in the cathedral of Oran, October 9, 1981.
5. "Le sens du dialogue islamo-chrétien" (speech to l'Institut musulman de la mosquée de Paris), in *La Vie Spirituelle* (October 1997): 705–6.
6. "Humanité plurielle," *Nouveaux Cahiers du Sud* (January 1996): 118.
7. "Que ton règne vienne!" *Le Lien*, October 1995, reprinted in *Lettres et messages d'Algérie* (Paris: Karthala, 1996), 210.

## Preface

1. Pierre Claverie, "Humanité plurielle," *Les Nouveaux Cahiers du Sud* 1 (January 1996): 113–14. This text is provided in an appendix, page 258.
2. This is the title of a biography of Professor Jean-Paul Grangaud, a pieds-noir of Pierre Claverie's generation. See A. Djelfaoui, *Grangaud d'Alger à El Djezaïr* (Algiers: Casbah, 2000). J.-P. Grangaud is a good example of the "liberal Christians" who chose Algeria and played a remarkable role there after independence.

## Chapter 1: From Happy Childhood to Youth as a Pied-Noir

1. "Le mot du P. Claverie à l'occasion de son ordination épiscopale," *La Vie Spirituelle* (October 1997): 701.
2. Ibid. In general, the quotations from Pierre Claverie will be drawn from those of his works easiest to consult, especially *Lettres et Messages d'Algérie*, revised and expanded edition (Paris: Karthala, 1997), and the special issue of *La Vie Spirituelle* dedicated to him (no. 721, October 1997). Some will also be taken from the monthly bulletin of the diocese of Oran, *Le Lien*, and also from his family correspondence, simply indicated by the date, as in "letter of . . . "
3. *Le Lien*, August–September 1999, 10.
4. Pierre Claverie recognized this debt, as shown by these comments from October 15, 1961: "Later [after I have left the priory], when I will have to deal with the real, concrete problems of the people to whom I will be sent, my love for them will have developed in the crucible of our love."
5. An allusion to the order's black and white habit, "penguin" was the term Papie ordinarily used to speak of the Dominicans.
6. The first volume of this correspondence has been published: *Pierre Claverie: Il est tout de même permis d'être heureux. Lettres familiales 1967–69* (Paris: Éditions du Cerf, 2003). The second volume, covering 1969–75, is *Cette contradiction continuellement vécue. Lettres familiales, 1963–1975* (Paris: Éditions du Cerf, 2007).

7. The character Cagayous was created by Auguste Robinet, known by the pseudonym of Musette. See A. Micaleff, *Petite histoire de l'Algérie (1830–1962)* (Paris: Karthala, 1998), which includes a delightful description of this working-class pied-noir world. *Kémia*, like Spanish *tapas*, was a dish of appetizers with such things as pistachios and spiced olives.

8. Albert Camus, *The First Man*, trans. David Hapgood (New York: Knopf, 1995).

9. *La Vie Spirituelle* (October 1997): 723–24.

10. *La Revue du Rosaire*, July 1991.

11. Ibid.

12. Ibid.

13. A high official, René Lenoir later became a minister in the French government, in charge of social action. Later on an advisor at the Élysée, he published a notable work on "the outcasts."

14. René Lenoir, *Mon Algérie tendre et violente* (Paris: Plon, 1994), 87.

15. *Le Lien*, September 1999, 11.

16. *Feux, Bulletin des anciens de la Saint-Do d'Alger* 306 (1996): 8.

17. The association of former members of the Saint-Do of Algiers still has three hundred members. In its most recent meeting, in June 2006 at Prouilhe, it celebrated the ten-year anniversary of Pierre Claverie's death.

18. *Feux* 315 (Christmas 1988): 15.

19. Ibid., 16.

20. See the special edition of *La Vie Spirituelle*, 831–36.

21. Albert Camus, *Noces*, followed by *L'Été* (Paris: Gallimard, 1947). "He had a profound attachment for the country, which I would call physical or conjugal," Camille Tarot writes of Pierre Claverie. See "Pierre Claverie, fils de l'Algérie et enfant de l'avenir," *La Vie Spirituelle* (October 1997): 648.

# Chapter 2: From University to Novitiate

1. "Humanité plurielle," *Les Nouveaux Cahiers du Sud* 1 (January 1996): 114.

2. See M. Harbi, *Le FLN, mirage ou réalité; des origines à la prise du pouvoir (1945–1962)* (Paris: Jaguar, 1990).

3. "Itinéraire," text of June 1990, *La Vie Spirituelle* (October 1997): 723.

4. Y. Courrière, *La Guerre d'Algérie*, 4 vols. (Paris: Fayard, 1968–71), volume two of which is entitled *Le Temps des léopards*. There are many works in French on the Algerian War. A good English-language overview is Alistair Horne, *A Savage War of Peace: Algeria 1954–1962* (New York: Viking Press, 1977).

5. "Read and have others read the best book that exists on the problem. A quick read, it's a sensational analysis of the ins and outs of the matter without political slant" (letter of January 30, 1958).

6. *Frangaos* was the insulting nickname for the French of the mother country who did not understand the French of Algeria.

7. In July 1957 there was a trial before the permanent tribunal of the armed forces of Algiers of what were called the "liberal Christians" or "progressive Christians," accused of supporting the rebellion. See H. Alleg, *La Guerre d'Algérie* (Paris: Temps actuels, 1981), 2:475.

8. One can see this in a passage from a letter of May 20, 1958, in reaction to the scenes of French and Algerian "fraternization" at the Forum in Algiers: "Here in France, our only hope is that you hold on at whatever cost because otherwise we are completely handed over to the commies who are carrying out an extraordinary level of activity right now..."

9. This was the case with Jean Scotto (parish priest of Hussein-Dey), Marie-Renée Chénée, Emma Serra, and Simone Galice, who opened the first private social centers, at Berardi. One should also mention Alexandre Chaulet, a union leader, whose family publicly supported the FLN.

10. On this subject, see A. Nozière, *Algérie: les chrétiens dans la guerre* (Paris: Cana, 1979).

11. "Humanité plurielle," 113.

12. The letter is not dated, but has on it the note "received October 20." Thus it was written in the period between his passing the written examination (October 10) and receiving the results of the lab exams that he failed (October 16).

13. In the summer of 1958, the entire Claverie family spent a happy vacation in Cagnes-sur-mer.

14. Friar Pierre Hugo, a former member of the Dominican community in Algiers, had sent the master of novices these simple words: "We send you a man of gold, who won't give you any problems" (letter of December 1, 1958, Archive of the province of France).

15. In January he took advantage of a visit from the provincial superior to get to know the plans of the province regarding the Dominican presence in the Muslim world. In March, he spoke again of his project to study Arabic as soon as he arrived at Le Saulchoir. In July, he presented a report on Islam. In September he read the Qur'an cover to cover and confided to his parents, "I can't wait to know if, intellectually and practically, I can join these students of Arabic. In any case, you can well imagine how I am drawn toward this goal! *Inch'Allah.*"

16. "If you really want to discover your religion, as I am doing every day, buy *right away Le Mystère pascal* (The Paschal Mystery) by Fr. Louis Bouyer... It's incredible to see how this convert from Protestantism has flashes of genius in his comprehension of our faith" (Easter letter, 1959).

17. *Ut sint unum, Bulletin de la province dominicaine de France* (July 1981): 80.

18. *La Vie Spirituelle* (October 1997): 648–49.

19. Interview with Radio Notre-Dame, September 16, 1989.

# Chapter 3: Le Saulchoir

1. From a letter of Étienne Claverie to his wife, October 9, 1962.

2. See François Leprieur, *Quand Rome condamne: Dominicains et prêtres-ouvriers* (Paris: Plon/Éditions du Cerf, 1989).

3. In 1959, Claverie had begun to practice yoga, making his evening prayer in the "perfect position" or the "dead leaf": "It's a great discovery..."

4. Yves Courrière, *La Guerre d'Algérie*, vol. 4 (Paris: Fayard, 1971).

5. See Léon-Étienne Duval, *Le Cardinal Duval, "évêque en Algérie,"* with Marie-Christine Ray (Paris: Centurion, 1984). See also: D. Gonzalez and A. Nozière, eds., *Au nom de la vérité (Algérie: 1954–62)* (Paris: Cana, 1982).

6. Like this reflection on the first visit of a delegation of the GPRA (Provisional Government of the Algerian Republic) to Paris: "The FLN has agreed to come to Paris. In the current situation, it appears that this is the lesser evil. Without over-stating the role of the GPRA, one can still imagine that it represents a little something, if only the handful of imbeciles determined to resist and who cause a hundred deaths per week" (letter of June 1, 1960).

7. Archives of the Dominican province of France, dossier Claverie III, M. 8.

8. Personal archives of Fr. Francis Marneffe, Paris.

9. Pierre Claverie, "Ce qu'un catholique attend du Concile," *Bulletin de l'aumônerie protestante du 23e CA*, May 1963.

10. The archetypical pied-noir family in French Algerian literature, a mixture of the multiple popular cultures of the Mediterranean.

11. Starting in the spring of 1962, Algerian families from the outlying districts began taking possession in the city center of "vacant" apartments, sold, or sometimes simply abandoned, by their owners. Unused to urban life, they quickly "ghettoized" the European-style buildings.

12. Letter to Fr. Marneffe, November 2, 1962.

13. Here is the account of Fr. Jean Mansir, O.P., who was ordained at the same time: "He remained a little outside our big debates about ideas, especially the philosophical ones, which were preparing us for the great events of May 1968. One had the impression that Pierre had a task to fulfill and pushed aside anything that could slow him down on his path. He wasn't conservative, absolutely not. But he had something else to do, a task of the church, in the large sense of that term. So our Marxist, Freudian, Nietzschean, linguistic critiques... irritated him a little. He was impatient to act."

14. An episode of which he spoke later illustrates this point: "When I was a deacon, I was asked to accompany a group of handicapped scouts. My first contacts with them were extremely difficult. Moreover, they wanted to "immerse" me in their life immediately, and the first night I spent in the camp, they put the orthopedic apparatuses of every kid who was there in the room where I was sleeping. I had nightmares the whole night! So, at first, I was shaken up, which was a good thing, because the next day, when I made contact with them again, I was much less sure of myself in my approach and so I discovered the wonderful way in which these young people communicated life to each other, whereas, full of health, very sure of himself, the deacon that I was ran the risk of passing by these others completely or of crushing them" (*Conférence aux Petites Soeurs de Jésus de la région d'Algérie*, summer 1995).

15. While attending a session for priests in Algiers, he developed a friendship with Fr. Scotto and other priests: "I've made the acquaintance of several White Fathers, Jesuits, and diocesan priests of Tunisia and the region around Oran: there are going to be some good things happening there! I hope that I can return to those areas" (letter of August 29, 1965).

16. In another literary genre, quite moving, Brother Paul Ferdinand, an old lay brother and friend of the elder Claveries, had predicted to them a brilliant future for their son, after he heard him speak on the Algerian question: "It is the first time that I have read or heard something accurate, thoughtful, charitable, and Christian on the question ... One has to accept the facts and later on people will have to say that I was right: this boy was born, or called from the moment of his birth, to honor the order of St. Dominic whatever path he takes. I would like to stay healthy and live a hundred years to see him become provincial superior on the way to becoming master of the order" (letter of May 25, 1961). In an earlier letter on the same theme, Brother Paul had added, "From there to a bishopric he would only need to take an easy step; if he read this, he would certainly get on my case" (letter of December 15, 1960).

17. Chronicle of the Dominican community of Algiers, Archives of the Province of France.

# Chapter 4: Toward the Joyous Encounter with the Other

1. "Humanité plurielle," *Les Nouveaux Cahiers du Sud* 1 (January 1996): 114.

2. In November 1968, he confessed that Atina had given him a talking-to, believing that he was spreading himself a little too thin.

3. "At the last reception, I was acclaimed in a completely unexpected fashion; I confess that it gave me pleasure ... In short, it was a good experience, which I leave with regrets ..." (letter of July 30, 1969).

4. In their memories of this period, the Lebanese sisters especially highlight the strong impression that Claverie's spiritual life made on them, as far as they could see, especially on Sundays, which he reserved as much as possible for solitude and prayer, according to Sister Houda.

5. "L'invité: Pierre Claverie, évêque d'Oran," *L'Actualité religieuse* 136 (September 1995). Reprinted in *Lettres et messages d'Algérie* (Paris: Karthala, 1997), 17.

6. "Le mot du père Claverie," *La Vie Spirituelle* (October 1997): 701–2.

7. See A. Nozière, *Les Chrétiens dans la guerre* (Paris: Cana, 1979).

8. In October 1999, Algerian president Abdelaziz Bouteflika, who had already given a major public eulogy of Cardinal Duval, several weeks later went so far as to demand his canonization while at a conference in Spain!

9. See, besides the work of M.-C. Ray cited above, Léon-Étienne Duval, *Au nom de la vérité* (*Algérie: 1954–1962*), edited by D. Gonzalez and A. Nozière (Paris: Cana, 1982).

10. Fr. Anawati, an Egyptian Dominican and founder/director of IDEO in Cairo, was regarded in both academic and cultural circles as one of the greatest experts on Muslim thought.

11. See J. Scotto, *Curé pied-noir, évêque algérien*, memories collected by C. Ehlinger (Paris: Desclée de Brouwer, 1991).

12. S. de Beaurecueil, *Prêtres des non-chrétiens* (Paris: Éditions du Cerf, 1968), 50. Many Algerian Christians appear in another book by the same author, *Nous avons partagé le pain et le sel* (Paris: Éditions du Cerf, 1965).

13. Marc Cote's very interesting work, *L'Algérie, ou l'espace retourné* (Paris: Flammarion, 1988) properly defines Algeria as "a land that turns its back to the sea"; its culture is more rural than maritime, despite the illusion made by Algiers.

14. Claverie's first "fundamental" articles date from this period, written for a Dominican review in Bologne: "La salvezza nell' Islam," *Sacra Doctrina* 62 (1971): 247–75.

15. An editorial in the June–July 1993 issue of *Le Lien* commemorating Scotto's death shows the affection and profound regard that Pierre Claverie had for Fr. Scotto.

16. For example, along with some allies he contested the agenda of the day: "We are taking affairs in hand and succeeded after a great deal of work that lasted partway through the night, in creating some work groups on real questions that priests and Christians of the diocese have to deal with. The bishop looks startled … And I am caught in the machinery again. Personally, I did not at all expect to be under attack at this post, and I have decided to quit if nothing specific is done at this first meeting" (letter of November 27, 1972).

# Chapter 5: The Time of Responsibilities

1. *Lettre interne des frères de la province dominicaine de France* 13 (December 1978): 39.

2. "He didn't ask for much advice and didn't share his questions," one of his collaborators reported. "In return," his brother-in-law Eric Gustavson emphasized, "Pierre had an astonishing ability to integrate other people's points of view in his own analysis." These are two important aspects of his personality.

3. *Lettre interne des frères de la province dominicaine de France* 13 (December 1978): 38.

4. A. Djeghloul, an Oran academic who regularly visited les Glycines during this period, gave Pierre Claverie this very beautiful tribute when his death was announced: "I remember that you, the Frenchman, the Christian, whom, as I can say today, I distrusted, you were able to hear my quest. You helped me. For long hours, you patiently guided me through your documentation, accumulated slowly but surely. Scandal of scandals, you allowed me to mark up these Arabic writings. My pride, I admit, took a heavy blow. You, the 'pieds-noir,' who after you had reached the age of reason had chosen our land, Algeria. You, who always remained 'Pierre,' you learned at Abdelkader to read Arabic texts, difficult for me. I never told you that Arabic, the language of my father and grandfather, was not my maternal language. You never made a comment. Only sometimes your sympathetic irony pointed to it. The nip of awareness passed without a word." A. Djeghloul, "Salut, Pierre Claverie," *Algérie-Actualité* (August 20, 1996).

5. "When I think," he wrote on January 27, 1976, "that, leaving our homeland, we never stop discovering the Arabic world and we measure the distance of civilization that separates us and the riches that unite us." Again we see his lively intuition of the road to take to encounter the other.

6. See B. Stora, *Histoire de l'Algérie depuis l'Indépendance* (Paris: Éditions de la Découverte, 1995), 25.

7. Letter of April 22, 1972, which begins, "It gives no end of trouble to those who try to imagine an open Islam."

8. An Arab political current that was born in Syria in 1947–50 and sought to promote a pan-Arabic nationalism on a socialist model. The Baathist party, in Syria and Iraq, provided to some degree an alternative to Islamism.

9. See two works that exemplify the debate: M. Lacheraf, *Algérie, nation et société* (Paris: Maspero, 1965) and Ahmed Taleb Ibrahimi, *De la décolonisation à la révolution culturelle* (Algiers: SNED, 1973).

10. J.-P. Durand and H. Tengour, *L'Algérie et ses populations* (Brussels: Complexe, 1982), 183.

11. Y. Turin, *Affrontements culturels dans l'Algérie coloniale* (Paris: Maspero, 1971).

12. The Algerian writer Rachid Mimouni, who died in exile at Tangiers, tells that he read the Qur'an with his son ever since the day that he realized that at school, during the instruction in Islam, it was being taught that "every year, for Passover, the Jews knead bread with a Muslim's blood." How many children had a father to correct these absurdities?

13. There was some *de facto* division of tasks: the technocrats undertook "serious matters," like petroleum and international trade; the Islamists were in charge of ideology in religion and schools. See A. Lamchichi, *Islam et contestation au Maghreb* (Paris: L'Harmattan, 1990).

14. Letter of October 14, 1975, which also reports the cardinal's remarks to the gendarmerie officer who commanded the basilica: "I have fought the OAS and I will fight you, too. If you are a soldier, be aware that I am a soldier of God and I will be stronger than you..."

15. His 1977 card of vows bears these simple words, in Arabic and French: "I abandon myself to God."

16. "Chrétiens en Algérie, réflexions et témoignages 1976–1979," mimeograph, Centre d'études diocésain, 1979.

17. See Jean Jolivet, "Averroès," in *Dictionnaire de l'Islam* (Paris: Albin Michel, 1997), 129.

18. The climate had deteriorated because of the explicit support President Giscard d'Estaing gave to Morocco, while the Front Polisario supported Algeria.

19. See *La Documentation catholique*, no. 1775.

20. H. Sanson, "Chrétiens en Algérie," *Christus* 86 (April 1975): 211–21.

21. H. Sanson, *Dialogue intérieur avec l'Islam* (Paris: Centurion, 1990), 17.

22. "Chrétiens au Maghreb, le sens de nos rencontres," *La Documentation catholique*, no. 1775, col. 1037.

23. The testimony of Roby Bois, March 3, 2000.

24. "Jacques Blanc trained me in all the services...It was a sort of Americanized Vatican, with ordainers, battalions of secretaries, cardinals in lounge suits...," Claverie commented in a letter of June 17, 1974, in which he appears both fascinated by this organized world and a little perplexed in face of "the dollar so present behind this façade."

25. Pierre Claverie, *Lettre interne des frères de la province dominicaine de France*, 13 (December 1978): 38.

26. Pierre Claverie, "Hommage au pasteur Jacques Blanc," November 1991. A posthumously published work traces this man's journey and his exceptional Christianity: Jacques Blanc, *Construire un monde solidaire. Une logique nouvelle* (Lausanne: Les Bergers et les Mages, 1992).

27. Letter of October 10, 1977 to Emilio Panella, general archives of the order, Rome.

28. It must be admitted that there were relatively few good Arabists among the priests of Algiers. One of them, Paul-Louis Cambuzat, a very promising Franciscan and professor of history at the University of Algiers, was killed in a car accident in January 1975, at the age of forty-three. Claverie wrote, "This is a heavy blow for the Algerian church, which can count its people of this quality on the fingers of one hand," on February 3, 1975.

29. A. Raulin, "L'institution dominicaine engagée dans le destin de Pierre Claverie," *La Vie Spirituelle* (October 1997): 683–89.

30. His return to Algiers was celebrated with a memorable dinner at *Chez Sauveur*, a seafood restaurant of La Madrague, a little harbor west of Algiers. Claverie said he was happy that he could immerse himself again in the ambiance of his Dominican community at Paris, happy to rediscover brothers who had been lost from sight for ten years, "but still more delighted to have made good my escape and to find myself today in Algeria" (letter of February 18, 1980).

31. In January 1977, the cardinal had already asked Claverie to replace Monseigneur Jacquier as bishop's representative to the major superiors, remarking to him humorously that it would be preferable to give such a position to a bishop!

32. Testimony of Gilles Danroc, "Le frère Pierre Claverie en Martinique," *La Vie Spirituelle* (October 1997): 679–83.

33. "To the unknown brother bishop, many greetings."

# Chapter 6: Bishop in Oran

1. Homily given at his installation in the cathedral of Oran, October 9, 1981.

2. *Le Lien*, September 15, 1981, 2. Cited by Mgr. Teissier, who tells of the event in *La Vie Spirituelle* (October 1997): 577.

3. In a letter to Wayne White, Pierre's faithful friend, Étienne Claverie reported wittily, "Not having had anything to do with any bishop until recently, I had only the slightest idea of what an episcopal ordination entailed, and still less that it would be Pierre for whom there would be such a demonstration! But I swear that it will be some time before we get over our emotions..." (letter to Wayne White, November 1981).

4. The full text was published in *La Semaine religieuse d'Alger,* November 19, 1981, and reprinted in *La Vie Spirituelle* (October 1997): 701–3.

5. "Which is unusual on such an occasion!" Cardinal Duval, who pretended surprise, said to Étienne Claverie (letter to Wayne White).

6. The report was written following a questionnaire where it is clear that the concerns of the various Roman dicasteries (i.e., offices and departments) were different from those the bishops encountered during their *ad limina* visit every five years.

7. That led Mgr. Teissier to suggest that there be found to succeed him "a pastor of non-French origin. It is time that the Christian community of Algeria be based upon a communion between groups of various nationalities" (*Présentation du diocèse d'Oran,* 6).

8. The importance of these diverse groups varied over the course of the years. One can find an essay on the subject by Pierre Claverie himself in *La Vie Spirituelle,* special edition, 731–39.

9. John Paul II was the victim of an attack in St. Peter's Square on May 13, 1981; the day before, Claverie had received the announcement that the pope had nominated him as bishop, which explains the influence of this event on him. See *La Vie Spirituelle* (October 1997): 674.

10. "What happiness to testify that Pierre appears so happy and free in spirit in his new office," wrote his superior, Jean-Pierre Voreux, to the Claverie parents (letter of November 2, 1981).

11. In the same letter, Pastor Butler adds, "My closest Protestant advisors being in Algiers or Constantine, Pierre's opinions and advice, especially on sensitive subjects, were always extremely precious to me."

12. *Le Lien,* June–July, 1984, 2.

13. See H. Remaoun, "Des roses rouges et blanches pour le cheikh Claverie," *La Vie Spirituelle* (October 1997): 631; A. Djeghloul, "Salut, Pierre Claverie," *Algérie-Actualité,* no. 1599, August 20, 1996.

14. "Like a good pied-noir, Pierre did not know how to say no," his vicar-general Jacques Bies commented benevolently, "which sometimes created difficult situations — for him, and especially for me, who had to arrange matters."

15. "All this took place very courteously and in Arabic," Claverie commented. "I promised to examine the question right away" (letter of October 13, 1982).

16. "I am beginning to prepare the diocese, which is near to understanding and has already accepted, except for certain irreducible nostalgia about French Algeria. I intend to give an interview to *La Croix* and to *Le Monde,* so that this matter can be clear on the other coast of the Mediterranean" (letter of December 27, 1982). In this period, certain associations circulated petitions to alert public opinion to this "treason."

17. See J.-M. Lancelot, "Vingt ans après, ils reviennent," *Le Lien,* May 1982, 15–16.

18. Bishop Scotto of Constantine was perplexed by these returnees, he who had suffered a great deal from the pieds-noir faithful during the Algerian war. Like Cardinal Duval, he came to be decried by those who had not forgiven him for pronouncing himself in favor of self-determination by the Algerian people. Besides the political disagreements, he was badly served by his unemotional demeanor, too cold for the taste of Mediterranean people.

19. "It appears that the folkloric aspect and political manipulations must now be separated from the pilgrimage; but they always exist, like the smell of sausage that floated over the procession, or the presence of various deputies at the Mass" (letter of May 2, 1992). Claverie himself gave an account of the journey to Nîmes in *Le Lien,* June–July 1992, 17.

20. Evoking the problems that he had had with his childhood milieu, Claverie added, "One always has the impression that I betrayed something by making the choice to return to Algeria" (speech to the Friends of Guy-Marie Riobé, Orléans, January 18, 1992).

21. *Feux,* no. 279 (1989): 12.

22. *Feux,* no. 283 (1990): 21.

23. Marino is one of the priests of the diocese, mentioned along with R. Tardy, T. Becker, and J.-L. Déclais in this letter. Jacques Biès was at that time vicar-general.

24. At this time, Claverie set himself to study English; later, he learned a little Polish.

25. On the evening of the diocesan meeting on Pentecost 1983, a thousand Christians of his diocese, of all nationalities, assembling, Claverie confided, "This evening, I am exhausted but happy because I knew nearly everyone and I am now like a fish in the water in the setting of this variegated crowd" (letter of May 23, 1983).

# Chapter 7: A Preaching Friar before All Else

1. See *La Documentation catholique*, no. 2017, December 9, 1990, and Jean-Louis Déclais, "Réponse au synode 1990," *Le Lien*, January 1991, 23–27. The editorial of January 1994 also addresses with astonishing frankness the multiplication of speeches, congresses, commissions, and entire weeks dedicated to ecumenism, and the difficulty of "being humble enough to desire unity beyond the duration of some speech."

2. See *Lettres et messages d'Algérie* (Paris: Karthala, 1997), 197–201. In another editorial from June–July of 1993, entitled "Deceived by the church," he concluded: "Not that I doubt my church: too many recent signs, here and in other places, lead me to think that it holds great promise. But I would like us, together, . . . to participate in the necessary renewal. There is still much to be done to scrape away from the icon of Jesus the centuries of encrustations that make it unrecognizable."

3. Homily of priestly ordination, Paris, Convent of the Annunciation, May 20, 1995. Reprinted in *Ut sint unum, Bulletin de la province dominicaine de France* (June–July 1995): 116.

4. "The pope is coming to Tunis on April 14. I don't think I'll go. For one thing, I have prior engagements in France at that time, and besides, this visit comes at the invitation of the Tunisian government, and there's no reason for me to join the delegation . . . Evidently the nunciature does not agree, and is pressing me to go" (letter dated March 27, 1996). The death of his father at the beginning of April would change his plans in every respect.

5. In November of 1995, while he was passing through Rome, he confided in me, "Some days I say to myself, 'Fifteen years, that's enough.'" It seems that he was more passionate about preaching than about management and diplomacy.

6. This documentation, which was meticulously compiled by Pierre Claverie himself, was systematically classified after his death by François Chavanes, at the prompting of Fr. Bernard Lapize, S.J., who at the time was the diocesan administrator. It is kept in the archives of the bishop's residence in Oran, and was very valuable in the process of writing this book.

7. "Je rentre du Liban," *Le Lien*, October 1982. Béchir Gemayel was assassinated on September 14. Israeli troops then entered West Beirut. Hundreds of Palestinians were massacred before their eyes, from September 16 to 18. See *Maghreb-Machrek* 98 (October–December 1982).

8. Letter from Sister Marie of the Incarnation to Claverie's relatives, September 1982.

9. [M.] Borrmans, "In memoriam," *Islamochristiana*, no. 22 (1996), 4.

10. Cassette recording contributed by Sister Thérèse Saad, who compiled a collection of recordings of Pierre Claverie's retreats.

11. "Autour d'une conversion," *Le Lien* nos. 115, 116, and 117.

12. Roger Garaudy, *Parole d'homme* (Paris: Robert Laffont, 1975). The archives of Pierre Claverie contain eighteen pages of handwritten notes on this book.

13. Pierre Claverie, "Autour d'une conversion," *Islamochristiana*, no. 10, 1984, 71–84. The IPEA has become the PIAIS, The Pontifical Institute of Arabic and Islamic Studies.

14. Entitled "De la différence . . . la coexistence," these five editorials would be reprinted by the *Bulletin du Conseil pontifical pour le dialogue interreligieux*, no. 61, 1986, 12–31, and also by *Documents Episcopat*, no. 4, February 1986. *Lettres et messages d'Algérie* (Paris: Karthala, 1997) also contains this important text (251–73).

15. "Une page nouvelle," *Le Lien* (August–September 1993).

16. "Au nom du Fils . . ." *Le Lien*, June–July 1990, reprinted in *Lettres et messages*, 89.

17. "Pourquoi?" "Qui sème le vent," and "Bravo" are published in *Lettres et messages*, 147, 171, and 213.

18. "Priez sans cesse," in *Lettres et messages*, 154.

19. "Un souffle de liberté," *Le Lien*, May 1996; reprinted in *Lettres et messages*, 241.

20. Henri Teissier, "Présentation du *Livre de la foi* des évêques du Maghreb," *La Vie Spirituelle* (October 1997): 837–48.

21. *Le Livre des passages*, unpublished manuscript, 1.

22. Ibid., 70.

23. The principal titles, in order of publication: "Chemins du dialogue islamo-chrétien," *Pro Dialogo, Bulletin du Secréteriat pour les non-chrétiens*, no. 61 (1986), CPDI, 12–31 (reprinted in *Lettres et messages*, 251–73); "Le sens du dialogue Islamo-Chrétien," *Documents SRI* 4 (October 1998): 10; "Chrétiens et musulmans, des chemins difficiles pour un dialogue nécessaire," *Documents SRI*, no. 10 (June 1991): 10; "Lectures du Coran," *Spiritus*, no. 126 (February 1992): 33–46; "Algérie: le désarroi," *Études* (September 1994): 149–59; "Le dialogue entre musulmans et chrétiens dans les Églises du Maghreb," *Chemins de dialogue*, no. 3 (January 1994): 105–26; "Islam et islamismes en Algérie," *Église et mission* (September 1994): 43–51; "Donner sa vie plutôt que de l'arracher aux autres," *Peuples du monde*, no. 275 (September–October 1995): 36–37; "L'Esprit Saint au-delà des frontières," *Spiritus*, no. 141 (December 1995): 401–6 (reprinted in *Lettres et messages*, 4th edition, 275–81); "Algérie, fin 1995," *Annuaire de l'Afrique du Nord* 34 (1995), 591–59; "La foi est un dialogue," preface to the *Missel des dimanches*, 1996, 5–6; "En Algérie, l'Esprit au-delà des frontières," *Mission de l'Église*, no. 118 (April 1998): 50–54. The Swedish journal *Signum* also published four articles by Pierre Claverie, translated into Swedish, from 1991 to 1999: no. 7 (1991): 211–15; no. 7 (1994): 225–29; no. 6 (1996): 175–76; no. 9 (1999): 40–43. Claverie also wrote a postscript for Gwenolé Jeusset's book *Rencontre sur l'autre rive: François d'Assise et les musulmans* (Paris: Éditions franciscaines, 1996). His text entitled "Humanité plurielle," which has been referred to here a number of times, was published by *Les Nouveaux Cahiers du Sud* 1 (January 1996): 113–19, later reprinted by *Le Monde*, August 4–5, 1996. Most of his articles were published in a variety of sources, which makes it a bit complicated to establish a systematic bibliography. Pierre Claverie's archives also contain the text of an extensively elaborated conference he gave at La Haye, which seems not to have been published: "L'Église et les droits de l'homme," Institut français, April 16, 1986, 16 pp.

24. Pierre Claverie, "Les derniers et le règne de l'homme," *Monoteismo e conflitto*, conference directed by E. Ferri, CUEN, 1997, 243–54.

25. Homily for diaconate ordinations, Strasbourg, published in *Ut sint unum Bulletin de la province dominicaine de France* (November 1983), and again in *La Vie Spirituelle* (October 1997): 779.

26. Ibid. A number of these ordination homilies can be found in *La Vie Spirituelle*, special edition. Claverie was also one of the co-consecrators of his friend Pierre Raffin, a fellow student at Le Saulchoir, who was made bishop of Metz in October of 1987. Albert de Monléon, bishop of Pamiers and then of Meaux, is another Dominican friar of the same generation. He would represent the bishops of France at the funeral of Pierre Claverie.

27. When a chapter meeting of the Dominican province of France declared in 1993 that it did not seem possible to guarantee replacements for the Dominicans stationed in the Maghreb, Pierre Claverie reacted vigorously and called upon his brothers to change their apostolic priorities. See *Actes du chapitre provincial de 1993*, no. 109. This decision would later be reconsidered.

28. See *La Revue du Rosaire* (December 1991).

# Chapter 8: Muslim-Christian Dialogue

1. Pierre Claverie, "Donner sa vie plutôt que de l'arracher aux autres," address to the Forum of Christian Communities, Angers, Pentecost 1994. Published in *Peuples du monde*, no. 275, September–October 1994, 36–37. Reprinted in *Lettres et messages d'Algérie* (Paris: Karthala, 1997), 24, and in *La Vie Spirituelle* (October 1997): 808.

2. *Nostra Aetate*, no. 2, in Austin Flannery, O.P., ed., *Vatican Council II: The Conciliar and Post Conciliar Documents* (Grand Rapids: William B. Eerdmans, 1992).

3. Ibid.

4. *Nostra Aetate*, no. 3, ibid.

5. *Lumen Gentium*, no. 8, ibid.

6. Apostolic Constitution *Pastor Bonus*, June 28, 1988, in *La Documentation catholique*, no 1970, 977.

7. Here are some of the topics discussed at the various meetings. Discussions sponsored by the Center for Economic and Social Studies (Tunis): *Consciences chrétiennes et musulmanes face au défi du développement*, 1974; *Sens et niveaux de la Révélation*, 1979; *Droits de l'homme*, 1982; *La Spiritualité, exigence de notre temps*, 1988; *La Participation des religions à la paix*, 1990. Discussions sponsored by Al-Azhar University: *Unité des croyants pour affronter l'athéisme*, 1966; *Pour une meilleure compréhension réciproque*, 1978. Discussions organized in Jordan by Al al-Bayt: *Problèmes et valeurs communes concernant la famille*, 1985; *Questions de pouvoir chez les chrétiens et les musulmans*, 1986; *Coexistence et valeurs communes*, 1987; *Droits de l'enfant et éducation chez les chrétiens et les musulmans*, 1989; *La Femme dans la société*, 1992. Discussions organized by Da'wa Islamyya (Libya): *Pour un renouveau de confiance*, 1976; *Missions chrétiennes et musulmanes*, 1987; *Coexistence entre chrétiens et musulmans: réalités et horizons*, 1990; *Médias et la présentation de la religion*, 1993.

8. [M.] Borrmans, *Orientations pour un dialogue entre chrétiens et musulmans* (Paris: Éditions du Cerf, 1981), 191.

9. The entire affair is presented in detail by M. Borrmans in "Le séminaire du dialogue islamo-chrétien de Tripoli (Libye)" (February 1–6, 1976), *Islamochristiana*, no. 2 (1976): 135–70. The same author provides an assessment in "Le dialogue islamo-chrétien des dix dernières années," *Pro Mundi Vita*, no. 74 (September–October 1978): 58.

10. The main centers of Christian study in the Muslim world were outlined by Jacques Levrat in *Une expérience de dialogue, les centres d'études chrétiens en monde musulman* (Altenberge [Germany]: Christlich-Islamisches Schrifttum, 1987).

11. A wonderful experience of "spiritual dialogue" had begun in 1979 around the figure of Christian de Chergé, a monk of Tibhirine, together with Sufi Muslims, in a group called the Ribât-as-Sâlam. See Marie-Christine Ray, *Christian de Chergé, prieur de Tibhirine* (Paris: Bayard/Centurion, 1998). Despite the excellence of this group and its spiritual depth, it must be noted that this is a solitary and very marginal initiative in the religious landscape of Algeria. It also brings up some complex theological questions, as the author implies.

12. This text can be found in its entirety in *Lettres et messages*, 251–73.

13. Pierre Claverie, "Humanité plurielle," 115.

14. This is what happened at the appearance of the book *La Bible, le Coran et la Science* by Maurice Bucaille (Paris: Seghers, 1977). After this, Pierre Claverie began producing an analysis of the nature of religious revelation.

15. El Hachemi Tidjani, "L'islam, présent et devenir," *Algérie-Actualité* (May 1985).

16. Mohamed Talbi, *Islam et dialogue*, Tunisian publishing house, 1972, 22.

17. Weekly magazine *Horizons*, May 18, 1988, 4.

18. See his interview in *L'Actualité religieuse dans le monde* (July–August 1988): 17–18: "Mgr Claverie, L'évêque d'Oran. Alerte aux polémiques antichrétiennes."

19. The complete text of the address was published in *Documents SRI*, October 1988, 10ff., and reprinted in *Lettres et messages*, 705–21.

20. *Hommes et migrations*, no. 1102 (April 1987), interview conducted by Ezzedine Mestiri.

21. "L'évêque d'Oran à la mosquée de Paris," June 15, 1988, a note of five pages, Claverie Archives, Oran.

22. "L'évêque 'd'Oran à la mosquée de Paris," 4–5.

23. The three texts summarized here are "Chemins du dialogue islamo-chrétien" (1985), in *Lettres et messages*, 251–73; "Le sens du dialogue islamo-chrétien," in *La Vie Spirituelle* (October 1997): 705–21; and "Chrétiens et musulmans, vivre ensemble?" ibid., 741–52. A presentation of the same topics was given a bit later in "Le dialogue entre chrétiens et musulmans dans les Églises du Maghreb," in *Chemins de dialogue*, no. 3 (January 1994): 105–26.

24. *Nostra Aetate*, no. 1, cited by Mohamed Talbi in *Islam et dialogue*, 36–37. (English translation from Austin Flannery, O.P., ed., *Vatican Council II: The Conciliar and Post Conciliar Documents* [Grand Rapids: William B. Eerdmans, 1992]).

25. *Gaudium et Spes*, no. 1, in Austin Flannery, O.P., ed., *Vatican Council II: The Conciliar and Post Conciliar Documents* (Grand Rapids: William B. Eerdmans, 1992).

26. Mohamed Talbi, *Islam et dialogue*, 24.

27. See his contribution to the plenary assembly of the Secretariat for Non-Christians in 1987: "Situation du dialogue interreligieux dans le Nord de l'Afrique (CERNA)," plenary assembly of April 1987, Rome, 9 pp., and also the interview given in 1988 to *L'Actualité religieuse dans le monde* (July–August, 1988).

28. Pierre Claverie, "L'Église et les droits de l'homme," Institut Français, La Haye, April 16, 1986, 16 pp.

# Chapter 9: Christians in the "House of Islam"

1. "Un grand abîme nous sépare," *Le Lien*, October 1986, reprinted in *La Vie Spirituelle* (October 1997): 784. N.B.: there are minor differences between the text published in *Le Lien* and the one reprinted by *La Vie Spirituelle*.

2. First letter to Timothy, 2:5.

3. A number of books have traced this contemporary pathway of the church in Algeria, in particular Henri Teissier, *Église en islam, méditation sur l'existence chrétienne en Algérie* (Paris: Centurion, 1984).

4. Vincent Cosmao, *Changer le monde, une tâche pour l'Église* (Paris: Éditions du Cerf, 1979).

5. Henri Sanson, "Chrétiens en Algérie," *Christus*, no. 86, April 1975, 215–16.

6. "Chemins du dialogue islamo-chrétien," *Pro Dialogo, Bulletin du Secrétariat pour les non-chrétiens*, no. 61, 1986, 21; reprinted in *Lettres et messages d'Algérie* (Paris: Karthala, 1997), 261.

7. "Noël 1994," *La Vie Spirituelle* (October 1997): 771.

8. Henri Teissier, "Une Église étrangère en pays socialiste," *Spiritus*, no. 66 (February 1977): 34.

9. Ibid., 36.

10. Cardinal Duval, *Lettre pastorale*, Lent 1980. "The future of the church is in the heart of the Algerians" is another of his sayings.

11. "Chrétiens au Maghreb, le sens de nos rencontres," *La Documentation catholique*, no. 1775, 1043.

12. Henri Teissier, "Chrétiens et non-chrétiens, accueillir ensemble le Règne de Dieu," *Spiritus*, no. 75 (May 1979): 179.

13. "Un grande abîme nous sépare," *Le Lien*, October 1986.

14. See Franceso Goia, ed., *Interreligious Dialogue: The Official Teaching of the Catholic Church (1963–1995)* (Boston: Pauline Books and Media, 1997), 566–79.

15. See Gioia, ed., ibid., "Reflections and Orientations on Interreligious Dialogue and the Proclamation of the Gospel of Jesus Christ" (usually referred to by the short title, "Dialogue and Proclamation"): 608–42.

16. The English version of this passage reads, "All Christians are called to be personally involved in these two ways of carrying out the one mission of the church, namely proclamation and dialogue."

17. "Dialogue and Proclamation," no. 82.

18. Pierre Claverie, "Dialogue et annonce. Pour une évangélisation 'dialogale,' " a text prepared for the Pontifical Council for Interreligious Dialogue, April 1987.

19. Pierre Claverie, "Nécessité et ambigüités du dialogue," Conférence au Congrès à distance CRISLAM, Madrid, November 1987, 2. Apart from these texts for the Pontifical Council for Interreligious Dialogue and for the North African bishops' conference, Pierre Claverie gave a number of conferences dedicated to this theme during these years.

20. Claude Geffré, "La théologie des religions non chrétiennes vingt ans après Vatican II," *Islamochristiana*, no. 11 (1985), 128. Pierre Claverie also brought Claude Geffré to his diocese for conferences during this period. He also references Joseph Gelot, "Vers une théologie chrétienne des religions non chrétiennes," *Islamochristiana*, no. 2 (1976): 1–57.

21. Citation of Geffré's article in *Islamochristiana*, reproduced by Pierre Claverie in his note for CERNA, "Islam et religion des théologies non chrétiennes" (December 1987): 4.

22. See Mohammed Arkoun, *Lectures du Coran* (Paris: Maisonneuve et Larose, 1982), 23.

23. Pierre Claverie, "Islam et théologie des religions non chrétiennes," a commentary for CERNA (December 1987), 6.

24. Jean-Louis Déclais, *Les Premiers Musulmans face à la tradition biblique, trois récits sur Job* (Paris: L'Harmattan, 1996); *David, raconté par les musulmans* (Paris: Éditions du Cerf, 2001).

25. See Étienne Renaud, "Le dialogue islamo-chrétien vu par les musulmans," *Islamochristiana*, no. 23 (1997): 111–38.

26. Pierre Claverie, "Le Salut par les religions. L'interpellation chrétienne," Brussels, 1988, 12.

27. "Un grand abîme nous sépare," *La Vie Spirituelle* (October 1997): 785 and 787.

28. "Un grand abîme nous sépare," *Le Lien*, October 1986. The version of this address in *La Vie Spirituelle* does a better job of retaining the oral character of the original (see 785).

29. Apart from his homily in Lille (1986), four other remarkable ordination homilies are reproduced in *La Vie Spirituelle* (October 1997): 779–804. The ordinations took place in Strasbourg (1983), L'Arbresle (1989), Froidmont (1990), and Paris Saint-Ignace (1995).

30. "Un grand abîme nous sépare," *Le Lien*, October 1986.

31. The Catholic Church continues to clarify its teaching on this point, as shown by the document of the International Theological Commission, published in 1997 under the title "Le christianisme et les religions." See *La Documentation catholique*, no. 2157, 312–22.

32. "Une religion de l'Esprit," *Le Lien*, May 1992.

33. English translation, *Jesus Christ at the Encounter of World Religions* (Maryknoll, N.Y.: Orbis Books, 1991). Dupuis later published a synthesis of his position as *Toward a Christian Theology of Religious Pluralism* (Maryknoll, N.Y.: Orbis Books, 1997).

34. "À la rencontre des religions," *Le Lien*, October 1991.

35. Ibid.

36. Ibid.

37. Ibid.

38. R. Gonnet, C. Brehem, and R. You, "Enquête sur le diocèse, dix ans après (1984–1994)," mimeograph, 12 pp.

39. Pierre Claverie, "25 ans après," *Le Lien*, June–July 1987.

40. Pierre Claverie, "Une page nouvelle," *Le Lien*, August–September 1987.

41. Pierre Claverie, "Un diocèse en pays musulman: diagramme," interview on June 23, 1990, reprinted in *La Vie Spirituelle* (October 1997): 739.

42. Letter for Christmas, 1993, *La Vie Spirituelle* (October 1997): 763–64.

43. Interview in *L'Actualité religieuse*, no. 136 (September 1995), reprinted in *Lettres et messages*, 11–20. Bishop Teissier made a similar statement when he said that "the excesses of fundamentalism bring Christians and moderate Muslims closer together." See "L'islam, défi pastoral; réflexions d'un pasteur à partir de la crise algérienne," *Prêtres diocésains* (August–September 1997): 342.

44. Interview in *L'Actualité religieuse*, no. 136; reprinted in *Lettres et messages*, 15.

45. Pierre Claverie, "Un diocèse en pays musulman: diagramme," *La Vie Spirituelle* (October 1997): 733.

46. Pierre Claverie, "Humanité plurielle," *Les Nouveaux Cahiers du Sud* 1 (January 1996): 119. Before the participants at a conference in Bastia in the summer of 1996, he remarked, "Algerian society is at a point of synthesis. Something entirely new could emerge from this bloody phase."

# Chapter 10: An Algerian Bishop in the Midst of Social and Political Debate

1. "Lecture d'événements: impossible démocratie?" *Le Lien*, June–July 1991; *Lettres et messages d'Algérie* (Paris: Karthala, 1997), 105.

2. "L'étape présente du dialogue islamo-chrétien en Algérie," *Le Lien*, March–April 1990, reprinted in *Lettres et messages*, 63–79.

3. See Sid Ahmed Semiane, *Octobre, ils parlent* (Algiers: Éditions Le Matin, Algiers, 1998).

4. Benjamin Stora, *Histoire de l'Algérie depuis l'Indépendance* (Paris: Éditions de la Découverte, 1995), 82.

5. Yasmina Khadra, *A quoi rêvent les loups?* (Paris: Julliard, 1999).

6. "L'étape présente du dialogue islamo-chrétien en Algérie," *Le Lien*, March–April 1990; *Lettres et messages,* 63–79.

7. Ibid., 63.

8. In two vigorous editorials for *Le Lien* in February and October of 1989, Claverie again reacted to Sheikh Al-Ghazâli's defamatory statements concerning Christianity: "Tolérable? Intolérable?" and "Plaidoyer pour le respect": "We undergo these assaults with sadness, and are unable to give our own interpretation of the actions or teachings for which we are reproached . . . Once again, I must express my dismay as a Christian at the one-sided and aggressive speech of the majority of the spokespeople for Islam in Algeria." See *Lettres et messages,* 44–45.

9. "Au nom du Fils . . . ," *Le Lien*, June–July 1990, reprinted in *Letters and messages,* 89.

10. That same year of 1990, he welcomed to his diocese one of the heads of Muslim-Christian dialogue for the church in France, whose approach he contested as too conciliatory. There was nothing to be gained from "saying only good things about Islam and refusing to address the flagrantly negative aspects," he told him. And by taking him to meet real people on their home turf, instead of the sort that frequented the dialogue meetings, he hoped to lead him toward more realistic positions.

11. Lahouari Addi, "Algérie: le dérapage," *Le Monde diplomatique* (February 1992): 20.

12. François Burgat, *L'Islamisme au Maghreb: la voix du Sud (Tunisie, Algérie, Libye, Maroc)* (Paris: Karthala, 1988).

13. Interview with the newspaper *Le Soir*, Marseille, January 10, 1992. The editorial "Au nom du Fils" from June–July 1990 conveys the same message. See *Lettres et messages,* 89–92. The archives of Pierre Claverie demonstrate that he was very well informed about these issues, in part by reading the books by Olivier Roy, a specialist in Iran and Islamism and the author of *L'Échec de l'islamisme politique* (Paris: Seuil, 1992).

14. "Raison garder," *Le Lien*, January 1992, reprinted in *Lettres et messages,* 114.

15. "Pouvoir, respect de l'autre, liberté," Conférence aux religieuses du diocèse d'Alger, February 7, 1992.

16. "Le Mouvement islamiste en Algérie, causes et effets," *USMDA*, March 26–27, 1992, an unpublished manuscript of 17 pages. His article "Algérie: le désarroi" (*Études* [September 1994]: 149–59) also provides an excellent synthesis of the political situation in the country since 1988, and analyzes the economic causes of the growth of Islamism.

17. This expression can be found in a May 1991 article for the Swedish journal *Signum* ("Chrétiens-musulmans, une humanité plurielle?"). The fullest expression of this theme is found in his article entitled "Humanité plurielle" in *Nouveaux Cahiers du Sud*, January 1996. Some political circles that included friends of Pierre Claverie were already using the phrase "société plurielle."

18. "Saladin n'est pas mort," *La Croix*, August 2, 1991, 15.

19. "Chrétiens et musulmans: vivre ensemble?" Conference given in Lille on January 16, 1992; *La Vie Spirituelle* (October 1997): 748.

20. "Lectures du Coran," *Spiritus*, no. 126 (February 1992): 33–46.

21. "Islamisme et islamismes en Algérie," *Église et mission* (September 1994): 44.

22. Ibid., 45.

23. "Au risque de la modernité," *Ut sint unum, Bulletin de la province dominicaine de France* (March 1992): 9.

24. "Islam et islamismes en Algérie," 51.

25. "L'Islamisme aux portes de l'Europe?" Address to the plenary assembly of the Pontifical Council for Interreligious Dialogue, Rome, November 1992, unpublished manuscript, 3.

26. "I have lived through the longest days of my life . . . and I still need much prayer and faith to accept this decision that the illness has forced us to make," he wrote on February 2 to Sister Jacqueline-Françoise, a member of the Little Sisters of Jesus who was very close to the Claverie family.

27. In September of 1988, he already noted, "I receive many requests, and refuse most of them." In December of 1992, he was invited to the Conference of Egyptian Patriarchs and Bishops, and

was encouraged to go by Bishop Teissier. He noted, "It is difficult to decide." His appointment books permit us to determine the exact number of his trips outside of Algeria: on an average, there were five of these a year, including the bishops' meetings. This figure would double during the last year of his life.

28. This is what led to his death, according to the Algerian Movement of Free Officers, a dissident branch of the Algerian army that publicizes its views on its own website (www.anp.org), which is administered from Madrid.

29. See *Lettres et messages*, 123.

30. "You realize, Louise, that he's coming from Oran just to see me," the cardinal said to his niece, who witnessed the admiration that Duval and Claverie had for one another. The quarrels that had at first characterized their relationship were long gone.

31. Published in *Le Lien*, August–September 1993, and reprinted in *Lettres et messages*, 125–26.

32. In replying to a letter from his sister, he wrote on April 12, 1993, "It is true that our entire family has the good fortune of this natural openness toward others! I still think about Mamie and her way of encountering everyone with such a presence of attention and friendship that any barriers could not last for long; this seems to me to be the right attitude for disarming the lack of trust and building bridges among persons and cultures. There are so many objective reasons to ignore and exclude one another without even understanding each other... Whenever I become unnerved or discouraged in this difficult mission in the Muslim world that is ours — especially now, with the stubborn entrenchment taking place on both sides — I call back to mind these utterly simple and spontaneous attitudes of friendship."

33. Mohamed Balhi, *Chroniques infernales (Algérie: 1990–1995)* (Algiers, Marinoor, 1997): 137. At Pierre Claverie's funeral, his friend Oum el Kheir would say, "Yes, my father, brother, and friend remained here for Alloula, for us, and for others" (*La Vie Spirituelle* (October 1997): 603.

34. Pierre Claverie paid homage to them in his homily broadcast by radio on January 1, 1994, breaking a general silence over this event. See B. Chenu, *Sept vies pour Dieu et l'Algérie* (Paris: Bayard/Centurion, 1996), 126–27.

35. See *Lettres et messages*, 142.

# Chapter 11: A Church on the Fault Lines

1. "Chrétiens en Algérie aujourd'hui," unpublished text of a conference given in Montpellier, February 1995.

2. As soon as he arrived in Algiers on May 9, Pierre Claverie learned that a Christian of his diocese had been attacked by terrorists: he made the return trip to Sidi-bel-Abbès in twenty-four hours to visit him before attending the funeral. Each day now brought a heavy burden of cares. His years of happiness were over.

3. "Priez sans cessse," *Le Lien*, June–July 1994, reprinted in *Lettres et messages*, 151–54.

4. Saïd Mekbel, "Mesmar J'ha," *Le Matin*, November 14, 1994.

5. The four were Frs. Christian Chessel, Jean Chevillard, Alain Dieulengard, and Charles Deckers. See A. Duval, *C'était une longue fidélité à l'Algérie et au Rwanda* (Paris: Médiaspaul, 1998), 19–148.

6. What was for some a step toward an end to the hostilities was, for others, "a major unilateral concession," as former prime minister Redha Malek stated to the newspaper *El Watan*.

7. Their questions convey the embarrassment of those in the midst of the situation: "You did not think it necessary to consult the local church, through its bishops, on the prudence of such an initiative... In holding your meeting in spite of the Algerian government's refusal to participate, you in fact take the side of those who oppose it, and provide a forum for those who are fighting against it... What can one expect from those who have recourse to violence, who have never shown proof of renouncing violence?..."

8. Being in Rome at the time, and with the assistance of a priest friend who was a member of Sant'Egidio, I was able to fax the six-page platform to Pierre Claverie during the hour following its signing.

9. For a detailed history of the community, see *Sant'Egidio, Rome et le monde: Discussion with Andrea Riccardi, Jean-Dominique Durand, et Régis Ladous* (Paris: Beauchesne, 1996). Another recent presentation can be found in *Télérama*, December 8, 1999, 10–18.

10. The secretary-general of Sant'Egidio, Marco Impagliazzo, had made a number of visits to Cardinal Duval, and had published a book on him: *Duval d'Algeria, una chiesa tra Europe e mondo arabo (1946–1988)* (Rome: Edizioni Studium, 1994).

11. "Veut-on, oui ou non, arrêter la guerre?", an interview with Mario Giro in *La Croix*, February 25, 1995.

12. Claverie's appointment books and correspondence give the dates of these contacts (for example, August 26, 1991). In November of 1993, the bishops had received members of Sant'Egidio in Algiers on the occasion of Cardinal Duval's ninetieth birthday. At that time, they had asked about what sort of welcome Sant'Egidio planned to extend to the Sudanese Islamist Hassan al-Tourabi in Rome.

13. The bishops released a statement after their visit to Rome: see *La Documentation catholique*, April 16, 1995. Not everyone in Italy agreed with the approach of Sant'Egidio, as seen in the debate with the Italian Committee for Solidarity with Algeria.

14. A more detailed analysis would show the danger of fostering the three main opposition parties involved in the talks at the expense of Algeria's nascent democratic movement. See the remarkable analysis by Jean Leca, "Mort d'un intellectuel algérien," *Commentaire*, nos. 77 and 78 (1997): 59–70 and 293–303.

15. The first issue of the journal *Les Nouveaux Cahiers du Sud* provides an idea of the forums in which Pierre Claverie participated with distinction: these included researchers, journalists, and personalities such as Fethi Benslama, François Burgat, Abed Charef, Selima Ghezali, and Mohamed Talbi. In an atmosphere of great intellectual freedom, they discussed the various forms of religious fundamentalism that were troubling the entire region of the Mediterranean.

16. The quotations are taken from an article by Ali Belhadj, the famous imam of Bab el Oued, in the newspaper of the Islamic Salvation Front (*Al-Munqidh*, no. 9).

17. Here is the passage he cited: "Until recent years, we have enjoyed perfectly agreeable relations … and now it all seems to be ruined, everything seems undone. We now find ourselves powerless before this afflicted people, and we ourselves are afflicted in our powerlessness, as when one watches over a person with a serious illness. We are giving of our time, of the last moments of our life, in nothing but being present … and this with no other intention than that of saying, 'I remain with you even now that the party is over; I want to stand with you and be present to you in your suffering.' This may be a useless presence, but it is a gift of presence that expresses genuine love." Pierre Claverie would cite this passage often, and Bernard Lapize, who was very close to him, would be chosen as administrator of the diocese of Oran after his assassination. See *Le Lien*, December 1994, 18.

18. Published in the August 9, 1996, edition of *La Croix*.

19. The article "Mgr Claverie s'insurge," in the April 15, 1995 edition of *L'Actualité religieuse*, is a response to the presentation of the Rome meeting in the journal's February 15 edition; see also "L'échec de Sant'Egidio," *Témoignage chrétien*, May 26, 1995; "Les accords de Rome ont échoué," *Jeune Afrique Économie*, June 5, 1995.

20. This is the case with the September 15, 1996 edition of *L'Actualité religieuse*, in which Paul Valadier, writing about Pierre Claverie, expressed his "boundless bewilderment at the fact that a bishop of his caliber would not meet and speak with another committed Christian like Andrea Riccardi" (16). Simple fact-checking would have shown that a meeting had taken place in Rome on January 30, 1995, but that it had been a complicated affair. For the sake of clarity, the editor in chief took care to explain that this in fact represented the newspaper's position. But this same editor would dedicate an entire editorial in November of 1996 to "the wizardry of Sant'Egidio."

21. "Ah, the press!," Pierre Claverie commented simply in his correspondence. The incident arose when the highly politicized account of his conference in Paris, published in the May 26, 1995 edition of *Témoignage chrétien*, was reprinted in the May 27, 1995 edition of the Algerian newspaper *Ouest-Tribune*. In Claverie's words, this earned him "congratulations and threats." In this same letter, dated June 17, 1995, in commenting on his two nieces' studies in the United States, he acknowledged that he had always been drawn to the subjects of culture and politics, and added, "My passion for religion (it doesn't matter which one) and my itch for political and social engagement make an amusing

combination that sometimes brings me trouble, but I think that these two are inseparable, at least in my way of understanding things." So he was clearly aware of what he was doing.

22. Elections held a few months later gave rise to a wider political landscape that brought fresh hope. It was then that many came to understand the limitations of the Rome platform. A journalist wrote to Pierre Claverie, "It is the triumph of your thesis." Claverie replied ("somewhat brusquely," as he later recalled), "It is not a triumph, because everything remains to be done on the government's side. And it wasn't a thesis, but merely conviction born from our deeply rooted solidarity with Algeria. End of story" (letter dated November 30, 1995).

23. "Lettre de Noël 1993," *La Vie Spirituelle* (October 1997): 763.

24. Pierre Claverie was very attentive to keeping his church from being taken over by a French mentality. Nevertheless he had a relationship of mutual trust with the French consul in Oran, Christine Robichon, who remarked to him in August of 1995, "We are the two highest-profile targets in the town of Oran." At a time when the Islamists were trying to make an impression on public opinion, this was not a misstatement.

25. François Chavanes, "Faits et réflexions concernant Pierre Claverie," memoirs from November 1995 to September 1999, archives of the Dominican province of France.

26. "Synthèse par le père Claverie," *Réunion USMDA*, Algiers, March 12, 1995, 1.

27. *Le Lien*, April 1995. Reprinted in *Lettres et messages*, 189–92.

28. Homily of ordination, church of Saint-Ignace, Paris, published in *La Vie Spirituelle* (October 1997): 803.

29. "Receive, O Father, in union with the sacrifice of the body and blood of Christ, and for the glory of your name, the offering of my life in immolation for my Muslim brothers and sisters, and for the whole world. I offer it also that my poor and oppressed brothers and sisters may find their true liberation in the justice and charity of Christ . . . "

30. The poem is dedicated to Fr. Charles Deckers and to his confreres assassinated in Tizi-Ouzou in December of 1994. Published in Brussels by *El Kalima*, in April of 1995, it was reprinted in *Le Lien* in June of 1995.

# Chapter 12: "The Combat of Life"

1. "Chemins de sainteté," *Le Lien*, November 1981.

2. I am grateful to François Chavanes, who read these files from beginning to end and made a summary of them that is the basis for this chapter. As he knew Pierre Claverie from 1954 until his death, and had lived with him for a number of years, he was more suited than anyone else to compile this accurate synthesis, extracts from which it would be interesting to publish someday. Most of the citations in this chapter have not yet been published, because notes from Claverie's retreats or on his editorials are not included in *Lettres et messages d'Algérie* (Paris: Karthala, 1996).

3. Pierre Claverie, "La Vie," unpublished address, 1979.

4. Ibid.

5. Testimonies from the Sisters of the Holy Hearts in Beirut and Bikfaya, collected in September of 1999.

6. Pierre Claverie, "Dialogue," unpublished address, 1985, 2–3.

7. Edmond Michelet, who resisted the Nazis in occupied France and was deported to Dachau, was the justice minister during General de Gaulle's administration.

8. Pierre Claverie, "La Vie," unpublished address, 1979, 6.

9. Pierre Claverie, "Béatitudes," unpublished address, 1982, 22.

10. Testimony of Sister Marie of the Incarnation and of the Dominican sisters of Notre-Dame-de-la-Délivrande.

11. 1982 retreat with the Dominican sisters of Araya, transcribed from cassette.

12. Pierre Claverie, "La Vie," unpublished address, August 1979.

13. Citation reprinted in *Le Lien*, March 1984.

14. Pierre Claverie, "Mémoire," 1980, unpublished address, 13–14.

15. Pierre Claverie, "Béatitudes," 1982, unpublished address, 18.

16. Pierre Claverie, "Dialogue," unpublished address, 35.

17. "Priez sans cesse," *Le Lien*, June–July 1994, reprinted in *Lettres et messages*, 154.

18. Pierre Claverie frequently quoted this Persian poet of the 13th century, Jalal ad-Din Rumi, a great Sufi mystical writer.

19. Pierre Claverie, "Vie religieuse," 1968, unpublished address, 27.

20. Pierre Claverie "Eucharistie," 1981, unpublished address, 8.

21. Pierre Claverie, "Mémoire," 1980, unpublished address, 38–40.

22. Homily for the ordination of the author of this book, given in L'Arbresle, June 24, 1989, published in *La Vie Spirituelle* (October 1997): 791.

23. Pierre Claverie, "Eucharistie," 1981, unpublished address, 38.

24. Pierre Claverie, "Avec saint Paul," unpublished address from an undated retreat, 22.

25. Recollection of Sister Marie-Danièle of the Little Sisters of Jesus, Oran.

26. Pierre Claverie, "Eucharistie," 1981, unpublished address, 71.

27. Homily of ordination, Froidmont, June 24, 1990; *La Vie Spirituelle* (October 1997): 796–97.

28. "Rester? Partir?" *Le Lien*, February 1995; *Lettres et messages*, 180.

29. Conference with the Little Sisters of Jesus of the Algeria region, on the offertory prayer, summer of 1995.

30. "Viens, suis-moi!" *Le Lien*, October 1994; *Lettres et messages*, 156.

31. Conference with the Little Sisters of Jesus, 14.

32. "Vivre et mourir," *Le Lien*, March 1996; *Lettres et messages*, 233–34.

33. Conference with the Little Sisters of Jesus, summer 1995, 15.

34. Ibid., 9.

35. Pierre Claverie, "Eucharistie," unpublished address, 1981, 48.

36. Pierre Claverie, "Vie religieuse et Islam," 1983, unpublished address, 12.

37. Ibid.

38. See R.-L. Moreau, "La Badaliya," *Parole et mission* (October 1966), reprinted in J. Keryell, *Louis Massignon, l'hospitalité sacreé* (Paris: Nouvelle Cité, 1987), 387–401.

39. "Chrétiens et musulmans, une humanité plurielle?" *Signum*, no. 7 (1991): 211.

40. Pierre Claverie, "Vie religieuse et islam," 1983, 11.

41. "Carême et Ramadan," *Le Lien*, March 1992. See also, on the same subject, *Le Lien*, February–March 1993; *Lettres et messages*, March 1995, 183–87, and February 1996, 227–31.

42. Pierre Claverie, "Vie religieuse et islam," 6.

43. Pierre Claverie, "Mémoire," 1980, unpublished address, 82.

44. "Rester? Partir?" *Le Lien*, February 1995.

45. See Bruno Chenu, *Sept vies pour Dieu et L'Algérie* (Paris: Bayard/Centurion, 1996), 212.

46. Extract of a letter to Sister Thérèse Saad, which may be the last letter Pierre Claverie ever wrote.

47. *Le Lien*, November 1981.

## Chapter 13: Witnessing the Greatest Love

1. See *Lettres et messages d'Algérie* (Paris: Karthala, 1997), 203–7.

2. In April of 1996, Pierre Claverie had launched an appeal to the Groupement fraternal, which represented the various Dominican women's congregations in France: "We cannot become very numerous, and we don't want to be. But we must assure the steady replacement of our numbers, from outside, in order to maintain our vitality over the long haul and to assure a future for the deep relationships we have established with the great majority of the Algerian people . . ." One religious sister responded to this appeal.

3. Pierre Claverie, "Note sur le colloque de Naples." An interview given in September of 1995 to *L'Actualité religieuse* confirms this momentary sense of discouragement: "In the Muslim world, it is not nationality that makes one belong, but rather religion. It is true that the longer I live in Algeria, the more I see, in spite of the solidity and depth of my friendship with Algerians, that I am a foreigner" (*Lettres et messages*, 20).

4. Dietrich Bonhoeffer, *Letters and Papers from Prison* (New York: Macmillan, 1972); Eberhard Bethge, *Dietrich Bonhoeffer: A Biography* (Minneapolis: Fortress Press, 2000).

5. M. Neusch, *La Croix*, October 3, 1995, 8.

6. *Le Lien*, October 1995, reprinted in *Lettres et messages*, 209–12.

7. See *Le Lien*, November 1995, reprinted in *Lettres et messages*, 213–17. "We are afraid for your sake when you write things like that," Sister Mireille, the secretary at the episcopal residence, told him. Pierre Claverie did not reply.

8. Pierre Claverie, "Événements et dialogue en Algérie," brief for the Pontifical Council for Interreligious Dialogue, Rome, November 17, 1995, unpublished, 2 pp.

9. See Enrico Ferri, ed., *Monoteismo e conflitto* (Naples: CUEN, 1997).

10. Pierre Claverie, "Les derniers et le règne de l'homme," in *Monoteismo e conflitto*, 253.

11. Ibid.

12. At his initiative, two evenings in homage to Claverie were organized in Rome in February and October of 1997. The text of the various addresses at these can be found in Enrico Ferri, *Ricordo di Pierre Claverie* (Naples: CUEN, 2000). The press coverage of the gatherings was remarkable.

13. Pierre Claverie, "Noël 1995, Lettre aux amis," *Lettres et messages*, 220.

14. The bibliography on the monks of Tibhirine is quite extensive. See in particular Bruno Chenu, *Sept vies pour Dieu et l'Algérie* (Paris: Bayard/Centurion, 1996); Marie-Christine Ray, *Christian de Chergé, prieur de Tibhirine* (Paris: Bayard/Centurion, 1998); and Robert Mason, *Tibhirine, les veilleurs de l'Atlas* (Paris: Éditions du Cerf, 1997).

15. Brother Christophe, *Le Souffle du don, journal du frère Christophe, moine de Tibhirine, 8 août 1993–19 mars 1996* (Paris: Bayard/Centurion, 1999), 41–42.

16. "Carême 1996," *Le Lien*, February 1996, reprinted in *Lettres et messages*, 229–31.

17. His editorial for March 1996 is entitled "Vivre et mourir...," *Lettres et messages*, 233–36.

18. Ibid., 234.

19. "Un souffle de liberté," *Le Lien*, May 1996, reprinted in *Lettres et messages*, 241.

20. Headline in the newspaper *La Croix* for April 18, 1996, which published extensive sections of the book.

21. To date, the book has sold nearly ten thousand copies.

22. Interview on the 8:00 p.m. television news broadcast on France 2, May 10, 1996.

23. "The journalists won't leave me alone, and I am beginning to fear this exaggerated publicity that is given to me," Pierre Claverie wrote to his sister, after his return to Oran, on June 10, 1996.

24. "Pierre Claverie, fils de l'Algérie et enfant de l'avenir," *La Vie Spirituelle* (October 1997): 646.

25. In a personal letter Pierre Claverie sent that day to Archbishop Teissier, one sees the role that the cardinal had for him: "With him we lose the spiritual founder of the church of Algeria, and we must now make the inheritance he left us bear fruit, with his courage, his firmness of mind, his farseeing faith, his accurate understanding of situations and persons, his delicacy, and his humility."

26. These repeated references to light show his irritation, shared by many Algerians, at the somewhat theatrical dousing of the seven candles representing the seven monks in the sanctuary of Notre Dame in Paris.

27. "In memoriam," *Le Lien*, June–July 1996; reprinted in *Lettres et messages*, 243–47.

28. Jean-René Bouchet, *Saint Dominique* (Paris: Éditions du Cerf, 1988), 36.

29. The complete text of this tremendous homily is found in the special edition of *La Vie Spirituelle*, 832–36.

30. Ibid.

31. Ibid.

32. He returned to this beautiful image from a text written by his friend and coworker Bernard Lapize. See page 277, note 17.

33. Ibid.

34. Ibid.

35. To Guy Maigrot, a childhood friend, who had come to meet him at the airport in Marignane, he remarked, "I will be killed, but I don't know when."

36. Recalling this final encounter, Jean-François Cota summed up Pierre Claverie in a few essential phrases: "Pierre was a man fully present, clear-sighted, and full of love."

37. All of his appointment books have been preserved, so the details of his activities can be verified.

38. Hervé de Charette, remarks made in *Paris-Match*, August 15, 1996.

39. R. You, "À Mohamed," *La Vie Spirituelle* (October 1997): 573. You adds, "Those who saw these two [Pierre and Mohamed] in their last months, and especially during their last days, could not help but think that they were sharing an 'agony,' a silent combat." In a small private notebook, found after his death, Mohamed had composed in his best Arabic script a sort of farewell to his friends.

40. Archbishop Teissier would later say of this funeral that it was "a unique assembly, such as has probably not been seen in the fourteen centuries during which Islam has existed: a Christian gathering in which most of the participants were Muslims weeping for and celebrating a brother bishop, whose ministry had held meaning not only for the Christian community, but also for many in the Muslim community" (Henri Teissier, *Lettres d'Algérie* [Paris: Bayard/Centurion, 1998], 75).

41. "God is love." It was a gift from the Dominican sisters of Notre-Dame-de-la-Délivrande.

# Epilogue

1. See Salima Tlemçani, "Révélations d'un émir du GIA," *El Watan*, July 2, 1998, and Patrick Forestier, *Confession d'un émir du GIA* (Paris: Grasset, 1999).

2. Jean Leca, "Mort d'un intellectuel algérien," *Commentaire*, no. 77 (Spring 1997): 59.

3. Enrico Ferri, "La concezione del dialogo di Pierre Claverie," *Ricordo di Pierre Claverie* (Naples: CUEN, 2000), 63–95.

4. Camille Tarot, "Pierre Claverie, fils d'Algérie et enfant de l'avenir," *La Vie Spirituelle* (October 1997): 647–48.

5. Oum El Kheir, in *La Vie Spirituelle* (October 1997): 604–5.

6. Abdelaziz Bouteflika, address to the French National Assembly, June 14, 2000, cited in *La Croix*, June 16, 2000.

7. Camille Tarot, "Pierre Claverie," 649.

8. Pierre Claverie, "Que ton Régne vienne!," *Le Lien*, October 1995; reprinted in *Lettres et messages* (Paris: Karthala, 1997), 210.

9. Pierre Claverie, Homily of ordination, church of Saint-Ignace, Paris, published in *La Vie Spirituelle* (October 1997): 803.

# Index

*Italicized page numbers refer to a photograph on that page.*

abandonment and commitment concepts, 217–21
*Actualité religieuse*, 122–23
Addi, Lahouari, 178
Algeria, 6–7
  anti-imperialism in, 92–93
  economic development of, 83–84, 109–10, 171
  independence and, 49–50, 52–55
  National Charter, 85
  nationalism, emergence of, 17–19
  October 1988 turning point in, 170
  "original sin" and, 37
  political turmoil in, xii–xiii, 82–83
  population of, 7
  schools, nationalization of, 156
Algerian church, 70–73
  Catholic Action movements and, 70–71
  as community in exodus, 155–57
  conversions and, 168–69
  mission of, viii, xi–xii, 102–5, 223
  "platforms of encounter and service," 111–12
  politics and, 91–93
  post-independence surveillance of, 86–89
  presence question, 202–4
  role of, 79–80, 88, 90–91, 102–5, 115, 154, 164–65
  turning inward, danger of, 167
  Vatican II and, 158
  violence and, 167–69
Algerian politics, Claverie on, 20–26, 32–33, 45–49
"Algerian question," 45–49
Algerian War, 18, 37
*Algerie en 57* (Tillion), 21

Algiers, 6–9
  Battle of, 16
  Dominicans in, 14–15
  independence and, 49
  violence in, 52–55
Alquier, Jean-Yves: *Nous avons pacifié Tazalt*, 21
Angèle-Marie, Sister, 225–26
Aquinas, Thomas, viii
Arabic, study of, 42, 48, 58, 64–69
  Lebanese sisters and, 68–69
Arabization, xii, 63–64, 85–86
assassination (of Claverie), vii, xi, 245–49, 254
Association des étudiants catholiques (l'Asso), 24
Atticha, Joseph, 34
Averroës versus Ghazâli, 88–89
Avril, Fr., 34

Bab el Oued, 7
Le Baut, Pierre, Fr., 48, 58–59
Beatitudes, 213
Bechtel Corporation, 83
Becker, Fr. Thierry, *247*
Ben Bella, Ahmed, 63
Benoît, Jean-Charles, 115
Bibiane, Sister, 225–26
Biès, Jacques, 107
bishop of Oran (Claverie as), 96–98
Blanc, Jacques, 71, 92
Bonhoeffer, Dietrich, 229–30, 252
  *Letters and Papers from Prison*, 229
Bouchikhi, Mohamed, vii, *247*, 248–49
Boudiaf, Mohamed, 184–85
Boumediene, Houari, 62–64, 82–86, 92, 155–56, 171
Boumendjel, Malika, 68

"Bravo" (Claverie), 231–32
Butler, David, 108

Camus, Albert, 7, 9
   *The First Man*, 7, 9
   *Summer*, 16
catechism (of Claverie), 11–12
Centre catholique universitaire (CCU), 24
Chadli, Bendjedid, 86, 171–72, 179,
   199–200
Chavanes, François, 13, 50–51, 133
Chenu, Fr. Marie-Dominique, 34, 152
   *Une école de théologie, le Saulchoir,* 38–39
"Chrétiens au Mahgreb," 158–59
Christian Committee for Service in Algeria
   (CCSA), 91–92
"Christians in Algeria today" conference,
   199–202
"Christians in the Mahgreb"(CERNA), 90
"Church and Human Rights," (Claverie),
   37, 150–52
citizenship, Algerian (of Claverie), 152–53
Claverie, Anne-Marie, 1, 3, 12
Claverie, Étienne, 2, 3–4, 23, 32, 52–54,
   97–98
   correspondence of, 4–6, 29–30
Claverie, Louise. *See under* Maillard
   Claverie
"colonial bubble," xi, 6–11, 7–9
Comité universitaire d'information
   politique (CUIP), 21–22
Conference of North African Bish-
   ops (CERNA): "Christians in the
   Mahgreb," 90
Constantine, 73–76
Constantine Plan, 19
conversion, 215–16
Cota, Jean-François, 12, 16
Couesnongle, Vincent de, 94
cross, theme of, 44, 135–36

Delalande, Fr., 30, 31, 32
democracy, 179–80. *See also* minority
   rights
*derniers et le règne de l'homme, Les*
   (Claverie), 134

dialogue, viii–x, 130–31, 137–53, 145–50,
   160–66, 179, 211, 232, 256
   conditions for creating, 150–52
   the "Other" and, 147–48, 160–61
*dialogue organisé,* 137–39
Djabali, Hawa: "Une longue fidélité,"
   206–8
Dominican order, 28–29, 241–45
   fraternity and, 134–36
   Les Éditions du Cerf, 39, 133
   post-war changes and, 38–40
Duployé, Fr., 34
Duval, Léon-Étienne, xii, 66, 71–73, 77,
   79, 86–89, 103, 240–41
   on Claverie, 94–95

Encounter and Development Association,
   71, 91–93
Etoile nord-africaine, 18
Eucharist, 198

Fadil, Atina, 65
family cell, 3–6, 184
family story, 1–2
*First Man, The* (Camus), 9
*Français d'Algerie* (Nora), 47
friendship, Algerian mission and, viii
Froidure, Michel, 32–33
Front nationale de libération (FLN), 19,
   47, 63, 171
funeral (of Claverie), viii–ix, xiii, 249

Garaudy, Roger, 233
   *Parole d'homme,* 130
Geffré, Claude, 161
*Glycines, les,* 78–82, 120
Grenoble, 20–26
   a true plan and, 26–31

Haubtmann, Georges, 24
*Histoire de l'Afrique du Nord* (Julien),
   68–69

"In the Face of Death" (Claverie), 188
"In the Footsteps of Saint Augustine"
   (Rahal), 254–57

Islam, ix–x, 259–60
  Algeria and, 86, 110–12, 140–43,
    166–69
  non-Muslims and, 156, 176, 183,
    251–52, 256
  politics and, ix–x, 131, 170–73, 175–76,
    179. *See also* Islamism (radical Islam)
Islamic Salvation Front, 171–72, 176–80
  in Oran, 179
  Sant'Egidio affair and, 197
  violence and, 185–88
Islamism (radical Islam), xii, 131, 178–80
  Christianity and, 168
  Claverie on, 150–51, 173–77, 181–83.
    *See also* violence

Jacquier, Gaston, 87
John Paul II, 252–53
Julien, Charles-André: *L'Histoire de
    l'Afrique du Nord*, 68–69

Khadra, Yasmina: *A quoi rêvent les loups?*
    174

*La Pensée catholique*, 15
"Least of All and the Kingdom of Man"
    (Claverie), 233–34
Lefèvre, Louis, 12–15, 28, 57, 114
Lenoir, René, 10
Leo XIII, 176
L'Espinay, Fr. de, 49–50
*Letters and Papers from Prison* (Bonhoeffer),
    229
*Lettres et messages d'Algerie* (Claverie),
    237–40
*Lien, Le*, 130–32
Lille, novitiate in, 31–35
*Livre de la foi, Le*, 132–33, 234
*Livre des passages, Le*, 133–34
"longue fidélité, Une" (Djabali), 206–8

Maillard Claverie, Louise, 2
Mandouze, André, 22
Merbah, Kasdi, 172–73
military service (of Claverie), 49–55
minority rights, 179–80, 192–93, 231, 256
Mosque of Paris address (Claverie), 143–45

*mouna*, 112–13
Mouvement des oulémas, 19
Mouvement pour le triomphe des libertés
    démocratiques (MTLD), 18
Muslim world, Christian presence in,
    221–24

Nora, Pierre: *Les Français d'Algerie*, 47
*Nous avons pacifié Tazalt* (Alquier), 21
novitiate (of Claverie), 31–35

Oran, diocese of, 105–7
ordination (of Claverie)
  episcopal, 100–102
  as priest, 57
Organisation armée secrète, 24–25
Organisation spécial (OS), 18
the "Other," xi–xii, 10–11, 24–25, 77, 113,
    198, 250–51, 258–61
  dialogue and, 147–48, 152, 160–61
  "diocese without borders" and, 198–202
  God as, 213–15
  self-effacement and, 223

"Papers on Islamology" (Claverie), 97
Parti du peuple algérian (PPA), 18–19
Paschal experience, 204–8
Pavat, Paul, 49–50
Perret, Michel, 32
personal traits (of Claverie), 50–51, 96,
    122–23, 251–52, 254–57
  "Claverie method," 177
  ideological confrontation, aversion to,
    15
  passion and, 224
"pieds-noirs," xi, 9
  racism and, 10–11
"pieds-rouges," 62, 92
Pontifical Council for Interreligious
    Dialogue, 138–39
  Claverie and, 139, 159–60, 232
  "Dialogue and Proclamation," 159–60
Pontifical Council for Interreligious
    Dialogue, 1995, 167
prayer, 34–35, 43, 81–82, 115, 193–94,
    214–17

preaching (of Claverie), 40–44, 52, 56–57, 119–36, 125–30. *See also* vocation(s)

Rahal, Redouane, 107, 110–11
  "In the Footsteps of Saint Augustine," 254–57
Raimbaud, Jean-Marie, *103*
*Revue de Presse*, 80
Robert, Joseph, 34
Rushdie, Salman: *The Satanic Verses*, 17

Sadou, Zazi, 249
Saint-Do, scouts of, 8, 12–16, 114–16, 241–45
Saint-Exupéry Club, 49–50
Saint-Raymond, Paul-Hélène, 190–93
Sant'Egidio affair, 194–98
  Islamic Salvation Front and, 197
*Satanic Verses* (Rushdie), 17
Saulchoir, le, 38–40
  Claverie's training at, 40–44
  Vatican II and, 55–56
schooling (of Claverie), 11
Scotto, Jean, 73–76, 97–98, *103*
Second Gulf War, ix
Shell Oil Company, 3, 6, 53–54
Soltani, Abdellatif, 85
spiritual experience, the, 209–12
Streicher, Abbé, 11–12
*Summer* (Camus), 16
Swaggart, Jimmy, 141–42

Teissier, Henri, 67, *75*, 78, 88, 97, 99–100, *103*, 158, 190
*Témoignage chrétien*, 22
theology of religions, 165–66
Tibhirine kidnapping, 237, 240–41
Tillion, Germaine: *L'Algerie en 57*, 21
tolerance, 102, 104–5, 142–45, 146–48, 201
  Islam and, 251–52, 256. *See also* the "Other"

*ulema*, 18, 181–83

Vatican II, 56
  *Ad Gentes*, 158
  *Dignitatis Humanae*, 137
  *Nostra Aetate*, 137–38
*venia*, 32
Vergès, Henri, 190–93
violence, 186–87, 192–93, 227–29, 231–33, 236–37
  culture of, 259–60
  and solidarity, 186–87
vocation(s)
  of the church, 160–61, 164–66, 199–201
  Claverie and, viii, xii–xiii, 27–31, 36–37, 89, 119, 125, 258

White, Wayne, 31

Zeroual, Liamine, 249